ROBERT LAIRD BORDEN

A BIOGRAPHY

ROBERT LAIRD BORDEN

A BIOGRAPHY

Volume I: 1854–1914

BY

ROBERT CRAIG BROWN

Macmillan of Canada/Toronto

ISBN 0-7705-1317-4

Printed in Canada for
The Macmillan Company of Canada Limited
70 Bond Street, Toronto M5B 1X3

To Gail and Bradley,
Brenda and Brian.

CONTENTS

List of Illustrations   *ix*
Preface   *xi*
1. The Roots of Ambition   *1*
2. The Future Guaranteed   *13*
3. The Tuppers' Choice   *28*
4. The Test of Leadership   *50*
5. Humiliation   *72*
6. Problems of Policy and Organization   *90*
7. Purity in Politics   *114*
8. The Naval Question   *142*
9. First Minister   *170*
10. Keeping Promises   *197*
11. The Great Debate   *230*
12. The Last Days of Peace   *248*
A Note on Sources   *264*
Notes   *269*
Index   *292*

LIST OF ILLUSTRATIONS

(Between pages 68 and 69)

1 & 2. Andrew Borden and Eunice Laird Borden
3. Robert Borden at age five
4. The Covenanters' Church, Grand Pré
5. The house where Borden was born (H. A. Buckmaster)
6. The Borden family home, Grand Pré
7. Robert Borden at age twenty-nine
8. Robert and Laura Borden, *circa* 1889
9. Pinehurst, Halifax (H. A. Buckmaster)
10. Halifax, 1887 (Public Archives of Canada)
11. John William Borden, 1907 (Public Archives of Canada)
12. Henry Clifford Borden, *circa* 1895
13. Robert's mother
14. Sir Charles Tupper (Public Archives of Canada)
15. Sir Charles Hibbert Tupper, 1894 (Public Archives of Canada)
16. Robert Borden, 1901 (Public Archives of Canada)

(Between pages 164 and 165)

17. Laura Borden, 1906 (Public Archives of Canada)
18. The second annual meeting of the Crown Life Insurance Company, 1903 (Crown Life Insurance Company)
19. Robert Borden, 1901 (Public Archives of Canada)
20. Glensmere, Ottawa, *circa* 1913
21 & 22. Interior views of Glensmere
23. Liberal election poster, 1904 (The Liberal Party of Canada and the Public Archives of Canada)
24. Sir Wilfrid Laurier campaigning, 1908 (Public Archives of Canada)

25. Sir Wilfrid Laurier at Mission City, B.C., 1910 (Public Archives of Canada)
26. Borden on his western tour, 1911 (Glenbow-Alberta Institute)

(Between pages 228 and 229)

27. Robert Borden, *circa* 1911
28. The Tories on tour, 1911
29. Planning the sweep of Ontario in 1911 (Public Archives of Canada)
30. Borden's first Cabinet, October 11, 1911 (Public Archives of Canada)
31. The Duke and Duchess of Connaught (Public Archives of Canada)
32 & 33. Robert and Laura Borden aboard the S.S. *Royal George*
34. Paddington Station, July 4, 1912 (Public Archives of Canada)
35. With Winston Churchill, July 1912 (Public Archives of Canada)
36. Borden in Windsor uniform
37. White, Borden, and Laurier (Public Archives of Canada)
38. Borden practising his golf swing (Public Archives of Canada)

PREFACE

Students of Canadian history remember Sir Robert Laird Borden as Canada's Prime Minister during the Great War, as the political leader who introduced conscription and who led the struggle for Canadian autonomy within the Empire-Commonwealth. Perhaps because the war so deeply touched the lives of all Canadians, and because conscription had such a lasting impact upon Canadian politics, little attention has been paid to the greatest part of Borden's public career, the years from 1896 to 1914 when he was first an unknown Conservative backbencher, then the leader of the Opposition for more than ten years, and finally, after October 1911, Prime Minister of Canada. Some of the story of the first sixty years of Borden's private and public life is revealed in the first volume of Sir Robert's *Memoirs*, edited by his nephew, Henry Borden, and published in 1938. Occasional glimpses of these years may also be found in *Letters To Limbo*, a series of letters of reminiscence and commentary written by Sir Robert in the mid-1930s, which Henry Borden edited for publication in 1971. The present volume, however, is the first attempt to reconstruct Borden's pre-war life which is based upon research in the Borden Papers and in a number of other private manuscript and public records collections. Like all biographies, this book is selective in content. It has not been possible to recount every detail of Borden's private life or every incident of his public career. What I have written about reflects my own judgment of what is most important and most interesting in Borden's life. A second volume will complete the study from 1914 to Sir Robert's death in 1937.

The list of people who have helped me in the preparation of this book is a long one. The staffs of public archives and libraries from Nova Scotia to British Columbia have all given prompt and generous assistance. But special mention is due to the Public Archives of Canada where Dr. Wilfrid I. Smith and his associates, especially the members of the Manuscript Division and Miss Barbara Wilson and Mr. Jay Atherton, have been unfailingly accommodating and helpful. The University of Toronto provided funds for research for this book and President Claude T. Bissell and Professor Donald F. Forster gave continual encouragement to the project. The Canada Council awarded me a Leave Grant in 1973–74 to enable me to complete a draft of the manuscript.

For some years, during the summer months, a number of talented graduate students, David Hall, Marion Lane, Margaret Davidson, Robert Bothwell, Ann Davis, Veronica Strong-Boag, John English, and Neil Semple, helped me collect and organize the vast amount of documentation for this book. Senator Eugene Forsey, Dr. D. A. Muise of the National Museum of Man, Blair Neatby and Richard Clippingdale of Carleton University, Terry Copp of Wilfrid Laurier University, Margaret Conrad of Acadia University, and my colleagues at the University of Toronto, Maurice Careless, Charles Stacey, Robert Bothwell, and Michael Bliss, have all read and criticized portions of the manuscript for this volume. My friends Ramsay Cook and John English read the entire manuscript and were exceedingly generous with their comments and suggestions. So too were Diane Mew and Kenneth McVey of the Macmillan Company of Canada. Betty Towne has been a patient reader and typist of my handwritten drafts.

Mr. Henry Borden has been a constant source of encouragement and information during my study of his uncle's life. Without his own detailed knowledge of Sir Robert's career, only a portion of which is directly acknowledged here, this volume would be much the poorer. He has given me complete access to all the Borden Papers which remain in his possession and he has read the drafts of this manuscript with great care. Mr. Borden has not attempted to influence my interpretation of Sir Robert's life.

My deepest debt is to my wife, Gail, and my children. The sacrifices they have made to assist me in the completion of this project are beyond enumeration.

Robert Craig Brown

CHAPTER ONE

THE ROOTS OF AMBITION

Grand Pré was a quiet, agricultural community overlooking the northern portion of the Annapolis Valley.* None of its hundred and more families was markedly more prosperous than any other; most enjoyed the simple amenities of mid-nineteenth-century life in rural Nova Scotia.[1] The houses were elegant frame structures, many of them two-storied, with commodious rooms to shelter large families. Fuel for the fireplaces, the cook stoves, and the base-burners, which afforded a measure of central heating, was laboriously gathered and cut in the winter months on the high hills surrounding the valley. Candles provided basic household illumination but kerosene lamps were coming into vogue. Large barns adjacent to most dwellings were used to store hay and grain and to give shelter to the family's horses, cows, and other livestock and poultry.

For those who had occasion to travel, Grand Pré, for many years, had had regular connections with Halifax by stage coach. By 1852 three steamers provided five-days-a-week service between Saint John, on the other side of the Bay of Fundy, and Annapolis to the west, and Windsor, a short fifteen miles to the southeast.[2] In 1854 Joseph Howe's government began the construction of the Nova Scotia Railway from Halifax to Truro. A branch to Windsor was completed by 1858. Six years later Charles Tupper's government authorized the construction of the Windsor and Annapolis Railway and in the summer of 1869 the line, with a station at Grand Pré, was opened. By December arrangements had been made for through trains to Halifax. Henceforth, the citizens of Grand Pré could travel to the provincial capital in modern com-

*In the mid nineteenth century the community was known as either Grand Pré or Lower Horton. The Post Office carried the latter designation.

1

fortable railway coaches pulled by engines bearing names recalling the history of the valley, the *Grand Pré*, the *Gaspereau*, and the *Evangeline*. In 1871 the railway brought the first large railway tourist party to the valley, four hundred visitors from Boston.[3]

Some of the visitors may have been surprised by the lack of public recognition of Grand Pré's rich historic past. Indeed, they may have had a more vivid, if imaginative, recollection of the community's past than most of the residents. For Grand Pré had been celebrated as the home of Evangeline in Longfellow's epic poem, written in 1847. In the village there were no monuments commemorating its settlement in 1685 by the Acadians. Only the meadow recalled the arduous work, in succeeding decades, of reclaiming the land from the sea. There was nothing to remind the visitors of the "massacre" at Grand Pré in the bitter winter of 1747 when a party of Canadiens and Indians drove New England soldiers from Acadian homes;[4] nothing of the expulsion of the hardy French-speaking settlers in 1755;[5] nothing of the tough capable New Englanders who had replaced them on the land.[6]

But the visitors would not have left Grand Pré entirely disappointed. The community did take great pride in its scenic location. From the yard of the Covenanters' Church on the hill the prospect was almost idyllic in every direction. In the south, South Mountain dominated the scene and below, between the mountain and the village hill, the turbid water of the Gaspereau made its way to the sea. From the church door, looking north, they would have seen, beyond the great meadow from which the village took its name, the sometimes glistening, often turbulent Minas Basin. Further in the distance, imposing Cape Blomidon was visible, and westward still the treed bulk of North Mountain closed the other side of the valley.

The land gave the families of Grand Pré their sustenance. On the meadow the farmers grew rich crops of hay and grain, of peas, beans, corn, and root vegetables. Farm homes on the adjoining upland were surrounded by orchards bearing an abundant harvest of apples, pears, and plums. It was true that a variety of other occupations were pursued by residents of the village. A doctor, two ministers, two teachers, and the principal of the local academy represented the professions. Two storekeepers, a widow who ran the hotel, four shoemakers, three blacksmiths, a mason, and two carpenters served the needs of the community. A small number of men worked as common labourers, and four householders took their living from the sea as mariners.[7] But most of the men of Grand Pré were farmers and agriculture dictated the pace and the habits of the community. Time was measured, work was done, by the rhythm of the seasons and the harvest, at "cherry time", or "haying time", or "apple time".

Each autumn the families of Grand Pré and their King's County neighbours celebrated their good fortune at the Windsor fair and the fruit show of the Nova Scotia Fruit Growers Association at near-by Somerset. After the railway was completed, visitors came all the way from Halifax on an excursion train to view the grand displays. During the morning the crowd milled around the outside of the exhibition hall while inside the judges gave solemn and weighty consideration to the merits of the more than sixty varieties of apples, all carefully labelled and polished, which filled the tables along both sides of the hall. It was, commented a contemporary observer, "a task of considerable delicacy as well as difficulty". At midday the multitude was let into the hall to appraise the farmers', and the judges', work. If God had been good and if a man had tended his trees with care, he might expect a prize. And so might his wife or his children to reward their diligence at gardening. For the tables at each end of the building groaned under the weight of the displays of prize vegetables grown in the valley.[8]

If the land was one determinant in the life of the people of the valley, the Lord was the other. The Protestant churches of King's County claimed the vast majority of the people as adherents. In Grand Pré the little church on the hill was Presbyterian. In the county about half of the more than 18,000 people in 1861 were Baptists and another 3,000 were Methodists. There were some 1,800 Presbyterians and slightly lesser numbers of Anglicans and Roman Catholics.[9] Whatever the denomination, one thing was certain: for the families of King's County and Grand Pré the church was the guidepost for their way of life and provided them with a source of fulfillment and community.

The children received their introduction to the formalities of education in Sunday School. And at least until 1864, when Charles Tupper's government passed the first provincial free public school act, it was not unusual for the village pastor to also assume the post of schoolmaster. Whether the children were taught by the local pastor or an itinerate teacher who "boarded around", a denominational catechism was often the most substantial reading given to them. "School books," a valley lad who went off to Harvard and a distinguished academic career recalled,

> were not bulky or numerous. Indeed it was not uncommon for a single book, and that a slender one, to include the whole course of a child's study. Such a comprehensive volume was "The New Guide to the English Tongue", by Thomas Dilworth, Schoolmaster! It began with the alphabet, then came the spelling of simple words, easy reading lessons, containing such moral precepts as "Do not tell a lie," and "Let thy hand do no hurt," and after that the spelling of longer words, of two, three, four or more syllables. Next came a treatise on English grammar, Latin words and phrases in common use, abbreviations used in writing, arithmetical tables, outlines of geography, advanced lessons in prose and verse, a compendium of natural history, illustrated selected fables . . . and finally a church catechism. . . . All this for one shilling![10]

Mid-century Grand Pré, then, was an unpretentious little village whose people lived by the laws of nature and God. Their livelihood came from the land and, for a few, from the sea. They had been brought up in the church. Throughout their lives the church would remain the centre of their community life, the arbiter of their values and attitudes.

Robert Laird Borden was born in Grand Pré on the 26th of June in 1854. It was almost a century since the first member of the Borden family had come to the Annapolis Valley, a little more than two centuries after Richard Borden had left Headcorn, Kent, in 1638 to settle in Portsmouth, Rhode Island. After the expulsion of the Acadians, Samuel Borden, Richard's great-grandson, a landowner and surveyor in New Bedford, Rhode Island, was commissioned by the Nova Scotia government to come to the province and lay out plots for some of the New Englanders intending to settle on the forcibly vacated lands. For his work Samuel received a parcel of land in Cornwallis from the government. But Samuel returned to New Bedford and it was his son, Perry, Robert's great-grandfather, who took up the land grant in 1760.[11] In succeeding decades the Borden families had made their modest contribution to the life of the valley as competent, hard working tillers of the soil.

Robert's father, Andrew, who was born on February 14, 1816, first married Catherine Fuller. She bore him two children before her death in 1847. In 1850 Andrew married Eunice Jane Laird. Robert, the first child of the marriage of Andrew and Eunice, was born in the small house next to the Covenanters' church on the hill. In 1858 Andrew built a larger house closer to the meadow to accommodate his growing family which then consisted of Robert's half-brother, Thomas, his half-sister, Sophie, and a younger brother, John William. Julia, Robert's sister, would be born a year later and Henry Clifford, his youngest brother, in 1870. Henry or Hal, as he was called in the family, was a frail lad, prone to all the usual childhood illnesses. But he had a sharp mind and a playful wit and of all the Borden children was Robert's favourite companion.

Robert's mother's family had also come to the valley late in the eighteenth century. Her grandfather had arrived in Nova Scotia from Scotland after a brief stay in New England. Her father, John Laird, was for many years the village schoolmaster in Grand Pré. He possessed a large library, much of it composed of the Greek and Latin classics, and was a classical scholar and a mathematician of some reputation.

Eunice Borden had a very strong influence upon her first son. She was a strong willed, outspoken woman, who, he later wrote, possessed a "highly-wrought nervous temperament", was "passionate but wholly just and considerate upon reflection", and was totally devoted to the well-being of her children. When, as a young man, Robert noted a friend's remark that "I wouldn't give my mother for 14 more than all the friends I have in the world", he added that his friend was "about right on that".[13]

Robert admired the qualities—"very strong character, remarkable energy, high ambition and unusual ability"—which he believed his mother had inherited from her father.[14] From her he learned a strict moral code of conduct, a commitment to duty and earnest endeavour, and the ambition for worldly success. To her he confessed his frequent fears of failure. "1876 is no more," he wrote from his Halifax room on a stormy New Year's Eve:[15]

I can remember of looking forward to it, in 1870, and thinking "how old will I be if I live till then." I determined to accomplish much before the time came round for I did not wish to be two and twenty and an ignoramous. Well the time

has come & gone, and how little has been accomplished. The
chariot wheels of time have rolled all too swiftly for my
tardy efforts.

Robert wrote no such letters to his father. Indeed, the family
letters that survive from his youth contain a large correspondence
with his mother and no letters at all between father and son.
Robert's estimate of his father's ability was respectful and qualified. He later noted that Andrew was "a man of good ability and
excellent judgment", of a "calm, contemplative and philosophical" turn of mind. But Andrew was less driven by the will to
succeed than either his wife or his son. Before Robert's birth he
had failed in a number of business ventures. "He lacked energy
and had no great aptitude for affairs," Robert observed. When the
Windsor and Annapolis Railway was completed Andrew secured
the position of Stationmaster at Grand Pré and he found the cam-
araderie and ease of the position a welcome relief from the travail
of the farm. The position was secure and not especially demanding; it afforded ample opportunity for friendly talk and specu-
lative musings, and it suited Andrew well. As a relative put it,
Robert's father was "so well posted on every subject and so com-
panionable".[16] Consequently, the major responsibility for the
management of both the farm and the family fell upon Eunice.

Robert's recollections of his childhood were dominated by
memories of a strict regimen of discipline and hard work. Once,
when Robert was between three and four years of age, the Anglican pastor from Wolfville, the Reverend John Storrs, came to
call. The visitor was very bald and Rob was so struck by the
novelty of a man without hair that he pulled a chair behind the
pastor's and climbed up to examine the strange phenomenon at
close range. The child's lively curiosity was quickly dampened by
a "stern reproof" from his mother. Some years later, when Rob
was a lad of eleven, the head of a prominent legal firm in the
county was invited to the house by Andrew to put the young
student "through [his] paces" in Virgil. The ordeal was unpleasant and taxing but the boy succeeded in convincing both his
father and the learned lawyer of his competence in Latin.

He was not nearly as proficient at farm work. He later recalled
that he failed to conquer "the mysteries of building a load of hay".
Removing stones from his father's fields and stowing hay in the
barn "are two impressions in my agricultural education to which

I look back with no pleasurable recollection". Hoeing potatoes was "extremely disagreeable". Sawing cord wood for winter fires was an "unpleasurable activity". The boy quickly decided that, despite family tradition, farming would not be his vocation. The rewards were meagre and "throughout the year, labour was severe and hours long".[17]

However different their temperaments and ambitions, Eunice and Andrew Borden shared an intense conviction that their son should have a good education. It began in the Presbyterian Sunday School in Grand Pré where Rob was introduced to the mysteries of the *Shorter Catechism* and the *Confession of Faith*. At home he was encouraged to read Bunyan's *Pilgrim's Progress* and he was delighted when his uncles came to read Pope's *Iliad* and Horace and Virgil to him. In due time he received lessons from the village school teacher. And in 1863, when he was nine, his parents enrolled him as a day student in the community's private academy, Acacia Villa Seminary. The school was run by Mr. Arthur McNutt Patterson, M.A., who himself had once been a pupil of Eunice's father, John Laird. Patterson's aim, he said, was "to fit boys physically, morally, and intellectually, for the responsibilities of life, to give a practical business education to those who desire it, and to prepare students to enter the several maritime provincial colleges".[18]

Thanks to the encouragement, the discipline, and the testing of his mother and father, the boy had already learned much more than most of his school mates. At Acacia Villa he studied the curriculum of a better than average elementary education. Like his parents, Master Patterson placed a heavy emphasis upon discipline, self-restraint, and moral development at his school. Each morning began with Patterson reading a chapter from the Book of Proverbs. The exercise, Robert later recalled, "instilled precepts and rules of conduct which were invaluable in later life".[19] Daily the students recited in Latin and Greek before Patterson or his assistant, James Henry Hamilton. Then there were the usual exercises in grammar, mathematics, literature, geography, and natural history. On Sunday afternoons throughout the year Rob joined a group of boys studying the Scriptures under Hamilton's tutelage. Hamilton soon had him poring over the New Testament in Greek and beginning the study of Hebrew.

Robert did well at Acacia Villa and his aptitude in the classics was soon recognized. When Hamilton suddenly left the school in the spring of 1869, Patterson promoted the fourteen-year-old from student to "assistant master" and charged him with the responsibility of drilling his school mates in classical studies. Doubtless Rob was flattered by the recognition from Patterson. But there was a practical advantage to be considered also. Will and Julia were also attending Acacia Villa and the cost was a heavy burden on the Borden family treasury. Rob's salary was meagre, but he could at least make a small contribution to the family finances. Patterson was satisfied with his work and Robert continued in his teaching position.

It was an important decision. Robert knew that his acquaintance with the world of ideas was still limited, that even in his field of special competence he had mastered more of the techniques of learning than of the contents of classical literature. And he recognized that to continue teaching would mean that his own aspirations for a university education would be unfulfilled. For the remainder of his life he would try to round out his own education by adopting rigorous programs of reading. Various schemes for self-improvement were carefully planned and started over the next few years. Each in turn fell victim to prior obligations, the preparation of lessons for his students and the continued unwanted but necessary chores of the farm.

Looking back more than a half-century later, he regretted that his education lacked the aid and challenge of "close and constant association with keen fellow students" and the "inestimable advantage" of the influence and leadership of "great teachers". But he also found much value, of a practical nature, in his own self-education. Above all else, he had acquired "an intense appreciation of the value of time. To waste it seems like wasting one's future." Moreover, his rigorous self-education had taught him valuable lessons not inherent in any university curriculum. "Assuming adequate intellectual equipment and essential moral standards," he told the graduating class at Acadia in 1932, "courage, patience, persistence and the saving grace of humour are perhaps the most useful qualities for one entering the lists of life . . . the most significant lessons of life are to be found in adversity. To agonize—that is to wrestle with oneself—in the intellectual and spiritual sense is an essential discipline."[20] These important though rather commonplace precepts may not have contributed much to an understanding of the world of ideas. But they were values which were essential to success in the day-to-day dealings of men.

In 1873 Robert received an attractive invitation from J. H. Hamilton, whom he had replaced at Acacia Villa. Hamilton was the master of another private academy, the Glenwood Institute, in Matawan, New Jersey. He asked Rob to join him there as an assistant master. Rob was anxious to accept. The work would be much the same as at Acacia Villa and he could renew his friendship with Hamilton. Hamilton may even have offered him a higher salary than Patterson was paying him in Grand Pré. But the most significant enticement was the chance to strike out on his own in a foreign but not unfamiliar land. His half-brother, Thomas, and his wife were living in New York, not far from Matawan. Other relatives were scattered throughout the eastern states. They would all provide him with a link with home. The challenge and adventure of the call from Hamilton was irresistible. And so the decision was made. In the fall of 1873 Robert Borden found himself in Matawan bearing the imposing title of Professor of Classics and Mathematics at the Glenwood Institute.

It was the first time he had ever been away from home for an extended period of time. Inevitably, Rob was dreadfully homesick. The sea voyage from Saint John to Portland and on to Boston in the company of Charles Hamilton, a King's County boy on his way to law school at Yale, was another first. It did not go well. The passage was rough and Robert was very ill. And such an inauspicious beginning intensified the young man's loneliness and despair. "I wish I could just step into [Grand Pré] tonight and surprise them all," he wrote in his diary. "However what cannot be cured must be endured. I will go to bed early and dream of home." For many weeks his infrequent diary entries always ended in the same resigned mood: *"Immerge, Etiam taci."*[21]

Still, there were brighter moments, especially during his first months in Matawan. Robert was impressed with the start he had made in a new land. "I had no very great inducement to come here, being able to do no more than support myself. . . . That, however, was about all I could do at home. I wished to try my hand in the world and if I wish to remain in this country I have not a bad beginning."[22] Matawan was a pleasant community of two thousand souls with Presbyterian, Baptist, Methodist, and Episcopalian churches and three public schools as well as the

Glenwood Institute. Robert took a room in a boarding house and met a public school teacher named Horner. Horner quickly introduced him to the community Literary Society and the Lodge of British Templars. In the fall, and again in the following spring, the young men rowed on the stream that passed through the village or "botanized" in the surrounding countryside.[23] On Sunday they sampled and criticized the homiletic skills of the village pastorate and attended morning, afternoon, and evening services, as often as not in the hope of meeting the attractive young ladies of Matawan.

Further afield, but only a convenient ferry ride away, was the exciting cosmopolitan city of New York. The young men often went there to visit its parks, museums, art galleries, libraries, and churches, and to attend temperance lectures. In Brooklyn Borden often stayed with the Samuel Harris', fellow Nova Scotians. And when his ship was in port, Robert regularly visited Tommie and his wife Sara. In short, life in Matawan became increasingly more pleasant and interesting and his early disposition to return home at Christmas was abandoned.

By late September Rob had settled in to his teaching duties. He had nine classes, most of them with less than a dozen students, and only two scholars in his Caesar class. He especially liked his group in Commercial Arithmetic. The work, itself, was hard, probably more taxing than it had been at Acacia Villa.

> I worked too hard this afternoon at reports &c. I was somewhat ill this evening about 7 o'clock. I must endeavour to take more exercise. There is so much infernal writing that one cannot find time for much else.

Or, again, "I feel very unwell tonight," he wrote. "My brain almost refuses to act. I must have less brain work or I will not be able to bear up."[24]

That hyperbolic outburst was typical; Robert would always be something of an alarmist about his health. It was not brain work itself that caused what he called "an incipient attack of congestion of the brain" on another occasion during the teaching year.[25] His work habits throughout his life would belie that. Rather, it was the dull daily routine of lesson preparations and of correcting the simple and repetitious reports of his young students which bothered him. More and more it became evident that he was bored. "Nothing of interest during the present week" became a frequent opening to his diary entry.[26] Less and less did he record his school duties, save for Hamilton's proclivity for foisting extra-curricular work off on his young assistant.* More and more he thought about his prospects at Glenwood Institute and as a teacher.

They were not bright. He knew only too well that his formal qualifications were few and that Canadians and Americans alike were becoming increasingly concerned about the low standards of public education. He could not afford to go back to school to complete his training. Staying in teaching meant a series of poorly paid posts as "Professor of Classics and Mathematics" in second-rate private academies, teaching comfortably dull and uninterested children. He was in the unenviable position of an amateur in an occupation that was increasingly thinking of itself in professional terms.

Perhaps it was one of the many chats with Charles Hamilton during their trip from Nova Scotia to New Haven which first drew Robert's attention to the law. He was probably not qualified to follow in Hamilton's path at Yale, but he did seek advice from his uncle in Ontario, William P. Laird, a solicitor in Strathroy, about the entrance requirements for the Ontario Bar. Laird asked the registrar of the University of Toronto to send him a list of the examination subjects and himself sent a long letter outlining the admittance procedure. When Rob informed his mother of his thoughts about going to Ontario she countered "that I should return home and study law in the office of a Halifax lawyer".

"I hardly know what to think of the proposition. I have asked for further particulars," Robert noted.[27] Certainly he was aware that legal training was not acquired quickly. In Ontario candidates without a university degree faced five years of drudgery under articles and rigorous preliminary, intermediate, and final entrance examinations.[28] Early in April, the eminent Halifax lawyer, R. L. Weatherbe, who had "one of the most conspicuous estates in the county" near Grand Pré,[29] answered an inquiry from Robert. The future looked brighter. In Nova Scotia candidates were required to serve under articles for one less year than in Ontario and there were only two sets of examinations. Weatherbe added "some idea of what the preliminary law examination [re-

---

*On October 21, 1873, he wrote in his diary that "I have been working at a confounded platform after school. If I have one more job of this kind, I think I will be apt to leave the place."

quires.] I think I would have no difficulty in passing it." Nova Scotia was surely the preferable locale to embark on a legal career. If successful it could be accomplished both more quickly and more cheaply.

After some further thought about the alternatives in his future, Robert made his decision. Between continuing in teaching and devoting four years of hard study to the intricacies of the law, there was little choice for the ambitious twenty-year-old. To carry on in teaching meant a life of mediocrity and subsistance living. But to break away and begin anew held out the potential of social eminence and wealth that no teacher, no matter how well qualified, could hope to achieve.

As soon as term was over Robert hurried home to Grand Pré, regretful of leaving behind a number of close friends but relieved of the burden of teaching. During the summer he immersed himself in the hard manual labour of the farm and, as time allowed, in studies for the Nova Scotia preliminary examinations. He passed the examinations in mid-July and a month later began work as an articled clerk in the office of Weatherbe and Graham in Halifax. He returned home for three weeks in September. And with the precision of a very practically minded young man, Robert Borden recorded the next step in his career:

> Commenced the study of the law by reading a small portion of Kerr's 1873 edition of the Student's Blackstone on Saturday evening, Sept. 19 at 8.45 o'clock.[30]

CHAPTER TWO

THE FUTURE GUARANTEED

Halifax was a small city nestled on the edge of the sea. Located on a peninsula jutting into a magnificent harbour, it was surrounded on three sides by water, on the fourth by the hills and forests that gave the city an almost insular character. For decades its economic and cultural livelihood had come from the great Atlantic world beyond its harbour. As a provincial capital, its governors had come from the mother country. As a military fortress, "The Warden of the Honour of the North" was the way Kipling described the city, its protection was guaranteed by Imperial forces and the Royal Navy. The men of the garrison and the ships of the Navy provided a handsome trade to the city's merchants. Halifax was also the base for a larger fleet of fishing schooners, the first mainland port of call for ships steaming the great circle route from Europe to America, and the home of a lively trade between British North America and the West Indies. Until Confederation its contacts with Canada were slight—almost negligible. It was a decade before the steel of the Intercolonial Railway tied Halifax to central Canada in 1876. And for most Haligonians the bonds of sentiment to the Dominion would be forged even more slowly.[1]

In the late nineteenth century all Canadian cities were dirty. But the combination of soot, fog, and salt sea air made Halifax uncommonly so. Most of its streets were unpaved, dusty in summer, muddy in spring and fall. Smoke poured from the stacks of steamers berthed in the harbour and from the chimneys of factories and mills scattered through and around the town. The long rows of unpainted houses lining the streets, the churches, stores, and public buildings all took on a deadening pall of grey.

In striking contrast to the gloomy appearance of its buildings was the welcome profusion of colours and delicate scents of the flowers lining the carefully planned walks and watercourses of the Public Gardens. The Gardens had been purchased by the city from the Horticultural Society in 1874, the year that Robert Borden came to Halifax to study law. In the years that followed the city steadily improved the facilities and attractions of the property. Space was set aside at the north-east end for croquet, archery, and tennis. In 1887 an ornate bandstand was built where the bands of the regiments at the garrison gave weekly concerts in summer. In September, during Exhibition week, Haligonians crowded the Gardens in the evening to watch spectacular fireworks displays. The pride of Halifax, the Public Gardens were a charming retreat from the grime and bustle of the seaport town.

Visitors were struck by the quiet pace of life of the city. An American traveller described it as a "dear old somnolent town" whose "ways of doing things was refreshingly un-American . . . all business is done in so quiet and leisurely a fashion". Another grudgingly admitted that it was "a city of great private virtue, and . . . its banks are sound". But Halifax was a "dull garrison town; probably there is not anywhere a more rusty, forlorn town, and this in spite of its magnificent setting". Still a third visitor criticized "the slow methods and unenterprising customs of the people of Halifax".[2]

The style of Halifax life was set by the traditional social and commercial alliance of military officers at the garrison and the leading business families of the city. What visitors decried as "slow methods and unenterprising customs" was for them a comfortable community of social and economic interest. After all, the garrison and the North American and West Indies fleet, stationed at Halifax from May to October, provided a dependable market for all sorts of goods and services. Along with the West Indies trade, victualling the mighty arm of Imperial power in British North America had long been the base of Halifax's commercial prosperity. By the seventies the West Indies trade was in decline, but the garrison and the fleet remained. And the merchant princes still catered to their needs with a propriety that reflected a more peaceful and orderly past.

Pushy traders from the Republic and "Upper Canada", obsessed with the harsh "progressive" realities of commerce in the age of steam and steel, found these mannered business methods bewildering. For their part the Halifax merchants regarded the upstart commercial travellers with their aggressive sales pitches and sharp practices as unwelcome intruders. The worst were the Canadians who looked upon the opening of the Intercolonial as an opportunity to expand their markets. A worried survey of Halifax businessmen quickly dubbed them as "thrusting drummers".[3] And their reputation would not die. A decade later the Halifax *Morning Chronicle* was still labelling the Canadian commercial man one of the more obnoxious banes of Confederation. "He spreads himself periodically throughout this province, in number he equals the locust and his visit has about the same effect," said an editorial in 1886. "He saps our resources, sucks our money and leaves a lot of shoddy behind him."[4]

By then, however shrill the complaint, however pervasive the nostalgia it evoked of better days in the province's Imperial past, the fact was that Halifax was benefitting from the ties of Confederation. From the mid-seventies through the nineties Halifax was a developing regional metropolis. "Progressive" businessmen, as they called themselves, used the shelter and encouragement of Macdonald's National Policy to expand and diversify the city's commercial and industrial base. The Army and Navy remained important, the dependence upon the Atlantic world continued. But the traditional sources of prosperity were augmented by ever stronger links to the inland provincial and national economies. One evidence of growth was the slow but steady rise in the city's population, an increase of about thirty-five per cent between 1871 and 1901.

In 1881 nearly ninety per cent of Haligonians traced their origins back to the British Isles, the Irish and English making up nearly three-quarters of the whole. The Roman Catholic Church claimed the largest number of adherents in the city, followed at some distance by the Church of England, the Presbyterians, the Methodists, and the Baptists. Half of the city's workers were of the industrial class; carpenters, clothiers, shipbuilders, other tradesmen and labourers. Mariners, merchants, clerks, and shopkeepers made up another quarter of the 13,000 strong work force and a fifth earned their living in some sort of domestic service. The professional class, the doctors and lawyers, government employees, clergy and teachers, formed a significant and increasingly influential minority of the people.

Halifax city and county attracted an increasing flow of investment capital for industrial development in the last decades of the nineteenth century. Some expansion occurred in the seventies, especially in the county. But its scale was small compared with investment in the eighties. The completion of railway links with central Canada, harbour improvements financed by the federal government, and the consequent growing number of trans-Atlantic shipping companies calling at Halifax, and the stimulus to industrial development given by the National Policy tariff, all added to the attractions of Halifax as a centre of industrial growth. The new capital was directed to secondary manufacturing, to the production of furniture, clothing, woodenwares, pianos, tobacco, refined sugar, and a host of other consumer goods for a society becoming more specialized in its livelihoods and more interdependent for both the necessities and the luxuries of life. Halifax's foundries increased their capitalization too, stimulating production of engines and machinery, tools, spikes, nails, and construction material. By the nineties the magical power of "white coal", supplied by the People's Heat and Light Company, drove the city's newly electrified street railways and factory machinery, and brightened the city's streets and public buildings and the homes of the well-to-do. And during the decade the West Indies trade was revived by the Black and Pickford Line. The city's banks followed the ships to the Indies, opening up branch offices to serve the trade. Halifax, then, was very much a participant in the industrialization of late-nineteenth-century Canada. The city's economy was diversified and strengthened. Its work force grew, responding to the new job opportunities and the improved skills required of an industrial age.[5]

Halifax was neither as "progressive" nor as hectic as New York or Boston, or even Montreal or Toronto. But that had its advantages, too, for a rural lad like Borden or the hundreds of others who came to the city to "get ahead" in these years. The competition for place and fortune was less severe but Halifax was still promising and prosperous; it was a good place for a new beginning. A young man with ambition and a willingness to work could soon find a niche for himself.

Another lure to the prospective Haligonian was the ever increasing diversity of the city's leisure and associational activities. Theatre and music, from the best American touring companies to numerous local groups of varying talent, was plentiful in offering and modest in price. The noted speakers of the day, from the righteous William Jennings Bryan to the scandalous Oscar Wilde all lectured on Halifax platforms. Debating, literary, and temperance societies—the latter more social than reform in motivation —abounded. Over the years more and more amateur athletic organizations came into being, promoting track racing, cricket, baseball, football, skating, hockey, tennis, golf, bicycling, and, naturally, rowing and sailing, for which the city was so well located. The latter, and especially rowing, were ever popular with Haligonians.

Most of these were the activities and diversions of Halifax's growing and increasingly influential middle class. Few of the city's large working class had either the time or the affluence to participate in these activities. And few working men would have found ready acceptance in the theatre and music groups, the literary and debating societies, or the golf and tennis clubs that grew apace with Halifax's expanding economy.

Borden was representative of many of the young men who came to the city from the provincial hinterlands. He sought a higher station in life than that of a labourer or a skilled tradesman, and the financial security that neither he nor his family had known in Grand Pré. And a career in the law had other attractions. The legal community of Nova Scotia was small* and, even in Halifax, where the greatest number of lawyers practised, associational ties were maintained after business hours. Social relations between senior and junior members of the bar, excepting, perhaps, the Provincial Justices, were relaxed and frequent. The Barristers' Society met regularly and among its gatherings was an annual winter outing of Bench and Bar at neighbouring Bedford. The judges in their impressive four-in-hands, the juniors following in their pairs or single-horse sleighs, drove off in grand array for an evening of dinner, toasts, and general conviviality, returning in the chill winter night guided by torchlight. Dependable, devoted, and especially eager to "get ahead", Robert Borden fitted easily into the companionship of the Bar and quickly rose to positions of leadership and respect.

Shortly after Robert Borden arrived in Halifax he was described in the city directory as a "student-in-law". His own description in later years of "apprenticeship" was closer to the mark. He was enrolled in service to the firm of Weatherbe and Graham for four years and, as he put it, "was entitled to be instructed in the

*There were 245 barristers in Nova Scotia in 1881.[6]

knowledge and the practice of law".[7] But instruction was minimal; formal training was non-existent. Law students in Nova Scotia in the 1870s, as they had always done before, learned their law by doing it, not by studying the discipline in any organized fashion. They were "articled clerks", engaged to prepare briefs and watch over the ordinary office affairs of the firms to which they were attached. Mastery of the great body of knowledge of the law, awareness of its intricacies, contemplation of its assumptions and its philosophy, was dependent solely upon the initiative of the "students" after the day's office work was done.

This was all very well. A modified form of English legal training, it had served the needs of the province for decades. But there was growing awareness of the inadequacies of the traditional mode of legal training among the barristers. A few worried that the best students left the province to pursue their education and careers elsewhere. "Some of our law students," observed one lawyer, "disgusted with the absence of any course of legal instruction in our colleges, or out of them, and unwilling to enter their profession without the advantages which these schools afford, have resorted to the neighbouring Union and from the law lectures of Harvard, or some other school of law in the United States, have learned to form a higher and a broader view of their profession than they could ever have attained from the instructive routine of a law office in Nova Scotia."[8] Others worried about the accumulating evidence of shoddy and incompetent practice in the profession, even of questionable and inadequate judgments from the Bench. "Our Judges are, with one exception, so poor," Wallace Graham noted in 1887, that "most of them could not make a living today in their profession."[9]

For Robert there would be time enough in the future to worry about the competence of judges. Nor was there any point in thinking about a more formal training. He could not afford to follow his acquaintance, Charles Hamilton, to Yale or to go to Toronto. And there would be no law school in Halifax until 1883. He would have to make the best he could of the opportunity afforded by working for Weatherbe and Graham. The two men had a large practice and Robert was never without an abundance of work. Some came from Weatherbe's political connections with the Liberal government of Alexander Mackenzie in Ottawa. As Halifax agent for the Department of Justice, the firm was given the task of preparing the Canadian case for the Fisheries Commission of 1877. Robert earned one hundred dollars for collecting materials for the case.

More important was the firm's extensive local practice which kept both the vain, demanding, and domineering Weatherbe and the sensitive junior partner, Graham, away from the office. Routine work—the preparation of briefs and office duties—was left to Borden and the clerks.[10] It was a dull, often frustrating grind. The senior members of the firm offered so little guidance. This was hardly the stuff of which youthful dreams of a brilliant career at Bar and Bench were made. Borden even thought of giving it up and accepting an offer to teach in the public school at Grand Pré.[11] But he stayed, practising the menial chores of his profession by day, studying at night.

There were plenty of diversions and some were unwelcome. Like most young apprentices away from home, he stayed in a boarding house with other young men seeking the foundations of a career. Naturally, their character and their habits ran the whole spectrum of human behaviour. Borden found his first "situation" friendly enough, but too diverting, and moved to another where only he and another law student boarded.[12] Much more pleasant were the occasional visits of Sophie, Julia, Hal, and his mother to Halifax. Then books were laid aside for a round of visiting with family friends and, perhaps, an evening at a local theatre or concert. Robert also found companionship in the militia regiment he joined a few days after coming to Halifax. Borden and his first boarding house mates, J. M. McGillvray and F. H. Simson, were in the Third Company of Halifax Rifles, each collecting a meagre but welcome six dollars for their twelve days of service. It was probably there that Borden also first met Charles Hibbert Tupper,* who was an officer in the regiment. Borden did another term in 1875–76 and a third in 1878–79, on the latter occasion receiving a fifty dollar bonus for qualifying

---

*Sir Charles Hibbert Tupper was the son of Sir Charles Tupper, the Premier of Nova Scotia at the time of Confederation, a prominent member of Sir John A. Macdonald's governments, Prime Minister of Canada from May 1, 1896 to July 8, 1896, and leader of the Conservative opposition from July 9, 1896 until February 5, 1901. Charles Hibbert Tupper was called to the Nova Scotia Bar in 1878. He was first elected to the House of Commons for Pictou in 1882 and he sat for the constituency until 1904. He entered Sir John A. Macdonald's government as Minister of Marine and Fisheries in May, 1888, and received his knighthood in September, 1893.

for a commission with a second-class certificate.[13] All in all, drill and rifle practice, and regular meetings of the St. Andrews Lodge of British Templars and of the Debating Society of the Y.M.C.A., proved a welcome respite from work and study during the winter months. In summer there was time for walking, for rowing, and for trips to the lovely North West Arm.

Borden's self-doubt and insecurity persisted throughout his student days. Though he was in his early twenties, he had accomplished so little, knew so little. "I cannot blame myself as a spendthrift of time," he wrote, almost too earnestly, "for I sincerely believe that I have worked as hard as my health would permit. And yet, when I look about me and see the boundless fields of knowledge that I have never yet approached, much less explored, it is with sorrow that I feel it necessary for me to turn away from them, a sorrow like unto that of the Lion-hearted King when he sadly averted his face from the Jerusalem he could not enter." And then, characteristically: "I must not be discouraged . . . I hope to learn much during the next ten years."[14]

At last, student days were done. Twenty-five candidates sat the Bar examinations in September, 1877, among them Charles Hibbert Tupper and Steve Rand, both of whom had studied at Harvard Law School, and many others who "did not[hing] but study up for six weeks previous to the Exam" [while] I never left the office for a day". The first inkling of triumph came after two anxious months when Borden discovered that the two lawyers on the board had given him a 92, "the next highest being 88". A few days later Robert proudly told his mother that the final examiner, Chief Justice Sir William Young, had not "docked" him. Instead, "mine is the only 1st in the number". Pluck and persistence had paid off; he had topped the class.[15]

Because he had written his papers a year early, Borden could not be admitted to the Bar until August, 1878. Already there were ambitious plans for the future. Rand, who was from Cornwallis, had proposed a partnership at Kentville. Both were Kings County boys and "our combined interest in the County and the fact that we would be the only legal 'Grits' in Kentville would be very largely in our favor," Borden told his mother.[16]

The plan to be the "legal Grits" of Kentville did not work out. But after a brief Halifax partnership with classmate John T. Ross, Borden went to Kentville as the junior partner of the Conservative lawyer, John P. Chipman.[17] Chipman, an able lawyer with

Harvard training, had a substantial practice. He turned his counsel work over to Borden. Robert quickly discovered attributes that would mark his whole professional career. He was good at counsel work. Perhaps because of his previous teaching experience, he was much more effective in the courtroom than he had expected to be. But it was terribly demanding upon his health. As he later put it, "I would be in a condition of such extreme nervous tension that I could hardly eat or sleep." By the greatest concentration of effort he prepared himself for argument, by the greatest concentration of will he managed to maintain "absolute self-control" before the Bench. But when it was over he was both mentally and physically exhausted.[18]

Wallace Graham kept an eye on his former pupil and noticed how quickly he had developed his professional skills in Kentville. In 1882 he sent Borden an irresistible invitation. Weatherbe had gone to the Bench as one of Mackenzie's "midnight judges" in 1878, and Graham had joined forces with J. S. D. Thompson and Charles Hibbert Tupper. The firm had become "law agent in Nova Scotia" for the now Conservative Ottawa government in 1881. Then, in 1882, Thompson joined Weatherbe on the Nova Scotia Supreme Court, and Tupper was elected to represent Pictou in the House of Commons. Charles Hibbert remained in the firm, but Thompson's promotion and Tupper's enforced political absence left too much work for Graham to carry alone. Would Borden care to return to Halifax and enter the firm?

There was hardly a moment's hesitation on Robert's part. Practice in Kentville was pleasant and initially had been challenging. But an offer to join a large, prosperous, and prominent Halifax firm could not be refused. Borden knew the work would be more demanding and that even as a junior member he would carry the heaviest counsel load of the partnership. But it would be worth the sacrifice. Graham offered professional prestige and financial security far beyond what Kentville promised. Robert readily accepted.

His expectations were fully realized. Borden immediately was assigned to a long list of cases before the Supreme Court at its Halifax sitting and others on circuit. His case load was heavy and grew annually. There was the work for the government, including preparation of the material for the "David J. Adams" and the "Doughty" cases, which concerned two American fishing vessels that had been seized for violations of the 1886 Fisheries Act.[19]

And the business of the firm continued to grow. More than any other professional group, the lawyers were directly involved in the industrialization of Halifax. Both the formation of new companies and the evolution of old family firms into publicly financed corporations required formal legal agreements and procedures. Capitalization, production, marketing, and management all became more intricate, more sophisticated, more intimately involved with the law and its practitioners.

Graham, Tupper, and Borden got more than their share of this work. But Graham was away much of the time, lecturing at the new law school at Dalhousie, arguing before the Supreme Court in Ottawa and, occasionally, the Judicial Committee of the Privy Council in London. Tupper took some cases before the Supreme Court but was principally occupied with his political career. There was too much for Borden to do by himself. So it was necessary to expand again and W. F. Parker, son of the prominent doctor and Conservative Legislative Councillor, Daniel McNeil Parker, was brought into the business.

Borden's reputation grew with the work of the firm. Late in 1887 Graham told him that he was about to be offered the deputy-ministership in the federal Department of Justice by John Thompson. Thompson had resigned from the Bench in 1885 and gone to Ottawa to assume political responsibility for the Department. His deputy-minister had resigned and Thompson had first offered the post to Graham. But Graham had declined, saying he preferred to wait for a possible vacancy upon the Nova Scotia Supreme Court. Thompson then considered Borden. He had been impressed by the young man's work before him during his judgeship and on the fishery cases, and he was anxious to have a young but proven and reputable lawyer to oversee his Department.

Robert sought Graham's advice, expressing concern about his competency for the post and whether, if he accepted it, his partner's elevation to the Bench would be jeopardized. Graham dismissed both considerations. But he plainly did not want Borden to leave the firm. Graham had told Thompson that Borden "is the fittest man for office I know of—his capacity for systematic work is unequalled—In fact he has been doing two thirds of the whole work of my firm and if you did offer him the position I would only have to implore him not to go".[20] The plain fact was that it was neither Tupper nor Graham but Borden who was expanding the firm's clientele and reputation. "[Your] future is guaranteed," Graham assured him. "Your position is better than that of anyone in the City." Did he really want to give that all up, to "leave your profession" for government service?[21] Finally Graham promised that if money was a factor, then "the division of the profits of our business . . . would be based to a greater extent upon the amount of time and work given to it . . . [and] would bring your remuneration up to a point that would leave the salary of the deputy a thing not to be coveted".[22]

Borden declined Thompson's offer, which was then made to and accepted by his friend Robert Sedgewick.[23] One reason, as he later wrote, was that he "felt it my duty to decline" because of Graham's generosity and friendship.[24] Perhaps another was Graham's opinion that the deputy-ministership was unlikely to lead to promotion to the Bench.* Most important, however, was the fact that by the time the offer came in early 1888 Borden must have known of other changes about to take place among his partners. Both the appointment of Graham to the Bench and of Charles Hibbert Tupper to the Cabinet were pending. Borden, with Graham's assurance that his position was "better than anyone in the City" clearly in mind, would succeed to the senior position in the firm and retain its large established clientele. From a professional point of view that was far more rewarding, financially and otherwise, than a deputy-ministership in Ottawa.

Tupper joined Sir John Macdonald's cabinet in May, 1888. Although at first he said he wanted his name to remain associated with the firm,[25] Charles Hibbert soon found his duties as Minister of Marine and Fisheries so consuming that his connection with the firm was dropped and Graham's promotion was delayed for a year. But by the fall of 1889, when Graham went to the Bench, Borden was ready to assume the leadership of one of the largest legal practices in the province.

Borden chose his new associates carefully. Parker, though his health was frail, was asked to stay on as a salaried member of the firm. Joseph Andrew Chisholm was a recent Dalhousie Law graduate, a Roman Catholic, and brother-in-law of Sir John Thompson. He left a practice in Antigonish to become another salaried member. The final man was William Bruce Almon Ritchie who had been trained at Harvard and had practised in Annapolis since 1882. A skilled and experienced lawyer, he would share the

---

*Borden later thought that it would and Sedgewick was eventually appointed to the Supreme Court of Canada.

counsel work and the net profits of Borden, Ritchie, Parker, and Chisholm. All of Borden's associates had firm connections with the Conservative party and the agency work for the Justice Department was carried over from Graham, Borden, and Parker.

Robert Borden was just thirty-five. He had made astonishing progress in the decade since he had been admitted to the Bar. He had won the respect of his profession and was well on his way towards a position of prestige and leadership within it. Already he was serving on the Council of the Nova Scotia Barristers' Society. He was one of the province's most promising young lawyers. He had carefully cultivated political connections. His future was assured. As Charlie Tupper told him, "You will (I know) soon get the silk."[26]

The doubts, the questioning, the insecurity of his youth were now gone. He knew he was successful and respected. He was confident about the future of his business. And he was now ready to enlarge and enrich his private life. Shortly before his new legal partnership was announced, Robert married Laura Bond. She was seven years younger than Robert, a bright, attractive, strong-willed young woman who was one of the daughters of Thomas H. Bond. Bond, who died a few years before the marriage, and may never have met Robert, had had a substantial hardware business on the corner of Duke and Upper Water streets. After his passing, his widow and daughters ran a boarding house on South Street.

When Robert first met Laura is not known. It may have been as early as his student days when Captain Berkeley Bond, Laura's uncle and Thomas's business partner, commanded Borden's Militia company.[27] Perhaps he met her after his return from Kentville, when he may have boarded for a time at the Bond's.[28] Or they may have met at St. Paul's where Laura occasionally played the organ for the Church of England services and Robert regularly attended.[29] In any case, the courtship began by mail in the summer of 1886 while Borden shared a cottage on the North West Arm with another young lawyer, "Ross", who may have been either his former partner, John T., or another Halifax barrister, William B. Ross. A chatty and increasingly affectionate correspondence developed with Laura who was vacationing in Antigonish. Her interest in music and theatre complemented his in literature. Both enjoyed tennis, golf, and water sports. They shared friendships in the younger business and professional community of the city. And over the next three years their affection grew into a deep and lasting love. They were married on September 25, 1889.

Robert and Laura did not buy a house immediately. Rather, they rented rooms in the centre of town in a district inhabited by merchants, clerks, insurance agents, and a scattering of prominent businessmen. Freed from many household obligations, more time could be devoted to the cultural life of Halifax and to travel. In the summers of 1891 and '93 the Bordens spent a number of weeks touring in England and Europe. Then, in 1894, Robert bought a large property with a commodious home on the south side of Quinpool Road. "Pinehurst" was in the developing western suburbs of the city, set back from Quinpool Road, surrounded by stately trees and on a bank overlooking the top of the Arm. Close by were Sir Charles Tupper's large home and the boating clubs of the Arm. The drive to town and Borden's office on Hollis Street, by coach, was pleasant, passing through the Common and around the imposing Citadel. There were no children and, sadly, there would be none. But the large house wasn't lonely. Robert's brother Hal was just finishing his law degree at Dalhousie and his easy and cheerful manner made him a pleasant companion to Robert and Laura at "Pinehurst".

The business of Borden, Ritchie, Parker, and Chisholm continued to grow, and with it Borden's reputation as a skillful counsellor. Most of his own case work was at the appellate level of jurisdiction, on referral from other lawyers and other firms, arguing Nova Scotia cases before the Supreme Court in Ottawa.[30] The work was both demanding and convivial. Insomnia and nervousness continued to plague him. "It is tiresome work but the longer I keep at it the easier it is in some respects," he told Laura in 1893. "One gets over his nervousness in the second case and when one's nervousness is less his sleep is better."[31] But there was also hearty companionship. Usually the Nova Scotia barristers took the same Intercolonial express to the capital for the high court sittings, whiling away the long hours of the journey with cards and professional gossip. In Ottawa the Nova Scotians were dined by Thomas Edward Kenny and John F. Stairs, the Halifax MP's. There were frequent lunches at the Rideau Club. And Borden was entertained by his old associates, Thompson, now Prime Minister, and Sedgewick, now on the Supreme Court Bench.

Especially pleasing was his close friendship with Charlie

Tupper and his growing family. There was always a place at Tupper's table, always a room in Tupper's home. In 1893 Robert and Laura became the godparents of the youngest member of the family, Reginald Hibbert. A year later Rob joined Charlie and his political cronies in Sir Charles' private car for a trip to Victoria, Borden's first visit to the Canadian west.[32]

In 1893 Borden argued the first of his two cases before the Judicial Committee of the Privy Council, acting for Pictou in *Municipality of Pictou* v. *Geldert*. Involved was an important principle concerning corporate liability. Geldert had been injured by driving into a hole in a bridge-approach in Pictou and had sued for damages. The municipality had made arrangements to repair the approach but the work had not been done. The Nova Scotia Supreme Court held that the municipality was not exempt from liability and that Geldert was entitled to more than seven thousand dollars in damages. On direct appeal to the JCPC Borden won. The question was whether a statute that conferred on a municipality the power and authority to repair roads also conferred an obligation to do so and its attendant liability for failure. No, said their lordships, public corporations were not liable to an action in respect of mere nonfeasance unless the legislature had shown an express intention to impose such liability upon them.[33]

The growth of the business of Borden's firm—"probably the largest practice in the Maritime Provinces"[34]—brought increasing financial security to Borden. It enabled him to lend financial support to his family, especially to his brother Will who was in business in Kentville. Robert invested his profits in mortgages, property, and a growing portfolio of stocks and bonds. His law firm represented a number of important Halifax businesses; Moirs, Nova Scotia Telephone Company, the Bank of Nova Scotia, and the Canada Atlantic Steamship Company, among others. Borden himself had become a man of comfortable wealth and considerable influence in Halifax. He sat on the Boards of Directors of Nova Scotia Telephone and the Eastern Trust Company and he had become a member of the Halifax Club. He would soon become a director of the Bank of Nova Scotia and, along with Sir Charles Tupper, a founder of the Crown Life Insurance Company.[35]

His prestige in his profession was reflected in his election to the vice-presidency of the Nova Scotia Barristers' Society in 1895 and to the presidency a year later. Under his leadership the executive of the society took the initiative in organizing the founding meetings of the Canadian Bar Association in 1896 in Montreal. The concern of the Nova Scotia lawyers for professionalism, evident in the founding of the Dalhousie Law School in 1883, was clear again in this attempt to found a national professional organization. As Borden's colleague, C. S. Harrington, explained to the first meeting, "there was need for some cohesive organization of the barristers . . . no profession needed such organization as much as did the legal profession." The profession itself was on trial. Different practices in the various provinces led to confusion and inefficiency in the conduct of legal business and the establishment of justice. Uniformity of legislation, of course, was not desired. And provincial autonomy would be respected. But what was necessary, and what was particularly apt for a national organization to oversee, was an upgrading of professional standards and an establishment of uniformity in legal practice. Harrington dwelt at length on "what the Association could do in raising the standard of legal education, in regulating and elevating the standards of professional honour and integrity, and in upholding the disciplinary rules of the profession". In short, the Nova Scotian argued, it was time for Canada's lawyers to put their house in order.[36]

That Borden agreed with these sentiments is beyond question. He took great pride in his profession. As his legal experience and education grew, as his practice enlarged from county to provincial to national and finally Imperial jurisdictions, he became ever more aware of and ever more impatient with the ineptitude, the crudity, and—in some cases—the simple dishonesty or incompetence he met with in some of his colleagues. The law, Borden believed, was a noble thing, a body of knowledge and experience worthy of the highest respect. Even more, the law was the cement of civilized society, the only true protection men had against their own and their neighbours' more barbarous instincts. But shady practitioners had and did besmirch its image. Society, rightly, was questioning the integrity of the lawyers, and, more ominously, of the law itself. It was, he believed, up to the legal profession to provide the corrective. They could do it best: by organization, by self-regulation, by disciplinary actions against their own members. The respect and honour of his profession was at stake. So too, ultimately, was the cohesion and strength of the social fabric of his country.

CHAPTER THREE

THE TUPPERS' CHOICE

As president of the Nova Scotia Barristers' Society Borden was not able to give as much time to the attempt to organize the Canadian Bar Association as he would have liked. A readjustment of his business affairs and a dramatic change in his personal life forced him to leave most of the work to his colleagues. In the law firm Parker was not well and could no longer carry his share of the work. Early in 1896 Borden asked Charles Hibbert Tupper if he would like to replace Parker. Tupper replied that it was unlikely that he would be returning to Halifax. There was going to be an election and Charlie thought the Conservatives' prospects were bright—"we will dish the Grits in '96 as well as we did in '91." So Tupper suggested that he might take on some of the firm's work in Ottawa. Borden agreed. Charles Hibbert would not become a partner, but would lend his name to the firm as an associate counsel.[1]

Tupper's association with Borden, Ritchie, and Chisholm did not mean that Robert would give up pleading cases before the Supreme Court. In fact, it was while he was in Ottawa that Tupper's father, Sir Charles, proposed that Borden run for Parliament. Robert was a guest at a dinner party at the elder Tupper's house on the evening of April 27, 1896. Sir Mackenzie Bowell had resigned the premiership that day and Sir Charles was about to become Prime Minister. Charles Hibbert may have spoken to Borden about his father's plans sometime earlier. But it was probably on that occasion that Sir Charles took Borden aside and asked him to stand for nomination as a Conservative candidate for Halifax in the forthcoming general election.

Tupper told him that he was completely satisfied with both of the Conservative representatives for the constituency, the Catholic member, Thomas Edward Kenny, who had held his seat since 1887, and his Protestant colleague, John F. Stairs. The problem was that Stairs, an influential Halifax businessman who had represented Halifax at various times since 1883, had so expanded his business and financial affairs in Halifax and Montreal that he did not want to run again. Sir Charles told Borden that Stairs would only stay out of Parliament for one term and then return to public life. Borden would be an ideal replacement. He was well-known, he had an impeccable reputation, and he would be especially popular with the business and professional community Stairs had so ably represented. When Stairs returned Robert could go back to his firm or, possibly, to the Bench.[2] Before he left the party, Borden accepted.* The following morning he took the train for Halifax where his nomination meeting was to be held on the last day of April.

Sir Charles Tupper's choice of Borden as a Conservative candidate for Halifax in 1896 requires some explanation. It is certainly true that, as Borden put it, "the thought of a parliamentary career had never entered my mind".[3] It is also true that many of the Halifax Conservatives were taken completely by surprise by Tupper's choice of Borden. One of them was furious. Charles H. Cahan, a lawyer and newspaperman who had led the Conservative opposition in Nova Scotia from 1890 until 1894 and had been an editor for the Conservative Halifax *Herald*, believed he was entitled to the nomination. He later claimed that he, not Borden, had the support of the local Conservative Association and ninety per cent of the nomination convention delegates, that a "stormy" scene had occurred at the nomination meeting, that after he had stepped aside "the Conservative leaders in four out of six city wards resigned, and refused to support Mr. Borden", and that Borden was a johnny-come-lately to the Tory cause who, until recently, had been a well-known Grit. "When I first entered political life in Nova Scotia, during the Repeal Campaign of 1886 until I resigned my leadership in the Provincial Legislature in 1894, owing to my defeat in Shelburne, . . . Mr. Borden, K.C. was President of the Young Men's Liberal Association of the City of Halifax, and was an active political associate and advisor of Mr.

---

*Borden later recalled that "at first I flatly refused" but "finally I consented". (*Memoirs*, I: 42) He may have been approached by Charles Hibbert before the party at Sir Charles' on April 27, but I think that Sir Charles persuaded him that evening to seek the nomination.

Fielding during the Repeal Campaign, and subsequently during the political controversy which developed over the legislation authorizing the organization of the Whitney Coal Combine in Cape Breton."[4] In short, Borden was a bare-faced opportunist who was misrepresenting his own political credentials so that he might sail easily into public office in Tupper's wake.

Dyed-in-the-wool Tories might well have wondered at the depth of Borden's conviction to Conservatism. Long after the party had selected him as its leader, the leading Nova Scotia Liberal, Finance Minister W. S. Fielding, twitted him in Parliament for his youthful Grit sympathies and his active "support of a Liberal candidate against the national policy". And Sir Charles Hibbert Tupper in a very angry letter in 1917 reminded Borden that "I served the interests both of yourself and the present Chief Justice of Nova Scotia (your personal friend) at the cost of both personal and political friends of my own. You and Graham were in those days both Liberals."[5] Finally, of course, Borden, himself, proposed to be a "legal Grit" in Kentville in 1877.

But the fact is that Borden had never had any reason to make a solid commitment to either political party. The idea of being a "legal Grit" in Kentville in 1877 was more a calculation of the opportunity open to a novice lawyer in a traditionally Liberal area than an expression of political ideology. It did not deter Borden from working with the Conservative Chipman. Robert did indeed speak—a five-minute speech—on behalf of a Liberal candidate in 1882. The candidate happened to be his cousin, Doctor Frederick Borden, Liberal MP for King's; and it was "the only political speech I ever made in my life up to 1896". He was not ashamed of having done so, he told Fielding in 1903: "if I were not so actively engaged in public life, personal considerations might induce me to support him again."[6]

In 1886, he wrote in his *Memoirs*, "I had ceased to be in sympathy with the Liberal party by reason of the Repeal campaign in Nova Scotia at the provincial election held in that year."[7] Fielding, then Premier of Nova Scotia, had campaigned and won on the proposition "that the financial and commercial interests of the people of Nova Scotia, New Brunswick, and Prince Edward Island would be advanced by these Provinces withdrawing from the Canadian Federation and uniting under one Government".[8] Borden did not agree—neither, for that matter, did most federal Liberals—and "ceased" to be a Liberal. There is no evidence that he was then President of the Halifax Young Men's Liberal Association, much less an "advisor of Mr. Fielding". He did, however, continue to act on his cousin's behalf. In 1887–88 he served as a reliable *via media* between the King's MP and the ruling Tory party in Ottawa. At the time Fred Borden was bargaining for a share of the patronage in King's in return for the support of Maritime Liberals for the Treaty of Washington[9] which was being considered by Parliament. And four years later Borden, Ritchie, Parker, and Chisholm refused to act against Fred Borden in the contested federal election cases after the general election of 1891. The truth is that Borden had "no political ambitions" and "was wholly devoted to [his] profession".[10]

On the other hand, Borden's professional interests were very closely tied to the federal Conservative party. The choice of Parker, Ritchie, and Chisholm as partners was no mere accident. It is worth recalling that all three were Conservatives, that Parker was the son of a distinguished local Conservative Legislative Councillor, that Chisholm was the son-in-law of Sir John Thompson. Again, the Halifax agency work for the Department of Justice up to 1896 was an important part of the business of the firm. While the offer of a partnership to Tupper in 1896 was certainly based on a long-standing friendship, it also had distinct business advantages for Borden's firm. Moreover, in the contested election cases of 1891 and 1892, Borden used his legal skills and a great deal of his own money to see to it that the cases of Sir Charles Hibbert and Sir John Thompson would not come to trial. Sir John A. Macdonald had died and the government was struggling under the leadership of Sir John Abbott. Thompson bluntly told Borden that "at the present stage of political affairs the Government cannot afford to have the slightest suspicion falling on ministers and even the unseating of Mr. Tupper and myself, (should the petitions have had that result), would have caused exultation among our enemies and depression among our friends which in ordinary times would not be realized."[11] Whatever Cahan may have said years later, it is ridiculous to assume that Tupper and Thompson would have entrusted their political careers to a man who did not have their complete confidence and trust.

The point is that in 1896 Borden had long established professional connections with the Conservative party though he did not have a public reputation as a party man. Two years before, at the time of the provincial election, he had refused to stand for the

Conservative nomination in his home county but he had been mentioned among the prominent men at the party's Halifax nomination meeting.[12] Sir Charles' selection of Borden, then, was as natural as it was unexpected. Outsiders in both parties who thought Tupper would choose a well-known party figure were caught off-guard. The Liberal *Morning Chronicle*'s feeble response was that Borden had undermined his "high personal character" and reputation for impartiality by joining forces with the Tories.

> By accepting that nomination he has placed himself before the people of this constituency in the attitude of deliberately endorsing the policy and the record of the government— their humbug national policy record, their appalling scandal record, their Manitoba coercion record, Mr. Kenny's shameful record of neglect towards the important interests of his constituency. Consequently, however friendly people may feel towards Mr. Borden personally, they have now to regard him as a Conservative politician, avowedly brought out in the interests of a government whose policy and record have brought disaster and shame upon their country.[13]

Unlike many party men with proven Conservative credentials, Borden did not hold as an article of faith that a Conservative victory would mean the continuation of progress and prosperity, that a Liberal victory would be the prelude to strife and ruin. He accepted Tupper's request out of respect for the father of a close friend and business associate. He accepted it because he believed that successful professional men had an obligation to public service, at least for a portion of their careers. He accepted it because, like teaching in Matawan, like studying the law, like moving from a comfortable Kentville practice to a junior partnership in a large Halifax firm, the offer was a new challenge, another opportunity to prove his worth. Finally, Laura hinted at another reason why Robert decided to stand for nomination in Halifax. She told Rob that Judge Weatherbe, who took his politics as seriously as he did his profession, was nearly beside himself when he learned that his former student was going into politics with such a gang of knaves. "I said you wanted to have some fun."[14]

The *Morning Chronicle* caustically reported that the nomination convention was "cut and dried", the expected result of the work of the Tory machine. Of course, Tom Kenny was renominated as the Conservative's Catholic candidate. As the Protestant flag-bearer, Borden won easily over Charles S. Hamilton, who received a few votes. "Another politician," the *Chronicle* added, presumably referring to the bitter Cahan, "who was anxious for nomination did not succeed in even having his name mentioned." Neither the *Chronicle* nor the Conservative *Herald* reported a "stormy" meeting or, in succeeding days, the refusal of Tory ward chieftains to support Borden. Both papers gave very partisan accounts of the convention. It was natural for the *Chronicle* to notice the routine nature of the meeting, the heavy hand of the party crushing the wishes of its local adherents and a "very small attendance". Similarly, the *Herald* ran a long front-page article under the heading "The Ticket That Will Sweep The County". Kenny, a proven winner, and Borden, who was expected to become one, had been nominated by "by far the largest, most representative, and the most enthusiastic gathering in that line that ever assembled in Halifax".[15]

Borden immediately returned to Ottawa to complete his Supreme Court cases. During the long journey he began to have second thoughts about his rash plunge into public life. "I think it will be possible to slide out before any great harm is done in case it is likely to prove disastrous," he wrote to Laura. "If I am going to win I want to win by a good majority as that would make things easier afterwards perhaps in case I wanted to give it up." But when he reached the capital his conversations with political friends convinced him he was on a winning ticket. The Tories may have come through five years of incompetent leadership and disastrous policies, climaxed by the unseemly spectacle of the withdrawal of the Manitoba School Remedial Bill and Bowell's replacement by Tupper. But they certainly were not downcast, not a bit of it. Charlie Tupper had said in January that they were going to whip the Grits again. In May the Ottawa contingent believed it more than ever. "The prospects of the Conservative Party being returned to power are very good," Robert reported.[16]

By the middle of May Borden was back in Halifax, ready for five weeks of campaigning when it did not interfere with his court work. In his absence Sir Charles Tupper's election manifesto had been published. Continuance and development of the National Policy headed the Conservative priorities, followed by Imperial preferential trade and the opening of a fast Atlantic steamship service. The Manitoba School Question came well down the list. The Tory members from Halifax had been National Policy

Conservatives. Both Kenny and Stairs were members of prominent Halifax merchant families, Kenny was president of the Merchants' (Royal) Bank and a director of Nova Scotia Cotton Manufacturing Company. Stairs was president of Consumer's Cordage, New Glasgow Iron, Coal and Railway Company, Nova Scotia Steel, Acadia Sugar Refinery, and the Eastern Trust Company. Borden fitted easily into this pattern. His business connections, his directorships, and his legal practice all linked him to the same National-Policy-inspired enterprises that his predecessor, Stairs, had represented.

He made the defence of the National Policy his brief campaign issue, especially emphasizing the development of Halifax as the nation's winter port on the Atlantic.[17] Throughout the last days of May Borden, Kenny, and Stairs, who had come in from Montreal to bolster the Conservative forces and publicly voice his approval of Borden, stumped the city and county pushing the soundness of their party's trade policy and warning that a Liberal victory would bring Sir Richard Cartwright to the Finance portfolio and spell the end of national development policies. When Sir Charles Tupper came to town to speak for Borden and Kenny on the third of June a great rally was held where the National Policy again had primacy of place.

Indeed, throughout the campaign, in Halifax and across the province, both parties skated warily around the most contentious issue in the election, the Manitoba School question. Neither party was anxious to debate the political and constitutional merit of federal intervention to restore public support for Manitoba's denominational schools where they did not have to. Nova Scotia seemed to be such a place. The separate school question appeared to be quite remote and unrelated to the needs of Canada's easternmost province.[18]

Borden said as little about the school question as he could. He had not studied, knew almost nothing about it. He was content to remind his audiences that the Judicial Committee of the Privy Council had concluded that the federal government did have the right to intervene on behalf of the minority in Manitoba.

> In so far as the privy council has decided that the compact made with the minority in Manitoba has not been observed, so far, I say, should every loyal citizen whether Protestant or Catholic, support the [federal] government in their desire to

remedy that which the privy council in so many words has called a grievance. Beyond this I do not go. Beyond this the policy of Sir Charles Tupper does not seek to go.[19]

For Borden it was not a question of the primacy of one race, or one religion, or one language over another. Rather, it was a relatively simple question of law, of the maintainance of the legal agreement between French and English-speaking Manitobans embodied in the Manitoba Act of 1870.

It is not a question of separate schools . . . it is one of good faith, of performing a bargain, of carrying out a compact which was entered into at the time Manitoba became a province. . . . It is not a question upon which any conflict ought to arise between the government of Manitoba and the government of Canada. It is a question which should be settled by mutual forbearance and mutual efforts for conciliation . . . any question of coercion is foreign to the subject.[20]

Frankly, he believed that the Manitoba School question was not very important, a waste of time, the product of selfish racial agitation. It was really a pity that the time and talent of Parliament had been squandered for so many months, nay years, discussing schools in Manitoba while the real business of the country went untended. "The time which has been devoted to it both in Parliament and in the press," he told a Dartmouth meeting, "is out of all proportion to its importance."[21]

Whether the electors of Halifax agreed is uncertain. What happened on polling day, June 23, 1896, was that Haligonians split their ticket for only the second time since Confederation. More important, the traditional pattern of electing one Catholic and one Protestant to represent the city and county of Halifax was broken for the first time. Both Catholic candidates, Kenny for the Conservatives and Keefe for the Liberals, were defeated. Benjamin Russell, a prominent barrister and professor at the Law School, would speak for Halifax on the government side and bring the favours of the new Prime Minister, Wilfrid Laurier, back to his constituency. Robert Borden topped the poll and it was a great personal victory for the political neophyte. But he had not anticipated the Liberal victory across the country. He had expected to be part of the Tupper tide which would again sweep the Conservatives into power. Instead, Borden was going to be a member of Her Majesty's loyal opposition, without power in Ottawa, without patronage in Halifax.

Borden knew Ottawa well. During his years of practice before the Supreme Court he had come to know the city and many of its more prominent residents. For the first parliamentary session he took up residence as a "privileged member of the [Rideau] Club".[22] In subsequent sittings he usually had rooms at the Gilmour so that Laura might join him for a portion of the long and lonesome sessions. Besides, the Gilmour was both more comfortable and less expensive than the Rideau Club and Borden retained a habit of extreme solicitude for his money despite his now very comfortable circumstances.[23] Many old friends were about, especially the Tuppers whom he saw frequently, though now their relationship was somewhat stiffened by the formal distinctions between junior backbenchers and party chieftains. And Senator David MacKeen, general manager of Dominion Coal, President of Halifax Tramways, and director of a number of Halifax corporations including Eastern Trust, was a frequent companion.

He made new acquaintances among the Tory backbenchers; Henry Powell, the Sackville lawyer, and a number of successful businessmen, Bennett Rosamond, the woollen mill owner who sat for Lanark North, Henry Craigie, MP for Bruce East and lumber manufacturer, James Clancy, farmer and lumberman representing Bothwell, and Alex MacLaren, the Stratford cheese manufacturer and exporter occupying the North Perth seat. There were new leisure activities too. He and Charlie Tupper were attracted by the current rage and took up bicycling. At first Rob used his brother's bicycle, Will having begun a long career in the Militia Department civil service in 1897 while cousin Fred was Minister of Militia and Defence. Soon Borden was very proficient at the sport and rode between ten and twenty miles a day when the Ottawa streets were not a sea of mud. "Up to date I have ridden 840 miles this year," he reported proudly to Laura in July, 1899.[24] And he played cricket when members of the Senate and Commons took on the experienced Rideau Hall team and whipped them soundly.

When the House was not sitting in the evening Borden slipped away to the Parliamentary Library or the Law Library to keep up with the work of his law firm. There some changes had taken place. It was certain that the new administration would not retain Borden and his partners as their Halifax agents. And shortly after the election the question of Charles Hibbert replacing Parker was reopened. Tupper thought he could bring the Allan Line business with him. In addition his father, Sir Charles, was going to Montreal and would ask the CPR and the Bank of Montreal "as to their business being thrown our way". Borden offered Charlie a quarter of the net profits in the firm. He reduced his own share from two-thirds to one-third because of his political commitments, and counted upon Ritchie and Chisholm to assume even more of the heavy case load of the partnership. Just before the new Parliament met in August Charles Hibbert accepted Borden's offer and moved to Halifax.*[25]

Neither his practice nor the business and social life of a parliamentarian could divert Robert from his loneliness. He and Laura had often been separated from each other before, but never for so long or so regularly. He constantly fretted at the deplorable mail service which delayed her anxiously awaited letters. When one arrived he immediately replied that it was "a great comfort to one so lonesome as I am". Without her comfort and companionship he was irritable and impatient. "I have only three [letters] from you although I have written every day since my arrival," he complained in August, 1896. He suffered from insomnia and indigestion. And he longed to be at home. "I would that I were with you in Halifax today and indeed always, dearest," he wrote. And again, "this political life seems to me most stale and flat and unprofitable. I am convinced that it is absolutely unsuited to a man of my temperament and the sooner I get out of it the better."[26]

Laura tried to busy herself with the work of the Victorian Order of Nurses and the Aberdeen Association, with visits to Lady Tupper and other friends in Halifax, and with her music and games of tennis. But she missed Rob as much as he missed her. She slept no better than he. "How glad I will be when you are home once more," she wrote in mid-June, 1897. "Come home soon dearie," she added a week later, "or I will have to come to you."[27] After 1896 Laura spent a portion of most sessions in

*In the fall of 1897 Charles Hibbert moved to Vancouver to become a partner in the firm of Peters, Tupper and Cassidy.

Ottawa with her husband. Both enjoyed the social life of Ottawa during the parliamentary sessions, the almost continual round of teas and dinners, the weekend sojourns to other members' homes in Montreal and Toronto or near the capital. During the dinner hour they would walk together by the river. Then Laura would go to the Gallery to watch the evening's debate.

When she was not there Borden would busy himself with professional affairs. "The manner of my daily life is this," he explained during the first session.

> I rise at eight and at 8[45] tea and toast are brought to my room. Until about ten I read and then make any calls at the Departmental office or elsewhere which are necessary in connection with my work. Then to the House of Commons where I receive any letters and write for an hour or thereabouts. Then for a short walk or go to the Library of Parliament or to that of the Supreme Court. After lunch we go to the House at three which occupies the time until dinner. Then if the House is not in Session read in my room or in the Library or chat with friends at the Club.[28]

The duties of a backbencher offered much work and scant reward. "It is a miserable irregular life that one has to lead," Borden complained, "and I am more than sick of it, I can assure you."[29] The demands from constituents were heavy and made more frustrating by the circumstances of opposition. Still, prominent constituents visiting Ottawa had to be seen and listened to, no matter how tiresome they were, and promises had to be made to do one's best for them. More pleasant, but still an obligation, was entertaining the Nova Scotia barristers during Court sittings, just as Kenny and Stairs had done for Borden and Russell in the past. And perhaps there was some comfort in knowing that Liberal backbenchers shared the same fate as Conservatives. One of them, a brilliant and charming young French Canadian, Henri Bourassa, boarded regularly with Borden during the last session of Robert's first Parliament. They often disagreed about policy matters, but they quickly gained a lasting respect for each other's ability and character. As Bourassa characteristically recalled it years later, "ever since we boarded together, some thirty five years ago, I have preserved the best remembrance of you & the highest regard for your person and *some* of your political achievements."[30]

Nor were first impressions of Parliament very favourable. Borden remembered that he had entered public life "with a rather lofty ideal of the dignity of Parliament as the grand inquest of the nation".[31] Doubts came quickly. The waste of time in Parliament, the onerous demands upon members, the iron-fisted control of the House by the Government to the point where debate seemed both mechanical and pointless, all added up to a feeling of frustration and uselessness. By his fourth session Borden had realistically concluded that Parliament was no different from other man-made, man-run institutions: a few men stood above the pettiness and commanded the respect of all, most wallowed about in their own frailties. "There are not many big men in the House," he told his wife. "Sir Charles Tupper on the whole is much the largest and next to him on the other side is probably Cartwright. Outside of these, the style of most of us is very parochial."[32]

Borden's early contribution to the debates in the House of Commons was slight. His first opportunity came on August 28, 1896, in a discussion initiated by Charles Hibbert on the apparently unwarranted dismissal of civil servants by the Laurier government. Of course, the Opposition implied that Laurier and his friends were making wholesale use of the spoils system and seizing every pretext to dismiss public officials who had worked for the previous administration. But what was at issue was an important point. Did any political activity at all on the part of a civil servant make him liable to dismissal; must civil servants be politically lifeless? Borden said no. As long as a civil servant participated in politics fairly and openly and without detriment to his assigned duties he had every right to do so, without placing his position in jeopardy. The danger of any other position was apparent.

> If the question of an official's politics is to be considered when the new government makes up its mind whether or not it will dismiss him from office, or if a government ventures to deal with these questions from the standpoint only of an official's political opinions, or if an official has given expression, even on the public platform, to his views on any public question—and if these things are to control in determining whether or not a man is to remain in the service, we shall have approached very closely to the American spoils system.
> . . .[33]

Later on he briefly intervened in a debate on the use of Governor General's warrants. The following year his major contribution was a legalistic speech demonstrating that the government's preferential tariff policy violated the Imperial treaties with Germany and Belgium and in 1898 he spoke on the Yukon Railway Bill, the acquisition of the Drummond County Railway by the Intercolonial—the fulfillment of a Liberal election pledge—and a few other matters. This did not mean that his responsibilities in the House were negligible. Far from it. More often than not Borden found himself in the Library preparing notes on this or that question, holding himself in readiness to speak if his leaders called upon him to do so. They seldom did; debate was dominated by the veteran established politicians. And he was more than happy to listen, and to learn.[34]

When he did rise from his chair it was usually to defend the interests of his constituency. His parliamentary interventions from mid-May to mid-June 1897 are a case in point. On May 13 he asked a question about the dismissal of a caretaker at the Halifax quarantine station for political partisanship. Five days later he spoke about similar dismissals of inspectors of weights and measures in Halifax and he asked a question concerning a Halifax immigration agent on May 25. On June 10 he inquired about a railway extension to one of the city's cotton mills. On the 15th he protested that a new thirty-five per cent *ad valorem* duty on "skates of all kinds, roller or other, and parts thereof" would throw more than a hundred men out of work in his constituency. Eight days later he was on his feet again, seeking clarification of the Laurier government's policy on government aid for wharfs.[35] It was necessary work, but it did not bring instant recognition as a brilliant parliamentary debater.

Where Borden's real talents were quickly revealed was in committee work. He was named to the Privileges and Elections, Railways, and Public Accounts committees. He was less nervous in these duties; the surroundings were somewhat more intimate and more familiar to him than the debates in the great public hall of the House of Commons. Committee work was often similar to courtroom proceedings and Borden's superior counsel skills were rapidly recognized. He was a faithful, steady, and reliable committee man and worked hard at his responsibilities. The minority report he and two other Conservative members of the Railway Committee presented in 1899 on the acquisition of the Drummond

County Railway formed the basis for a long speech. He attacked the government's generosity to its friends, who just happened to own the railway in question, and moved on to condemn the Government's decision to develop Saint John rather than Halifax as the major ocean terminal for the Intercolonial.[36] Later in the session Borden forced the Committee on Privileges and Elections to examine the conduct of the West Huron and Brockville by-elections and a long and gruelling investigation took place.[37]

By now he was speaking more frequently on a wider range of topics in the House. His contributions were sharper, more confident, and gaining more respect from his colleagues. Tupper was placing ever greater responsibility upon him. "Sir Charles is cutting out plenty of work for me," he told Laura early in July, 1899. "Another all night session!" he reported a few days later. "I went home about eleven with everything looking peaceful. At five this morning I was summoned to the house and have been here ever since."[38] The extra work brought recognition in the formal ways of the House of Commons. Borden was moved up to the front bench, a clear indication that he was being groomed for a more prominent role in the party's affairs. Certainly he was needed. Rumours of an election were about and the Conservative's image was not strong. Most of the front benchers, men like George Foster and Rufus Henry Pope, were hardy veterans of political wars long since forgotten—Tupper himself had been in the service of the party since Confederation. Others had not carried the party standard for so long but were worn out and not very reliable when it came to the dull details of everyday Commons work. Fresh talent was at a premium in Tory ranks and when it appeared it was only natural that the leader would make the most of it.

When Parliament reconvened in February, 1900, it was nearly certain that a pre-election session was beginning. Tension was high in the House. The Opposition was sharply critical of the government's acts; even more so of its failures. After Ben Russell extolled the virtues of Liberal trade policy, his Halifax colleague countered with a demonstration of the merits of the National Policy as conceived by its founders, the Conservatives. Charles Hibbert Tupper and Borden probed, with singular lack of success, for weaknesses in the government's Yukon administration policy. The by-election investigation of the previous year had not been completed and Borden tried to get it reopened. He was not successful in his first attempt. But when he threatened to bring the matter up in Supply, he forced the Liberals to put off a Supply debate for a month and a half. Eventually Laurier agreed to a judicial inquiry into the election cases and Borden had to be satisfied with it. The inquiry, not unexpectedly, was never held.[39]

Family matters were a more immediate concern. His father, Andrew, died late in March and Borden went home for the funeral and to attend to the rearrangement of affairs at the farm. Eunice and Julia would stay on at the farm but would need extra help and financial support to keep it up. In 1897 Frederick Borden, Robert's cousin from Canning, who was Minister of Militia and Defence in the Laurier government, appointed Will to an accountancy in the Department. Will had gotten on well and was now the Department's Chief Clerk and Accountant. And Hal, who was working in Robert's law firm, had just been married to Mabel Barnstead, the sister of a fellow graduate of Dalhousie Law School, Arthur Barnstead. As before, Robert's mother and sister looked to him for support. He readily gave it, but it was one more problem to worry about.

He was concerned about his growing parliamentary responsibilities which had forced him to return to Ottawa almost immediately after the funeral. He continued to carry a heavy load of counsel work for his firm, both in Ottawa and from one end to the other of Nova Scotia. And he fretted over the major alterations being made at Pinehurst in his absence. The result was more frequent and more prolonged attacks of insomnia and more irritability in his behaviour. It had been revealed in a letter to Laura the preceding summer where the usual expressions of affection and longing were overshadowed by a testy outburst of self-rightousness. Robert wanted a new study as part of the Pinehurst alterations. But it was not enough to simply say so:

> My present study doesn't suit me in many respects, as you know it is not really a study but a sitting room. There are many times when I come from work tired, nervous and over-wrought; or it may be that I wish to do work or read some book requiring close concentration of mind. On such occasions it has very often happened that any guests who are in the house come to my so called study and engage in general conversation. . . . I must confess to you that this has been most irritating and annoying to me. I desire and I think I

have earned the right to a room in which I shall not be so disturbed. . . .[40]

Robert quickly apologized for the sharpness of his letter and the incident was forgotten. But both he and Laura were increasingly concerned about his health. They agreed that he should go to New York to consult a physician about his condition. He made two trips in April and May, 1900, and was examined by Dr. Nesbit "who is said to be a specialist on disorders of the stomach".

Nesbit carefully reviewed Borden's medical history. In 1891 a Halifax doctor had told him that his heart "was in bad condition" but later in the year an English physician had not confirmed that diagnosis. Between 1891 and 1896, his condition, "so-called flatulent indigestion", improved "owing to a gradual lightening of work and living in the country". Since he had entered Parliament, however, it had gotten worse again. Dr. Nesbit told him that he had "acid catarrh of the stomach and intestinal indigestion, enlargement of the liver to a extent of three fingers and slight enlargement of the spleen, hydrochloric acid 36 whereas it should be 20". By the second visit to New York the enlargement of the liver had decreased and he felt somewhat better. But he was not well, "still suffers from the same disorder and particularly suffers in loss of sleep thereby occasioned and in consequent nervous exhaustion". Nesbit put him on a limited diet, eliminating spices, sauces, and fatty foods, which he maintained for the rest of his life. For a time Borden gave up tobacco, as was also suggested. But the most important prescription, aside from some temporary medicinal treatment, was another matter. "Decrease of work," Nesbit ordered, "particularly not to work in the evening; to avoid excitement etc. as the patient's nervous system was said to be in a very low condition."[41]

The essence of the prescription was simple enough; get out of politics. Borden was undoubtedly inclined in that direction. Repeatedly he had hinted to Laura that his first parliamentary term would be his last. "Unless I alter my mind greatly, nothing will ever induce me to again become a candidate," he had written in July, 1899. "I want to be rid of it and I am becoming convinced that my health won't stand it," he added a few days later.[42] There would be no financial problems if he gave up public life. Indeed, he would be better off if he did leave and devote full time to his law firm. And healthier too! But perhaps his illness was not quite so serious as he sometimes thought, perhaps he made too much of it when it conveniently served as a plausible excuse from some objectionable task. His insomnia was real enough, as was the stomach condition which precipitated it. But if he took hold of himself, if he was determined to accommodate his living style to his condition, he could certainly carry on. It wouldn't be entirely comfortable. But neither would retirement from politics where his friends thought he was badly needed.

"The men whose good opinion I value most" had been increasingly urgent in their appeals for him to stay on.[43] Borden was beginning to make a mark for himself and Sir Charles Tupper was especially anxious that Borden run in the now-certain fall election. It would be a bad blow for the party, he said, if Borden, of all the Nova Scotia candidates, chose to retire.[44] More than that, Tupper wanted him to organize the Tory campaign in the province. So despite his illness, despite his family and business concerns, Borden yielded. Gone from his letters to Laura were thoughts of resignation. As the 1900 session drew to a close they were replaced by news of his preparations of campaign literature and the dozens of other tasks necessary to an election. The flattery was welcome, the appeal to his pride and to his usefulness to the party had worked. Borden would again stand for Halifax City and County.

The Conservatives faced a formidable foe in Nova Scotia and across Canada. In 1900 the country was prosperous and the Liberals took full credit for the good times. True, the Laurier government had borrowed many of its development policies from previous Conservative administrations. But Laurier's cabinet of all talents had a potent boast: *they* had made the policies work! Immigration was at an all-time high, so too was trade, and Liberal budget surpluses were favourably compared to the Tory deficits of a few years before. Industry and agriculture were booming. Even the despatch of Canadian volunteers to the South African War in October and December, 1899, had caused hardly more than a ripple of discontent. In Quebec Henri Bourassa had resigned his seat in protest and had been returned again, unopposed, by acclamation. In Ontario Goldwin Smith thundered away about the sinister forces of Imperialism in the columns of the *Weekly Farmers' Sun*. But most Canadians who cared about such matters, and they were not many, took Canada's involvement in the war as evidence of the country's growing maturity and national achievement. "Four years of peace," Finance Minister Fielding proclaimed, conveniently ignoring the Canadian boys in arms in South Africa, "four years of progress, four years of such prosperity as this country never before knew."[45] Who could doubt it? And who would doubt that the Liberals were responsible for the good times?

Few did. The Conservatives, under Sir Charles Tupper's leadership, blundered badly. They provided no convincing counterargument, much less an appealing alternative governing party, to the promises and personnel of the Liberals. Their campaign was haphazard and unorganized. In central Canada they tried to play anti-Imperialist French-Canadian sentiment off against its Ontario counterpart. The strategy backfired, leaving the party with an image of appeals to prejudice that would not soon be forgotten. Everywhere they sniped away at the government party on a plenitude of petty and confused issues. "Of all the issues which Sir Charles Tupper delights to restate, there is not one which the Canadian elector can declare to be of surpassing importance," a writer for *The Canadian Magazine* observed.[46]

In Nova Scotia Borden had to contend with Fielding's claims of peace, progress, and prosperity, with the organizational skills and patronage of the Minister of Finance and of his cousin, Frederick Borden, and with the provincial Liberal machine that Fielding had constructed and passed on to his protégé, Premier Murray. In 1896 the Conservatives had won ten of the province's twenty seats and a bit more than half of the popular vote. In 1900 they took only five seats and their popular vote dropped noticeably.

In Halifax Borden's running mate was again Tom Kenny. William Roche and W. B. Wallace stood for the government. Borden conducted a set-piece campaign. He said scarcely a word about Canada's involvement in the South African War. In speech after speech he emphasized two points: if victorious the Conservatives would implement a fast Atlantic steamship service; if defeated, Haligonians could expect more scandals from the Liberals, more corrupt by-elections, more corrupt administration in the Yukon, more shady railway deals like the acquisition of the Drummond County line. As in 1896 the city and county of Halifax electors split their tickets and elected the two Protestant candidates, Borden and Roche. "We cannot congratulate Halifax on what it has done," the *Chronicle* gloomily observed after polling day. Roche and Borden were both "good men" but they were "permanently paired" and "Halifax is out of it for the next five years".[47] Robert's own election was uncomfortably close. "The country districts saved me," he told Charles Hibbert.[48]

On election night, November 7, Borden spent an hour with Sir Charles Tupper at the Halifax home of their mutual friend, Senator David MacKeen. Borden was downcast as the gloomy news came in. The defeat was a party disaster. It wasn't just that Laurier had a majority of 55. More important, Tupper's strategy had been to run his key veterans against Liberal chieftains. This too had backfired. George Foster had been defeated by the Minister of Railways, A. G. Blair, in neighbouring New Brunswick. Clifford Sifton had humiliated Sir John A. Macdonald's son, Hugh John, in Brandon. Sir Adolphe Caron and J. G. H. Bergeron were gone from Quebec as was Borden's friend Henry Powell from Ontario and the colourful Nicholas Flood Davin from the Territories. Worst of all, Tupper, himself, had been turned out in Cape Breton. In short, the party's front ranks had been purged.

The old man, however, was his ever cheerful and confident self. He intended to leave immediately for the West Coast to campaign in postponed elections in British Columbia constituencies. He was ready to go on fighting. But he also seemed relieved of a great burden. Tupper hinted that he did not want a seat found for him. He would see the campaign through and then he was done. As Sir Charles described the evening: "Telegraphed to my wife that I was now honourably released from public care and could devote the evening of my days to her and our children. Went to bed & slept soundly."[49]

Charles Hibbert Tupper, who had won his Pictou seat again, joined his father on the western trip. There was much to talk about as the train chugged across Northern Ontario and the prairies. But foremost in the Tuppers' minds was the succession to the leadership. One thing was clear. Charles Hibbert could not be a candidate. He would not only keep his own enemies in the party but inherit all of his father's. Nor did he want the job. His financial situation was very poor. He would finish out this Parliamentary term and then devote his life to the law and politics in his new home in Vancouver. Other leadership possibilities were canvassed. Foster, as an experienced former cabinet minister and one of the most formidable debaters on the Conservative benches, had a strong claim. But he was without a seat and, more important, like the Tuppers, was a part of the old gang, veterans of the interparty battles up to and during 1896. And the same was true of Clarke Wallace.

More names came to mind: Thomas Chase Casgrain of the old Quebec Bleu faction; Frederick Debartzch Monk, who had entered Parliament in the same year as Borden and who promised to represent new trends in Quebec Conservative thinking; E. F. Clarke, the former mayor of Toronto and prominent Orangeman; and William F. "Billy" Maclean, the impetuous publisher of the Toronto *World*. But all had their faults. Casgrain would alienate Monk and his followers. Monk would alienate Casgrain and the other Bleus. Clarke would alienate the Catholics. And Billy—well—sooner or later Billy would alienate everybody! There remained Robert Borden. Shortly after the Tuppers reached the coast, Charles Hibbert, with his father's blessing, put the idea to his former law partner.

That Tupper should select the Conservative member for Halifax illustrated the depths to which the once great Conservative party had fallen. Certainly the election defeats of 1896 and 1900 by the Liberals were serious blows. But the mortal wounds had been self-inflicted since the deaths of Macdonald and Thompson by the party leaders as they squabbled and scrambled for power. What remained was a quarrelling collection of jealous, disorganized, and dejected factions. Borden's chief attraction to the party leader was that he had taken no part in the party strife, had not knowingly offended anyone. Because of his youth and inexperience he had committed no political sins, made no political enemies. He was loyal to his leader and did not hesitate to acknowledge his admiration for Tupper's ability and long service to the party.[50] He had proved to be an able and conscientious worker and had willingly accepted the increasing responsibilities Tupper had assigned to him. In short, in his first term in the House of Commons Borden had acquired the skills of a competent parliamentarian.

Leading a national political party was quite another matter. Borden may have been, as the *Herald* enthusiastically proclaimed during the election campaign, "in the front rank of the parliamentarians of the day".[51] But a party leader had to combine subtle persuasion and cold ruthlessness in his dealings with other men. For the interests of the party stood above the whims and fancies of any of its members. The leader held the welfare of the party in trust. Ultimately, the usefulness of all of his followers to the party depended upon his judgment, his tact, his decisiveness. Borden's legal career and his all-too-brief political life gave few hints that he possessed these traits. There was much to prove his success as a self-made man; there was little to suggest that he would be a successful leader of men. And yet, there was also nothing to prove that he would not be or could not be a leader. Given the state of the Liberal–Conservative party in 1900, that was enough to make the Tuppers' choice seem both reasonable and wise.

Borden was truly surprised when he received Charles Hibbert's letter in mid-November. Though he denied that he "regarded the matter seriously", he took almost three weeks to consider "my acceptance of the leadership" and then replied that he would not. His reasons were truthful enough. "I have not either the experience or the qualifications which would enable me to successfully lead the party," he told Charles Hibbert; "it would be an absurdity for the party and madness for me." But Borden did not flatly refuse. The closest he came to it was an admission that he "could not" give up his law practice "to give his whole time to the undertaking". He concluded with the suggestion that Charles Hibbert's ability, experience, good judgment, and aggressiveness made him the logical man to succeed his father as party leader.[52] But Borden knew that Tupper could not afford to give up his law practice in Vancouver and move back to Ottawa to live on an MP's $1,500 annual indemnity. He also recognized that if Sir Charles chose his son as his successor all the old divisions and rivalries that had grown up among the senior members of the party would be perpetuated. The party needed a leader who had not been involved in the quarrels of the past and who could gain the respect and loyalty of all its members. Apparently nothing more was said, though Sir Charles may have talked with Borden when he returned from his tour of British Columbia. The Tuppers still wanted Borden; and Borden had not quite declined to accept their nomination.

Early in February, 1901, a disheartened group of Tory MP's and senators met in Ottawa to receive Sir Charles Tupper's formal resignation and to select a new leader. The first day was largely taken up with bidding the old man farewell and the Conservatives went through the ceremonies with the respect due to the man who had played a leading role in their party since Confederation. Such excitement as there was centred on the succesion question. All the men the Tuppers considered came to the meeting with some support: Charles Hibbert, himself; Foster, of course; and Wallace, Clarke, Maclean, Monk, and Casgrain. Sir Charles Hibbert broke through the atmosphere of "desultory discussion" with a motion supporting Borden. Support for the other men, especially Foster, persisted. But Foster was out of Parliament. And over the night of February 5–6, the Tuppers used their great powers of persuasion on Borden's behalf. Yes, they granted that their man was inexperienced and unproven. But he was responsible, hard-working, honest, and promising. And he was a new man who would give the party new life and a new image. That did it. When the caucus reconvened on the 6th the Tuppers' choice was ratified as leader of the Conservative party of Canada.

Borden acted out the necessary formalities of surprise, consideration, very reluctant acceptance, and two conditions.[53] His term, he said, would be for one year and he would demand a committee of the party to select a permanent leader. He then accepted. The temporary nature of his appointment was never made public; his demand for a committee to select a permanent leader was quickly forgotten. It was a neat demonstration that he was beginning to understand how to manipulate political power.

CHAPTER FOUR

THE TEST OF LEADERSHIP

Robert Borden's first responsibility was to rebuild his party. One manifestation of the difficulty before him was the sparse attendance at the leadership caucus. Just over seventy of the one hundred and twenty MP's and senators had bothered to come to Ottawa to bid Tupper farewell and to choose a new leader. Another was the uneven distribution of Conservative party representation in the House of Commons. For practical purposes, the Tories were an Ontario party; fifty-five of their eighty members came from that province. The next largest group was the tiny eight-member delegation from Quebec, a pitiful but accurate reflection of the decline of the party's power and prestige in French Canada. Scattered representation from the other provinces made up the remaining seventeen Conservative seats. Still more evidence of weakness was to be found in the absence of the great voices and commanding personalities of the past from the Tory benches. A number of men of local prominence remained and there were some promising newcomers. But there were no men of the stature or reputation of Tupper or Foster or even Hugh John Macdonald. No one, including Borden, was instantly recognized as the leader of the party in fact as well as in name. In the House of Commons Laurier was forceful, confident, gracious; Borden was a mere shadow in his presence. The handsome and eloquent Prime Minister stood at the head of a loyal and disciplined army with a majority of fifty. Borden led a weak, divided, and dispirited band of hesitant followers.

The prescription for the restoration of the party's health was obvious. Most important, Borden had to make himself known and respected as leader by both the party and the public. Then it was necessary to pull the party together, to unite its localized factions into a functioning national organization, to direct its energies away from the personal feuds and past quarrels that were the characteristic indulgences of the beaten. The ultimate goal, turning out the Laurier government, could only be achieved by a party whose faith in itself had been restored, whose confidence in its leader had been established. But defeating the Grits required even more. The party's strength in traditional centres of power, like Quebec, had to be revived, and strong support created in the growing Territories, soon to become provinces, of the prairie west. Finally, though no less important, the party had to come to grips with the rapid industrialization of twentieth-century Canada and to reassess the role of the party and of government in an increasingly complex economy and diverse society. It was not good enough to claim that the policies responsible for the creation of the new Canada were Conservative policies, which the crafty Laurier had adopted as his own. It was not good enough to recall that the National Policy was a Conservative policy and that they were the party of development and prosperity. The great rhetorical flourishes had worn thin with endless repetition. Macdonald was dead. And memories of Macdonald's promises were no competition to Laurier's free-wheeling, high-dealing accomplishments. In short, if the Conservatives were to regain power, they had to shake loose from the past. They had to compete with the Liberals in the planning and promise of the future.

Borden sensed that his work would be slow, demanding, often discouraging. He recognized that it would call for patience and understanding far beyond what he had been called upon to exhibit in his legal career. He suspected that it would require endless negotiation and skillful compromise in a host of areas where his knowledge and experience were limited. The security of the law, of its established precedents, of its traditional procedures, of its professional respect, had no real equivalent in politics. Party leadership meant dealing with men with vague principles, variable moral standards, strong emotions, with men whose reason was shackled by the lure of power. Politics was a game of chance. The players were tough, ambitious, often unscrupulous. The rules were peripheral and the security was minimal. The rewards of victory were enormous but the penalties of defeat could be crushing.

The weeks immediately following his selection as leader were occupied by the first session of the new Parliament and by Borden's continuing obligations to his law practice. But it was imperative that he go before the public, make his person and his views known to them. Among countless invitations, he accepted one from Toronto for his inaugural address. In May, 1901, before a large and enthusiastic audience at Massey Hall, Borden began with a sampling of the expected Conservative platitudes. But he went on to warn that reliance on past policies designed for past problems would not do. Conservatives had to recognize that they were in "a new age" which demanded new thinking about the nature of the state, of the economy, and of society. Among the most important of the new problems was the rise of corporate wealth. Its capacity to enhance efficiency and productivity were granted. But its great power was also dangerous to society and ways had to be found to keep it in check.[1]

Other appearances followed, including a splendid banquet in his home city on July 1. There Borden stated that it was necessary "to advance and develop" the party's fiscal policy "so as to meet new conditions" and he criticized the indiscriminate immigration policy of the Liberal government. "Canada should look to quality rather than quantity," he observed; her future citizens "should be of the same or similar race to those which now inhabit the country, and should be at least of a strain which will readily assimilate with our own people."[2] Then, more frequently as the year drew to a close, there were meetings of another sort; quiet affairs out of public view where the leader was introduced to or got better acquainted with the party's acknowledged managers in Quebec and Ontario.[3]

Reasonably enough, his initial visits were concentrated in Ontario where his party's strength was great and where success was most assured, and in Quebec, where his party had its greatest problems. The following year Robert and Laura embarked upon a grand tour of the emerging, confident, and prosperous Canadian West. The trappings were tailored to the task. The leader, the local notables, a group of "prominent" fellow parliamentarians, and the politicians' ladies were all prepared for the grand ceremonial performances demanded of them. They travelled in a sleeping car hired from the Canadian Pacific. At each stop the local faithful waited with a line of carriages to take the procession of visitors to the place of the meeting. Speeches of welcome were followed by words of wisdom from the prominent MP's. Then the new leader explained his policy and purpose and sought the earnest support of the audience. His style was ponderous and heavy but sympathetic reporters had the good grace to call it "reasoned" or "intellectual". Finally local dignitaries concluded the meeting with speeches of thanks. If the party was staying over the night, a banquet and yet another round of oratory followed. At long last the people went home and Borden and his colleagues collapsed, exhausted, into their berths. The same formula, the same words, soon worn and tiresome to the travelling Tories, would have to be repeated next day.

In Vancouver, early in September, Borden began with a staple of the tour. "Adequate protection" was essential to the development of Canadian industry. He quickly turned to another subject of western interest. His party was not and would not be indebted to the CPR; "no corporation will control the principles or policy of the party". And amidst loud cheers, he denounced the Laurier government for its repeated disallowance of the Asiatic exclusion laws passed by the province.

In the Territories the standard fare was spiced with a vigorous demand for the immediate grant of provincial status. At Winnipeg, as the tour drew to a close, Borden was feted at a sumptuous banquet where Sir Charles, Premier Roblin, Monk, and Foster celebrated his political virtues. The Winnipeg Theatre "was packed to its utmost capacity" to hear Borden return to one of the most popular topics in western Canada, Chinese immigration.

> I am satisfied of two or three things about this Chinese immigration. In the first place, I am satisfied that the Chinese for the most part do not become permanent settlers in British Columbia; in the second place, I am satisfied that they do not assimilate with the people of British Columbia; the people do not desire them to assimilate, and the Chinese do not desire to be assimilated; in the third place, I am satisfied that the greater portion of their earnings go back to their own country, and that they themselves live in the hope and expectation of going back. In the fourth place I am satisfied that the standards [sic] of living which they maintain is one which tends to degrade white labor wherever it is placed in competition. (Cheers).[4]

The tour was an extremely trying experience and it was rather too elaborate in the planning. Almost inevitably, the "representative" delegation of prominent MP's fell to quarrelling and petty jealousies after nearly two months at such a pace at such close quarters. More important was the impact of the new leader upon the westerners. Some were not impressed, perhaps more than either they or the party cared to admit. There was some grumbling about Borden's vigorous defence of tariff protection, but that was matched by a grudging admiration for his "courageous" defence of protectionism in an area where free trade was an article of faith. No, the essence of the matter, it seemed, was not party policy, but the man who proclaimed it. "Mr. Borden and his lieutenants offer a sad contrast to the men who so recently used to champion the Conservative Party," one local politico wrote to Sir Charles Hibbert Tupper. "The leader himself appears to be an able and courteous gentleman, but with no force at all compared with such giants as your good old father and his colleagues."[5] The remarks were probably exceptional; the sentiment behind them probably was not. It was one measure of how far Borden would have to go to lure his party's loyalty away from his predecessors and the past.

Whatever the private reservations, the outward appearances were good. Borden had been well-received, even warmly received in western Canada. The tour had been boomed by Conservative newspapers across the land and, as it drew to a close, more and more often it was described as a "triumph". The giant celebration at Winnipeg was repeated by and for the faithful in Montreal and in Halifax where a huge torchlight procession accompanied the weary leader to his home.

There were other, more tangible results from the tour. In Winnipeg Premier Roblin was favourably impressed by his talks with Borden, thus solidifying the provincial party's support behind the new leader. At Revelstoke Borden had attended the leadership convention of the British Columbia Liberal–Conservatives. A year later the party assumed power at Victoria and Richard McBride became premier. On the prairies Borden's conversations with the leader of the Territorial government, F. W. Haultain, won that important western political figure over to the Conservative cause. The following March Borden advised R. B. Bennett, a prominent Calgary Conservative, that the forthcoming

Territorial convention of the party should restrain its criticisms of Haultain's administration. In federal politics, Borden wrote, "we should invite his cooperation and assistance as long as he is disposed to remain with us."[6] To the convention itself the leader addressed a letter stressing the importance of thorough party organization. He reminded the delegates that political organization brought the party into intimate contact with the people, made it responsible to the people, and lessened the chance that the party would become the creature of self-serving professional politicians. "If the people remain inert," Borden wrote, "the Government naturally falls into the hands of professional politicians, men whose chief interest is their own political existence, men accustomed to rely upon the unscrupulous methods of the machine."[7]

All of this was unquestionably important. Showing the flag in the west, and in the Maritime provinces, where Borden toured in 1903, was a necessary duty of a national party leader. But Borden knew that governments were made and broken not in the west, nor in the Maritimes, but in Ontario and Quebec. And for him Quebec and its Conservative members were a perpetual source of puzzlement and frustration. The heart of his problem was his relationship with Frederick Monk.

When Borden accepted the leadership he appointed Monk leader of the party in Quebec. Why he did so is not entirely clear. Perhaps he recalled the old alliance of Macdonald and Cartier which had been the key to the success of the party in Quebec a generation before. Perhaps Monk's appointment was a tacit acknowledgement by Borden of his own unfamiliarity with the political problems and aspirations of French-speaking Canadians. Certainly the appointment was recognition of the fact that Monk was the ablest of the small group of Quebec MP's and that Monk had had some support for the party leadership. Moreover, Borden probably knew Monk much better than the other French-speaking Quebec Conservatives. They had shared a front-bench desk in the last Parliament. Like Borden, Monk had had a distinguished career in the law and he hoped to use his political career as a stepping stone to the Bench.[8] Both men were first elected to Parliament in 1896; both had quickly risen to prominence in party circles. Both men were temperamental, sensitive, not prone to accept criticism easily. Both men looked to the day when their party would be rebuilt around a generation of younger men dedicated to public service. Borden, then, chose a man very much like himself to be his Quebec lieutenant.

And Monk's task was even more difficult than Borden's. He had, at one and the same time, to follow Borden and to speak for a tiny warring faction of Quebec MP's. He wanted to give a fresh voice and a new outlook to Quebec Conservatives. He quickly angered the old party regulars in the province. Casgrain complained that Monk "constantly sought the advice of men who had not yet acquired that experience in political life which gives to their judgment preponderating weight in the solution of difficult questions, he altogether neglected and even appeared to shun the counsel of those whose years of training gave them a right to be called to the deliberations of the Party."[9] When the regulars appealed to Borden, he too quickly accepted their accounts of Monk's failures and inadequacies.

By its very nature, the relationship between the party leader and his Quebec lieutenant was difficult and confusing in the best of circumstances. The dual leadership lent ambiguity to the role of the party leader in Quebec politics and to the responsibilities and privileges of the Quebec leader in the national party. To be successful, the relationship required three qualities which neither Borden nor Monk was noted for: long experience in practical party politics, the desire to understand the other man's point of view, and the willingness to cooperate with each other. If the arrangement worked well the potential benefits to the party would be great. If it did not, the existing rifts and rivalries in the party would be exacerbated.

Unfortunately, Monk's relations with Borden steadily deteriorated. Borden was offended when Monk did not join him on the western tour though Monk had a very reasonable excuse. The Quebec leader stayed home to oversee a series of important by-elections and then rushed to Winnipeg for the triumphal celebration that concluded the tour.* By the summer of 1903, with the possibility of an election pending, Borden was thoroughly exasperated by Monk's conduct. "Monk has been here only three days in the past three weeks," he noted in early July. Some days later the complaint was reversed. Monk's presence had thrown a damper over an otherwise successful organizational meeting:

---

*Many years later Borden acidly recorded that Monk made "some convenient excuse" for not joining the tour (*Memoirs*, I: 88).

"My Quebec lieutenant, however, was in a very morose mood and did not succeed in impressing any of us with a sense of his largeness of soul." And finally, on the 24th, Borden told his wife that "Monk spends the most of his time in brooding over imaginary conspiracies which he thinks are being hatched against him on every side. Hence he is not of much assistance to me at present. In fact my work would have been infinitely easier during the present session if he had never entered the Chamber."[10]

The comments reveal much about the extreme sensitivity and self-righteousness of both Borden and Monk. Neither man could work easily and continuously with the other. The selection of Monk as party leader in Quebec had been a mistake. But having made his choice, Borden should have honoured it and given Monk his unswerving support in what was, after all, a well-nigh impossible job. Instead, in the fall of 1903, the party leader stripped Monk of his major responsibilities, appointing L. P. Pelletier and M. F. Hackett as provincial organizers and giving them a great deal of independence from the Quebec leader.[11] Little wonder that Monk complained of "conspiracies". The appointments of Pelletier and Hackett were serious enough. But Borden's simultaneous wooing of Joseph Israel Tarte left Monk with no choice but to question the loyalty of his leader to him.

Tarte was so different from Monk. He was an acknowledged master at political affairs, both seemly and unseemly. He was a skilled organizer, a magnetic speaker, an enthusiastic professional player at the game of politics. Once a Conservative, he had bolted the party and become Laurier's chief Quebec organizer in the 1896 and 1900 campaigns. He was rewarded with the politically important portfolio of Public Works. By 1902 Tarte had become increasingly concerned that his colleagues might bow before a growing public clamour against tariff protection. While Laurier was in London attending the Imperial Conference, Tarte went on the stump to drum up protectionist support in the government camp. Within days a public rift had developed in the Liberal ranks and charges of treachery were being hurled at Tarte. When Laurier returned Tarte was dismissed, less, apparently, for his protectionist convictions—he was replaced by the equally ardent protectionist J.-R. F. Prefontaine—than for his unauthorized campaign.

Borden believed there was much political capital to be made out of Tarte's dismissal. He gave no thought to replacing Monk as titular Quebec leader with the ex-Minister. But if, short of that, some working agreement between Tarte and the Conservatives could be arranged, all sorts of possibilities might open up for the party both in and outside Quebec. Tarte was a proven winner in the fiercely partisan battles of the province. He possessed the personality and the organizational talent that Monk and the Quebec party so sadly lacked. Equally important, Tarte and Borden agreed upon the role of the federal government in national development. Like Borden, Tarte believed that the government should pursue a broad ranging, integrated transport policy. Railways were important, of course, but future railway policy should be tied to harbour improvements, improvements in the St. Lawrence water route, and the establishment of a Canadian merchant marine. The great public works of the country should take advantage of all of its physical assets to provide the cheapest and quickest Canadian transport possible for Canada's growing foreign trade.[12] Similarly, they saw eye-to-eye on the tariff. Tarte's letter of resignation to Laurier had pointedly referred to the need for tariff revision, "with the view of giving a more adequate protection to our industries, to our farming community, to our workmen".[13] It was an echo of Borden's own words. The potential pay-off, then, of a Borden–Tarte alliance was immense. A talented French-speaking advocate of Borden's own policies would not only be useful in Quebec where protectionist sentiment was strong, but could strengthen Borden's claims with the carefully protected industrialists of Ontario who were all too readily giving their party contributions to Laurier's men.

Such thoughts reckoned neither with the feelings of the Quebec Conservatives in general nor with Frederick Monk in particular. To most French-speaking Conservatives, at least, Tarte's protectionist sympathies were less important than two other facts about his career. First, he was an unreliable turn-coat who had originally bolted from their party and now—if you believed his claim that he resigned rather than that he was fired—from the Liberals. Second, it was Tarte who had engineered, by fair means and foul, Laurier's great victories in Quebec. And not a few important French Conservatives had painful personal knowledge of Tarte's tactics. Not unnaturally, to them Tarte was more an untrustworthy intruder than a potential party Messiah.

For Monk the matter was more personal. In January the party

had arranged a grand testimonial banquet for him in Montreal where Borden had paid him eloquent tribute in his first speech in French.[14] But for months there had been talk of and some pressure for an arrangement with Tarte, especially among the English-speaking Conservatives in the province.[15] Borden did nothing to discourage it, or to reassure Monk that his own position was secure. By June, 1903, Tarte was suggesting tactical manoeuvers in the House to Borden.[16] In August, Brenton Macnab, the editor of the Montreal *Star*, informed Borden that Hugh Graham, publisher of the *Star*, had seen Tarte. An election seemed imminent and "Israel will take off his coat for the balance of the campaign". While Tarte was talking with Graham, Monk had dined with Pelletier and Hackett and told them "that he should not be asked to speak on the same platform with Israel; but professed his willingness to stand by and allow the procession to march along, with Israel in it, helping in every way possible otherwise".[17]

The understanding had been consummated, significantly, by Graham and Macnab at the *Star* rather than by Borden, himself. Monk, apparently, had been handed a *fait accompli*, again not by Borden, but by the two men Borden had appointed to assume responsibilities that were titularly Monk's. By early September Tarte was appearing on Conservative platforms with Pelletier and Casgrain. Then, in November, after it had become clear that there would be no election until 1904, Borden, Tarte, and Monk all appeared together at the Monument Nationale in Montreal.[18] In January, 1904, the three men toured the Eastern townships.[19] So far as the public could see, all was well. But it was not. Tarte, who was not the Quebec leader, complained about the appalling lack of organization in the province, about the lack of leadership in Quebec. The Quebec leader complained about the lack of organization, about Tarte, and about the obvious confusion in party ranks in the province. Monk had had enough. Not without reason, he resigned from his now meaningless post as Quebec lieutenant in mid-January.

The Conservative members of the House of Commons and the Senate set the party's style and controlled its power. Unlike the Liberals, the Conservatives had never held a national convention where a great gathering of the faithful, representing both the federal and provincial elements of the party, had thrashed out the party's policy. Instead, the MP's played a major role in determining and in modifying party policy. As the duly elected representatives of the people, they were the repository of the party's philosophy and program. And insofar as the party had a rationale for its organization, it too was based upon electoral success at the constituency level. The MP's were the national organization and represented a curious blend of individual and local halls of power and union for national purpose. Prominent defeated candidates and major party contributors would be listened to and, on occasion, could exercise great influence in party affairs. But the continuous and most powerful determinate in party business was its collective representation in Parliament and especially its membership in the House of Commons.

The party leader was the creature of this group of men. They had, after all, selected him to lead them. His role was flexible, but a priority on strong leadership was implicit in the system. Macdonald, in his day, had always had his problems with "loose fish" at the beginning of a new Parliament. And though the terminology might have changed, and general party identification become more fixed in succeeding decades, the role of the leader remained essentially the same, to unite the representatives of a multitude of local and parochial interests into a coherent body of men capable of debating national problems and legislating in the national interest. A broad perspective on national issues, persistence, skillful persuasion, an independent power base and confidence were all demanded of the party leader. If he had these strengths he could, over time, mould his Parliamentary party into an effective fighting force. If he was weak, the party could destroy him and, in turn, itself. The measure of Borden's leadership would be how soon and how well his influence over his parliamentary colleagues would surpass their influence upon him.

Borden moved cautiously, moderately, with respect for the power of his assembled followers. It was evident in his selection of his Whips. The veteran George Taylor was selected as Chief Whip. The regional Whips were Henry Corby from Ontario, Rufus Pope from Quebec, Gilbert Ganong from the Maritimes, and W. J. Roche from the west, all long-standing influential members of the parliamentary party.[20] Similarly, when he was asked to nominate fifteen MP's to the executive of the Ontario Liberal–Conservative Association, the leader weighted his selection with prominent veteran members including Ned Clarke, Tom Sproule, Clarke Wallace, Sam Barker, John Haggart, and Colonels Tisdale and Hughes.[21] Clearly, Borden was not going out of his way to antagonize the party regulars.

Borden made no attempt to emulate the style of his predecessor in the House of Commons. It would have been foolish to try to follow Tupper's colourful posture. The booming challenges, the heavy partisan thrusts echoed through the Commons chamber no more. Instead, the new Leader of the Opposition was the very essence of reasonableness; questioning the government almost too politely, prodding its members ever so slightly, issuing few challenges to government policy. He avoided ringing pronouncements on broad issues and delegated a good deal of responsibility for critiques of general policy to some of his more experienced colleagues, like John Haggart, a former Minister of Railways.

The tenuousness of his own position in the House and in his party was a partial explanation for his approach. But there was more to it than that. It was consistent with Borden's conception of what the business of Parliament ought to be and how it ought to be conducted. Since he had first entered the House of Commons he had had an evident distaste for the petty partisan wrangling that predominated in debate. It wasted so much time, it distracted the members from their responsibility to legislate for the development of the country. Partisan rhetoric was appropriate, even necessary, in an election campaign. But once the people had expressed their will it was the duty of their representatives to get on with the business of the country.

Moreover, Borden believed that certain issues were of such national significance that partisan debate was inappropriate. He might have added, though he did not, that the same issues were so charged with emotion that they threatened the fragile unity of his own parliamentary party. One of these was the bi-racial character of Canada. In the past, debate upon the differing perceptions of roles of French- and English-speaking Canadians in the country's affairs had been the cause of deep hostility between parties and within parties. Borden found it difficult to understand the intensity of feeling the subject engendered among his colleagues and in the public mind. "I think we are all content to be Canadians," he told the House of Commons. "It is not of any importance that we should look back and say that our ancestors were English or French or Irish or Scotch. It only tends to keep alive ideas which really have no useful place in the life of this country."[22] The intrusion of racial bias and religious quarrels into the national forum had never been for the public good. Obviously the differences would come up again; it was not possible to govern Canada without taking account of them. But Borden believed that distinctions rooted in the past were less important than, and potentially destructive of, the common purpose of the present.

Much of the same reasoning governed his approach to Imperial relations. It too had been the cause of vicious differences between and within the parties in the past. And while Canadians would continue to differ in their attitudes to the Imperial relationship, the subject was of such common concern to all of them that it should stand well above the field of party advantage.[23] This did not mean that Borden and his colleagues would sit mute when Imperial affairs were brought before the House. Nor did it mean that they regarded the present relationship to the mother country with satisfaction. Canadian participation in the South African War had raised the whole question of change in the relationship. The nature of the change and the government's attitude toward the change was a very proper subject for debate.

In fact, though both parties claimed to put Canada's interests first in any consideration of Imperial relations, they did differ considerably in their conceptions of what Canada's interests were. Laurier and his followers seemed to regard a passive attitude as the best possible stance for Canada in Imperial affairs. The Conservatives, though they differed sharply among themselves on details, thought that Canada's rapid growth should be reflected in a steadily evolving role of responsibility in Imperial affairs. Laurier's reluctance to deal with Imperial defence at the Imperial Conference of 1902 was taken as one evidence of his irresponsibility. "Canada must herself deal with the subject of contribution to Imperial defence," Borden argued. "The parliament of Canada is the proper tribunal to deal with that."[24]

Similarly, after the Alaska Boundary Tribunal had decided in favour of the United States, Laurier had talked vaguely about acquiring full treaty-making powers for Canada. Borden did not dispute the general idea: "I will stand for any greater powers which may be required for the fuller development of our national life." But Laurier's protestations were a case of closing the barn door after the horse had gone. During the negotiations preceding the Tribunal Laurier had not properly exercised the power he had; he had casually surrendered the initiative to the Foreign Office. "Canada must have the right to be consulted, fully and absolutely consulted, in all treaties that concern her interests," Borden argued. Laurier had not insisted on consultation, had allowed the negotiations to slip out of his control, and the ultimate result was a sacrifice of Canadian interests.[25]

Of more importance was the preference given to products of the Empire in the Fielding tariff. The subject was full of difficulties for the Conservatives. The first was the embarrassing fact that the Liberals had artfully stolen this plank of Conservative policy and implemented it in the tariffs of 1897 and 1898. A twenty-five per cent tariff reduction on Imperial goods had been granted and no reciprocal demands had been made of the mother country. The second was that advocacy of mutual preferential tariffs within the Empire could lay the Conservatives open to the charge of meddling in the internal affairs of the mother country. And that became a very delicate problem in 1903 when Joseph Chamberlain resigned from the British government and began his celebrated tariff reform campaign. More difficult still was the fact that if the British ever did take up the subject of mutual preferences, they might demand even further concessions for their manufactured goods in the Canadian tariff. This would be unacceptable to the Canadian business community.

Not surprisingly, the Conservative policy was exceedingly equivocal on the preference. Their 1902 resolution was typical. It first reaffirmed a belief in the principle of tariff protection and then added that

> while always firmly maintaining the necessity of such protection to Canadian interests, this House affirms its belief in a policy of reciprocal trade preferences within the empire.[26]

How the Conservatives might achieve a balance between an Empire scheme of tariff preferences and protection of Canadian industries was not clear. But Borden did emphasize that they were not willing to surrender much to Imperial sentiment. "I do not believe," he said, "in dealing with it by adopting a preferential tariff which will shut up mills in Canada and give increased profits and outputs to some manufacturers in Yorkshire."[27]

The preference question was a clear example of the kind of issue Borden conveniently regarded as being of such national importance as to be above partisan debate. Though the 1902 resolution said very little, indeed, it had been the cause of heated debate within his party. "We were greatly divided in our opinion as to whether we should say anything in our resolution respecting mutual trade preference within the Empire," he confessed to John Stairs. "Eventually we thought it better to include a short reference to that for this reason. On two occasions at least we have affirmed our belief in that policy by a resolution in the House and on many occasions by the speeches of our leading men. To omit all reference to it at this juncture when the subject is about being [sic] discussed at the approaching conference in London would indicate we had abandoned the policy."[28] The resolution, then, was neither a hearty endorsement of the principle of mutual Imperial trade preferences nor a strong alternative to Laurier's preference policy. Rather, it was a hesitant attempt to reconcile present doubts about the preference with past party policy, a compromise to quiet the divided voices within the caucus. And it was a hint of the delicate balancing act Borden had to perform in his caucus on the larger question of fiscal policy.

Part of Borden's problem was personal, almost petty. George Foster, a former Minister of Finance and later financial critic for the Opposition, had been defeated in 1900. A choice vacancy on the Opposition front benches was thus opened and there were many aspirants for the seat. Great jealousies and rivalries quickly surfaced among Borden's colleagues. The leader was forced to take on the additional chores of financial critic to keep peace within his caucus.[29] But more than recognition within the party hierarchy was involved. The old regulars of the party had been brought up on John A.'s National Policy and believed they owed their political careers to it. For them the National Policy took on something of the aura of sacred script and they fought with the tenacity of old believers for its place in party policy in its purest form. But many younger members sensed a staleness and sterility in the protectionist rhetoric of the 1880s and 1890s. Certainly none of them questioned the general principles of protectionism. But they argued that the promises of the National Policy had now become an accomplished fact, due, with no little irony, to the adoption of the policy by the Laurier government. It was time to modify the policy, to bring it up to date, to mould it to the reality of a twentieth-century industrialized Canada.

The solution was to adopt the phrase "adequate protection", a clear compromise between the two contending views within the party. It was as meaningless or as meaningful as any observer wished to make it. It satisfied the old regulars' insistence upon doctrinal purity but hinted at a flexible tariff policy consistent with the present and future needs of the country. In the House of Commons Borden took great pains to see that it implied the inadequacy of the government's tariff policy. Further than that he would not go. In January 1903 he told an Amherst, Nova Scotia audience that

> It means protection sufficient to maintain in Canada industries in competition with those of other countries. It means a protection which gives a fighting chance to every legitimate industry in Canada. It means a protection which will enable the resources of this country to be developed along all legitimate lines.[30]

A few months later, in response to Fielding's 1903 budget, Borden enumerated the objectives of "adequate protection". First, it should ensure the survival of "legitimate" industries in Canada in depressed as well as prosperous times. Second, the policy should be so framed as to attract both capital investment and labour to develop Canada's resources. Third, "adequate protection" must protect the Canadian market for Canadian industry. It was also important to insure that Canadian workers were paid "a fair living wage. . . . We do not want our labouring classes to compete without protection against the pauper labour of any country." Nor did the Conservatives like the export of Canadian raw materials for manufacturing abroad. "It is surely bad policy to export our raw material, to send our labouring classes abroad to another country to find work in its manufactories and to send after both our money to pay for the finished product which we require." And finally, Canada's farmers "are entitled to every possible protection and assistance".[31]

Borden's cautious approach to traditional issues of party policy was a conscious attempt to win the support of the veteran Conservative MP's. He was equally cautious about railway policy, the great subject of debate in the ninth Parliament. The veteran Haggart retained his post as official Opposition critic on railway matters. But gradually, as Parliament debated the merits of building a second transcontinental railway, Borden's own opinion became the policy of the party. No one disputed the need for a second transcontinental; repeated blockages of grain shipments from the west had demonstrated the inability of the Canadian Pacific to handle the vast growth in freight traffic. What was debatable was who would get the contract for the new line and upon what terms.

By 1902 there were three claimants for government sanction and assistance. The Trans-Canada, a Quebec syndicate, had little experience and less financial support behind its plans for a railway from Quebec City to Port Simpson on the Pacific.[32] Mackenzie and Mann's Canadian Northern line, with headquarters in Toronto and strong backing from the Canadian Bank of Commerce, already had more than 1,000 miles of road completed from Port Arthur to Winnipeg and in Manitoba. They were building towards the Pacific and had authorization for construction to Quebec City.[33] The other contender was the Grand Trunk with its extensive system of lines in eastern Canada and American outlets in Portland and Chicago. Its management had been revitalized, its lines and equipment modernized, its profits increased. Its policy was confident and aggressive, and its political influence was enormous.

Borden had no strong ties to any of these companies. The Canadian Pacific, a traditional ally of the Conservatives, retained a friendly interest in his party, but not to the extent of impairing its very practical relationship with Laurier's government. Borden, therefore, had a relatively free hand in developing his own railway policy. He believed that criticism of Liberal policy, however it developed, would not be enough; that his party should present a constructive alternative policy of its own. He sought advice from trusted friends within and outside the party, seeking a stronger position than the inevitable compromise that would emanate from his caucus. And by the end of 1902 the main points of his policy began to take shape. Government aid should be moderate. Land subsidies should not be given to the successful bidder. The eastern terminal for the railway must be in Canada. Capitalization should be reasonable and not be the cause of an excessive rate structure when the line was completed. And the government might insist on "the right to take over the undertaking after a certain period of years at a valuation to be determined by arbitration or otherwise", as a step towards "a possible future policy of government ownership".[34] He was aware of a growing sentiment in favour of government ownership and he recognized its advantage to the country. But he was not yet ready to commit himself or his party to the idea.

Meanwhile the government was dealing with the competitors for the franchise. The flimsy Trans-Canada proposal was quickly dropped. And some effort at a reasonable compromise between the other two companies was made. Laurier put pressure upon Mackenzie and Mann, strong in the west, to combine forces with the established eastern line, the Grand Trunk. Both were too confident of their own resources and potential to work together and Laurier was forced to choose between them. The long-established and very respectable Grand Trunk got the prize. In July, 1903, after some very successful hard bargaining by the railway and the resignation of the Minister of Railways, A. G. Blair, the Prime Minister announced his railway policy. The western section of the new railway would be built and operated by the Grand Trunk Pacific Railway. There would be no land subsidies granted by the Government of Canada. Instead, the government would guarantee the bonds of the Grand Trunk Pacific and pay the interest on the construction costs of the mountain section. The eastern portion of the railway would run from Winnipeg across northern Ontario and the Quebec hinterland to Quebec City and then to the eastern terminus at Moncton. It would be constructed by the Government of Canada at undetermined cost and, when finished, leased for fifty years to the Grand Trunk Pacific for operation.[35]

The proposal was breathtaking in its simplicity. But even the passionately patriotic rhetoric of the Prime Minister could not hide its defects. His calm assurance that it would cost the country a mere $13 million—the interest on construction costs of the mountain section—was incredible. The equally bland assumption that the lease of the eastern section at 3 per cent per annum of an unknown construction cost would work and would recoup the public treasury was also incredible. There was no assurance that the Grand Trunk–Grand Trunk Pacific would route its traffic through the political terminus at Moncton instead of its existing Atlantic terminus at Portland, Maine. Nor did the plan take any account of Mackenzie and Mann who were determined to build their own transcontinental in direct competition with the government's line.

Borden thought the plan was disgraceful and irresponsible.

This would be a political railway beyond compare, replete with unannounced payoffs for the government's friends, full of un-acknowledged liabilities for the country and its taxpayers. His own policy was announced on August 18. Borden argued that the most rational use should be made of the nation's existing trans-port system. Only such additional lines as were demonstrably necessary and profitable should be built. The Intercolonial, which had recently gained access to Montreal, should be extended to Georgian Bay by the acquisition of J. R. Booth's Canada–Atlantic line. The Canadian Pacific line from North Bay to Fort William should be purchased—the President of the CPR, Sir Thomas Shaughnessy, had approved the proposal in consulta-tions with Borden—and be run by an independent commission with running rights granted to the CPR, the Grand Trunk, and the Canadian Northern. The Grand Trunk should be allowed to build north of Mackenzie and Mann's Canadian Northern Railway from Winnipeg to Edmonton. The National Transcontinental line from Winnipeg to Quebec City should be delayed. To complete the plan, extensive improvements should be made in the connecting Great Lakes and Atlantic ports and the St. Lawrence route to provide an integrated all year rail and water transport system.[36]

Borden's policy received qualified approval from "independ-ent" businessmen whom he had consulted prior to its announce-ment. One of them, Joseph Flavelle, was enthusiastic about Borden's plan for eastern Canada. It seemed much more business-like than the government's sketchy Winnipeg to Moncton pro-posal. In the west, however, Flavelle was taken by the grandeur of the Grand Trunk Pacific scheme.[37] After the announcement the Conservative leader took heart from the praise for the construc-tive stance he had taken, "in strong contrast in spirit to the spirit of the utterances of the [other] speakers on the Conservative side".[38] But he soon realized that his policy was not going to "take" with the public. There was a patchwork, piecemeal quality to it that had none of the appeal of Laurier's nebulous but con-fident policy.

His caution ran against the temper of the times. Even his own constituents in Halifax were lured to Laurier's policy by the prospects of extensive government spending in the Maritimes.[39] And a Montreal Conservative properly caught the public mood: "This proposal will give us good times for at least ten years and after that I do not care."[40] It was clear that Borden would have

1, 2 & 3. Andrew Borden and Eunice Laird Borden, Robert's parents. (Left) Robert at age five

4 & 5. (Above) The Covenanters' Church in Grand Pré. (Below) A recent photograph of the house in Grand Pré where Robert Borden was born in 1854

6. The Borden family home, Grand Pré, *circa* 1909, to which they moved when Robert was four

7. Robert Borden at age twenty-nine

8, 9 & 10. (Above) Robert and Laura Borden, taken about the time of their marriage in 1889. (Right) Pinehurst, in Halifax, Robert and Laura's first home. (Below) Halifax in 1887

11 & 12. Robert's brothers, (left) John William in 1907, and (right) Henry Clifford, *circa* 1895

13. Robert's mother in her later years

14. Sir Charles Tupper in court uniform

15. Sir Charles Hibbert Tupper
in 1894 when he was Minister
of Marine and Fisheries

16. The new Leader of the Opposition, March 1901

to go further, would have to convince his party to take an advanced stand that would at once be a sensible alternative to Laurier's policy and capture the public imagination. He knew that the government's plan would be sent back to Parliament in 1904; many of its details had been left to be settled in further negotiation with the Grand Trunk Pacific. That would be his opportunity.

In fact, when the government presented the contract revisions to Parliament in 1904, they were even more favourable to the railway and less protective of the public interest. A carefully orchestrated response came from the Conservatives. In April, Borden declared that the best means of obtaining cheap transportation for Canadian products across Canada to Canadian ports would be the development and extension of the existing government railway system.[41] Then Ned Clarke proposed that the question of government ownership be submitted to the people and Haughton Lennox and W. H. Bennett moved that an expropriation clause be inserted into the Grand Trunk Pacific contract. Finally, on May 26, Borden rose on third reading of the railway bill to advocate the government ownership and operation of the new transcontinental.

He had been thinking about a government-owned line since 1902. His 1903 policy for the eastern portion of the transcontinental was based upon the extension of the government-owned Intercolonial and the acquisition by the government of the Canada–Atlantic and the North Bay–Fort William section of the Canadian Pacific. Now he stood before the House quoting lengthy passages from learned authorities on the efficacy of public ownership of railways. He went on to trace the details of the successful operation of state railways in other countries. In sharp contrast were the glaring deficiencies of the government's plan. It was a plan without planning, without careful calculation of costs, with hastily presumed benefits. At bottom, the Grand Trunk Pacific contract was an unsavoury agreement between the government and a giant corporation which callously neglected the peoples' interests.

> The people of Canada, if they realize their own strength, will be greater than any corporation—greater than all corporations. . . . If it is the will of the people of Canada, as declared by their voice at the next election, then another railway from ocean to ocean shall be built, owned and controlled by the

> people of Canada, and not by the Grand Trunk Pacific Railway Company . . . the Conservative party if returned to power, is prepared . . . to place upon the statute-book of Canada such legislation as will enable that result to be accomplished with the least possible delay.[42]

To no one's surprise, the Grand Trunk Pacific contract revisions were approved by Parliament. And public reaction to Borden's bold stand was mixed. Generally, the Conservative press applauded. But some staunch Conservative businessmen were shocked.[43] It was rumoured that the Canadian Pacific would join forces with its old rival, the Grand Trunk, to fight his government-ownership policy at the coming election.[44] On the other hand, Watson Griffin of the Canadian Manufacturers' Association bubbled with enthusiasm. "Mr. Borden's strength is in large measure due to the fact that he does not feel bound to stand still where the Conservative party stood a few years ago," he wrote. "He is not afraid to take more advanced ground than his predecessors. He has shown this spirit of progressiveness not only in his bold advocacy of public ownership of railways, which I believe to be in accord with the sentiment of the Canadian people, but also in reference to tariff revision. No previous Conservative leader has taken such advanced ground in favour of the protection of all Canadian interests."[45]

During the first four years of his leadership Borden had worked hard to establish his position within the party and in the public mind. Public speeches and political tours had familiarized him with local party workers across the country and kept his name in the public press. He had not challenged the status of his senior parliamentary colleagues but he had, gradually, modified the tactics of the Opposition in the House of Commons. Fiery partisan sallies had given way to reasoned argument. He had carefully avoided contentious positions on the traditional issues of party politics both because he believed them not to be in the national interest and because he recognized that they could split his own party. French-English questions and the Imperial relationship had been handled with delicate caution. He had resisted the urgings of some of his colleagues to accept the participation of Canada in the South African War as the occasion for a radical revision of Imperial affairs. And he had eased his caucus towards the acceptance of an implicitly more flexible tariff policy.

But it was his 1904 railway policy that most clearly revealed Borden's growing power in his party. Opting for government ownership was a bold stroke, a challenge to the economic philosophy of his caucus and the public. It was true that his railway policy left as many questions unanswered as Laurier's; how government ownership would be implemented and how much it would cost was no clearer than the real costs of the Grand Trunk Pacific–National Transcontinental scheme. But it was a startling alternative to Laurier's grand design. And his colleagues responded with evident delight. "Our members in the House of Commons are so much pleased with our position," he reported, "that some of them are asking why we did not take this stand immediately upon the announcement of the Government's policy last year."[46] Some of them, of course, didn't accept the principle of government ownership and never would. But that was less important than the fact that their leader had taken a stand, that he was leading them, and that he had provided them with an issue upon which they could do battle with the government. The choice before the people in 1904 would be clear cut. In Borden's words, they would have to decide whether they wanted "a government-owned railway or a railway-owned government".

CHAPTER FIVE

HUMILIATION

Memorable campaign phrases do not win elections. Nor do spectacular policy planks. Both are useful, indeed necessary, to attract public attention to the party which proclaims them. But they represent only the surface of the electoral struggle. Beneath are the multiplicity of organizational details that determine the party's fate in each constituency. Candidates must be selected and their individual efforts coordinated into regional, provincial, and national campaign strategy. Public meetings must be arranged, party propaganda must be dispensed, tours by prominent party figures must be organized. Each and all of these activities, in turn, require funding by party supporters whose contributions are motivated by incentives ranging from high principle to gross expectation of future favours. Then, too, a host of intangible factors enter the equation of success or failure. The comparative attractiveness of the opposing national leaders, the influence and respect of the local candidates, the party heritage of the voter and his family, and the weather on polling day are but a few of them.

Generally, the party in power has the advantage in the contest. And 1904 was no exception to the rule. As in 1900, the times were good and the Liberals again took credit for prosperity. The party had at its command a huge store of patronage and had the support of all but two of the provincial governments. The government claimed to have fulfilled its past promises and for the most part it had. The clear implication was that it could deliver in the future. Contemporary newspapers caught the spirit of the times in their repeated references to "big men" who could "get things done". Laurier's party, unlike Borden's, had "big men" who had gotten "things done". And the party's greatest asset was its leader.

He convincingly cultivated the image of statesman; his every aspect looked the part, his every word and action played to the part. He was gracious and magnetic on the platform. He was tough, calculating and realistic in the party corridors. The defections of Tarte and Blair were a minor embarrassment to the Liberals, an expected occurrence in a powerful, long-lived Ministry. Sir Wilfrid was at the peak of his power and he expected to win again.

Borden was not ready for an election in the early months of 1904. In the west there were some encouraging signs. Richard McBride in British Columbia and Rodmond Roblin in Manitoba had both won elections in 1903. Their governments were not yet prepared to swing their full weight behind the Conservative leader, but at least some Liberal influence would be dispelled in those provinces. On the other hand, the party organization in the Territories had been disrupted by the recent Redistribution Act which added six new seats to the Territorial representation.[1] A 1903 tour of the Maritimes by Borden had been a public relations success, but it had not been followed up with any significant organizational effort.[2] The organizers for Ontario had resigned in 1903 and it was not until September that they were reappointed by Borden.[3] In Quebec, Monk severely embarrassed Borden and the party by publishing his letter of resignation in January. It precipitated a public quarrel among the contending Quebec factions which lasted for months. "Our friends in Quebec are as lively in fighting with each other as ever they were," Borden told his wife.[4]

Clearly, an early election would be disastrous. The government was rumoured to have just such thoughts in mind—a tidy little session and a whirlwind campaign. But Borden was determined to delay the business of the House to give his party time to pull itself together.[5] By the end of July his mood had changed. The warm reception of his railway policy by the party completely altered his outlook. He apparently assumed, however naively, that a fighting slogan would compensate for the party's continuing organizational chaos. He told Laura that the prospects were "looking better every day". "I really think that we stand a fairly good chance of beating them by a small majority."[6]

Dissolution was announced at the end of September. By then Borden already had a month of campaigning behind him. His campaign began at Saint John early in the month. The following week Laura joined him for a tour of Ontario which lasted until mid-October. There was at least one speech a day in support of a local candidate, often more.

Each visit conformed to a predictable pattern. Early in the afternoon Robert and Laura and Foster, Sam Hughes, Ned Clarke, or some other well-known Ontario MP would be met at the railway station by the local candidate and the prominent Conservatives of the town. The big-city journalists and the local reporters hovered at the back of the platform waiting for something unusual to happen which might give them a fresh lead for their daily despatch. Borden would be whisked away to party headquarters to hear a tale of woe about the difficulties of the local campaign and a seldom-accurate assessment of the candidate's chances. Laura, who did not especially enjoy her role as a public figure, might be left in peace at the town's hotel. But more often than not she would be asked to give the "women's viewpoint" of the national election to the local reporters. After a dinner with the town's distinguished citizens, at which the nervous party leader seldom ate, there would be a parade to the Opera House or arena. The party's chances might be gauged by the decorations; autumn flowers and boughs and large bright banners reflected optimism, a sparsely decorated stage and a bare lectern hinted at a Grit victory. Around eight the speeches began. The chairman of the meeting, a well-known manufacturer or doctor or lawyer, maybe the local undertaker, perhaps even the mayor if the town had Tory leanings, made the ritual introductions. The local candidate followed. Then it was time for the man the crowd waited for, the party leader, to speak.

Borden was dressed in a black suit and white shirt with upturned collar and black tie. He put on his spectacles and turned to get a reassuring smile from his wife, who was trying desperately to look enthusiastically interested at this repeated performance. Gravely, he stepped to the lectern. A few good words for the local candidate were always the first order of business. And sometimes it was pretty heavy going to find something that could be said. On one occasion he acknowledged that his colleague seldom said anything in the House, but quickly added that when he did he "was always listened to with respect and attention". And then Borden launched into the serious matter of the day, an hour or two of exposition of the horrors of the government's persons and policies and of the unparalleled promises of his own platform. His voice was deep and resonate, his manner serious, his delivery slow but more confident than in the past. He paused for the audience to cheer at every appropriate catchword in the Tory vocabulary. He was patient with hecklers, sure in the knowledge that the local partisans would quickly descend upon them and roughly escort them from the hall. When he was done, he returned to his seat, and steeled himself to sit through a fire-eating speech or two by one of his oratorically gifted parliamentary colleagues. Between eleven and midnight the meeting would close. After a light supper the national party would be escorted back to the sleeping car, dead of body and of mind.

Borden found this part of public life no more enjoyable than he ever had. The hours were appalling, the pressure intense, the local company seldom stimulating. Little wonder that the progress became mechanical; the actors, almost like children's toys, performing their predictable gestures, mouthing their predictable words. Only rarely was the tedium interrupted by a different question that might occasion a fresh, though not especially enlightening, response. Once, at Blenheim, the Baptist minister, amidst a clamour of voices that he be still, asked for Borden's views of the prohibition question. The party leader allowed that he was no teetotaller. He seldom drank but not from reasons of principle. Evasively he added that the public had been hoodwinked by Laurier's national plebiscite in 1898, that the question was within provincial jurisdiction in any case, and that public opinion was not ready for prohibition. "I do not believe in this Canada of ours in passing any law until public opinion has been brought up to the standard of enforcement."[7]

But these variations on the script were exceptional. After a great rally in Toronto's Massey Hall on October 4, the *News* gave a capsule version of the Conservative gospel as proclaimed in Ontario:

> A national policy in finance of adequate protection for Canadian industries; a national policy in transportation, a transcontinental railway built and operated by the people for the benefit of the people, and the upbuilding of Canadian ports; the placing of the Intercolonial Railway under a Commission of non-partisan businessmen to operate it on a business basis; the cleansing of the Government patronage from party considerations; negotiations with the Mother Country and

the other colonies for mutual preferential trade; purified elections; in short, a free, clean and progressive Government for the people of Canada.[8]

Borden's reception in Ontario was expectedly heartening, though press reports varied wildly in their accounts of his meetings. The despatches in the Toronto papers from his Stratford meeting were typical. It "began in an enthusiastic manner", *The Globe* observed, "but before it was over many had left the hall, and there was no enthusiasm during the exposition of the Opposition policy." The *Mail and Empire* countered with a report that "the Opera House was packed with an enthusiastic crowd, most of them being young men". And the professedly independent *News* described it as "an enthusiastic meeting and [the crowd] applauded heartily and frequently, whistling vigorously when its feelings grew too deep for utterance by mere applause".[9]

From Toronto the party moved into eastern Ontario and then Quebec. In Montreal two carefully arranged meetings were very successful. Tarte, who was not running for re-election, was on the platform. So too was Monk, clearly loyal in his own independent way and showing no sign of disaffection from the party leader. They were joined by dozens of other prominent men, French and English, including businessman and Alderman Herbert Ames*, the candidate in Montreal–St. Antoine, in a skillfully organized display of Tory power. Local conditions demanded a variation on the platform themes. Montreal was the headquarters of the Canadian Pacific and the Canadian base of the Grand Trunk. When it came to railways, Montreal was decidedly not a "government ownership" town. So the leader began with and emphasized tariff policy; his transcontinental plan took up a few minutes of the second hour of his speech. In Quebec a few days later, Pelletier rallied his troops for a huge cheering parade. Borden warmly responded with speeches in both French and English. It was one of the few memorable occasions of the campaign and Robert wished that Laura, who had left the tour, had been there to share

---

*Herbert Brown Ames was a Montreal millionaire who retired from business to devote his life to political reform. He wrote *The City Below the Hill*, a pioneer study of the living conditions of the working class in Montreal, and a number of articles advocating the reform of municipal and national politics. He was a Montreal alderman from 1898 to 1906 and was first elected to the House of Commons for Montreal–St. Antoine in 1904.

it with him. The meeting, he wrote, "was simply magnificent and the demonstration was far more enthusiastic than any I have yet encountered. Pelletier and Casgrain sat in the cab with me and said 'Are we dreaming, or is this really Quebec'?"[10]

Another two weeks and the campaign was over. There were the usual daily meetings in scattered Maritime centres outside Halifax which meant that Borden could only spend a few hours in his own constituency. Overall the prospects seemed good. Borden had nagging doubts about Quebec; the one-shot demonstrations of support were no substitute for solid organization. "Our friends have been underestimating their strength," he observed. "If they had put candidates in the field four weeks ago there would have been some surprises."[11] But reports from the west were good, Ontario was solid, and Borden thought that Fielding's claim that Nova Scotia would only elect one Conservative[12] was nonsense. The leader was confident. With a little luck all the varied elements in the election would combine in a successful formula.

It was not to be. Borden was at home on polling day, November 3. In the evening his driver took him in the carriage from Pinehurst to party headquarters downtown. There he waited with E. C. Tanner, the provincial organizer, J. C. O'Mullin, his running mate in Halifax, and his local supporters for the results to come in over the wire. The reports from his own province were a prelude to an unfolding disaster. Fielding had accomplished more than he had claimed; the Liberals had won every seat in Nova Scotia, including Borden's. Hours later Borden learned that they had also engineered a complete sweep in British Columbia. The Conservatives gained one seat each in New Brunswick and Prince Edward Island, and captured four seats in the Territories and the Yukon. In Quebec they also gained three seats, giving the party a total of eleven representatives from the province. Ontario returned forty-eight Conservative MP's to retain its overwhelming dominance of the parliamentary party. But even that was a loss of seven seats from the results in 1900. Similarly, the Conservative share of the popular vote dropped sharply in Nova Scotia, significantly in Quebec and marginally across the nation. There was nothing indecisive about the result. When Laurier first met the tenth Parliament he could count on an increased majority of sixty-four.[13]

Borden's disappointment was beyond measure. He had worked so hard, for so long. He had established a reputation of deliberate, sound, and constructive leadership. He had given the party a fighting slogan for the election, the people a real choice in railway policy. And he had lost. He was especially bitter about the result in his own constituency. It was, he told Donald MacMaster, "entirely unexpected". He felt betrayed by his own friends. "On account of my absence in other parts of the Dominion I was obliged to rely entirely upon the reports of my friends who gave me most positive assurance that my colleagues and myself would be elected by considerable majorities."[14] He also thought his opponents had used unfair and illegal means to defeat him and he considered contesting the Halifax result. But whatever the outcome, the defeat was very embarrassing to the party leader. For the moment all he wished to do was get away, to go to the South with Laura for a much needed rest. He hoped the humiliation of the 1904 election was at an end. It wasn't. The press had attached his name to an election scandal during the campaign.

Rumours of the *La Presse* affair were circulating in private and in the press even before the election campaign began. In August the *News* carried a story about A. G. Blair, who had resigned from Laurier's cabinet in 1903 and who had very similar views to Borden's on railway policy. The *News* said that Blair, who had been appointed chairman of the Railway Commission in the fall of 1903, was about to resign and cooperate with Borden in the expected election campaign. A few weeks later Blair's associate, Montreal financier David Russell, after a vigorous fight, gained control of two Saint John newspapers. Russell began to boom William Pugsley, New Brunswick's Attorney General, for a cabinet post in the Dominion government. Both actions were designed to thwart the interests of Blair's successor in Laurier's cabinet, H. R. Emmerson of Moncton, and to deprive Laurier of newspaper support in Saint John. Then on October 17, 1904, *Le Nationaliste* announced that two prominent Montreal Conservatives, the publisher of the *Star*, Hugh Graham, and Rodolphe Forget, had purchased *La Presse*, the great Liberal paper in Quebec. The same day the Toronto *Star* reported that Russell and J. N. Greenshields had purchased *La Presse*. The following day Blair resigned his chairmanship of the Railway Commission and it was immediately assumed that he would take the stump against Laurier.

Gradually the pattern of a complicated plot against the Laurier government was emerging. The Russell-Blair interests had gained control of two Saint John dailies and the largest French-language (and Liberal) daily in the country. Blair remained an influential figure in the Maritimes and could be damaging to Laurier on the stump everywhere. Russell's money could be put to all sorts of interesting purposes. And the Conservatives were said to be involved in the scheme. Blair and Russell were alleged to be connected with a New York syndicate which wanted a controllable Railway Minister in either a Laurier or a Borden government, a minister who would grant it Grand Trunk Pacific construction contracts. Moreover, Railway Minister Emmerson now charged, Borden had recently joined Russell and Greenshields in their private railway car at Fredericton and travelled to Halifax with them. Yet another story reported that the same New York syndicate and Russell and Blair were prepared to spend huge sums to elect Borden. In return, they expected to receive construction contracts from his government railway scheme.[15]

On October 24th Borden publicly denied that his party either had been or could be bought by any vested interest.

> [T]he Conservative Party will receive subscriptions only from those who favour its general policy, that such subscriptions are not to be understood as creating claims to consideration for any interest likely to be affected by any special feature of that policy, and that no subscriptions are solicited from any such interest. Such a declaration is deemed desirable in order that the Leader may have an absolutely free hand in framing his policy in the interest of the whole country upon the return of the party to power. If any subscriptions have been given in other spirit they will be returned on application to James Crathern, Treasurer, Montreal.[16]

Borden probably believed that the matter would end there. But after the election the rumours of the *La Presse* affair continued to dominate the public interest. Maclean's independent paper in Toronto, the *World*, and *Le Nationaliste* in Montreal led the continuing press speculation. Blair, Russell, Greenshields, who was Mackenzie and Mann's Montreal lawyer, and Graham were the central figures in the drama. But the implication that Borden was somehow involved did not die. On December 6, shortly after his return from his southern vacation, Borden issued a categorical denial.

> I wish to say that that [Blair's] resignation came as a great surprise to me. I did not directly or indirectly suggest to him or ask him to resign. I held out no inducement to him to resign. I had no interviews with him upon the subject, nor did any one on my behalf approach him on the subject. In short I had nothing whatever to do with his resignation and I was thoroughly surprised when I heard of it. I had no connection with, and I knew nothing of any negotiation respecting the alleged change of ownership of *La Presse*, and I had nothing to do with such change, if it took place. I never had an interview or communication with any English or American capitalists, or with any other person, with respect to proposed contracts for the building of the Grand Trunk Pacific. I never even heard of the alleged construction syndicate. No one approached me with any proposal respecting the construction of the railway. Any statement or suggestion to the contrary is utterly without foundation.

Finally, Borden denied having received "any contributions for any purpose from Mr. Russell or any of the other sources mentioned".[17]

In fact, Borden was involved, almost certainly more involved than he himself realized, in the affair. Extensive communications from Hugh Graham, disguised in a childish code, and later correspondence between Borden and officials of the Bank of Nova Scotia make this clear beyond any doubt.[18]

The sordid little scheme had its origin in 1903 when Blair resigned from Laurier's government. It was the brainchild of Hugh Graham. As early as May 1903, Graham was wooing the Minister of Railways to aid the Conservative fight against Laurier's railway policy. Blair wanted "a certain paper's support and co-operation in organizing certain features". If the attack were successful, Blair or his nominee could become Minister of Railways in a Conservative government. In addition, the Canadian Pacific Railway was going to be involved in the fight against Laurier's railway policy. Borden, it should be remembered, made a point of clearing his 1903 policy with its president, Sir Thomas Shaughnessy, before it was announced.[19] Mackenzie and Mann also were approached, but they decided to continue supporting Laurier.[20] In September, 1903, Graham's editor at the *Star*

Brenton Macnab, told Borden that Russell and Blair had had a falling out over the support which Russell's Saint John *Telegram* was giving to Laurier's railway policy. Macnab added that Blair had been offered the chairmanship of the Railway Commission by Laurier. Macnab thought that ultimately Russell could and would control Blair and that "any *further* advance made to B. by the Cons. will be met instantly with a favorable response".[21] The scheme fell apart when Blair accepted Laurier's appointment and when the Prime Minister delayed the election because of continuing difficulties in the Grand Trunk negotiation.

The plot became more complex when it was revived in 1904. Blair, unhappy in his Railway Commissioner's post, again resigned. Now another of Russell's associates, New Brunswick Attorney General William Pugsley, also became involved. Apparently Russell was hedging his election bets. If Laurier won, Pugsley would be his man in the Railway's ministry; if Borden, Blair. By now Russell's newspaper ambitions had also expanded. Government papers would be bought and forced to reverse their editorial positions on railway policy shortly before the coming election. The revelation of scandals by these papers would force the resignations of Sifton, Prefontaine, and Fitzpatrick from Laurier's cabinet. And Liberal candidates would be bribed to withdraw from the contest in some Quebec seats. As before, support was expected from both the CPR and the CNR. By October 1904, Russell controlled two Saint John papers and had held a great banquet at his Caledonia Springs hotel to boom Pugsley. Borden was invited but declined. However, many prominent Montreal and Maritime Conservatives joined a number of Liberals in attendance.[22]

On October 17 a syndicate headed by Hugh Graham and David Russell purchased *La Presse* for $750,000. Both the Canadian Pacific and the Canadian Northern were to be part of the eventual financing of the takeover and the CPR was expected to offer a million dollar bond issue after the election to cover various bank loans and the rearrangement of the paper's finances. Blair left the chairmanship of the Railway Commission the next day.

Again the scheme collapsed. The story of the purchase of Quebec's largest French newspaper by English-speaking capitalists got out. The ever politically sensitive Canadian Pacific beat a hasty retreat with Shaughnessy professing no involvement in his letters to Laurier.[23] Russell and Blair had another quarrel. Along the way Pugsley had had second thoughts and rushed off to

Ottawa to tell all to Laurier.[24] Laurier immediately saw Blair and forced his silence in the election. And eventually, in January 1905, Russell and Graham, on the edge of financial embarrassment, sold out their interest in *La Presse* to Mackenzie and Mann. Laurier and Clifford Sifton acted as intermediaries in the sale and all parties agreed that *La Presse* would continue to be a Liberal organ.[25]

Part of the initial financing for the *La Presse* purchase was a note of Graham's in favour of Russell for $100,000. At a meeting between Graham, Borden, and Russell, before October 17 and perhaps during Borden's campaign visit to Montreal, it was decided that the note should be discounted by the Bank of Nova Scotia because that institution had no connection with the Liberal party. Borden was a director of the bank. On the 16th or 17th Borden wrote to H. C. McLeod, General Manager of the Bank in Toronto, giving his personal recommendation that the bank discount the note. The Manager in Montreal, W. P. Hunt, had sought advice from his superior in Toronto before carrying out the transaction and Borden's recommendation was influential in McLeod's decision to allow Hunt to discount the note.[26]

On the 19th, the day the Bank of Nova Scotia approved the discounting of Graham's note to Russell, Borden wrote to Graham:

> Mr. Macnab has just apprized me of certain proposals for negotiation which have recently been made to you. I shall be glad if you will take the matter up. I cannot depart in any way from the pledges which I have made to the people, but subject to that consideration I am willing to endeavor to arrive at any preliminary understanding and would confirm any preliminary arrangement approved by yourself and Barker of Hamilton [who] understands the situation most thoroughly.[27]

This letter *probably* refers to a "preliminary understanding" and "certain proposals for negotiation" with Blair, who had resigned the previous day, and not to the purchase of *La Presse*. If it does, Borden's later denial of any involvement with Blair is true in its most literal sense, i.e., that Borden did not know about the resignation before it happened and was surprised by it. It does not account for what he did *immediately after* Blair's resignation. Furthermore, the very carefully worded statement of

December 6 conveyed the impression that at no time in the past had Borden "directly or indirectly" approached Blair. But Blair had been negotiating with the Conservatives before his resignation in 1903 and Macnab had informed Borden of the negotiations.

Borden's statement that "I had no connection with, and I know nothing of any negotiation respecting the alleged change of ownership of *La Presse*" is difficult to understand. Admittedly, the evidence which survives regarding the purchase of *La Presse* is partially circumstantial and inferential. Borden's own letter to McLeod in Toronto does not exist. In 1907 he apparently tried to get it back from McLeod. McLeod replied that he had destroyed it, but sent copies of the remaining correspondence related to the discount of Graham's note to Borden.[28] That correspondence shows clearly that Hunt in Montreal believed that Borden was aware of and involved in the *La Presse* purchase. McLeod, in Toronto, clearly worked upon the same assumption. It is possible, even probable, that Borden's letter to McLeod simply affirmed Borden's confidence in Graham's credit standing. There was no reason for McLeod to know why *La Presse* was being purchased. But I think it is most unlikely that Borden would write his letter unless he knew why *La Presse* was being purchased. It was not in his nature to make a recommendation on a $100,000 transaction casually, or to exercise his responsibility and influence as a director of the bank lightly. At the same time, there was nothing illegal about the purchase of *La Presse*. And from the bank's point of view, it was a straightforward business deal; their only concern was the strength of Graham's credit.

Borden's statement that he had nothing to do with any prospective Grand Trunk Pacific contractors is almost certainly true. He did, by accident, meet Russell and Greenshields at Fredericton Junction and rode to Saint John with them. There is no evidence that they discussed such matters or that Borden promised them anything.

Borden's final denial of receiving contributions to his election fund from "Russell or any of the other sources mentioned" is, I think, misleading. No evidence survives to indicate that he received any contributions from Russell. But the "other sources" publicly "mentioned" in the affair did include Hugh Graham. And Graham was a regular and substantial contributor to the party. "If you see your way to carrying out my suggestion," i.e., allowing co-operation between Tarte and the Quebec Conservatives,

Graham told Monk in May 1903, "I will begin at once to aid you, and will use my utmost endeavours to strengthen the hands of our friends."[29] In July 1903, Graham offered Borden "ten thousand dollars, with a strong probability that it will be greatly increased before the campaign is over . . . upon condition that active campaign work be begun all over the Dominion immediately".[30] A year later he told the Conservative leader that "I can do as I have been doing in the past,—borrow on my personal responsibility from the Bank to meet what you want".[31] A month before the 1904 election Graham proposed to visit "Ampersand" (Shaughnessy?) "with a view to getting him to do better. I will promise to double my own provided he will add fifty or more."[32] And so it went on through the campaign. How much Graham contributed is not known. In 1917 he claimed that his election expenditures in 1904 had been over two hundred thousand dollars, at least a portion of which was in loans. On the first of November, two days before the election, repayments had reduced his total contribution to $161,306.63. It is clear that his contribution was very substantial and that it was used not simply in Quebec but throughout the Dominion. "Every penny of what we received outside our Province came from you," Charles Hibbert Tupper told the Montreal publisher in December.[33]

Why did Borden issue the December statement? The evidence in the Borden Papers in part confirms that it was a misleading account of his involvement in the *La Presse* affair. Encouraging Blair to come out against Laurier would have been a dirty trick on the Liberals but good politics for the Conservatives. It had been tried before, and would be tried again, by both parties. The problem was that it didn't work. Facilitating the financing of *La Presse* was the same sort of thing. Trying to gain control of the other party's papers had also been tried before, and would be tried again. It was certainly naive to expect that the Liberals would allow their main French-language organ to pass from their hands without exposure, and to suppose that the change of ownership would enhance Conservative fortunes with the French-speaking electorate. But as the whole *La Presse* affair demonstrated, the naiveté of the principals in the enterprise knew few bounds. Finally, accepting large political contributions from men like Graham was hardly unusual. It had no better or no worse connotations to it than did the acceptance of contributions from other wealthy men by both political parties. True, taken altogether, and linked to the allegation that Borden would make pay-offs to potential Grand Trunk Pacific contractors, the elements of the *La Presse* affair could easily be regarded as a conspiracy by the public press. But there is no evidence to support the charge that Borden had or would have made any deals with Grand Trunk Pacific contractors. The worst that could be said of the rest of it was that it was a political plot of sensational proportions. And it is closer to the mark to say that the other components of the scheme were common parts of the electoral game. What made them notable was the ineptitude and the flair for bumbling exhibited in their execution.

Borden might just as well have kept silent. There was no more obvious reason for him to speak out in December than there had been in October. But speak out he did. Two thoughts probably motivated his statement. The first was that as long as Billy Maclean's *World* and *Le Nationaliste* kept public speculation on the *La Presse* affair alive, his indirect link to the seamy side of politics was going to be kept before the public eye. Borden never denied that there was another side to politics, the world of the politico and the machine. But he had tried very hard to establish an image as a political leader committed to eliminating these very practices from the political landscape. The longer the rumours and insinuations went on, the more his reputation, already dealt a severe blow by the election, suffered. The other point was that he did not know how far the *La Presse* affair went. Certainly there was more to it than he was aware of. Even the details of the scheme that he did know had been presented to him during the last hectic days of the election campaign, when he was preoccupied with more immediate problems. He had had no time to reflect upon their implications for the reputations of his party and himself. Nor was it in Graham's nature to tell all to anyone, even Borden. And Borden was doubtless eager to be assured by Graham that all was well and under control. It was only later that Borden realized that the amateurish plotters, Graham and Russell, might have made any number of embarrassing political commitments in his name. Perhaps they, too, would find their way into the press. And so, fearful of what might yet be revealed, fearful of a smear upon his political honour, and suddenly realizing that some of his political friends were probably his worst enemies, he struck back with a dubious statement to save his public reputation.

Borden's immediate reaction to the election was that he had had enough. His own defeat in Halifax was an especially bitter blow; he regarded it as a personal rejection of his leadership and his policies by his own constituents. "I see very great difficulties in the way of my continuance in public life and they seem to me insuperable," he wrote to Sam Barker.

> How can a party keep at its head a leader who has been unable to carry a single seat in his own Province and who has himself been defeated? It seems to me madness to consider the suggestion. You know I am not very fond of public life and besides personal affairs have been very much neglected and are by no means in a satisfactory condition. You have splendid debating power in the present Opposition. I want to do my full duty to the party which has been so loyal and devoted during the past four years but I think my duty to the party as well as to myself calls for my retirement.[34]

And he told George Taylor that Laura "did not greatly regret the loss on our own account".[35]

Both letters were intended to test the political waters in Ontario, to elicit the opinions of two of the party's senior spokesmen on his standing with his followers. But they were, nonetheless, sincere. Borden was deeply humiliated and really doubted whether he should carry on. During his vacation he had reflected on his future course. There had been much hardship and sacrifice in the past four years. As party leader his personal political expenses had increased considerably at the same time that his income from his law firm had diminished. Before 1896 he had received about thirty thousand dollars annually from his law firm. In 1901, when he took over the leadership, his share of the firm's profits had been eighteen thousand dollars. But in the last two years he had received very little income from the practice.[36] It had been hard enough to devote the necessary time and energy to his practice as an ordinary member of Parliament; as party leader the demands of his practice always had to take second place. One or the other had to go. Each was a full time job.

Still harder to bear were the enforced separations from Laura. She travelled with him on his political tours and spent portions of each session with him in Ottawa. But when she was not at his side his letters were filled with the pain of loneliness, of the awful emptiness of living in rented rooms, of heartlessly nibbling at solitary boarding-house meals. And the party leadership offered no real compensations for the sacrifice of home and business security. The moments of accomplishment and praise were few, the hours of frustration and complaints many. So few of his colleagues shared his devotion to duty; so many blatantly used their parliamentary position solely for personal advancement, neglecting even the minimal responsibility of attendance at the sittings of the House. "While our men in the House are very loyal and true, they are extremely lazy," he told Laura before the election. "It is discouraging beyond measure that matters of moment should be continually neglected."[37]

The election results were the final blow. For weeks he had spent his every waking hour campaigning for others, trusting in his subordinates to carry the responsibilities for organization and promotion of his cause in his own constituency and province. The results were disgraceful to them and to him. Similarly he had let his friends, more skilled than he in the nether world of politics, involve him in a cheap little game of political trickery at the expense of legitimate organization in Quebec. It had been quickly exposed. He was tied to it, but he did not know even yet the extent to which deeds had been done and promises made in his name. Was not a quiet retirement, then, his only honourable choice?

But there was another side to the question. There had, after all, been many good days in his public life. He enjoyed the recognition that a party leader naturally received. He liked the continual association with important men of affairs that was part of his responsibility as party leader. And he believed that he had done well in his position. Gradually he had won the confidence of both the public and his parliamentary companions in his leadership. He had been praised for the high tone of his policy positions, admired for the courage of the challenging alternatives he posed to government policy. Obviously, if he stayed on, there was much still to be done to weld his party into an effective fighting force. It was especially important to give it the vigorous organizational structure it still so sadly lacked. If he was really committed to this, if he really believed this to be in the best interests of his party and the nation, then he certainly could not achieve it by quitting.

He was not a quitter; nor had he ever failed in a task he had been committed to. Could he now retire so easily, return to his law practice and forget his public past? Was it not, in fact, the courageous course to accept defeat and carry on? After all, defeat was a common part of political life. The true test of the commitment of a public man was that he accepted it and fought on for the principles he believed in. If he really believed in his railway policy, if he really believed that he could offer his country better government than Laurier could, if he really believed that his party's ramshackle structure should be replaced by an efficient and honest organization that reflected the will of the people, if he believed that *he* could effect these objectives, then he clearly had to stay in public life.

The indications that his party wanted and needed him at the helm came quickly. Even before he returned from his vacation nearly a dozen seats had been offered to him in Ontario, Sam Hughes being the first to indicate his willingness to step down in Victoria–Haliburton for his leader.[38] When he reached Montreal, on December 4, he was met by twenty-five of his MP's and other party powers who implored him not to resign.[39] Some days later Borden told Richard McBride that he still had not made up his mind. But the appeal of resignation had clearly weakened. "There are many serious personal reasons which deter if they do not altogether forbid me from continuing in public life. On the other hand I wish to do my full duty to friends who have very loyally supported me." Just before Christmas Borden decided to stay on and instructed his secretary in Ottawa, A. E. Blount,* to begin preparations for the first session of the new Parliament.[40]

The appropriate formalities had to be engineered in the caucus, scheduled to meet on January 10. Borden would present a formal resignation. The caucus would pass the necessary resolutions rejecting his resignation and begging him to resume his post.[41] Edward Kidd would resign his seat in Carleton and, until Borden was elected there, George Foster, the party's senior Privy Councillor, who had been returned for North York, would serve as temporary House leader. Blount advised that there was no point in coming to Ottawa before the caucus met. But "it might be well to have your business engagements in such shape that you could come on short notice if necessary." He added that the only

*Austin Ernest Blount was born in Stanstead, Quebec, on May 30, 1870. In 1896 he was employed by Sir Charles Tupper as private secretary to the leader of the Opposition. Besides handling the leader's voluminous correspondence, his duties included assisting the leader in all aspects of party business. Borden retained Blount to perform the same services for him after he was elected party leader.

apparent challenger to Borden's leadership, Billy Maclean, who had been a contender in 1901 and had assiduously kept the *La Presse* affair alive in the Toronto press after the election, "will have no backing at the caucus and I doubt very much if he attends. There is a disposition among several of the members that he should be read out of the party."[42]

The "several personal reasons" which had been the main consideration for resigning in mid-December were disposed of with equal dispatch. Most serious was the regular enforced separations from Laura. "We cannot continue in this way for another year," he had told her in the summer of 1904. "Either I must give up the leadership or remove to Ottawa." The Prime Minister graciously arranged for his election by acclamation in Carleton on February 4. On the ninth Robert told Laura that he had been house hunting and that Ottawa prices were "very excessive". It would be another year before they finally found a suitable house and moved into the impressive residence on Wurtemburg Street that they would occupy for the rest of their lives. In the meantime Laura would prepare Pinehurst for sale and join Robert in Ottawa late in 1905. And by the end of March he had given up his interest in his law firm.[43] He had made a clear break with the past. He was ready for a fresh start, more wary of his friends in public life, more determined to achieve his own goals. "My habit of mind," Borden told John Willison,*

> is to dwell upon the past only so far as may be necessary to point the path for the future. One who believes in what he has advocated and who has used his best energies, however imperfect they may be, in that advocacy has little cause for regret. Indeed to lose thus is not far from success, however overwhelming the defeat may seem.
>
> From a purely personal standpoint there were many cogent reasons why I should remain out of public life and for a long time I more than hesitated. Having returned I have put all the hesitation and doubt behind me and I shall endeavour to do my full duty.[44]

---

*John Stephen Willison was the editor-in-chief of the Toronto *News*, which was owned by Joseph Wesley Flavelle. Before Flavelle hired him to run the *News* as an "independent" newspaper, Willison had been editor-in-chief of the Toronto *Globe* from 1890 to 1902.

CHAPTER SIX

PROBLEMS OF POLICY AND ORGANIZATION

When Borden resumed his seat in the House of Commons in February 1905, he anticipated that the first session of the new Parliament would be dominated by routine business. Laurier's government could be expected to introduce the ordinary legislation necessary for the carrying on of the country's business and it might bring forward bills fulfilling one or two of its minor election pledges. Both parties needed time to mould their members into disciplined debating corps. And the election results could be interpreted as a triumphant vindication of the status quo; the voters evidently wanted no dramatic changes in either the personnel or the policy of the Government of Canada.

He did not expect that he would be embroiled in the most important debate of the session just two weeks after his election. Nor did he know that before he could turn his full attention to the contentious problem of granting provincial status to Saskatchewan and Alberta there would be a tragic death in his family. On the morning of February 22, just as he was trying to formulate an Opposition policy on the Autonomy Bills, he received word that Hal's young wife, Mabel, had suddenly taken ill and died of pneumonia. Hal was left with the care of three small children, Eunice, Henry, and baby Mabel who had been born the preceding October. Robert left immediately for Halifax. At Springhill Junction he was stranded for three days by snow blocking the railway. When he finally reached Halifax he found his younger brother distraught and alone; their mother and sister had been unable to leave Grand Pré because of the storm.

Despite the shock and sorrow of Mabel's death, plans for the future were imperative. Hal acknowledged the precariousness of

his position. Robert's own firm was in the process of winding up
its affairs and another position would have to be found for Hal.
The three young children had to be cared for. In desperation the
two brothers considered breaking up the family. Eunice might
accompany Robert and Laura in their projected move to Ottawa.
Henry could also come to Ottawa and live with William and his
wife and Robert's mother and sister could look after baby Mabel
in Grand Pré. But to be deprived of both his wife and children
was more than Hal could bear. He insisted that his family be kept
together.

Robert arranged a place for Hal in the new firm of his former
partner, W. B. A. Ritchie. The children would go to Grand Pré for
the summer months and in the fall Hal's sister-in-law, Ethel
Barnstead, would move to his house to look after the three
children.¹ Then he rushed back to Ottawa and the growing
clamour over the Autonomy Bills. There he found a few callous
press reports complaining that he was neglecting his political
responsibilities by his absence from the House. He was deeply
hurt by the attack. On March 6 he angrily explained that he had
been called away by the death of "a very near and dear relative".
The suggestion that he had conveniently disappeared to avoid
taking a stand on a contentious issue was offensive. "I do not
think that in my public life I have usually been found wanting in
my attendance on Parliament; nor do I think that anything has
been displayed in my public career which would lead any journalist of even the most suspicious type to suppose that I would
have gone to Halifax on this particular occasion if it had not been
absolutely necessary, in my judgment, that I should do so."²

The explanation was hardly necessary. Even the most un-
sympathetic of his parliamentary colleagues would not have
believed that Borden had deliberately shirked his parliamentary
and party duties. And in other circumstances Borden would not
have risen to the unfair taunt. But he continued to worry about
Hal and the children. Indeed, throughout the first session of the
new Parliament his brother's welfare dominated his thoughts.
"Poor Hal [is] in an exceedingly depressed and nervous condition," he told Laura in June. "He is living alone as I understand
and it is most injurious to have him brooding with no companion save his own sad thoughts."³ Laura, who remained in
Halifax to oversee the coming move to Ottawa, knew this all too
well. She was doing what she could to look after Hal, but he

plainly did not want to share his sorrow and grief. When she had asked him to move back to Pinehurst, his reply was almost distant. He was, he said, going to "think it over". Robert felt equally helpless in Ottawa. He had thought of sending for Hal to come and join him, "but it seems almost useless as my time is so occupied".[4] The best that could be hoped for was that Hal would improve in the fall with Ethel's help and the return of the children. In the meantime, Robert's concern for his family was distracting his attention from the debate on the creation of the new western provinces.

Borden had been committed to provincial status for the Northwest Territories since the beginning of his leadership. And Laurier had made it a promise in his 1904 election campaign. Both men knew that provincial status for the vast expanse of land between Manitoba and the Rocky Mountains could no longer be denied. The number of settlers was growing by leaps and bounds; the prairie agricultural economy was exceeding the fondest expectations of the most optimistic proponents of western development. Between 1901 and 1911 the population of the area that became Saskatchewan and Alberta grew by more than seven hundred thousand. In the same decade nearly one hundred and fifty thousand farms were created in the prairie provinces. Farm acreage increased by forty-two million acres, wheat production jumped more than seventy-seven million bushels, cattle production rose by more than five hundred per cent.[5] Provincial status would put the final seal of accomplishment upon the development policies of the Laurier government.

Laurier's railway policy was working. The voters might have found Borden's policy interesting, but Sir Wilfrid's was convincing. His transcontinental scheme was going ahead. And during the session the Liberals teased the Opposition by setting conditions upon the takeover by the Grand Trunk of the Canada-Atlantic which had, at one time, been a key link in the railway policies of Borden and Blair. Under the new legislation the government was allowed to run through freight and passenger trains and to do local passenger business over the Grand Trunk's new property.[6]

Tariff policy was successful. There was some murmuring about the tariff, just as there always had been. The woollen and lumber industries believed themselves to be hard-pressed and demanded tariff relief. The Canadian Manufacturers' Association gave them vigorous support and added its own worries about the apparent trend towards an unfavourable balance of trade with the United States. The increasing importation of American consumer goods, it was argued, denied production to Canadian factories and jobs for Canadian workers. The Trades and Labour Congress, with connections with the American Federation of Labor, flatly declared against a tariff increase which, it said, would raise profits for manufacturers and prices for workmen and consumers. But the rival National Trades and Labour Congress, starting from the premise that the most desirable objective was "the manufacture in Canada of everything we are capable of producing in order to make employment for workingmen", appeared to favour any tariff increases that would result in increased employment of Canadian workers. To all this, and the usual pressure from agrarians for lower tariff schedules, the government responded cautiously. The Minister of Finance announced the appointment of a Tariff Commission which would hold hearings in all the principal cities of the country.* Until it reported, no major changes in the tariff would be in order.

The administration of immigration policy by Clifford Sifton, the Minister of Interior, was the most notable achievement of the Laurier government. It was transforming Canada into a new nation with diverse tongues and talents and with uncounted ambitions. By a happy coincidence of favourable economic conditions, reformed administrative procedures and an aggressive program of attracting prospective immigrants in Great Britain, the United States, and Europe, the annual rate of immigration had risen from less than twenty thousand in 1896 to over one hundred and forty thousand in 1905.[7] Britons, Americans, and Europeans were literally rushing into the country at Halifax, Quebec, Montreal, and Vancouver and dozens of official and unofficial points of entry along the United States border. Sifton had promised to settle the wheat lands with strong-backed producers of Canada's major export commodity and eager consumers of Canadian manufactured goods. He had done just that.

---

*The members of the Commission were W. S. Fielding, the Minister of Finance; Sir Richard Cartwright, the Minister of Trade and Commerce; William Paterson, the Minister of Customs; and Louis-Philippe Brodeur, the Minister of Inland Revenue.

Save for a preference for agricultural immigrants, Sifton's policy contained few restrictions. It reflected his strong faith in the ability of the country to absorb the newcomers, whatever their origin, in the ability of the newcomers to become solid and respectable Canadian citizens. One key to the process was to give them work to do, preferably on the land, to give them a stake in Canada's future. The other was the school system. The varied heritages of the immigrants would broaden and enrich the cultural life of all Canadians, but the schools were vital to the assimilation of the immigrants into the Canadian way of life. But Sifton's critics, men of a decidedly less optimistic turn of mind, became increasingly concerned as his policy prospered. The huge numbers involved, and the lack of selectivity in the immigration process, gravely worried those who doubted the ability of Canada to "Canadianize" the newcomers. The latent distrust of these "foreigners", wherever they came from, was widespread. At one end of the scale were the Britons and Americans who it was assumed would assimilate Canadian ways with relative ease; at the other were the Asians. Borden's view that the Asian immigrants were not capable of assimilation was atypical only in its relative mildness. There were few Canadians who did not believe that the country's interests would be best served by exclusion of Asian immigrants.

Between these two views was a spectrum of shades of doubt and distrust about the place of the European immigrants who entered the country. Group settlements of Doukhobors and Mennonites (and of Mormons from the United States) and thousands upon thousands of Ukrainians, Russians, Austrians, Swedes, Germans, and Belgians had found new homes on the prairies. They were hardy settlers who were becoming first-rate farmers. But they spoke a babel of tongues and followed a plethora of beliefs and cultural practices that native Canadians found at least confusing and more often frightening. As early as 1903 the fears were starkly revealed in a debate in the House. Thomas Sproule, Borden's colleague and a prominent member of the Orange Order, summed up his complaints against Sifton's policy with characteristic crudeness: "Canada is today the dumping ground for the refuse of every country in the world." Frank Oliver, the Liberal MP for Edmonton who would find himself in charge of immigration policy before the 1905 session was done, was more polite though no less anxious. "It is a question of the ultimate results of the efforts put forward for the building up of a Canadian nationality," he had said. "This can never be accomplished if the preponderance of the population should be of such a class and character as will deteriorate rather than elevate the condition of our people and our country at large."[8]

To these fears were added others, resurrected from past national quarrels. Ontarians worried about the growing numbers of "foreigners" moving into their cities and industrial towns. They increasingly complained about their isolation as the west became more and more "un-British" and as strange and incomprehensible as was Quebec at their eastern gate. In Quebec French-speaking Canadians thought that Sifton's policy was undermining their claim to a rightful place in western development and threatened the rights and privileges of French Canadians living in the west. In 1899 Borden's desk-mate, Monk, had reflected that concern by suggesting that western lands be reserved for settlement by the two founding races.

As the new settlers poured in, the already precarious position of French-speaking Canadians in the west became ever more tenuous. In the Territories the official recognition of the French language had been abolished in 1893. By 1901, with the passage of new ordinances by the Territorial government, the separate school system granted in 1875 had all but vanished. The ordinances proclaimed that all schools had to be public schools with the same regulations and curriculum. Religious instruction was permitted only at the end of the school day and the wishes of the majority in the school district would determine whether teachers were Roman Catholic or Protestant. The minority might establish its own school with teachers of the other faith. But the minority schools still had to conform to the Territorial regulations and curriculum. In the eyes of English-speaking Canadians, the ordinances were necessary to establish one efficient school system that could assimilate the growing number of "foreigners" into Canadian life. But French Canadians saw them as another threat to their rights and privileges. They questioned the worth of an immigration policy whose consequences undermined their own cultural heritage. By 1904 Henri Bourassa, who originally supported Sifton's policy, shared Monk's fears. "It was never in the minds of the founders of this nation," he told the House of Commons, that "we ought to change a providential condition of our partly French and partly English country to make it a land of refuge for the scum of all nations."[9]

Many Canadians, then, did not share Sifton's faith in his immigration policy. They might agree that it was an economic blessing; but it was also a cultural curse. And its ultimate result, the grant of provincial status to Saskatchewan and Alberta, crystalized all their doubts and fears about the new Canada Sifton had built.

Three plans had been considered for the disposition of the Territories. Frederick Haultain, the able leader of the Territorial government, wanted one province. Others urged that Manitoba's western boundary be extended and two provinces created between the Red and the Rockies. Finally, Laurier's government decided on a third plan, the formation of two new provinces between Manitoba and British Columbia and extending from the United States border north to the sixtieth parallel. Reasonably generous financial terms were established for the new provincial governments. At Sifton's insistence, and following the Manitoba precedent in 1871, the federal government retained control over public lands so that they might continue to be used to promote immigration.

Though Borden heartily agreed to the creation of the provinces of Alberta and Saskatchewan, he did not like the way in which the legislation had been drawn up and introduced to the House of Commons. Haultain, by design, had not been consulted while the bills were being drafted nor had he been shown the legislation until a few short hours before it was presented. Similarly, Laurier had failed to observe the customary courtesy of showing the legislation to the leader of the Opposition before it was introduced. Copies of the Alberta bill, the first to be considered, reached Borden's desk just minutes before Laurier rose to make his introductory speech.[10]

Even a cursory glance during Laurier's speech revealed two troublesome proposals. The first was the retention of control of the public lands by the Dominion government. Sifton had argued that to turn the lands over to the new provinces "would be ruinous to our settlement policies and would be disastrous to the whole Dominion".[11] But Borden was on record as favouring the surrender of the public lands to provincial control and he had not changed his mind. Their retention by Ottawa, he said, was an unnecessary infringement upon provincial autonomy.[12] "The people of the Northwest when they are granted provincial rights are fully capable of dealing with these lands," he argued later in the debate. "They are entitled to the control of these lands just as much as the people of the eastern provinces of Canada are entitled to the control of their provincial domain."[13]

The other, and much more serious problem, was the clause relating to public schools. As soon as it was learned that the government was considering the grant of provincial autonomy, the "school question" became a subject of public debate. Westerners assumed that their schools were under local control and would remain so. G. H. V. Bulyea, the Territorial Commissioner of Public Works, told the *Globe* in early January that "We have no school question on our hands . . . and [we] do not expect any." But Ontarians were not so complacent. They pressured Laurier's government to insure the unfettered control of education by the provinces. Local control, they argued, was consistent with provincial autonomy; more important, local control meant what westerners called "national schools", a single state-controlled, English-language system which would guarantee the assimilation of western immigrants into English-Canadian culture. French-speaking Canadians and the Roman Catholic Church, on the other hand, just as strongly desired a restoration of the minority's school rights and privileges in the new provinces.

The two views were mirrored in an intense struggle within Laurier's cabinet. Sifton was just as opposed to separate schools in the new provinces as he had been to separate schools in his own province of Manitoba throughout his political career. He was willing to have the federal government guarantee such privileges as remained to the minority under the 1901 ordinances, but would go no further. Charles Fitzpatrick, who had recently been appointed Minister of Justice, a post Sifton coveted, was anxious to placate the Roman Catholic hierarchy by improving the status of the minority's Catholic schools in the new provinces. While Sifton vacationed in the South, Fitzpatrick was entrusted with the task of drafting the schools clause. Fitzpatrick worked in close consultation with Henri Bourassa and Mgr. Sbarretti, the Papal Delegate to Canada. His clause was ambiguous in wording, but clearly open to the interpretation that the completely separate school system of 1875 was being restored and guaranteed under Section 93 of the British North America Act.

Borden refused to commit himself on the school clause on first reading of the Alberta bill. He knew little about the question itself and all too quickly asserted that "up to the present time there has been really no school question, to use the common expression, in the Northwestern Territories of Canada". After a quick glance at the clause he feared that it might engender a debate about schools "which happily has been entirely absent there in the past". But he hoped it would not be so. He was acutely aware of the trouble the "schools question" could cause in his caucus and his party. His Ontario members, the dominant force in his caucus, would, almost as much by instinct as by conviction, be pitted against his followers from Quebec. He hoped, he told the Commons, "that on both sides of the House we will not seek to make this a political question in any sense".[14]

He must have known that it was a vain hope. What could a debate on separate-school status in the new provinces be if it was not a "political question" in every sense? It went to the very heart of the differing conceptions of French and English Canadians of their respective roles in Confederation. It raised the central question of the nature of Confederation itself. It aroused all the emotions that the Manitoba school question had raised just over a decade ago. And, though Borden failed to realize it, by its very nature the "schools question" had been present in the Territories since the inception of territorial government. The progressive limitations imposed upon the minority school system by the various territorial ordinances had kept it very much alive in government offices in Regina and Ottawa and in clerical circles in eastern and western Canada.[15]

The months that passed between first and second readings of the autonomy bills proved just how political the school question was. Sifton returned from his southern vacation to discover that he had lost the cabinet debate over the school question. Like many others, he read Fitzpatrick's clause as a device to restore denominational schools to equal status with public schools in Alberta and Saskatchewan and promptly resigned. Publicly, Sir Wilfrid Laurier professed bafflement at what all the fuss was about and claimed that the school clause simply entrenched the existing school system under the 1901 ordinances. But the threat that Fielding would also resign and a strident outcry from the Grit press in Ontario forced the Prime Minister to finally concede the ambiguity of the clause. He did not ask Sifton to withdraw his resignation, but he did assign him to the task of redrafting the school clause. Sifton's handiwork eventually made clear what Laurier said he had wanted all along, a perpetuation of the existing territorial system under the protection of Section 93 of the British North America Act.[16]

Meanwhile Borden's caucus struggled with the school question. There was considerable pressure from the party press and the Ontario members for a straight party position on the issue.[17] But the views of his Ontario and Quebec members could not be reconciled and a party position would have inevitably meant the adoption of the Ontario view and a split in Conservative ranks. Borden freed his followers to vote on the school clause as conscience dictated. His decision was at once consistent with his plea that the members of Parliament not make the schools question a "political [i.e., party] question" and a convenient escape from the imposition of an Ontario view upon his Quebec members. Furthermore, he would take his own position on the question and tell the caucus of his decision the day before he spoke in debate. He would not "announce it as a matter on which they should dictate to me but as a matter on which I had made up my own mind".[18]

The debate on second reading and in committee proceeded, for the most part, on a high plane. Borden, as he had forecast in his remarks on the public lands question, cast himself as the ardent champion of provincial rights. He argued that the original schools clause was an unwarranted interference in what was properly a provincial affair. The issue, Borden said, was not "a question of separate schools, but a question of provincial rights".

> I . . . am standing on the rock of the constitution, as I understand that constitution: I simply desire that the domination of the parliament shall not in any way destroy or undermine that foundation upon which the provincial rights of this country rest. . . . In . . . Quebec, there is . . . a strong spirit in favour of provincial rights. And it is because I interpret the constitution in the light of that spirit that I take the stand upon this question which I take today . . . education should be left absolutely to the control of the people of the new province.[19]

Education was a provincial affair. And public lands also should be. To confine the province's jurisdiction in the first, and to deny the province's jurisdiction in the second matter, completely upset the allotment of jurisdiction in the British North America Act. Laurier's Autonomy Bills, in essence, "completely transpose and reverse the entire scheme and compact of confederation. . . . We have no duty, nay, we have no right or power to shatter the foundations then laid, or to rewrite the compact into which we then entered."[20] He concluded by moving an amendment demanding that the provincial legislatures-to-be should have "full powers of Provincial self-government, including power to exclusively make laws in relation to education".

Borden's position won him no friends in Quebec. His Quebec members wanted more than the freedom to vote as they wished from their leader. They wanted, at the very least, a restatement of the Conservative position on the Manitoba school question in 1896, that the federal government had both the right and the duty to intervene in provincial educational affairs to protect the rights of the minority. They did not get it. Instead, their leader said the very opposite, that "education should be left absolutely" to the control of the provincial legislatures. Both Ames and Bergeron supported Laurier's policy and Monk went further afield, demanding positive safeguards for the rights of the French-speaking minority in the new provinces. Monk was so incensed by Borden's statement that he was reported to be telling his colleagues that Borden's stand on the school question had set the Conservative cause back fifteen years in Quebec.[21] Casgrain wrote that he understood how Borden had acted "from a sense of duty" and coolly added that "your conduct will not lessen the sincere regard which I have for you".[22] Another Quebec Tory reported that efforts to raise a mere four thousand dollars to give a more favourable interpretation to Borden's position were hopeless.[23]

Borden was hurt by these criticisms. After all, he thought, where were provincial rights more jealously guarded than in the province of Quebec? How better to protect Quebec's interests than by standing on the "rock of the constitution"? If a defence of provincial rights on the school question happened to coincide with Ontario's case for "national schools" in Alberta and Saskatchewan, as it did, that defence also meant protection for Quebec from federal interference in its affairs. As he pointedly argued to a Quebec City audience two years later, defending his position on the "school question", "Your rights in the Province of Quebec, the rights which you so zealously cherish and so stoutly

maintain, are dependent upon [the] constitution."²⁴ Fundament-
ally, Borden believed, the position of his Quebec members was
constitutionally inconsistent. They seemed to want the sanctity
of provincial rights for their own province and the right of the
federal government to override provincial rights in the other
provinces when the rights of the French-speaking minority were
threatened. "One cannot say a single word in defence either of the
constitution or the principle of national schools without at once
being charged with fomenting religious discord and racial
hatred," Borden sourly observed. "The attitude of the French
Canadians has always been a little peculiar in this respect."²⁵

Borden simply could not understand either the fears or the
aspirations of his Quebec colleagues. For years he had argued
that both English and French-speaking Canadians should all be
"content to be Canadians". A perpetual concern with whether
one's "ancestors were English or French", he had said in one of
his early speeches as leader of the party, "only tends to keep alive
ideas which really have no useful place in the life of this
country".²⁶ But for his French-speaking colleagues the matter
was not quite that simple, nor was it only a question of defence
of provincial rights. In order to be "content to be Canadian" they
had to battle constantly for their rights and privileges as a
minority. The constitution may have given them their rights and
privileges both in Quebec and everywhere else in Canada. But
they had to use their political power to protect and defend them.

Borden's amendment was defeated, with thirteen of his followers voting with the government. Laurier's party carried second
reading early in May. A month later, while debate on the autonomy bills continued, the school question was submitted to the
Ontario electorate in the London and North Oxford by-elections.
The big guns of both parties entered the contest. Borden's candi-
dates got heady rhetorical support from both Haultain and R. B.
Bennett, a prominent Conservative member of the Territorial
Assembly. But to no avail. The defeats broke the spirit of the
Opposition. "Probably the session will be little shortened as our
members will not now take the same interest in the Autonomy
Bills. Our men are very much disappointed," Robert told Laura.²⁷
At the end of June, Sifton's amended school clause was introduced
and a few days later the great Autonomy debate was over. Alberta
and Saskatchewan became the eighth and ninth provinces of
Canada.

Both parties paid dearly for the rounding out of Confederation. Laurier's initial support for Fitzpatrick's school clause cost him the services of one of his most talented ministers. His support for Sifton's amended clause hastened Bourassa's disaffection with Laurier Liberalism. Borden's failure to force a unified party position on the school question struck some of his more ardent Protestant followers in Ontario as a sign of weakness. Joseph Flavelle, for example, claimed that the Conservatives lacked courage in their reluctance to stand up to a Roman Catholic Church "arrogant with the sense of its power, and operating through a Prime Minister her own son".[28] At the same time, Borden's personal defence of provincial rights opened a wound in his relations with his French-Canadian colleagues that would never heal.

The members of the House of Commons were exhausted, their last ounce of political enthusiasm played out by the Autonomy debate. But there was one last bit of contentious business to deal with; an increase in their sessional indemnities. Before the indemnity issue was finally resolved it occasioned a minor crisis in the Conservative party. The Tory MP's did not object to an increase in their indemnities from $1,500 to $2,500 per session; the matter had been discussed throughout the session and a "round robin" favouring a salary increase had been signed by most members. Nor was an increase in the salaries of judges and of the Prime Minister and the provision of annuities for Privy Councillors who had served for five years as Cabinet members in dispute. What was novel and debatable, though not in the House where all the proposals passed without division, was the inclusion of an additional "Sessional allowance" of $7,000—the equivalent of a Cabinet member's salary—for "the recognized position of Leader of the Opposition".

Borden favoured all of the increases, though at first he had been unaware that the "round robin" included a special allowance for him.[29] Borden told the Prime Minister "that I would not consider in connection with any of these matters or as part of any 'deal' or arrangement, the subject of a salary to the leader of the Opposition; that this must be considered apart from other matters and solely upon its merits, that I would not discuss it at all myself. Accordingly I appointed Foster, Barker, Stockton and

Lake as a committee to represent the Conservative party in dealing with this question."[30] A committee of Government and Opposition members then proposed a special indemnity of $5,000
for him. This he flatly refused. "If there was to be a special indemnity," he said, "it should be not less than the salary of a
Cabinet Minister. His labours were certainly as arduous as that
of any member of the Government with the exception of the
Prime Minister." Borden, always solicitous of his own financial
well-being, undoubtedly preferred the equivalent of a Cabinet
member's salary, $7,000, to the committee's proposal. But it was
the principle, not the money, that mattered. He did not need
the money. His investments in stocks, bonds, and real estate
brought him a very comfortable income. In fact, though only a
few close friends knew it, throughout the tenth Parliament he
turned over his regular indemnity to Edward Kidd, who had given
up the Carleton seat to him.[32]

Borden's support for the indemnity increase was based both on
the fact that the annual sessions of Parliament were getting longer
each year and that the matters before Parliament had grown ever
more complex and interrelated. Aspects of economic, fiscal, and
social policy that had scarcely been imagined proper subjects
for federal government action a short decade before were now
commonplace items of deliberation. Borden frankly believed that,
on the whole, the capacity of the members of the House of Commons had not kept pace with the business of the country. What
was needed was a means to attract more skilled men of affairs
into politics, men anxious to devote their attention to the on-
going development of the country by efficient means, men who
had no interest in the parochial politics of the past.

The indifference of business and professional men to the affairs
of state, Borden thought, was one of the most dangerous consequences of the prosperity the nation enjoyed. He decried it in his
remarks at Saint Francis Xavier College when he accepted an
honourary degree in September. "The people are the true guard-
ians of their own rights and liberties; but how inefficient must be
that protection if the better elements of our population absorbed
in their own pursuits remain indifferent to the conduct of public
affairs," he observed. "Power involves duty. The privilege of
citizenship imposes a certain responsibility. . . . In a democracy
the great vice as well as the great danger is the indifference of the
individual citizen."[33]

But he also realized that the kind of people he wanted to see in Parliament, or, for that matter, on the bench, would have to incur substantial financial sacrifices if they accepted public office. Time and time again he had pleaded with prominent men to join him in political life. Time and time again, they had refused. "Those who are opposed to any increase of indemnity might have their views altered if they had undergone my own experience in endeavouring to get representative men to enter public life," he wrote in July. "This is rapidly becoming impossible under present conditions."[34]

The public reaction to the passage of the indemnity legislation in 1905 shocked the leader of the Opposition. In Halifax the Conservative paper denounced the measure as a "treasury raid". In New Brunswick the party executive passed a resolution condemning the increased indemnity, the pension scheme and the special allowance of $7,000 to Borden. Hugh Graham's Montreal *Star* said the indemnity increase was "the most shameless salary grab on record" and the party paper in Victoria, the *Colonist*, spoke of "a wholesale and reckless raid on the Treasury planned in the dark and suddenly sprung upon the country".[35] Billy Maclean was particularly incensed. Ostentatiously, he gave his indemnity increase, $1,000, to the Hospital for Sick Children at the end of July. A week before, his Toronto paper carried a bitter denunciation of the indemnity legislation and singled out Borden, "the Tupper nominee", as the villain of the piece. "The regeneration of the Conservative party must start from the outside and start soon," cried the *World*. At Wexford, in early August, Maclean charged that the special allowance to Borden made him "practically an appointee, certainly a payee of the Government of the day".[36]

"My friend W. F. McLean [*sic*] with his usual fairness is endeavouring to place the blame upon my shoulders for that which the Government has initiated and is responsible for," Robert told Laura in July.[37] Maclean's personal attack stung enough that Borden finally replied in a major address in Toronto in mid-December. He denied any personal involvement in the "special allowance" proposal. And he asserted that the "special allowance" was, properly interpreted, both legitimate and salutary to the interests of the Opposition party of the day. Hitherto circumstances dictated that the Opposition leader be either a rich man or dependent upon party gifts and "under obligation to its wealthy members". The "special allowance" gave the party much broader scope in its choice of a leader. It was "paid by the country, not the Government", and there was no more reason to assume that the leader of the Opposition would thereby be sub-servient to the government of the day than there was to assume that the nation's judges were.[38]

But that was not the end of it. Early in the new year Borden sought the advice of some of his parliamentary colleagues and a few other prominent Conservatives. Though he did not like it, he suggested the repeal of the pension scheme and the "special allowance" and postponement of the increased indemnities until after the next election.[39] To his dismay, most respondents indi-cated continued opposition to the indemnity measures. Premier Whitney of Ontario supported the increases but thought that both parties had badly bungled the affair. Premier Roblin accepted the indemnity raise but opposed the special allowance. So too did Charles Hibbert Tupper, who firmly believed that it was the responsibility of the party, not the country, to support its leader. And great exception was taken to the pension scheme by most of the respondents.[40]

Tupper's letter is especially interesting. He and Borden were contemporaries in age. But their contrasting views on the special allowance to the leader of the Opposition revealed much about the differing attitudes of the older and younger generations of politicians in the Conservative party. Tupper clearly reflected a traditional attitude in his inability to draw a distinction between the government and the governing party. He believed that accept-ance of payment from one meant subservience to the other. "I am opposed to it in the interest of the Party; it must weaken the Leader who without it can acquire a stronger claim to public attention and consideration than he otherwise would do. It virtually makes him an unattached member of the Administra-tion," he wrote. Tupper concluded that "the Party ought to be able and willing (and I think it is) to supply the amount named to a Leader who has now to devote his whole time to the Party's services".

Borden made the distinction that Tupper could not. He believed that the independence of the Opposition leader was much more likely to be compromised by his own party than by the govern-ment of the day. "The duties, if properly discharged," he told Joseph Flavelle, demand the entire time of any man occupying so important a position. To restrict it to the choice of men of ample fortune seems to limit it unduly. If provision must be made it is infinitely better, in my opinion, that it should come as a provision from the country for public service than as a contribution from party funds. In the latter case the leader is in effect a pensioner of a few men of wealth within the ranks of the party. This condition is obviously not a desirable one. It does not seem to me that the independence of a leader is in any way affected by a special indemnity payable out of the Exchequer. The independence of members in Opposition is surely not affected by an indemnity paid in the same way.

Borden was committed to the principle of a state-financed special indemnity to the leader of the Opposition. And he was impatient with his colleagues who thought otherwise. "It is intolerable to have within the ranks of my own party men whose opinions on the subject are strongly opposed to the provision which has been made and who are inclined to suspect improper motives on my part," he told Flavelle. It seemed that there was only one way out. "This provision should be either repealed or postponed during my service as leader."[41]

Late in the spring of 1906 the indemnity legislation was debated again in the House. In May, Maclean's bill to repeal the sessional indemnity was defeated 167 to 9. Seven other Conservatives and one Liberal voted with Maclean. The only casualty of the debate was the annuity scheme for ex-Cabinet Ministers. At the end of June a government bill repealing the pension scheme was carried. The other measures, including the special allowance to the leader of the Opposition, stood. And so did the sneers, public and private, within the party, that Robert Borden was the "paid servant" of Sir Wilfrid Laurier's government.

The extraordinarily long parliamentary session gave Borden little time to think about other party business. A very welcome bit of news was the word of James Pliny Whitney's victory in the Ontario election of 1905. In the years to come Whitney would become a most valuable ally. But Borden's interest centred on the federal party. The rout of his forces in the election of 1904 had demonstrated that a fighting issue and a vigorous campaign by the party leader were not enough to win a political contest. The *La Presse* affair proved that political tricks were no substitute for sound and constructive organization. Borden was ready to give the lead. But would the party follow him? He made it clear that it had to if it wanted him to continue in the leadership. Except for the caucus, there was hardly any continuing organizational structure at all. Borden, who was responsible for leading both the Opposition in Parliament and the party at large, received able assistance from Blount. Blount directed political traffic, looked after all the details of Borden's endless round of appointments and meetings, and supervised the countless minutiae of party business. But there was just too much work for the two men to do by themselves and Borden complained to his secretary that "it is useless to continue in public life unless the party awakens to the necessity of activity and organization".[42]

Throughout the early months of 1905 the problems of building an effective organization were discussed in party circles. What Borden had in mind was an elaborate organizational structure, rooted in the constituencies and based upon democratically elected party officials, with clear lines of authority from the constituencies to the national leader. That, of course, would take time to construct. It would also temper the power and influence of individual MP's in their own constituencies. And other party members were speculating about an easier, flashier route to organization of the party. There was much talk of a convention, perhaps modelled on the great Liberal convention of 1893. It would, some thought, be a convenient way to hammer a party platform into shape. Others expressed skepticism about a policy convention but hinted that a national gathering of the faithful might be a proper place for a purge of the party leadership. Among them was F. H. Haultain, in Ottawa for the Autonomy debates. He may have had Borden in mind when he hinted darkly that a convention could get "the party leadership into proper hands". "The party needed," he told a reporter, "four or five first-class funerals."[43]

Talk of a party convention was premature. To hold one without an established organizational structure for the party and without a good deal of prior planning would be worse than doing nothing at all. Borden liked the convention suggestion well enough, but only in due time. In April, a committee which had been considering the idea reported to caucus. It recommended that the MP's from each province be responsible for organization in their respective provinces. They were to organize each electoral district and have it select a delegation for a provincial convention to meet, if possible, before the end of the year. Each provincial convention, in turn, would elect delegates "to a Dominion Convention which shall be held at such time and place as the Central Committee shall decide". The Central Committee would be composed of about 25 members initially selected by Borden and the provincial conventions would either ratify or replace his nominees when they met. Eventually the Dominion Convention would either endorse or replace the members of the Central Committee. The Central Committee would then become the chief organizational body of the national party. The caucus approved the plan on April 12 and later in the day Borden nominated the members of the provisional Central Committee. Except for Nova Scotia and British Columbia, which had no Conservative representation in the House of Commons, every province had at least one member on the committee.[44]

By the end of the year provincial conventions had been held in Nova Scotia, Quebec, Saskatchewan, and Alberta, and another was due to meet in Manitoba in January, 1906. There had been no convention in Ontario, perhaps because Premier Whitney distrusted such gatherings, but an elaborate scheme of organization had been proposed for the province. The federal constituencies in Ontario were divided into twenty-five regional groups, each represented by a committee made up of officers of the local Conservative Association or the sitting members of the federal and provincial legislatures, or, failing either, the most recent federal candidates. The federal leader would select a person from each regional committee to convene a meeting to choose a group executive committee and adopt rules and procedures for annual meetings. In addition, there would be a "Central organization" composed of federal MP's from Ontario, the group presidents, the federal leader, and five other persons selected by him. The "Central organization", in turn, would have a seven-man executive committee. Finally, the federal leader would "appoint a Secretary for the party within the Province of Ontario, and from time to time prescribe his functions and duties within the Province".[45]

During 1905, then, very considerable progress had been made in the planning and implementation of a national party organization. What was most notable about the scheme was the party leader's control of the party apparatus, if he chose to exercise it.

The Central Committee for the convention was his creature. And in the largest province in the Dominion he would have direct links to each group executive, could exercise enormous influence in the "Central organization" and would appoint and prescribe the functions and duties of the provincial party secretary.

But there were set-backs and disappointments too. Certainly the by-election losses in London and North Oxford had not helped. In the new provinces, both conventions had been pre-occupied with the immediate issue of the first provincial general elections and the election results at year's end were scarcely encouraging. In Alberta, R. B. Bennett had been selected as party leader. He lost his own contest and only two Conservatives were returned in a twenty-five seat legislature. In Saskatchewan Haultain chose to fight on a non-partisan Provincial Rights plat-form. He was supported by the local Conservatives but did only a bit better than Bennett in Alberta. Eight Provincial Righters were elected to the Legislature.

Both Bennett and Haultain were supported by the national party. Blount made two quiet scouting expeditions to the west and came back with an estimate that $1,000 was needed for legitimate expenses in each of the fifty seats. Large amounts of money went forth from Ontario. And Premier Roblin was en-couraged to send his skillful organizers, led by Robert Rogers, the Manitoba Minister of Public Works, to lend a hand. When the elections were over, reports varied as to the amount of eastern Conservative money used in the campaign. Some said that Haultain had gotten the full $25,000 needed in Saskatchewan, but the local MP, R. S. Lake, named a lower figure. Whatever the case, the significant fact was that despite considerable effort, the party had lost another contest to Laurier.[46]

And the pot of disaffection continued to boil merrily in Quebec. As always, a host of differences large and small created an un-bridgeable gap of understanding between Borden and his French-speaking colleagues. Two incidents were typical. The first was the Jacques Cartier Club affair. The Montreal club had a long standing affiliation with the party and for years had received financial assistance from party funds. Early in 1905 it requested $4,000 from the party. With the treasury depleted after the election, and with no evidence that the club had contributed any worthwhile effort during the contest, Borden refused the request. Then, in October, the club gave a banquet to Whitney and Dr. J. O.

Reaume, the Ontario Minister of Public Works. Borden was not invited. When Whitney discovered this he refused to attend. Borden interceded and Whitney eventually went. Whitney forced the club to send a formal invitation to Borden who, in turn, sent his regrets.[47]

It was a very petty business but it had momentous overtones. It signalled a complete breakdown in the relations between French and English-speaking Conservatives in Quebec. A Conservative who had attended the Whitney banquet and heard reports of a speech Thomas Chapais had made to the Club Lafontaine reported that "it was quite within the bounds of possibility that the Quebec Conservatives would have to constitute themselves into a separate body of their own, as recent events, and much that was said in Parliament during the last session, had rendered their position most unsatisfactory, and had greatly crippled their influence amongst their fellow countrymen."[48] Hugh Graham relayed a report from Pelletier of the affair. "If Ameer [Borden] should not be invited down goes the club," said Pelletier. "If he accepts Zandright [Monk] will probably leave the banquet hall on Ameer entering it."[49]

Gossip about the French-speaking Conservatives withdrawing from the federal party circulated during the provincial convention in December. The need for a provincial leader for federal purposes also was discussed. Monk ambiguously discouraged both propositions with the statement that "as a Federal party there was an organization with a Leader for the whole Dominion, and he strongly deprecated any attempt to cut off the Province". But Borden again was not invited, apparently sent no message to the convention, and his existence was scarcely acknowledged by it. The convention drew up platforms for both levels of government, the federal document generally echoing national party policy. But its first plank went to the heart of the on-going dispute between the party leader and the French-Canadian Conservatives. "The interests of the country require," it declared,

> that minorities should be treated with full justice in the exercise of all their civil and religious rights. Any violations of rights that are founded upon the Federal constitution and upon pledges entered into by the Crown is contrary to the British institutions under which we live. These rights are inviolable.

Borden and the French Conservatives all agreed with the general principle. The problem, as the Autonomy debate made clear, was that they had very different conceptions of what constituted the inviolable rights of French-speaking Canadians.

As serious as the Quebec problem was, it did not detract from Borden's determination to proceed with the organization of the party. In fact, he was even confident that when a national convention was called, as Blount told C. F. Hamilton, the Ottawa correspondent of the *News*, "they will have no difficulty in having a harmonious Quebec contingent".[50] On December 14 the party leader was banqueted by the Borden Club in Toronto. Borden defended his stand on both the Autonomy Bills and the indemnity question. But his main theme was organization. "Our platform may be all that we wish, our policy all that could be desired, yet without thorough organization we cannot succeed. A party armed with good policy but destitute of organization, is like an army supplied with excellent ammunition but entirely destitute of rifles." Then he surprised at least some of his listeners by announcing that the party would hold a national convention during the coming year. It would be an open convention; every party matter would be considered from platform and policy to "full liberty to consider the question of leadership".[51]

At the beginning of 1905 Borden had been determined to stay in public life. He had given up his law practice in Halifax and started to look for a house in Ottawa. He had told John Willison that he had put "all the hesitation and doubt behind" and that he was ready "to do my full duty" to the Conservative party. But by the end of the year he was questioning the wisdom of his decision. On the positive side, he was sure that he had made the right decisions on both the Autonomy bills and the indemnity question. He had not forced his colleagues to follow him in either debate and had expressed his own beliefs clearly and unequivocally. And he was quite satisfied with the progress that had been made with the plan he had initiated for a national organization.

But his stand on the "school question" in the new provinces had revealed the great gulf in understanding the aspirations of French Canada between himself and his French Canadian colleagues. That gulf contributed to the continuing problems with party organization in Quebec. The provincial party convention had been an all-Quebec affair; he neither attended the convention nor was his leadership of the party more than politely acknowledged. Moreover, some party members and party papers, a minority to-be-sure, continued to blame him for the "salary grab" of 1905. They were right in believing that the indemnity measures would not have been passed without his cooperation. He was right in arguing that there was "no good reason why we should not do what is no more than justice (in most cases) in the resolutions" and that "the Government must bear the chief brunt" of responsibility.[52] In both debates, Borden's determination to stand for what he believed in had alienated influential people and groups in his party.

In addition, though Hal's condition seemed better at year's end, Borden knew that the solution to his brother's family problems was, at best, temporary. Ethel wanted to go to nursing school in Montreal and though she was happy enough to assume the obligation of caring for her late sister's husband and children, everyone recognized that it would be unfair to detain her for long from her goal. Permanent arrangements for the future of Hal and his children would have to be made sooner or later. One way out would be to resign the leadership, get out of politics, go back to Halifax and reopen his practice with Hal as a member of his firm. It would certainly appeal to Laura. She much preferred the security, order, and relative anonymity of professional life to the continuous public exposure and hazardous uncertainty of Robert's political career. More important, she worried about the effect of the endless hours of preparation for debates, caucuses, committee meetings, and party conferences upon Robert's health and disposition. Time and again she and Robert had doubted the worth of it all. On the evening of February 11, 1906, she left a note on his desk:

> I hereby give my consent to your getting out of politics—and quick.
>
> Laura Borden.

There was a hint of jest in it, but not enough to conceal her concern for her husband's future.

In public Borden revealed none of the doubts he had about his future course, save for the cryptic reference in his Borden Club speech to opening up the leadership question at the coming national convention. By mid-January his differences with his French Canadian followers appeared to be patched over. He shared the platform with Monk and Bergeron at a meeting of the

Montreal Conservative Club and urged better party organization upon his listeners. A few weeks later he carried the same message to the Ottawa Conservative Club. "Good organization and clean elections" should become the party's rallying cry.[53] Once again he had put his doubts behind him. He had found a chink in Laurier's armour, a weakness in Laurier's government that could be exposed without danger to his own party. In fact, he believed that the issue of purity in politics, if properly exploited, could unite his own party, discredit the Laurier government, and carry him to the premiership.

CHAPTER SEVEN

PURITY IN POLITICS

Once the provinces of Saskatchewan and Alberta had been created, the major work of the tenth Parliament was done. The great plan of national development, so cherished by both parties since Confederation, had been rounded out. Autonomous and in some cases very powerful provincial governments spanned southern Canada from sea to sea. In the north a vast domain remained under federal jurisdiction, a northern frontier which would be largely ignored by citizens and government alike for decades to come. There was, in fact, much left to be done in Canada "south of 60". Thousands more immigrants were yet to arrive from Europe, from the Mother Country, from the neighbouring Republic to join the hundreds of thousands who had already come. All of them had to be accommodated, provided with a livelihood, and assimilated into the Canadian way of life. The two new railways had to be completed. Roads and canals, factories and grain elevators, schools and homes had to be built. But the grand design was an accomplished fact.

The work of the remaining sessions of the tenth Parliament was more hesitant than imaginative. The creative energy of earlier Laurier governments, with admitted assistance from a decade of relative peace and great prosperity, had initiated a process of change in Canadian society and Canadian values scarcely foreseen by the legislators and administrators in Ottawa. Both the economy and society had acquired a progressive impetus of their own, which challenged the government's ability to control them. No longer was the stimulation of growth the first priority of policy-makers. Rather, influential groups in society were demanding consolidation and regulation of the growth they had set in train. Many Canadians believed it was time to reconsider the values that underlay large scale development policies. Bigness, profit, and material success had become the worldly goals of Canadians. But many questioned whether they should be. The traditional virtues of honesty, thrift, morality, duty, and even religious conviction seemed to have been swept aside in a hurly-burly world of competition, pleasure, and greed.

Three acts of the tenth Parliament indicated the faltering response of both the government and the Opposition to the demands for more effective social and economic policy. The Lord's Day Observance Act of 1906 sought to reassert the traditional Christian values of Canadians, at least on Sunday. The 1907 tariff revisions were designed to enhance the competitiveness of Canadian goods in changing world markets without endangering the manufacturers control of domestic markets. And the Industrial Disputes Investigation Act of 1907 was an attempt to check the growing antagonism between capital and labour. In none of these did the government exhibit the forceful imaginative policies that had characterized its development strategy; nor did Borden and his followers offer any constructive alternatives to government policy.

Like most agitations for the legislative control of moral values, the demand for a federal Lord's Day Observance Act was driven by a combination of sincere social and religious concern, self-interest, and petty grievances. Members of the Lord's Day Alliance and other citizens were anxious to guarantee a day of rest for Canadian workers. But many English-speaking Protestants also sought a way to curb the lax observance of the Sabbath by Catholic immigrants and French Canadians, by rich Canadians who frequented golf-and-country clubs on Sunday, and by people who subscribed to Sunday newspapers. In its own way, the demand for strict observance of the Lord's Day raised issues as fundamental and as controversial as the school question, issues which neither Laurier nor Borden were anxious to resolve. Though the federal legislation had the support of Archbishop Bruchési of Montreal, there was no getting around the fact that the most active support came from Canadian Protestants and that opposition could be expected both from powerful business interests like the railways and the Canadian Manufacturers' Association and from many French-speaking Canadians.

The businessmen made their protest in representations before a special committee of the House of Commons. Tarte told the readers of *La Presse* that "never has the liberty of the subject been so disregarded" as in the Lord's Day Bill. Bourassa and the prominent Quebec Conservative, L. T. Marechal, told a Montreal audience that the bill would "impose on the Province of Quebec a law contrary to the customs, sentiments, the interests and the civil rights of its inhabitants". In the House of Commons Bourassa acidly commented that "we cannot expect the working people to stay at home and read books of philosophy or even the publications of the Lord's Day Alliance" on Sunday.[1] Borden explained to Marechal that the federal government had been forced to act when a recent decision of the Judicial Committee of the Privy Council declared a similar Ontario law beyond the jurisdiction of the province. But he confessed that his caucus was divided on the issue. "It is so difficult," he wrote, "to make men of one Province understand the habit and mode of thought of those residing in another Province and brought up under the influence of different customs and traditions."[2]

Much to Borden's relief, the government presented the bill as a non-party measure, freeing MP's to vote, as Borden had done to his caucus on the school question, as their consciences dictated. Employment and business and commercial transactions were prohibited on the Lord's Day. So too were public games, excursions, and performances for hire. The sale or distribution of foreign Sunday newspapers and the publication of Canadian Sunday newspapers were forbidden. Numerous necessary exceptions were written into the bill, particularly in the fields of transportation and essential public services. But there was no denying that it was a sweeping measure which could drastically alter the Sunday habits of many Canadians.

Borden unsuccessfully tried to get Jews and Seventh Day Adventists exempted from the force of the legislation. His general stance on the bill, however, was equivocal, reflecting the delicate balance of forces and views in his caucus. He agreed that federal legislation to provide for a general day of rest was desirable, especially in light of the Privy Council decision. But he thought the bill should set out general principles and leave the details of observance of the Lord's Day to the differing convictions of the people of the various provinces.[3] His advice went unheeded in the House of Commons. However, the Senate amended the bill to allow the provincial Attorneys General discretion in the prosecution of the Act. In its own tortuous way the amendment made

the point he had urged throughout the debate, that there could be
no common standard for observance of the Lord's Day applied to
all the provinces. The leader of the Opposition sourly concluded
that the final legislation was less a statement of principles for a
general day of rest than "an Act for the benefit of the legal
profession".[4]

The 1907 tariff revisions were an even more hesitant response
to change. As the Minister of Finance admitted, when he introduced the tariff, "we are adopting new forms of schedules but,
after all, it will be found that no very great and no very radical
changes are being made". After a laborious cross-country inquiry,
after listening to scores of representations from manufacturers,
farmers, and consumers, Fielding had little to propose. Given the
inevitable contradictions in the representations made to the
Tariff Commission, and the apparent health of both the economy
and the Liberal party, the government concluded that it was best
to leave well enough alone. One small change decreased the
amount of the British preference on a substantial list of manufactured goods. More novel, but of less significance in terms of
total trade, was the introduction of an intermediate schedule
between the general and the preference levels of the tariff. A
slight reduction on the general rates, the intermediate schedule
was a bargaining tool, to be implemented by order-in-council, in
future negotiations with countries willing to grant Canada
reciprocal concessions. Neither the farmers nor the manufacturers were particularly pleased with the tariff revisions. The
former had wanted much lower, the latter much higher, rates in
the general tariff. The intermediate schedule promised little to
the agriculturalists and the Canadian Manufacturers' Association, with predictable alarm, said that if it was ever used "it
would deal a blow to Canadian enterprises and prove disastrous
to many lines of industry".[5]

The Conservative response was singularly feeble. One reason
was that the Tories had nothing better to propose. Foster, who
had resumed his post as party financial critic after his election in
1904, did fear that the intermediate schedule might be used to
open extensive trade talks with the United States. But he devoted
most of his reply to a set-piece condemnation of government
extravagance and fiscal irresponsibility. Borden's most significant contribution to the debate, during a discussion of farm
implement duties, was unusually fatuous: "Adequate protection

I stand for as much as I ever did; but I do not stand for adequate protection under conditions which will make our people pay more than they ought to pay for agricultural implements, or anything else."[6] The other reason for Conservative reticence was that the party had nothing to gain by siding with either the manufacturers or the farmers. The farmers would not accept "adequate protection" and the manufacturers still benefited from Fielding's clearly protectionist policy. So much so that a suggestion that the Conservatives urge higher duties to win support from the manufacturers brought a sharp response from Borden. "I do not propose to contend for higher duties which will better business conditions for men who belaud the Government with extravagant praise, who declare that the tariff is out of politics and whose practical sympathy on all occasions is given to the Government and not to the Conservatives," he wrote. "Those gentlemen have conceived the idea that they hold the Conservative party in the palm of their hand and can afford to treat the party, as they have treated it, with contempt. Eventually they may discover the error of their ways."[7]

A coal miners' strike in Lethbridge, which lasted from March to December, 1906, and which severely threatened prairie fuel supplies for the winter of 1906–7, set the stage for the debate on the Industrial Disputes Investigation Act.[8] In January 1907 Borden made a major speech in the House of Commons on the growing crisis in industrial relations. He rehearsed the dismal statistics of industrial unrest since the turn of the century; there had been more than a hundred strikes and lockouts in every year from 1901 to 1904 and nearly as many in 1905; the militia had been called out to aid the civil power in curbing industrial violence every year and in every section of the country.[9] The fact that the situation was steadily deteriorating was highlighted by the fuel crisis caused by the Lethbridge strike. All strikes and lockouts were unwelcome. But Borden especially worried about interruptions in the service of public utilities and stoppages of "the supply to the public of commodities which . . . are absolutely necessary for the public comfort". Neither the Conciliation Act of 1900 nor the Railway Disputes Act of 1903 had proved to be effective countermeasures to industrial unrest and violence.[10]

Borden moved that a select committee of inquiry be established by the House of Commons to investigate the matter. He was not committed to any particular solution to the problem. He was not ready, for example, to endorse compulsory arbitration, but he did favourably review the New Zealand labour legislation which included provisions for compulsory arbitration by the courts. He did stress the importance of labour unions. It was essential that labour be as thoroughly organized to protect its interests as capital was organized for its interest.[11] But neither capital nor labour could hold the country at bay: "We cannot permit employers on the one hand and employees on the other hand, to hold up the whole country while they are settling disputes between themselves by a costly and unreasonable method, while those disputes might be terminated, it seems to me, by some method of arbitration to which the parties ought to consent and to which the state should oblige them to consent."[12]

Borden, then, seemed to be prepared to use the power of the state to stop strikes in the public utilities sector if other methods failed. The government was not prepared to go that far. Its solution was the Industrial Disputes Investigation Act, drafted by the Deputy Minister of Labour, William Lyon Mackenzie King, and carried through the House by his minister, Rodolphe Lemieux. But it was Laurier who set the limits on government policy. The act was intended "simply to make an investigation compulsory", the Prime Minister said. "We do not propose to make arbitration compulsory. We say that it will be sufficient for the time being to provide for a compulsory investigation." The Act would apply to the coal mining, transportation, and public utility industries. Laurier was convinced, as was King, that concerned public opinion, guided by the disclosure of the facts of a strike from a compulsory investigation, would force a settlement. "The investigation takes place," Laurier explained. "The public will follow the investigation from day to day and satisfy themselves as to the merits of the case as it unfolds. I believe this is a great guarantee of the final settlement of the dispute."[13]

In fact, Borden's position on the Industrial Disputes Investigation Act was not as clear as his January speech. It became evident that the distinctions between compulsory arbitration, which he appeared to advocate, and compulsory investigation eluded him. By February he was backing away from compulsory arbitration. "I . . . would strongly deprecate the enactment of any compulsory law, any law imposing compulsory arbitration in advance of public opinion or against the protests of those interests [who are the parties to a dispute]." He even suggested that the government's provision for investigation of a dispute before a strike was very close to compulsory arbitration in disguise. The fact that under the new Act neither party in a labour dispute was obliged to accept the report of the investigation board did not bother him. That the Act did not prevent employers from discharging employees or from hiring strike-breakers drew no condemnation from him. At best, Borden's support for organized labour and for real collective bargaining in industrial disputes was just as ephemeral as was the government's. Neither party was prepared to put serious limitations upon the privileges of capital and management. And many years later, Borden's retrospective judgment was that the Lemieux Act "had served an excellent purpose".[15]

Neither party and neither party leader, then, was ready to respond forcefully to the changing social and economic conditions of the country. There was much to be said for permitting provincial variations in the observance of a general day of rest, but the device used to permit provincial discretion, either Borden's suggestion or the Senate amendment, was also a very convenient way for both parties to avoid another challenge to the different cultural habits of English and French Canadians. The party positions on the tariff were so similar as to be scarcely worth debating. Neither party was ready to make any significant concessions to employees in industrial disputes that would threaten the powers and privileges of employers. Both party leaders were very much aware of the individuals and groups in Canadian society which were demanding new government initiatives in social and economic policy, but both replied with hesitation and caution. Moreover, for Borden, questions of social and economic policy were a distraction from the course he had set for his party. In January 1906, he had decided to commit the full resources of his party to another task. The Conservatives were going to discredit the Laurier government.

Borden's plan was explained in a letter to his colleagues in the House of Commons. Quite naturally, a strong government had a great advantage in the normal conduct of the business of the House. But if the administration of its policies could be exposed as corrupt and inefficient, then doubt could be cast upon the prestige and integrity of the government. Borden reminded his followers that "several administrative scandals were unearthed" during the previous session, enough to suggest that diligent digging would turn up much more dirt. The public had been "aroused" by the initial revelations and "the country is at present in a very receptive mood". A scandal campaign could only redound to the benefit of the Conservative party. The public expected honesty and action from their political representatives. The Conservatives would give them both. "There is reason to believe," Borden wrote,

> that a far reaching system of corruption—a thorough going scheme of exploitation of the public resources and revenues for private gain—pervades more than one Department of the Government. Let me urge upon you to investigate wherever possible any manifestation of this. A slight appearance of decay on the surface often indicates thorough rottenness beneath.
>
> Reasonable effort should enable us to present and discuss a fresh scandal in each week of the session. The supply is undoubtedly abundant. Some cases will demand not only discussion but investigation.[16]

So began the party's "purity in politics" campaign, which continued throughout the remaining sessions of the tenth Parliament. The intensity of the attack increased annually, reaching a climax of invective and innuendo in the pre-election session of 1908. As the editor of the *Canadian Annual Review* observed, "it was a stormy Session and filled with angry debates and prolonged discussion and personal charges; it was a scandal Session teeming with Opposition allegations of corruption and maladministration".[17]

Borden, Monk, Foster, and their colleagues concentrated their fire upon the Departments of Interior, Marine and Fisheries, Railways and Canals, and Customs. The Interior Department's secret contract with the North Atlantic Trading Company, an organization established to secure European immigrants, and the allegedly corrupt activities of W. T. R. Preston, a Liberal immigration official in London, were hotly debated in each session. Borden accused the Department of maladministration in its land management and disposal policies in 1906 and a whole team of Conservatives followed up with detailed charges of mismanagement and corruption in 1907 and 1908. Herbert Ames and Borden revealed allegedly corrupt railway land transactions in Moncton and demanded inquiries into the collapse of the Quebec Bridge and the construction contracts on the National Transcontinental Railway. An investigation into the affairs of the Department of Marine and Fisheries, forced by the Conservatives, brought to light gross inefficiency and corruption in that Department. An investigation of the Militia Department highlighted deficiencies in the Ross rifle. And charges were made against the Customs Department and against the administration of the Yukon Territory.[18]

It was not possible for Borden's men to produce a fresh relevation of scandal every week in any of the parliamentary sessions, but their persistent questions and charges did turn up instance after instance of careless management of the public's affairs and money by the Laurier government. They forced investigations of Departmental administration that eventually led to the Civil Service Amendment Act of 1908 which established a Civil Service Commission to supervise recruitment into and promotion within the civil service.[19]

Moreover, the scandal campaign inspired Borden's colleagues with unaccustomed vigour and unity on the opposition benches. "The Opposition are in markedly better form this session," the Ottawa correspondent of the Toronto *News*, C. F. Hamilton, reported in March 1906. "The rank & file are showing more willingness to work, and support each other better."[20] An unexpected benefit of the campaign was that Bourassa, his friend Armand Lavergne and Alphonse Verville, a prominent figure in the labour movement in Quebec, frequently voted with the Conservatives on these matters.[21] But the most important effect of the scandal campaign was that it enhanced Borden's reputation in his caucus. A persistent complaint among the Tory members had been that their leader was much too reasonable—too indecisive, some said —in the House of Commons. Now, Hamilton observed, "they seem to have a new idea on the subject of Borden's leadership. All I speak to speak very highly of him & his leadership. His authority seems at last to be fairly established." And Borden responded enthusiastically to the successful implementation of his strategy. "Borden is speaking far better, with much more fire and directness."[22]

Nonetheless, a strategy of scandal mongering was a dangerous device for the Opposition party to adopt. It quickly became apparent, for example, that the Conservatives were much better at alleging than confirming wrongdoing in the Canadian government. The Tory force had to be spread thinly over a broad field of investigation and the ineffectiveness of the Conservative members on the various investigation committees of the House was soon evident. Hamilton, who very much wanted to believe that every Conservative allegation was true, complained that "Monk would be good if he had the courage & persistence, but he is a coward & wilts when things get squally. Barker is very ineffective with a witness & they have to use lightweights like Northrup."[23] More serious was the suggestion that the campaign was not having the desired effect upon the public. Borden's object was to discredit his opponents. But as week after week of debate in the House of Commons was taken up with angry charges and counter-charges, there seemed to be a growing conviction among the public that no politician could be trusted. One worried correspondent told Borden that "the whole House has suffered, and until one or two guilty people are punished, the public confidence will not be restored".[24]

The most damaging blow to the Conservative cause came when the Government's Royal Commission on Life Insurance charged that George Foster, one of the leaders of the Tory campaign, was himself up to his neck in shady dealings. One of the companies investigated by the Royal Commission was a fraternal organization, the Independent Order of Foresters. The IOF had established a trust company, the Union Trust, to handle the investment of its funds. Foster was the General Manager of Union Trust. Two weeks before the Royal Commission was announced, Sam Barker warned Borden that the impending investigation would be used, *inter alia*, to discredit Foster and a number of other Conservative MP's and, if possible, Borden. "I was told in Toronto today that an attempt would be made during the investigation of the Foresters to fasten some land purchase scandals on several of our party friends—Foster, Fowler, Pope, Lefurgy, Bennett, Clare et al—that Aylesworth is at [the] back of the attempt . . . it all has an ugly look, & my informant said they had tried to get you in with them but he was pleased that you had firmly refused."[25] Later on Borden acquired evidence of partisan bias by the Royal Commission in the form of a letter from "a very important member of the Government" telling George

Shipley, Chief Counsel for the Government, to "explode the bomb against Foster".[26]

Foster, Fowler, Lefurgy, and a number of IOF officers testified before the Royal Commission in October 1906. The facts of the case appeared to be that Foster, in his position as General Manager of Union Trust, invested IOF funds in a land syndicate of which Pope, Fowler, Bennett, and Lefurgy were members. The syndicate controlled a large block of land along the route of the Canadian Northern's transcontinental line. A similar investment of IOF money was made in timber lands in British Columbia in which Fowler was also interested. The Union Trust made handsome returns for itself and its client, the IOF, in the transactions. The rub was that Foster was alleged to have pocketed considerable profits himself and to have accepted large commissions from the syndicates for turning Union Trust (IOF) business to them.

Immediately cries for Foster's scalp appeared in the Liberal press. They were echoed in some Tory papers like Graham's *Star* and in Flavelle's "independent" *News*. The reports added insinuations of Borden's involvement. Borden admitted that he had indeed been asked to join the syndicate while he was on his 1902 western tour, but that he had refused. His denial was readily accepted.[27] But Foster was not so fortunate. His own explanations of his actions were tortuous and involved, not unnaturally in what was a complicated business affair. But they tended to cast doubt upon his denials of improper business conduct or of receiving commissions from the syndicate. As well, his own pious lectures and partisan sallies over the years made it unlikely that opponents or independents would take the man at his word. As one disgruntled Liberal journalist put it, "it would be mighty impressive and useful if both Foster and Fowler could be delicately strangled by the neck . . . Fowler . . . cheated his associates, and Foster . . . was d – d loose in his ethics touching the fiduciary duty. Everybody—I mean all reasonable beings, who drink, smoke, gamble, and generally enjoy life as she is to be had, hate Foster anyhow."[28] No recommendations for action against Foster were made in the report of the Royal Commission when it was tabled in the House in the Spring of 1907. But the allegations remained in the summary evidence the Commission had gathered.

That was bad enough. But Fowler, who also believed that he had been grievously wounded by the Royal Commission, took the occasion to launch a furious counterattack in the House which precipitated a heated debate where the whole matter was aired again. If the Government was going to sanction an inquisition into his personal affairs, Fowler said, then "I shall discuss the characters of hon. members opposite whether they be Ministers or private members and their connection with women, wine and graft."[29] Bourassa then demanded a thorough investigation of both the Liberal charges against Foster and his friends and the Fowler charges against the Liberals. Much to Foster's dismay, Borden led the Conservative support—albeit in a losing cause— for Bourassa's motion. Borden defended Foster in a speech more notable for its revelations of the unfairness of the Commission's procedures than for its assertions of his confidence in the probity of his colleague. The debate ended with Foster and Aylesworth trading inconclusive verbal blows and with Foster's reputation in doubt.

Borden's speech went to the heart of the matter. Right or wrong, Foster's own denials had not been accepted. The man, nonetheless, had not been given the advantage of defence procedures open to him in a court of law. He had been charged but neither acquitted nor convicted. The indictment would shadow him for the rest of his days. And because he was so prominent a figure in the party, it shadowed the Conservative party too. Exploding "the bomb against Foster" had been designed to discredit the prolonged Tory scandal campaign. It worked. It cast a pall over the sincerity of the men accusing the government of malfeasance in office. Borden and his colleagues would remain convinced of the sincerity of the charges they levelled against Laurier's government. But the allegations against Foster made their own efforts seem hypocritical in the public mind. Still, the Conservatives could not back away. To give up the scandal campaign would have been taken as a tacit admission of guilt, a silent confession that the accusers were as corrupt as the accused. Their crusade was tainted, but they would have to go on.

The scandal campaign was directly linked to the on-going work of party organization and the formulation of party policy. Thorough and efficient organization, Borden had always believed, lessened the opportunities for shady and corrupt transactions in the business of the party. An integrated party organization composed of democratically elected party officials and following a carefully constructed party platform were essential to the electoral success. Neither could be achieved easily; both would have to be worked out in long negotiations with his followers.

During 1905 the organizational work had gotten off to such a promising start that in December Borden called for a party convention in 1906. His parliamentary colleagues were taken by surprise and few of them responded enthusiastically. During the 1906 session a caucus committee "to consider and report upon the advisability of holding a Dominion Convention" concluded that a convention would be inappropriate. Late in the year Borden asked the committee to reconsider the question and, in January 1907, it reported informally to him that a convention should be convened in June. Before the recommendation was taken to caucus Borden sought extra-parliamentary support for the convention plan. Letters to McBride, Roblin, Whitney, and a number of other prominent Conservatives "earnestly" asked them to "support the proposal and give us a promise that you . . . will be present".[31]

The initial response was favourable. The President of the Conservative Union in Montreal reported that a few months before he had been opposed to the idea because of quarrels among the Quebec Tories. "Now the people here seem to be disposed to look for the future of the party and let bygones be bygones" and a convention would be very much in order. His opinion was seconded by the Executive Committee of the party in Quebec who favoured a convention and appointed Bergeron and Ames as their delegates to an organizing committee.[32] But Premier Whitney had "very strong doubts". He would go along with the idea and would attend if there was to be a convention. But he clearly did not like leaving the determination of policy (and perhaps the leadership) in the hands of an uncontrolled mass gathering of the party. "I am afraid the Convention will take these matters into its own hands when it meets and that perhaps the conclusion of the majority will be neither wise nor conclusive as to the views of the rank and file of the Party."[33] W. B. Ross and Charles Tanner both added a Nova Scotia voice of opposition. Ross thought a convention only of interest to "faddists" and Tanner bluntly said that it was "not a safe or satisfactory body to entrust with the duty of determining a policy". On the other hand, W. L. Walsh of Calgary and McBride and Roblin all gave enthusiastic support to the idea, with Roblin adding a number of policy planks to be considered.[34]

Borden shelved the convention plan. He told a disappointed Roblin that "the Quebec Conservatives would decline to attend"[35] and a convention without them was unthinkable. But the record suggests that there were other reasons for dropping the convention proposal. A. E. Blount later recalled that it was not the Quebeckers who were opposed to the convention; "the Quebec men were quite willing to see it called."[36] Instead, the caucus was very leery of the idea and the party bosses outside Parliament were sharply divided. The enthusiasm of the westerners was balanced by the coolness of the Nova Scotians. And Whitney's disapproval was probably decisive. A convention with the blunt and outspoken Premier of Ontario in reluctant attendance would be as unsatisfactory as a convention without Quebec representation.

Other organizational work produced more disappointing results. In the west, Premier McBride confidently promised "all 7 B.C. seats" in the next general election[37] and Premier Roblin and his Minister of Public Works, Robert Rogers, could be expected to perform equally well in Manitoba. But Saskatchewan and Alberta remained Liberal fortresses and, in British Columbia, Charles Hibbert Tupper was engaged in a bitter fight over patronage and organization with McBride's henchmen.[38] In Nova Scotia the surprising victory of John Stanfield in the Colchester byelection of 1907 was mitigated by rumours of extensive electoral corruption and by continuing evidence of dissension in the province's Conservative ranks.[39] And Borden's repeated pleas for a joint national-provincial organizational effort in Ontario met with friendly agreement in intention and polite evasion in practice from Whitney.[40] By late summer 1906 Whitney had appointed his own provincial organizer and any pretence of a joint organization structure was given up. In May 1907 Borden appointed J. S. Carstairs secretary and organizer for a new federal party organization, the Dominion Liberal-Conservative Association for the Province of Ontario.[41]

Whitney's reluctance to cooperate in organizational matters did not indicate any lack of regard for Borden personally or for his leadership qualities in federal politics. Quite the contrary. The two men worked together in the acquisition of the Toronto

News by Frank Cochrane, the Ontario Minister of Lands and Mines, from Joseph Flavelle in 1908. Both men had been dissatisfied with the work of the *Mail and Empire* as the principal Ontario party paper and Whitney proudly told a friend that the formerly "independent" *News* would now be a "straight Conservative organ".[42] Equally important, when the former MP from Quebec, Rufus Pope, hinted to Whitney in June 1907 that he should replace Borden as party leader, the Ontario Premier sharply replied that "at any luncheon or demonstration where I speak, I shall feel impelled to refer to [Borden] and his leadership, *past and future*, in terms of the highest approbation".[43]

Pope's suggestion was evidence of the persistent ambiguity of Borden's role in Quebec Conservative politics. Younger Quebec Conservatives asked in January 1907 "that Mr. Monk be elected chief of the Province of Quebec". Borden ignored the request and appointed an "Executive Committee" for organization in the province. Bergeron was named convener of the committee and its other members, Ames, R. Forget, Leonard, Marechal, Monk, and Pope, were a deliberate mix of traditional and new and French and English-speaking Quebec Tories. There would be no Quebec *chef*. Instead, Borden hoped to use the committee to exert more direct influence himself over party matters in the province.[44]

A more interesting development in Quebec in the summer of 1907 was an approach to Borden by Henri Bourassa. Bourassa and Armand Lavergne planned to resign their seats in the House of Commons and the former was preparing to enter Quebec provincial politics. He had reached an agreement with J. M. Tellier of the provincial Conservatives that if Premier Gouin's Liberals could be beaten "a Liberal-Conservative coalition would be formed to carry on the affairs of the province". In July he approached Brenton Macnab of the Montreal *Star* and outlined a platform for reform which, Bourassa admitted, had been deeply influenced by the progressive economic legislation of the Whitney Government in Ontario. Bourassa wanted the support of the *Star* in the coming provincial campaign. More important, he wanted "an alliance—not open, but real—with Mr. Ames" of the federal party and he told Macnab that he wanted to see Borden "as soon as possible, with a view to enlisting the latter's good offices in the campaign".

There is no evidence that Borden did meet Bourassa to formalize an alliance in 1907. Bourassa did tell Macnab that though "he objects to certain elements in the party", he "wants to aid the Cons." federally as well as provincially.[46] In the late spring and early summer of 1908 there were persistent rumours in Tory circles that "a Bourassa-Conservative alignment is practically settled" or "is pretty close now".[47] In the 1908 provincial election the provincial Conservatives and Bourassa forces openly co-operated and both probably received financial assistance from the federal Conservative party.

Bourassa's objection to "certain elements" in the federal party, doubtless men like Foster, Hughes, and Thomas Sproule, made an open alliance with the federal party impossible. But Borden welcomed whatever "aid" Bourassa could give to the Conservatives in Quebec. Anything Bourassa could do to shake the faith of Quebeckers in Gouin and Laurier would help the Conservatives. But there was more to it than that. Both men were disgusted by the growing evidence of corruption in politics. Bourassa's campaign against Gouin provincially was motivated by much the same reform impulse as Borden's strategy in federal politics. And though it was only a coincidence, it is interesting that Bourassa presented his platform for provincial reform to Macnab just when Borden was putting the finishing touches upon a reform platform for the federal Conservative party.

There was no question about the need for a new statement of party policy. The main plank of the 1904 platform, "a government owned railway", had been rejected by the people. Both those who favoured and those who opposed a convention had told Borden that a fresh approach to party policy was needed. Borden himself harboured no illusions that party proclamations were the key to electoral success. But he believed that they did play a necessary educative role in the political process and they did indicate the different attitudes of the parties on great national issues. "In a time of great prosperity no government which is reasonably honest and efficient can ever be defeated by a declaration of policy on the part of the opposition," he told Premier Roblin, suggesting the relationship between the scandal campaign and policy formation. But, he added, "I do not minimize the importance of having an effective and honest rallying cry which will appeal to the more progressive spirits and communities."[48]

Among the party potentates Roblin took the lead in urging Borden to announce a constructive Opposition policy. "A policy of negation, and a policy based largely on the traditions and record of the past, always coupled with the maladministration of the party at present in power, is not sufficient to either create [*sic*] enthusiasm among our own followers, nor yet warrant us in hoping to recover the positions we lost in 1896," he wrote in early 1906. The need to break with the past was especially important for Conservatives in the west, but hardly less so for the national party. Roblin suggested that reciprocity with the United States in natural products should become a central feature of party policy, and Conservatives should declare themselves in favour of an elective Senate and of rural free mail delivery. These planks in a party platform would "crystallise [*sic*] or arouse public opinion to the point that the party is not tied to the traditions of the past but is ever on the alert for new fields in which to add to the avenues of trade and other matters which give wealth and contentment to the people".[49]

Roblin's letter was sent to a number of important Conservatives for comment. Once again Borden received contradictory advice. Only Monk favoured a reciprocity plank; indeed, he bubbled with enthusiasm for all of Roblin's proposals. A. C. Bell, a former Nova Scotia member, A. B. Ingram from Elgin East and Andy Broder from Dundas favoured an elective Senate. (Borden himself told Senator Ferguson that "if any change should be made in the Senate I would rather prefer the United States system of an election by State legislatures". He added that "the present system would be better than any that has been suggested" if partisanship could be eliminated from the appointments.)[50] Foster expectedly denounced reciprocity, apparently believed the Senate and mail delivery proposals not worth comment, and lectured his leader on the need for a plank on administrative reform. There was even disagreement on the need for a party policy. Ingram's support for a "nifty catchy policy" was echoed by Foster, Senator Ferguson, Broder, and Monk. But Broder and A. E. Kemp thought the scandal campaign was an even more effective device for promoting party popularity and Bell entered a plea for greater organizational effort.[51] One thing was clear; the "advanced" ideas of the Manitoba Premier had not struck a responsive chord in eastern Tory thinking. More significant, the negative reaction and the traditionalist bias were most apparent in the Parliamentary party.

By the summer of 1906 there were strong indications that

Borden was going to dictate a new comprehensive policy to his party. During a Maritime tour he developed two themes in his speeches. The first, expectedly, was the need to rid the country of the dreadful corruption of the Laurier government. The second was the desirability of government ownership or operation of public resources. The party would not depart from its "best traditions", he told a Truro audience, but new conditions demanded new policies. The Conservatives had always emphasized national development, but in the new century the administration and the disposal of the public domain had become a central issue of public policy. Natural resources, national franchises, and public utilities all had to be approached upon the assumption that they were "the property of the State, and they must be administered and exploited for the public benefit". That, he suggested, could best be achieved by "Government ownership or operation". True, the concept was "repeatedly challenged because of incompetent or corrupt administration". But that argument was weak and there was "no other argument against it". Incompetent and corrupt administration was just as evident in private as in public enterprise. "But shall all private enterprise be condemned because of insurance frauds or business failure, or corporate graft?" he asked. Of course not. Similarly, "the principle of state ownership is no more to be condemned for defects or errors of administration than is the general principle of responsible government. The remedy is to amend the methods."[52]

The Truro speech produced cries of alarm from many of the party faithful. A month later in Pembroke, Ontario, Borden reverted to his 1904 position, government ownership of railways, with only hints that the concept might be extended to other areas of public concern.[53] The Pembroke speech upset the President of the CPR who complained vigorously to Charlie Tupper. The CPR was safe, Borden told Tupper in December; Shaughnessy had been "unduly alarmed" by the "exaggerated" report to the Montreal press. "The position which I took would affect capitalists who expect to receive a great public franchise in the future and it would also affect the action of the Government in relation to their transcontinental railway policy although in that instance a contract has been made which must be sacredly kept."[54] In short, profitable private enterprises serving the public interest would not be tampered with and contracts were sacrosanct. He did not back away from his belief in the reasonableness of the principle of government ownership. He had not thought through all the implications of the concept. He had not resolved the difficult question of whether public control of public resources and franchises was more effective through government regulation or through government ownership and operation. But to even suggest that public resources could be exploited just as efficiently by public managers as by private businessmen placed him far in advance of most of the members of his party. Not Roblin, however. The Manitoba Premier urged him to be more explicit in his policy pronouncements. "I would declare unequivocally and without limitation for public ownership of such utilities as were necessarily a monopoly and would specify by a declaration for a public constructed and operated national Telegraph and Telephone."[55]

Borden's thinking was definitely influenced by Roblin's advice. Roblin's government had instituted a publicly owned telephone system in Manitoba. Equally important, Whitney was moving towards public ownership in hydro electricity, railways, and mining operations in Ontario. He admired both men as courageous innovative leaders who were willing to use the powers of the state in the public interest. Like him, neither man was strong on economic theory nor cared much for political ideology. Like him, their interest was in practical answers to practical problems, in "method" rather than philosophical abstraction. And a most telling point: they both led strong governments with broad support.

Borden unveiled his Halifax Platform before an enthusiastic audience in his home city on August 20, 1907. He regarded it as "the most advanced and progressive policy ever put forward in Federal affairs". The first four planks were his alternative to the corruption and inefficiency his party was exposing in the House of Commons. The Conservatives promised honest appropriation and expenditure of public monies, appointment of public officials on the merit principle, and civil service reform. In his speech Borden advocated an elected Senate, but the platform itself more cautiously called for Senate reform. Borden also demanded a more selective immigration policy, "restoration" of public lands to Alberta and Saskatchewan, the "unimpaired maintenance" of provincial rights, the non-partisan management of government railways, the "promotion" of Imperial preferential tariffs and, "after proper inquiry as to cost", free rural mail delivery. The cherished term "protection" was omitted from a tariff plank which called for the promotion of Canadian production "of all useful articles" which could be "advantageously produced" from "our natural resources".

In his speech Borden reiterated his defence of the principle of government ownership. But the scary words did not find their way into the platform. There he suggested that public participation in the disposal of public franchises be limited to a share of the stock issue. This would ensure, he said, "that while the capitalist will receive not only a fair but a generous reward for his enterprise, the people will also participate in the profit which arises through national development and progress." Beyond that, the Railways Commission ought to be made a Public Utilities Commission with power to regulate telephone and express companies as well as the railways. Eventually, a system of national telegraphs and telephones should be established, but due care should be taken to protect "capital already invested in those enterprises". Canada, Borden reasoned, was and would continue to be dependent upon foreign investment capital for development. Therefore, an attractive climate for investment was essential. The sanctity of contracts "must always be respected" and the use of the state's powers to confiscate private businesses without compensation as a step towards government ownership was unthinkable. It "would be the worst possible service that any government or parliament could render."[56]

Borden left Halifax immediately after his speech on a grinding two and one-half month cross-country "educational" tour. With the exception of his stop in Quebec City, where he devoted his whole speech to a defence of his position on the Autonomy bills, his text was the Halifax Platform. Press reaction was predictable: Tory journals proclaimed the dawn of a new political era; Grit papers, with one or two notable exceptions like the Toronto *Star* and Montreal *Herald*, scoffed at Borden's platform as the usual set of Conservative platitudes.[57]

The Halifax Platform received a mixed reception in party circles. Sir Thomas Shaughnessy broadly hinted at his skepticism by not providing a private car for Borden and his entourage.[58] In fact, all the Montreal men were nervous about Borden's unorthodox ideas and some were appalled. The ambiguous phrasing of the tariff plank left them wondering about where the party was going. Borden's ideas about public participation in national franchises was positively frightening. They were particularly offended by the proposal for a system of national telephones and telegraphs. "The commercial and financial men," Ames warned, "condemn this plank as a step towards socialism," "a bit of 'Rooseveltism'"! When Borden reached Montreal he discovered that Ames had arranged some Labour Day hand-shaking and a "kodacked" session with labour leaders and a St. James Club luncheon with "about a dozen of our old time stalwarts who are a bit dubious in regard to the Conservative platform".[59]

In Winnipeg the local bosses and MP's were also disturbed. Like many other Conservatives, they had been taken completely by surprise by the Halifax Platform. Borden had not presented it to his caucus; in fact, only a tiny handful of Conservatives, including Ames and John Willison of the *News* in Toronto, had been consulted at all by Borden. The westerners angrily complained that Borden had not consulted them. Borden lost his temper and asserted that when all "sections" of the country "were challenged to name new planks they wanted, they could not mention any".[60] He then grandly proclaimed that the Halifax Platform "had been accepted by the party throughout Canada".[61] His meaning was crystal clear; the party could either accept his platform or find a new leader. "The delegation," he smugly recalled, "went away not only satisfied but enthusiastic."[62]

Despite these irritations and the inevitable discomforts of a political tour, Borden's trip was very successful and he returned to the last session of the tenth Parliament in a confident mood. The scandal campaign, even after the embarrassing revelations of Foster's involvement with the Union Trust, was going well. Organizational work had not progressed as rapidly and as smoothly as Borden had hoped, but there had been one significant advance there too. In May of 1907 the party had accepted his proposal to set up a National Finance Committee with L. J. Forget as Chairman.[63] And the Halifax Platform had been well received, except in Montreal. Whitney was especially enthusiastic. What pleased him most was the way Borden had taken matters into his own hands. "I cannot avoid saying here," he wrote, "that I think the platform is distinctly better than anything which would have been the outcome of that fearful and wonderful thing, a convention."[64] Borden, in fact, could look back on the last three years of his leadership with considerable satisfaction. Even with the many setbacks and disappointments, it was clear that the party's organization was in better shape than it had been in a decade. The Halifax Platform was another testament to his leadership. It was his platform and he had outlined the party's goals for the future. His colleagues in the House were anxious to begin their final assault upon the Laurier government and Borden was ready for an election.

The last session of the tenth Parliament set the tone for the 1908 general election. Party animosity reached fever-pitch as Borden and his followers hammered away, day after day, and week after week, at the alleged iniquities of the Laurier government. It was, of course, a game at which two could play. And the Prime Minister's party struck back hard with a flagrantly partisan clause in its proposed Dominion Elections Act.

Most of the bill was made up of modest reforms which outlawed some of the more obvious electoral abuses without seriously disturbing existing electoral practices, reforms upon which both parties agreed. The offensive clause was a partial repudiation of a basic principle of Laurier Liberalism; that the provinces should control the franchise for Dominion elections. It proposed that there should be separate federal electoral lists, established by Ottawa, for the provinces of British Columbia and Manitoba, and for the northern regions of Ontario and Quebec. It was no mere coincidence that three of the affected areas were ruled by Tory governments in Victoria, Winnipeg, and Toronto. In a surprisingly blunt admission of his government's motive, Laurier told the House that the question reduced "itself to this, that you gentlemen on the other side of the House, do not want to go before the country on electoral lists prepared by your opponents and we, on this side of the House, do not care to go the country on electoral lists prepared by our opponents".[65] In May the enraged Conservatives decided to obstruct supply votes until the government backed down. By early June only a small portion of the government's estimates had been passed. Laurier then had a long meeting with Roblin and Rogers from Manitoba and a series of conferences with Borden. In July the Conservatives accepted a compromise which retained the provincial lists for federal elections in Manitoba and Ontario under the supervision of County or District Court judges. The lists in British Columbia and northern Quebec remained in provincial hands.[66]

The bitterness of the scandal session and the Elections Act debate carried directly over into the early fall election campaign. The political atmosphere was filled with charges and counter-charges of dishonesty. Liberals gleefully disseminated a pamphlet entitled "Foster the Forester". Laurier told an audience at Jackson's Point, Ontario, that "I do not pretend to be a moral reformer, but I do think that I am as good a man as Mr. Borden and as good a man as George Eulas Foster". "Sir Wilfrid says that no man can be half as honest as I talk," Borden acidly replied in Peterborough. "Let me tell him that we will no more put up with his shoddy politics than we will put up with his shoddy morality."[67] At Massey Hall Borden carefully defended Foster's public career, deliberately evading the point of the Grit attack on "Foster the Forester". "I have yet to know where any man can place his hand on one spot in Mr. Foster's public career which was not straightforward, honest and creditable to himself," he said.[68]

There were the usual campaign promises from both parties, though none captured the political imagination and became great issues as the second transcontinental had done four years before. Borden, without explaining how he would do it, pledged restitution "from those who had pilfered from the public treasure".[69] Laurier, scorning his doubters—"Oh ye of little faith"!—promised the construction of the Hudson's Bay Railway and *La Presse* predicted that it would transform Fort Churchill into the New Orleans of the North![70] An unusually clean election in Halifax, where Borden was running,* was the exception to the continuing rule of the politics of whiskey and money. More typical was the election in Quebec West where Billy Price won a hot contest with William Power by a mere two votes. The election there was dominated by "playful but practical politicians, who enjoyed down-to-earth campaigning", Power's son later recalled. "The gospel was spread on both sides in the most unholy manner."[71] A scurrilous editorial, "The Duty of the Hour", by Conservative H. C. Hocken in the Orange *Sentinel* again raised divisions of race and creed. Reprinted in pamphlet form, "The Duty of the Hour" was used with unpredictable effect by both parties.[72]

In the end the election boiled down to two simple themes. "Let

---

*Borden ran in both Halifax and Carleton in 1908 and won both contests. His running mate in Halifax, Adam B. Crosby, was also elected. Borden resigned his Carleton seat and the former member, Edward Kidd, was returned in a 1909 by-election.

Laurier finish his work!", "Let Borden keep on with his talk!", cried the Liberals. The Conservatives were expected to counter with Borden's Halifax Platform. But as Borden toured from the Maritimes through Quebec and into Ontario his speeches were lightly laced with his program and heavily laden with charges against the government. "As a matter of fact," the editor of the *Canadian Annual Review* observed, "the campaign of the Opposition was based almost entirely upon a strongly professed principle of political purity and vigorously-urged charges against the Government of political corruption."[73]

Why Borden decided not to emphasize his own program is not clear. He knew, of course, that portions of it were unpopular in Montreal and the stubborn "independence" of Graham's *Star* during the campaign was trouble enough without the tycoons worrying about Borden's "Rooseveltism". (Graham was rewarded for his "independence" by a knighthood from Laurier.) But he could safely assume that the Halifax Platform would be no less enthusiastically received in the rest of the country than it had been during his 1907 tour. It is more likely that he counted too much on the popularity of his Platform. And he was clearly determined to discredit Laurier. He told Willison that his Halifax speech at the beginning of the campaign was "designed to emphasize both the 'boodling' and the bungling of the present administration; and I do not intend . . . to discuss at any considerable length the platform which I laid down last year and which is pretty thoroughly understood by the people at large."[74] The electors were left with a list of petty promises and partisan charges from both parties. The Liberals made much of the Tory connection to the Foresters affair. Of the Conservatives who were allegedly involved, only Foster retained his seat. Some political observers thought that that was more a curse than a blessing to Borden. Undoubtedly the image of "Foster the Forester" compromised Borden's purity campaign. "Foster lost us Ontario and conceivably the election," Hamilton wrote. And Willison was scarcely more kind in reply: "Mr. Foster has no gift of popular leadership and for the time is perhaps more discredited than he deserves to be."[75]

On the eve of the election Borden jubilantly told a group of reporters that "This is 1878 over again". That was a far cry from the private predictions of his secretary a year before. Then "Blount admitted that [Borden] has no hope of a Conservative victory [in the] next general election."[76] But in the meantime the tide seemed to turn in Borden's favour. Both John Stanfield's by-election victory in Colchester and Douglas Hazen's rout of Pugsley in the New Brunswick election in March 1908 were omens of good fortune in the Maritimes. Whitney's overwhelming victory in Ontario in June appeared to be proof that the Liberals were on the run. In Vancouver the *World* switched from the Liberal to the Conservative camp. In Toronto, the acquisition of the *News* as a party organ countered the declining influence of the *Mail and Empire* and the independence of Maclean's *World*. ("I'm a Conservative, but also a free man," Maclean said. "The party system's all right, but I am not a machine.")[77] In Quebec, late in the campaign, Bourassa announced his neutrality. But his lieutenant, Armand Lavergne, supported William Price, appeared on the platform with Borden and campaigned against Laurier in his paper, *Le Nationaliste*. For a while it even seemed possible that Borden's old friend and partner, Sir Charles Hibbert Tupper, might be at his side in the new Parliament. Tupper agreed to run again in Pictou and also was endorsed as a candidate in Vancouver. But then a faction-fight with McBride's forces and the virulent opposition of the Orange *Sentinel* forced him to withdraw from both seats. Still, the prospects were very bright. The Tory provincial premiers and their colleagues had campaigned vigorously with Borden. Borden thought that his platform was "pretty thoroughly understood by the people at large". And the shoddy politics and morality of the Laurier government had been revealed.

For the second time in his party leadership Borden's electoral prediction was wrong. The Laurier government was returned to power. Borden was elected in Halifax, as was his running-mate, A. B. Crosby, and the Conservatives took four other seats in Nova Scotia. In New Brunswick the forecast that Hazen's provincial victory would carry federal Tories to success was dashed. Only two Conservatives were elected there and one in Prince Edward Island. In Quebec the party held its own with eleven seats to Laurier's fifty-four. British Columbia with five and Manitoba with eight Conservatives delivered well for Borden and Alberta's three seats and Saskatchewan's one added up to important Conservative gains in western Canada. But, as in 1904, Ontario held the key to Conservative success. Substantial gains were expected in Whitney's province, but did not materialize. In fact, Ontario returned exactly the same number of Conservatives, forty-eight, to the House of Commons that it had in 1904.

Borden was saddened by the loss of some of his colleagues, especially Bergeron and A. E. Kemp who had figured prominently in his organizational efforts in Quebec and Ontario. But there were good signs too. The Conservative percentage of the popular vote had gone up in Nova Scotia, Ontario, Manitoba, and British Columbia. In the western provinces the two parties had come to a draw in the contest; each had seventeen members in the new House of Commons. Excluding Quebec, the government majority was a scant seven seats and Laurier's over-all majority had been reduced by thirteen. Borden let it be known privately that he was "well satisfied on the whole".[78]

So was Whitney, who had become one of his most trusted advisors. The Ontario Premier had "no doubt whatever that many Government supporters were ready to transfer their allegiance, but felt that there was not much to choose between the two sides, having regard for the conduct of half a dozen Candidates of the Conservative party who had been members of the Commons". Save for Foster, whose reputation had been viciously smeared but who had been convicted of no wrong-doing, they were now gone. And both Whitney and Borden were delighted by the return of a very promising group of Conservative members including C. J. Doherty, T. W. Crothers, Charles Magrath, Arthur Meighen, William Price, W. B. Nantel, and Martin Burrell. Whitney was confident that "Mr. Borden is practically certain to succeed at the next appeal to the Country".[79]

Borden shared Whitney's confidence. His mood after the 1908 election contrasted sharply to the despair and resignation that had characterized his reaction to defeat in 1904. One reason for the difference was his personal victory in Halifax where he had been beaten four years earlier. Another, and more important, was that he was no longer torn by the demands of two full-time professions. He had cast aside his first career and first love, the law, and devoted all his energies to politics and public service. Symbolically, the decision was clear when he and Laura had moved into their new home on Wurtemburg Street in Ottawa in the summer of 1906.

Robert and Laura spent nearly a year looking for a suitable home in Ottawa. When no appropriate house seemed to be available, Borden bought a lot on Marlborough and planned to have a house built on it. But just as the plans were being completed, Laura attended the wedding of the daughter of the Chief Justice of the Supreme Court, Sir Charles Fitzpatrick. Fitzpatrick was living in a large home on Wurtemburg Street owned by Mrs. Hayter Reid. The property was not in good repair, nor was the street and surrounding area. But when Laura attended the reception she was immediately taken by the possibilities of making Glensmere into a comfortable and attractive home. At her urging, Robert discovered that the property was for sale and that Fitzpatrick was not interested in buying it. Borden bought Glensmere in April and took possession at the end of June.[80]

Over the next few years Robert and Laura spent many of their happiest leisure hours improving the property. Between the back veranda and the Rideau River at the rear of the lot they cleaned out a scraggly jungle of bushes and weeds and replaced it with pleasant walks sloping down to the river bordered by various gardens. Robert found a welcome respite from politics by caring for all the gardens, including a vegetable garden in the extreme south-east corner of the lot. But his favourite was his wild garden bordering the walkways. In the house itself additional radiators had to be installed and the rooms redecorated to Laura's taste. The rooms were large and well-suited to the entertaining that was expected of a political leader and his wife. To the right of the entrance hall there was a drawing room and to the left, the library, dining room, pantry, kitchen, and the maid's sitting room. Upstairs Robert's bedroom was above the drawing room. On the other side of the upstairs hall were Laura's sewing room, bedroom, and study and then the maid's quarters.

The purchase of Glensmere lifted a great personal burden from Borden's political life. The dreary months of living in rented rooms and the long separations from Laura that had been so much a part of the first decade of his political career were over. Now he could fulfill his responsibilities to his party with Laura at his side. Now they could participate together in the social life of Ottawa that was so much a part of the capital's political environment. Now Robert also had a comfortable retreat from politics when he needed it; he could repair to his study or his garden for a few quiet hours of thought and reflection. In all of these ways Glensmere made his political career more bearable, even enjoyable. He looked back beyond the defeat of 1908 to the past four years with assurance and resolution. His efforts had given his party the beginnings of an organizational structure, a vigorous opposition strategy in the House of Commons, and a new party platform. He had made the Conservative party his party, he had established himself as its leader. "I had developed through experience," he later remembered,

> had become a more effective speaker and had gained in large measure the confidence of my parliamentary following. During the same period, I had got in touch with the people of the country through constant campaigning and in this way, as well as through my work in Parliament, I had acquired increasing influence, and in some measure had won the confidence of the rank and file of my party, and of many men not actively affiliated with either party.[81]

After the 1904 election Borden was ready to give up and get out of politics. After the election of 1908 he was more determined than he had ever been to carry on.

CHAPTER EIGHT

THE NAVAL QUESTION

In January 1909, the new Parliament began in the same acrimonious spirit with which ·the old had closed. There was an
exception. Borden, who had been elected in both Halifax and
Carleton, decided to sit for his original constituency. In Carleton,
perhaps after an arrangement with the Liberals, Edward Kidd,
who had given up the seat in 1905, was returned by acclamation.
But the general tendency of the parties was to rehearse old
charges, to maintain sharply partisan stances. After all, both
Liberals and Conservatives read the results of the election as a
vindication of their positions; the Government had retained
power, the Opposition had reduced the Liberal majority. With
no great public issues before the country, the parties quickly
resumed their accustomed roles.

In his own ranks Borden saw promise in some of the new MPs
and problems with his veteran colleagues. He was aware of, and
perhaps even shared, the party's resentment of his most prominent lieutenant, George Foster. "The feeling against Foster on the
part of the Conservative rank and file is intense," C. F. Hamilton
reported. "They feel that they lost the election between him and
Hocken; in British Columbia even he lost them votes."[1]

Equally troublesome, many Ontario Conservatives were anxious to challenge Laurier's nomination of Charles Marcil as
Speaker of the House of Commons. Marcil, they charged, had
been re-elected for Bonaventure in 1904 primarily because he had
been able to demonstrate that he was responsible for bringing
more than $600,000 in government grants to his constituency.
Willison was especially upset. He fussed and fumed about "the
wholesale use of public money for purposes of bribery",[2] and
unkindly intimated that it would be no easy matter for the leader

of the purity in politics campaign to condone Marcil's electoral practices. But all the Quebec members, sensing that there was more to the attack on Marcil than his ability to acquire government largesse, opposed a division of the House on the issue.[3] "Our friends in the Province of Quebec are extremely sensitive in matters of this character and one must give a certain amount of consideration to their opinions. The cry continually comes to me from that Province that our friends, fighting against great odds, are handicapped by the position taken in the House of Commons by more or less influential members of the party," Borden explained. "Anything which by the wildest conception can give ground for appeal to the sensitive imagination of the French Canadian habitant is distorted by the Liberal press and produces unfortunate results."[4] Moreover, the evidence that Marcil had conducted himself in similar fashion in 1908 was suspect and as Deputy Speaker in the last Parliament Marcil had earned the respect of both parties. "His record in the House shows that he had discharged his duties with dignity and impartiality."[5] When Parliament opened Borden lamely protested that it would be better to follow the British practice of continuing the previous Speaker in office and that Marcil's appointment might encourage the bribery of constituencies with public funds. Neither he nor his party opposed Marcil's nomination.[6]

On safer issues the Conservatives revived the tactics of the last Parliament to harass the government. They vigorously attacked the government's proposed loan of ten million dollars to the Grand Trunk Pacific to facilitate construction of the railway's Prairie section in a series of resolutions designed to force modification of the terms of the loan. Borden believed the government proposal further committed the public to responsibility for completion of the Grand Trunk Pacific and released the Grand Trunk from obligations to its offspring. His determination was strengthened by bitter memories of the Grand Trunk's support of the Liberals in the last election and of a promise it had given to the Conservatives and then broken. "The alliance of the Grand Trunk with the Government is pretty permanent under present conditions," Borden retorted to Willison, who supported the loan.

Their interference in the recent contest was undoubtedly due to a corrupt agreement for the assistance now proposed. They had no warrant for opposing the Conservative Party in that contest. I had taken the trouble to announce on several occasions in the House of Commons, and on many public platforms that the Conservative Party, if returned to power, would deal with the contract in exactly the same spirit as if it had been made by a Conservative administration. The management of the Grand Trunk gave us to understand that they would not interfere in the recent contest. Unless these huge railway corporations are restrained from such interference I see no limit to the unfortunate results which may ensue.[7]

The debate on the Grand Trunk Pacific loan went on intermittently for more than a month. In the end the government had its way and the loan was approved. But Borden felt vindicated too. For five years he had charged that the government's cost estimates for the project were unrealistic, if not ridiculous. Now he took great pleasure in suggesting how right he had been. He predicted that the whole National Transcontinental–Grand Trunk Pacific scheme was going to be enormously expensive—"its probable cost will be about $280,000,000."[8]

He took a more positive approach to two other important debates in the eleventh Parliament. The discussion on conservation of the country's natural resources and the debate on the Combines Investigation Act both illustrated the growing concern of the parliamentarians about their ability to control the course of Canada's industrial economy. In February 1909, Borden moved that a select committee of the House of Commons be established to study the conservation question. In a long, carefully documented and able speech, he argued that the time had come for the government to encourage the efficient use of the nation's natural wealth. Much attention had already been given to agriculture, and properly so; it "must be the principal basis upon which the future wealth of this country depends". But the emerging industrial economy was using more and more of Canada's forests, minerals, fisheries, and water resources. It was imperative that they too be used wisely, that they not be wasted and depleted, and that they be passed on to future generations in a useful state.

Like many of the American authorities he quoted, Borden stressed that conservation and development were not contradictory but complementary ideals. Indeed, they "should be the watchwords of the country with regard to its natural resources".

> Conservation does not mean non-use; on the contrary, it is
> consistent with that reasonable use of these great resources
> which is absolutely necessary for their development. And,
> on the other hand, development does not imply destruction
> or waste; it ought not to imply destruction or waste, but
> these great resources should be both developed and con-
> served, so that they may be of the greatest possible advantage
> to the present generation and may also be handed down as a
> continuing heritage to those who come after us in the work
> of upbuilding this Dominion and the British Empire.[9]

Sir Wilfrid Laurier's suggestion that a number of committees
be appointed to study particular resources was readily accepted
by Borden. Then, just a few weeks later, Sydney Fisher, the
Minister of Agriculture, and Clifford Sifton returned to Ottawa
from President Roosevelt's North American Conservation Conference armed with a recommendation that each North American
nation appoint a permanent commission to guide the conservation of the natural resources. Laurier acted quickly on the
recommendation. Legislation was passed by Parliament and in
September 1909 the members of Canada's Commission of Conservation, chaired by Clifford Sifton, were announced.[10]

The Combines Bill was introduced by William Lyon Mackenzie
King, the recently appointed Minister of Labour, in January 1910.
It was the government's response to growing public concern
over the rising number of industrial combines and mergers and
their alleged responsibility for the rapid increase in the cost of
living. King was not prepared to outlaw combines. He believed
them to be an inevitable stage in the evolution of an industrial
economy, and he was quite ready to believe that the rationale of
industrial mergers, to increase the efficiency of production and
thereby reduce costs, could be a beneficent result of industrial
organization. The problem was that there was no guarantee that
combines would pass on the savings to their customers. Moreover, these concerns were becoming so large and so strong that
they could eliminate competition and set prices solely in their
own interest.

King explained that his legislation—*An Act to Provide for the
Investigation of Combines, Monopolies and Mergers*—"is not
aimed against combines and mergers as such, but rather against

the exercise on the part of combines, mergers or monopolies, in an unfair manner, of the powers which they may get from that form of organization".[11] The emphasis, as the title suggested, was upon investigation and, even more, publicity. By a very complicated process six persons could initiate an investigation of an apparently offending corporation. A series of steps of investigation and review could eventually lead to a fine against a corporation acting in restraint of trade or engaged in price fixing. But King stated his belief that it would seldom come to that. He believed that the adverse publicity of an investigation would be enough to force the offending corporation to cease and desist from activities contrary to the public interest.[12]

Like King, Borden believed that combines were an inevitable development in industrial capitalism and, in the long run, beneficial to an industrial economy. The goal of the age was efficiency and the way to achieve it was through large-scale organization, be it either of capital or labour. But, like King, he recognized the need for some measure of control over corporate organization, and he supported the purpose of King's bill. He did not believe, as did many of his followers inside and outside the House of Commons, that King's legislation would undermine the whole structure of the capitalist economy. Nor did he accept Flavelle's implied charge that King had surrendered to the pressure of "inflammatory agitators". "The lesson which the present agitation [and King's bill] says we should learn," Flavelle wrote, "is that you should get after the big fellow who is organized in this manner by calling him a trust, or a combine, or a corporation, or a merger, and having succeeded in convicting him under laws specially devised to meet his iniquity, you should hold him up to the public as an example of total depravity."[13]

Borden had only one fundamental objection to the bill. It was a flabby, toothless, inadequate, and innocuous piece of legislation. The basic problem with existing legal restraints against unfair trade practices in the criminal and common law and in the tariff act was that the government had failed to provide adequate machinery for their enforcement. Precisely the same fault was present in King's bill. "It is perfectly idle to put this law or any other law upon the statute book in respect to a public evil of this kind unless proper provision is made for the administration of that law," Borden told the House in April. King's bill had no enforcement provisions

except such as may arise from the unorganized energies of
the public at large; . . . the difficulty which will probably
arise under this statute is, in the first place, that what is
everybody's business may prove to be nobody's business,
and that skilful and powerful combines may entirely escape
the remedy which . . . is to be enforced against them. . . . Not
only that, but there seems to be a danger that the provisions
of this measure may be used oppressively and maliciously. . . .
I believe that the measure is capable of becoming useless on
the one hand, and of being abused on the other hand. . . . It
is my own belief that in respect of measures . . . designed to
apply a remedy to a great public evil, officers should be
appointed whose duty it is, representing the public, to en-
quire into these conditions and to bring such matters before
the proper tribunal.[14]

The tribunal should not be some nebulous conception of public
opinion but a court of law. If King was really sincere in his
desire to protect the public from potential abuses of corporate
power, if the Laurier government believed that the danger
implicit in great industrial combinations was everybody's business, then clearly it was the government's business to assume
responsibility for protecting the public. To leave so serious a
matter to the whim of the "unorganized public" was an evasion
of the government's public duty. King might rest comfortably
upon his faith in the power of rational, fair-minded public
opinion. But Borden doubted that the Combines Investigation
Act would work. He wanted rigorously drafted legislation with
strong provisions for enforcement and he was convinced that the
Act was a spineless measure, which would neither cure a public
evil nor enhance the public welfare.

The Opposition attacks on government railway bills, the establishment of the Commission of Conservation, and the passing of
the Combines Investigation Act were but passing episodes in the
life of the eleventh Parliament. Suddenly, without warning, the
parliamentarians found themselves face-to-face with a great
public issue which made all others seem insignificant. They were
unprepared, they were hesitant in response, and soon they were
divided into intensely hostile camps. For nearly a decade both

parties had studiously avoided taking a defined position on imperial relations, preferring ambiguous platitudes to contentious principles. Neither could do so any longer. In the spring of 1909 Canada learned that the Empire was in danger.

The naval crisis of 1909 was a rude and unwelcome surprise to both Laurier and Borden. Because the Royal Navy was so essential to the preservation of the integrity of the British Empire, because it was the first line of defence of every portion of the Empire, the news that its superiority was threatened by the aggressive program of building capital ships by the German navy was particularly frightening. What Canada could do and what Canada should do in the naval crisis raised even more fundamental questions about the nature of Canada's imperial responsibilities in peace and war. There were no easy or ready answers. Canadians had very different perceptions of the proper Canadian commitment to imperial defence.

French Canadian nationalists, for example, argued that the best Canadian contribution was the maintenance of a strong and united Canada and an adequate defence of their own country. They had vigorously defended imperial interests in Canada before and they would do so again. Armand Lavergne put their case clearly in a speech to the Military Institute in 1910: "The Nationalists of Quebec today are willing and ready to give their last drop of blood for the defence of the British flag and British institutions in this country."[15] But military commitments beyond Canadian shores were quite another matter and the Canadian contribution to the South African War a decade before had been, at best, a dangerous precedent.

English-Canadian imperialists, however, read other lessons from the experience of the South African War. For them it was evidence of Canada's willingness to assume a greater responsibility in all imperial affairs, military, political, and economic, and proof of Canada's maturity as an equal nation in the British Empire. They argued that there should be no backsliding from the commitment of 1899. Instead, the time had come for Canada to assume a full share of the imperial burden. "We are henceforth a nation," wrote Principal Grant of Queen's University, one of the most eloquent of Canadian imperialists. National dignity required that the country increase the efficiency of the militia, create a naval reserve, and defend its own coastlines. Grant concluded that "the party that does not understand the necessity of action is not loyal to Canada, or it is blind to the signs of the times".[16]

Sir Wilfrid steered a cautious course of compromise between these equally persuasive but very different roles for Canada in imperial relations. To adopt either one, he reasoned, would threaten national unity and thus impair any Canadian contribution. He politely but firmly rejected proposals for political centralization of the Empire in the immediate aftermath of the South African War. And after the Liberals came to power in Britain in 1905 he welcomed their doubts about imperial political centralization. He supported a series of policies in military affairs which could be interpreted both as contributions to imperial defence and as steps toward Canadian autonomy. Among them, the most important was the assertion of Canadian responsibility over the affairs of the Canadian Militia. In the process two British-appointed General Officers Commanding the Militia were virtually dismissed at the request of the Canadian government for overstepping their authority, Colonel Hutton in 1900 and Lord Dundonald in 1904. And as early as 1902 Laurier had promised to formulate a policy of naval defence for Canada.

Robert Borden, in the luxury of opposition, could afford to be less definite than Laurier on imperial questions. He had supported the Canadian contribution to the South African War, but he had contributed nothing substantial to the ensuing debate in Parliament and across the country. He had retained a mutual imperial preference plank in his party's platform but had seldom emphasized it. He had criticized Laurier's apparent lack of commitment to imperial affairs at Imperial Conferences, but carefully refrained from offering any alternative policies. In 1904 he briefly toyed with the idea of making Lord Dundonald's dismissal an election issue but only for domestic partisan purposes. Numerous pleas to Borden for support from advocates of imperial centralization had elicited deliberately vague and non-committal replies. In fact, over the years of his leadership he had given little thought to detailed questions about the imperial relationship. Like Laurier, he recognized that imperial questions were best left ambiguous by party leaders. In his own party the discussion of imperial issues would inevitably lead to a direct confrontation between his French- and English-speaking colleagues.

On the fundamentals of imperial relationship, however, his mind was clear. It was, of course, an evolving relationship, reflecting the growth of Canada to national maturity. The evolution would continue, would be gradual, and would be determined by circumstance. There would be no sudden change, force-fed by the elaborate theories and plans of imperial centralists. It was "idle to speculate" on the nature of the future imperial relationship, he had told a Lindsay audience in 1902. The goal was "a perpetual alliance", but the terms of the alliance would always be flexible, a mix of traditional bonds and present necessities. Most important, the "right of self-government" was at the heart of the relationship. Self-government "conferred upon the colonist a strong sense of responsibility and a desire to make his country worthy of the place which it holds in the Empire".[17]

Self-government was the cement of the union. Canadians would perpetuate it and would modify it as their own interests dictated. Borden believed that proposals for imperial institutions which might limit Canada's determination of her own affairs were dangerous. One such scheme, the establishment of a system of imperial loans administered by an imperial council, was put to him by L. S. Amery* early in 1909. Borden's response was decidedly cool. He foresaw "great difficulty" in the project. Colonial aspirations and imperial responsibilities would necessarily conflict. "Every colony," he warned, "would naturally be anxious to secure the most favourable terms for its loans, but on the other hand the responsibilities of a financial council or authority, whose endorsement might be required, would be very considerable, and any refusal to endorse a particular loan would undoubtedly create friction."[18]

And self-government was the right of the union. All too easily and automatically the imperial government amended imperial legislation without prior consultation with the colonial nations. Borden acknowledged that Westminster had the legal power to amend any imperial statute, including the British North America Act. But, he claimed, it did not have the constitutional right to do so; it was implicit in colonial self-government that the colonies must be consulted before legislation was passed which affected their interests. He made the point in 1908 when Louis Brodeur

*Leopold Stennett Amery was a member of *The Times* editorial staff from 1899 to 1909. He was an ardent advocate of imperial centralization. In 1911 Amery was elected to the House of Commons as a Unionist and Tariff Reformer for South Birmingham. In 1917 he became Assistant Secretary to the War Cabinet and the Imperial War Cabinet.

proposed changes in the Canada Shipping Act occasioned by recent imperial legislation. "There is a vast difference between the legal power to pass a statute or to perform a legislative act and the constitutional right to do it," Borden proclaimed.

> While the imperial parliament has the absolute technical right to repeal the British North America Act, *pro tanto*, in respect of legislation affecting this country, I would respectfully submit that it has not the constitutional right to do so, without first consulting the government of this country and ascertaining whether or not the proposed legislation will meet and fulfil the wants and requirements of the people of Canada.[19]

In short, self-government fulfilled the "wants and requirements of the people of Canada"; it was the bond which maintained and enriched the imperial relationship.

Correspondingly, self-government, Borden had said, "conferred upon the colonist a strong sense of responsibility". It was this thought which motivated Borden's approval of a resolution for coastal defence Foster proposed moving in February, 1909. There was no crisis, there was no alarum. Rather, Foster and Borden believed that it was high time for Canada to assume a share of the burden of defending her coastlines. There was a hint of partisan advantage in the resolution, a gentle reminder to Laurier that his 1902 pledge to build a Canadian naval force remained unfulfilled. But the essence of the matter was that Canada was mature enough to maintain her own coastal defence force. "In view of her great and varied resources, of her geographical position and national environment, and of that spirit of self-help and self-respect which alone befits a strong and growing people," Foster's resolution read, "Canada should no longer delay in assuming her proper share of the responsibility and financial burden incident to the suitable protection of her exposed coast line and great sea-ports."[20] The Foster resolution was an attack on Canadian complacency, upon the easy assumption of many Canadians that the great power of the Royal Navy would always protect their shores, upon the belief by others that they were sheltered by the shield of the Monroe Doctrine and the growing strength of the United States fleet. Either or both might be true. But neither was worthy of Canadians in the twentieth century.

In mid-March, before Foster's resolution was debated, news of the naval crisis reached Canada. Canadians had been vaguely aware of the growing tension between Great Britain and Germany, of the developing naval rivalry, of the increasing expenditure of the two powers on construction of capital ships. But to many the European naval race seemed a remote problem, and the idea that any power could seriously challenge the supremacy of the Royal Navy seemed so unreal. Canadians did not know that the Admiralty believed the challenge to be very real indeed, that the apparent acceleration of German naval construction would undermine the British two-power standard in capital ships by 1912. Nor did they know that the Admiralty believed Germany might even have more capital ships than Great Britain by 1912. The compensating increase in British expenditure for Dreadnoughts was announced at Westminster on March 16. Soon New Zealand offered a dreadnought to the imperial fleet and Australia planned a contribution. In Canada the first reaction, an observer of public opinion recalled, was "one of doubt and astonishment".[21] All the major Toronto papers responded with predictable excitement and weighed in for a Canadian contribution to the Imperial fleet. The Ottawa *Citizen* and Montreal *Star* called for either a contribution or some other positive action by Canada. But the Ottawa *Free Press*, the Kingston *Standard*, and *La Presse*, among others, opposed any Canadian action.[22]

Even before the announcement of the naval crisis the French-Canadian members of Borden's party, ever wary of any proposal that implied a change in the imperial relationship, were worried about the Foster resolution. With the crisis revealed, and with the Toronto papers fervently demanding a contribution to imperial defence, Foster's resolution took on even more ominous tones. Casgrain, speaking for himself and Monk, warned Borden that the resolution was "useless and inopportune". Casgrain noted the enormous sums Canada was spending in national development to "make it a valuable part of the British dominions" and the militia force maintained "at the expense of the Canadian taxpayer". "We are all in our own way devoted to the Empire, and if the occasion arose, I am sure that we would vie one with the other in maintaining its integrity and its greatness," he wrote. But he did not believe Canada was "now in a position to spend any money in building Dreadnoughts or in assuming directly any part of the expense to which Great Britain is being put by reason of the peculiar position which she occupies amongst the European nations".[23]

Borden immediately replied, assuring Casgrain that neither Foster nor "any other member of the party proposes that we should spend money in building Dreadnoughts" and that they would "not be carried away by the excitement of the moment". The resolution had not come up for debate yet and Casgrain had misunderstood its purpose. It was neither a frenzied response to the immediate crisis, nor was it intended to bail the Mother Country out of her apparent difficulties. Rather, the resolution dealt with Canadian coastal defence.

> The subject must be approached as one of Canadian rather than Imperial concern. The protection of our coasts and the safeguarding of our commerce are matters to which Canada cannot afford to be indifferent irrespective of Imperial interests altogether. Unless we are to relegate ourselves to the status of a Crown colony, or assume the position of vassals of the United States, we shall be obliged in the early future to do something in the line of defence not only on shore, but on our coast and in the Gulf of St. Lawrence. We claim the freedom of self-government as a right, and not of grace, but the exercise of that right implies some corresponding responsibility.[24]

Casgrain was not convinced that the distinction Borden made between coastal defence and the naval crisis could be maintained. "We are allowing ourselves to be carried away by a passing sentiment," he replied. Borden might stick to the original purpose of the Foster resolution. But its mere presence on the order paper was encouraging his colleagues, swept up in the emotion of the naval crisis, to demand much more than the creation of a coastal defence force. "The party," he wrote, "owes no thanks to the gentleman [Foster] whose sole aim seems to be to put us in the hole and keep us there."[25]

On March 29, after establishing a unified party position in caucus,[26] Borden and Foster led the party in the debate on Foster's resolution. Both men rejected a policy of a Canadian contribution to imperial defence. Both men strongly favoured the establishment of some form of Canadian naval force. Both men said they would support an emergency contribution if, in fact, the present or any future crisis proved so grave that no alternative

policy would do. But neither they, nor any other of the partici-
pants, suggested an immediate contribution of either ships or
money.[27]

After Foster's initial speech the Prime Minister offered an
alternate resolution to the House. It had three key points. The
first was that "the payment of any stated contribution to the
Imperial treasury for naval and military purposes would not . . .
be a satisfactory solution of the question of Defence". Secondly,
it asked the House to approve "any necessary expenditure designed to promote the organization of a Canadian naval service
in cooperation with and in close relation to the Imperial Navy".
Finally, the House affirmed "that whenever the need arises the
Canadian people will be found ready and willing to make any
sacrifice that is required to give the Imperial authorities the most
loyal and hearty co-operation in every movement for the maintenance of the integrity and honour of the Empire".[28]

Borden thought that Laurier's resolution was even better than
Foster's. It was more detailed, more specific on the question of
coastal defence, and it also recognized the naval crisis. He suggested two amendments. The substitution of the words "the payment of regular and periodical contribution" for "the payment
of any stated contribution" would clarify the contributions clause
and leave open the possibility of an emergency contribution. And
the insertion of the word "speedy" in the naval service clause, so
that it would read "any necessary expenditure designed to promote the speedy organization of a Canadian naval service", would
be more in keeping with the spirit and intent of the Foster
resolution.[29] Laurier readily accepted Borden's suggestions,[30] and
the amended Laurier resolution was unanimously passed by the
House of Commons.

Borden was pleased with the result of the debate on the Foster
and Laurier resolutions. Members on both sides of the House had
acquitted themselves with uncommon dignity and responsibility.
Both sides had judged the Foster resolution inadequate in the
crisis atmosphere at the end of March and were committed to the
"speedy organization of a Canadian naval service" after detailed
consultation with Imperial authorities at a hastily called Imperial
Defence Conference in the coming summer. Both parties had
opposed "the payment of regular and periodical contributions"
to imperial defence but seemed to be ready to accept the idea of
an emergency contribution if the crisis proved to be as grave as

it appeared. It was true that Casgrain's prediction had proved correct; the emotional response to the naval crisis had turned the thoughts of the Parliament from coastal defence to more ambitious projects. But the unanimous vote on the Laurier resolution suggested that French- and English-speaking Canadians could unite in common purpose when the Empire was in danger.

It took less than twenty-four hours for Borden to discover that unanimity in the House of Commons did not mean unanimity in his party. The very next day Premier Whitney announced that he favoured a policy of contribution "of a Dreadnought". Premier Roblin told the Toronto *Star* on March 31 that he favoured "a Dreadnought being at once built and presented to the British Government". On April 17 Roblin called the Laurier resolution "cheap and wishy-washy". Four days later Premier McBride endorsed the resolution but asked, in addition, for "an immediate and unconditional gift to the Imperial Navy". Premier Hazen, never one to commit himself with unseemly haste, waited until December to announce his support for "a direct contribution of either money or ships". By then Haultain in Saskatchewan and Bennett of Alberta had long since joined the English-speaking Conservative provincial leaders in the contribution chorus.[31]

Borden was not moved. The Laurier resolution, he admitted to L. S. Amery in April, "did not meet my own personal views to the fullest extent". He carefully avoided, however, any explanation of where the resolution fell short of his own ideas. Instead, he emphasized the importance of unanimity in the passage of the resolution. His support of the resolution had aroused a "good deal" of criticism in Canada. But he believed it to be "the most important step" Canada had taken in defence policy for many years. "It thoroughly commits the Liberal Party to a policy to which hitherto it has been unalterably opposed," he wrote. (This, of course, was palpably untrue.) More important, "it unites both parties in a common declaration; and the language is sufficiently broad and comprehensive to justify every possible effort for the Empire's safety and the maintenance of Imperial ties."[32]

"Every possible effort for the Empire's safety" meant that Borden could conceive of circumstances where an emergency contribution would be necessary, but he was not prepared to commit himself. The press reports from London in the weeks following the March 29 debate made the gravity of the crisis hard to measure. Spokesmen for Asquith's government suggested that the crisis had been overcome by an accelerated British naval construction program. Critics of Asquith's government claimed that the inadequate plans of the Admiralty left the Empire in peril. So the questions remained. What constituted an emergency grave enough to warrant a contribution from Canada? If such an emergency did exist, what form should the Canadian contribution take? Should it be ships? Should it be money? How should it be arranged?

These questions were to plague Borden throughout the years of the naval debate. Eventually they would divide his party into hot-tempered contending factions on the naval question. As party leader, Borden could not make quick decisions based on senti-ment and immediate partisan advantage. His provincial col-leagues, devoid of any responsibility in the matter, could easily decide that a grave emergency existed and that the immediate grant of a Dreadnought or two should be the minimum appro-priate Canadian response. But he had to be more cautious; his obligations were broader, more complex. He had to try to keep his party together, to act responsibly and reasonably in the national interest. His amendment to the contribution clause had left open the possibility of an emergency contribution. That was as far as he could go in the March debate in the House. Privately, his first definition of a crisis serious enough to warrant an emergency contribution was severely limited. "An emergency contribution, *in the case of war*, would not only be within the scope of the second paragraph, but is in effect promised by the concluding paragraph of the resolution," he wrote to Amery in April. A month later he was more ambiguous. His amendment, he told the editor of the *National Review*, left "open the door to a money contribution in time of peril".[33] But what was a time of peril?

Publicly he stood by the House of Commons resolution. During a trip to England in the summer of 1909 he told a London audience that the resolution, "while its terms might not upon their surface seem as significant at the moment as the offer of one or two Dreadnoughts would have been, laid down a perman-ent policy for the Dominion of Canada upon which both parties united and which would serve a more practical purpose than any such offer of Dreadnoughts".[34] At Halifax, on October 14, he again spoke of naval policy and imperial relations, but did not even mention the contribution question. Then, two weeks later, Borden issued a statement to the press that suggested a change of position. Party policy, he said, "rests to-day exactly where it did when the unanimous Resolution of Parliament was passed". But now he talked openly of the emergency contribution, saying —as he had not said for months—that the resolution permitted "a special contribution in time of emergency". The decision as to what constituted an emergency, however, did not rest with him. "Whether such emergency existed then or is imminent to-day is within the knowledge of the British Government and the Canadian Government."[35]

Borden's gradual shift of position on the contribution question was not brought about by a continuing crisis in the Mother Country. There the naval debate had subsided by mid-summer. By the end of 1909 the British government realized that the German naval construction program had not been accelerated.[36] But in Canada the debate had been kept alive, even intensified, by the visits of prominent British spokesmen drumming up support for the imperialist cause. Admiral Lord Charles Beresford, who had recently given up command of the Channel Fleet in a bitter dispute with the First Sea Lord, Lord Fisher, opened the Canadian National Exhibition on August 30. The Toronto audience, knowing nothing of his quarrel with Fisher over naval policy, and not suspecting for a moment that Beresford had any personal axe to grind in the naval crisis, naturally assumed that if anyone knew the gravity of the crisis, the Admiral did. "Our supremacy at sea has been threatened in language that is unmistakable," he told them. He had generous words for Laurier's proposed naval service. But at no point in his extended tour did he attempt to belie the impression that the crisis remained.[37] In September Lord Northcliffe, the famous British publisher, warned a Winnipeg gathering that Germany was going to attack Great Britain as soon as she thought she could be successful.[38] And the most prominent British resident in Canada, the Governor General, played his part in keeping the agitation alive. Lord Grey identified Quebec as the broken link in the chain of Canadian Imperial enthusiasm. He pressured French-speaking MP's and other prominent Quebeckers to assist in establishing branches of the Navy League in the province.[39] "One German cruiser in the mouth of the St. Lawrence," he maladroitly warned Monk, "would put every Quebec farmer out of business." Monk was not impressed. "His mind appeared to me to be unbalanced by a Party Hatred of Sir Wilfrid Laurier," Grey gloomily told Borden.[40] All of this drumming by British imperialists only served to encourage the native naval experts. In October, Roblin denounced the Laurier scheme as a "toy navy"; by December it had become the "tin pot" navy.[41]

The propaganda campaign for an emergency contribution confirmed the darkest suspicions of the French-speaking Conservatives. When Borden was preparing to leave for England in June 1909, William Price told him that the "Quebec attitude on Naval Defence" would be "all right if properly handled".[42] But Borden could not check the enthusiasm within his party for an emergency contribution. During his trip to England the public statements of the contributionists became more and more extreme. When he returned Monk warned that he was going to have to reply to the contributionists. Monk said he would "be as guarded as possible" and "try to avoid expressing views which might clash with those of our friends". But, he added ominously, "you know what my opinions have always been upon this subject."[43]

On November 8, at a Lachine Conservative Club banquet, with the full approval of Senator Landry, W. B. Nantel, and J. M. Tellier, Monk soundly denounced the Laurier resolution and the proposed Canadian naval force. He stated that it would be a flagrant violation of Canadian self-government if the navy question were settled "without submitting it to the judgment of the electorate".[44] Monk's "guarded" remarks placed the blame for the continuing naval debate in Canada on Laurier's naval policy. In effect, he demanded a plebiscite on the naval question. Publicly, he avoided the emergency contribution issue. Privately, he conceded that it had been necessary to give unanimous support to Laurier's resolution in March. "If the same thing happened again," he told Borden, "I think we should pursue the same course."[45] But he made no such admission to his Lachine audience. Instead he sought to silence the contributionists and satisfy his French-Canadian supporters by demanding a plebiscite on naval policy. Monk had declared war on Laurier's navy. And Borden's party, united in March, had come apart.

The general results of the Imperial Defence Conference of 1909 had been made public before Parliament reconvened on November 11. It was known that the Canadian representatives, Sir Frederick Borden and Louis Brodeur, had rejected an Admiralty suggestion that Canada provide an Imperial fleet unit stationed on the Pacific coast. That was politically impossible. ("It would not satisfy in any regard the ambitions of the Canadian people to place a Naval unit on one ocean and rely entirely upon the protection to be derived from the great Navy on the other ocean," Sir Frederick had told the Conference.)[46] Instead, Canada was going to have a two-ocean navy, however large or small it might be. None of the Conservatives found satisfaction in the little they yet knew about Laurier's plans. But they were deeply divided among themselves, and it was only with difficulty that Borden persuaded them "to leave Naval matters alone on the Address debate".[47] Borden was bidding for time, for an opportunity to seek advice outside the caucus.

Borden told the men he was consulting that Laurier's estimate of a three million dollar expenditure for naval construction in the next fiscal year would "entirely fail to meet the present emergency". It would be ten "and probably twenty" years before Laurier's navy "could be made reasonably effective as a fighting unit of the Imperial fleet", but the "North Sea Crisis will be solved in one way or another within five years". This, then, was the nature of "the present emergency". If the Conservatives were in power, they would have a three-point policy. There would be "a sufficient and generous emergency contribution to the Imperial Treasury". Similar contributions would be given "from time to time while the emergency remains imminent and menacing and until a Canadian unit or section of the Imperial Navy can be relied upon as an effective fighting force". Finally, they would "proceed cautiously and by slow beginnings toward the construction and the establishment of such a unit which must be under Admiralty (or some thoroughly effective central) control for fighting purposes, and must to all intents and purposes be an integral and constituent part of a great Imperial fleet". Though his policy was entirely in line with the March resolution, he said, "the vital question is as to our duty today, not what we were prepared to do a year ago". And not being in power, the question became what position should the party take on Laurier's soon-to-be-announced proposals "upon considerations of patriotic action as well as those of political strategy". He suggested two alternatives. The party could accept Laurier's anticipated plan "under forcible and earnest protest as an exceedingly inadequate instalment of what might have been expected". Or, because "a warfare of naval construction is now being waged by the Empire in anticipation of the actual warfare which may follow at any moment", it might declare its own policy and "vote against the Bill; in other words to move the six months hoist".[48]

Borden had finally come to terms with the emergency contribution question. Just weeks before, he had said that it was up to the governments in Ottawa and London to determine whether there was, in fact, an emergency. Now he had decided that there was. There was no longer a crisis in London, nor any reflection of an emergency in Laurier's anticipated naval policy. But the crisis atmosphere persisted in his party and he accepted it. As he defined it, his "emergency" was plausible. No one doubted that the "warfare of naval construction" continued. If that was the essence of the emergency, then the crisis would be resolved "within five years". But the Conservatives believed that it would be at least ten years before the Canadian navy could become "reasonably effective as a fighting unit of an Imperial fleet". If anyone doubted that, they just had to look at Fielding's paltry three million dollar estimate for construction. So defined, the emergency outlined in Borden's memorandum brought him into line with the contributionists in the party while holding out the hope that even Monk might stay in line. Had Monk not said that "if the same thing happened again", if, in other words, an emergency did exist, he would follow his leader?

The replies to Borden's memorandum were hardly surprising. Richard White of the Montreal *Gazette* advised against any contributory policy. A. F. Wallis of the *Mail and Empire* suggested that Borden allow his members a free vote on the naval issue.[49] Willison, Flavelle, Roblin, Whitney, Bennett, Sir Charles Hibbert Tupper, and Kemp all favoured some form of contributory policy though Flavelle cautioned there was little popular support for it. All were opposed to the six-months hoist. Rather, Borden should accept Laurier's plan and better it by adding an emergency contribution. Only Casgrain, in a series of letters, favoured the six-months hoist as a device to keep the party together. What was most striking in the replies from English Canadians was the advice to Borden not to bow to Quebec. Flavelle suggested that the party would not stand for a "policy which cribs, cabins and confines the actions of the Conservative Party upon public issues of high importance within the limits set by Quebec". Tupper was more blunt. "If Quebec is to be a 'canker'," he asked, "why not meet the difficulty and have it out?"[50]

Laurier presented his plan for a Canadian Naval Service on January 12, 1910. The Canadian Navy would be composed of five cruisers and six destroyers, with some ships stationed on each coast. There would be a permanent naval force of regular and reserve units, both recruited by voluntary enlistment. The Canadian Navy would be under Canadian control. "In case of emergency," the Navy could, by Order-in-Council, be placed under imperial control. If that happened, Parliament would immediately be asked to give its approval. Laurier flatly rejected the idea that these provisions meant that Canada's Navy could stay out of an imperial war. "When Britain is at war Canada is at war; there is no distinction."[51]

Borden's initial reply was very general. He did not like the idea that Parliament must consent to handing control of the navy over to the imperial authorities. It meant "the absolute and complete independence of Canada from the British Empire". Still, he acknowledged the difficulty of the control problem. Would it not be better resolved, he asked, by some sort of "Defence Committee, or an Imperial Conference having special jurisdiction over defence matters"? "I thoroughly agree," he said, "that if we are to take part in the permanent defence of this great Empire we must have some control and some voice in such matters." The leader of the opposition made it clear that he was absolutely opposed to a policy of permanent contributions. "Go on with your Naval Service. Proceed cautiously and surely," he told Laurier. But in a desperate effort to keep his own party together, he would go further. "Lay your proposals before the people and give them, if necessary, the opportunity to be heard," he urged for Monk's benefit. For the contributionists he asked Laurier to remember that "we are confronted with an emergency which may rend this Empire asunder before the proposed Service is worthy of the name". "Immediate, vigorous, earnest action" was necessary and it should take the form of a cash equivalent grant of a Dreadnought to the Admiralty.[52] It was a speech designed to please everyone, to quell the warfare in his own party. It didn't work.

In the weeks that followed a special committee of the caucus groped for a policy "by which we might score off the Government and combine in some feasible way the conflicting views of our men".[53] Second reading of the Naval Service Bill was scheduled for February 3. That morning there was another acrimonious caucus over whether Borden should move a six-months hoist or a "resolution for Dreadnoughts". By then Borden already knew that his Quebec supporters might bolt. Neither of the special committee's proposed resolutions mentioned a "referendum" on naval policy and Monk, Paquet, Nantel, Blondin, and Lortie found it "impossible" to support either one.[54] Rather than bring the dispute to a vote in caucus, the decision was left to Borden alone. He agreed to announce the party's policy in his speech that afternoon.[55]

Borden again denounced the government's concept of parliamentary control of the navy in time of war. He tried once more to reconcile the conflicting views of his caucus. He rejected a six-months hoist. His amendment condemned the government for not following the advice of the Admiralty, for threatening the unity of the Empire, for affording no effective immediate aid. To Monk's surprise, Borden included a clause supporting approval by the electorate of Canada's permanent naval policy. The amendment concluded with a demand for an emergency contribution sufficient to provide two Dreadnoughts for the imperial fleet. Behind him feet stamped, hands pounded on desks, and voices roared as he droned out his proposals. "We out cheered the beggars all through the game," Martin Burrell wrote, "and the scene was a corker when we started God Save the King at the conclusion of Borden's speech."[56]

Monk followed, describing the Naval Service Bill as a thinly disguised "Imperialist scheme". He submitted an amendment of his own demanding a "plebiscite" on Laurier's bill. The debate went on periodically for more than a month. Monk's amendment was defeated on March 9, 175 to 18.* Borden's amendment was defeated the same day, 129 to 74. Again the Tories sprang from their seats to sing "God Save the King". For practical purposes, the navy debate was over. W. B. Northrup moved a six-months hoist the following day and the motion was defeated 119 to 78. In April, on third reading, Borden caustically referred to a Cana-

---

*Monk's amendment was supported by 16 other Conservatives; Blondin, Broder, Chisholm, Currie, Doherty, Forget, Herron, Jameson, Lewis, Lortie, Nantel, Paquet, Sharpe, White, Wilcox, and Worthington, and by one Liberal, Verville.

dian navy in time of peace, an "Order-in-Council Navy" in time of war.[57]

There would be a Canadian Naval Service. But it would not be the Canadian Navy unanimously supported in the March 1909 resolution. The naval crisis of 1909 had become, in no small measure, a political crisis for the Conservative party in 1910. In 1909 there had been an impressive display of non-partisan resolve. In 1910, Burrell observed that "Laurier made a miserable party affair of it and we intend to hand the stuff out as hot as we can all along the line". But the truth was that, to use the words of Borden's November memorandum, both parties paid more attention to "political strategy" than to "patriotic action". For Conservatives the Canadian Navy would henceforth be "Laurier's Navy", an "Order-in-Council Navy".

There was no way Borden could lead his party through the naval debate unscarred. With equal sincerity his French- and English-speaking followers came to opposite conclusions about the seriousness of the 1909 naval scare. All his followers had to rely upon confused and contradictory accounts in the press or by spokesmen of varied vested interests. The issue was doubly complicated because of its highly emotional character. For both French-speaking nationalists and English-speaking contributionists the naval question was less an issue of the relative strengths of the Imperial and German fleets in 1909, or in 1912, and more a matter of the integrity of their conceptions of the past, present, and future of their country. Borden eventually accepted most of the contributionist's argument. But he knew the danger of both positions. The full logic of the nationalist position threatened the imperial connection; the full logic of the contributionist argument threatened Canadian self-government. The two were inextricably linked, a threat to either threatened both, and, hence, the very essence of the Canadian identity. His own preference was, in fact, much closer to Laurier's solution of the problem, a middle way, the creation of a naval force that was at once Canadian and part of a larger Imperial force. Because of this he defended the March 1909 resolution as long as he could. In the end he had to give way. He had to choose between the contending groups of his followers, less because of an apprehended naval emergency than because of a real crisis in his party. The choice was invidious; whichever position he took, the proponents of the other would be estranged.

Politically, there was much to be said for casting his lot with the contributionist faction. He would solidify his support from the Conservative provincial premiers and give them an added incentive to turn out the vote for his party in the next election. And there was even an unexpected bonus. In March 1910, Sam Hughes told him that some of the most important Toronto Liberal businessmen were very sympathetic to his policy. He suggested that Byron Walker, W. K. George, E. R. Wood, W. T. White, and W. M. Clark might all be lured away from Laurier's party.[58] There were even hints that Clifford Sifton, who had close contacts with a most unlikely trio of Tories, Hughes, Willison, and Billy Maclean, could be brought into the fold.[59] But Borden's commitment to an emergency contribution cost him the support of the French-speaking Conservatives. His support for a plebiscite on permanent naval policy was a desperate and unsuccessful attempt to hold them in line. The repercussions were severe, in Quebec and throughout the party.

Borden was optimistic about the state of his party at the beginning of 1909. He and Monk had reconciled their differences and Monk was reinstated as Quebec leader, a post that had been vacant since early 1904. Old sins of omission and commission were forgiven on both sides and Borden pledged that he would "accept and cooperate with, to the fullest extent, the chosen leader of the Conservatives in that Province". There was even more. Thomas Chase Casgrain accepted the post of Chairman of the Executive Comittee, reconciling the differences between the old Bleu and younger nationalist groups in the Quebec party. And there were hopeful signs that an alliance might even be made with Bourassa. It was agreed that "without making any alliance with him for the present we could work on parallel lines".[60]

The reconciliation held through the March naval debate and was still intact when Borden left for England in June. When Borden returned, while he still was giving unambiguous support to the March resolution, he confidently announced that the party would hold a national convention in 1910.[61] Whitney still opposed a convention. But "McBride, Roblin and Hazen, especially the two former, are entirely of the opposite opinion." Borden believed that pressure for a convention was "so strong . . . throughout the country" that he could no longer delay calling one. He strongly

17. Laura Borden, 1906

18. The second annual meeting of the Crown Life Insurance Company, Toronto, March 1903. Sir Charles Tupper, the president, is second from the left, and Borden is fourth from the right.

19. (Right) Borden in 1901

20. Glensmere, the Bordens' Ottawa home, *circa* 1913. In the driveway is the electric automobile presented to Laura by the ladies of the Conservative Party.

21 & 22. Two views of the interior of Glensmere taken before the Bordens bought the house. (Above) The entrance hall and (below) the living room with the music alcove

23. A Liberal poster from the 1904 election

24 & 25. (Above) Sir Wilfrid Laurier campaigning in 1908. (Below) Sir Wilfrid at Mission City, B.C., in August 1910 during his western tour.

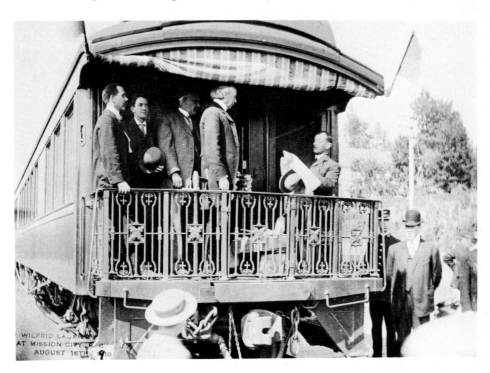

WILFRID LAURIER
AT MISSION CITY, B.C.
AUGUST 16TH 1910

26. Borden speaking from the platform during his western tour, June 1911

favoured it himself. A national convention would "make the Conservatives realize their strength and . . . impress those who are critical and indifferent with the fact that the party is still possessed of abundant life and energy and proposed to win at the next general election".[62] In January of 1910, before his commitment to an emergency contribution was known to anyone except the recipients of his November memorandum, he appointed a committee of party members to plan the meeting. On February 3, Borden and Monk offered their separate amendments to the Naval Service Bill. Monk's action infuriated the English-speaking Conservatives. "It almost justified the reading of Monk straight out of the party," said Martin Burrell.[63] The party fat was again in the fire.

On March 1 a delegation of Montreal Conservatives demanded that Borden postpone the convention for a year. Otherwise, Quebec would boycott the gathering. By the end of the month word had been leaked that the convention was off. Borden appointed a small committee to resolve the differences between the French and English Conservatives. Charles Magrath, T. W. Crothers, O. S. Crocket, and Martin Burrell were asked to negotiate with a group of Quebec Conservatives including both Bleu and nationalist representatives.* The heart of the problem was the naval issue. The Quebeckers were dismayed at the way in which Borden had handled the Conservative side of the debate. Burrell reported that they "agreed as to opposition to the Naval Bill, and agreed on the desirability of giving a contribution in case of emergency, but [were] not agreed on the fact of emergency".[64] At the end of March Borden publicly acknowledged that his Quebec followers did not accept his definition of an emergency in the naval debate. "The chief, if not the only difference of opinion between my colleagues from Quebec and myself," he told a Halifax audience, "is in the estimate of the gravity of existing conditions. I believe that an emergency has arisen which makes it the imperative duty of Canada to proffer immediate and effective aid, to offer it now, and to stand shoulder to shoulder with our fellow Dominions. The French-speaking Conservatives from Quebec are not satisfied that such an emergency exists."[65]

The Quebeckers used the negotiations to air a host of older,

---

*The Quebec group included Lacoste, Casgrain, C. Beauvieu, Louis Coderre, Nantel, Blondin, and D.-O. L'Esperance. Perley and Doherty occasionally attended the meetings. Apparently Monk was not a member of the group.

long-standing, and deeper grievances. Sam Hughes' regular "utterances on French questions", the dislike and distrust of Foster, and Borden's stance on the Autonomy Bills were all rehearsed again with evident passion. So too were the ineffectiveness of Borden's front bench, the inadequacy of George Taylor as Chief Whip and, as Burrell put it, Borden's "own limitations (temperamental)". It boiled down to this: the Quebeckers were dissatisfied with Borden's leadership. Both the Quebec men and Borden's committee talked of a complete reorganization at the top of the party, of bringing in McBride as leader or, at least, as Borden's lieutenant and eventual successor.[66] "What would suit us all would be that Borden should be big enough to stay in the House with you as Leader," Burrell told McBride. "This would satisfy all malcontents and would put such life into the party as to mean, I verily believe, victory next time we went to the country."[67]

Once the dam had been breached, a great flood of discontent in the parliamentary party broke loose. Many parliamentarians deeply resented the way Borden had treated his colleagues over the years. He had been distant, moody, imperious, sometimes almost scornful of their worth. He had seldom consulted with them. If a caucus was stormy he might go away and not call another for the remainder of the session. From the beginning of his leadership he had made policy by memoranda with outsiders; businessmen, journalists, provincial potentates, men who understood little and cared less about the demands, the whims, and the welfare of the parliamentary party. And now all the long smouldering unrest came out in a great disorganized rush of revolt. The Quebeckers had wounded the leader. The malcontents moved in for the kill.

On April 7, 1910, the Toronto *Star* broke the whole embarrassing story in a long article headed BORDEN'S WANT OF TACT STARTED THE DISCONTENT. The *Star*'s staff correspondent in Ottawa had gotten the cause right enough. But he was a little too enthusiastic in identifying "Seven Different Factions Within the Party". There were, in fact, three identifiable groups of discontented parliamentarians and a few scattered individuals opposed to Borden. The French Canadians, led by Monk, who appears to have let his colleagues confront Borden while he stayed in the background, had, from their point of view, understandable grievances. The motives of a second group, William Price, William Northrup, and J. D. Reid, were less clear, but they probably objected to Borden's apparent vacillation on the naval issue. A letter from Northrup to some party members in October 1909, before Borden committed himself to the emergency contribution, charged the leader with a "cowardly desertion of the Empire".[68] All three believed Borden was an incompetent leader and had to go.[69] A third group was led by Thomas Crothers who was said to have the support of Major Thomas Beattie of London.[70] Then there were the scattered individuals, among them Billy Maclean and Rufus Pope, who had never accepted Borden's leadership. "Borden was no good, we must have another leader," Pope told Burrell early in March.[71] And Burrell recalled many years later that a number of others, though not willing to challenge Borden's leadership directly, "felt restless, and felt that they were not in touch with you, that reorganization was necessary, and especially, that there ought to be a change in the Chief Whip".*

Borden discussed the revolt with his negotiating committee, Magrath, Crothers, Crocket, and Burrell. He considered stepping aside for McBride but no one knew if the British Columbia Premier would accept a call. In fact, he would not.[72] McBride had been told the previous year that he suffered from a terminal illness and he could give no thought to a new political career.[73] Borden also suggested putting his resignation in the hands of the caucus. His colleagues were opposed but it was the most effective way of resolving the leadership crisis. On April 6 he handed a letter of resignation to George Taylor, the Chief Whip.

Borden had no intention of resigning. Rather, his letter was an invitation to a test of strength with his caucus. He was determined to have it out with the malcontents. Before the sixth he had informed his non-parliamentary supporters of his intention to retire, fully expecting they would rally to his leadership.[74] Hugh Clark, an Ontario Conservative MPP, had assured him "that every member of the Whitney government and every Conservative member of the Legislature is heart and soul with you. Every man of them believes that your retirement from the leadership of the party would spell *disaster* to the party."[75] Roblin also replied immediately, telling him "a leader must be absolute in authority".

*This letter was written at Borden's request when he was preparing his *Memoirs*. BP, 294, Burrell to Borden, October 17, 1932, no. 172623-27.

> I would stand at my post and I would have the courage of a
> lion, and face of flint and exercise my rights as leader in as
> autocratic a manner as does the Czar of Russia. . . . Spit upon
> your hands, take a fresh hold, bare your muscles, bare your
> chest to the wind and not only request, but demand from
> every man who assumes to be a follower, his allegiance and
> his willingness to discharge any duty that may be put upon
> him and to call upon your friends from the Atlantic to the
> Pacific to rally around you in your patriotic effort to promote
> such legislation as will foster and develop the moral, social
> and material life of the people of Canada. . . . In other words
> be boss; exercise your power, and then when you have done
> this, call upon men like myself, McBride, Whitney and Hazen
> and any others . . . for work and such assistance as will
> strengthen your hands.[76]

Roblin's bluster could not hide the importance of his message.
He and Whitney were backing Borden.

Borden met his caucus on the morning of April 12. Burrell
recalled that Borden spoke at length,

> saying that you were anxious to retire, and realized the lack
> of support amongst many, and the talking behind your back
> and so on. You stayed for a time, and then retired from the
> meeting, which continued till one. There was apparently
> much frank talk and finally Doherty, while agreeing that
> there was some dissatisfaction and a strong feeling that
> some change was necessary, moved a resolution of confidence
> in you as leader, coupled with a request for reorganization,
> and several of those present—friends of yours—expressed
> the feeling that the leader was the only one who could deal
> with the reorganization question. At last the motion was put,
> and carried, all standing up. I have a note saying that various
> men (whose names I will not permit myself to mention) got
> up "with evident reluctance".[77]

The revolt had been put down. With the exception of the
French Canadians, who would remain at odds with the leader, the
malcontents had been disorganized and had lacked any clear
objective or an alternative to Borden as leader. In an open test
of strength they were hopelessly weak. The great majority of the
parliamentarians may well have had grievances against Borden,

but they were not prepared to throw him out. Equally important, Borden had the undeniable support of the provincial premiers and their powerful organizations. It is reasonable to assume that not a few MP's were made aware of that blunt fact before the caucus on the 12th. The message was clear enough. Their own careers were in jeopardy if they persisted in their opposition to both the national leader and the ruling provincial parties.

The next morning, April 13, another caucus received a report from the committee on preliminary arrangements for a national convention. There would be no convention because, as Borden's secretary carefully put it in letters to party members that afternoon, "requests had been received from nearly every section of the country asking that the Convention be postponed".[78] Borden agreed to reorganize the parliamentary party. When the caucus met the following November, at the opening of the new session, Borden announced that all the key positions in the parliamentary party would be assumed by men who were not only loyal to the leader, but close friends. George Perley was the new Chief Whip, Charles Magrath was permanent chairman of the caucus, and Herbert Ames was chairman of a committee on party reorganization.[79] The party, it seemed, was again in his control.

CHAPTER NINE

FIRST MINISTER

The support of the Conservative provincial premiers had been the decisive factor in Borden's defence of his leadership at the April 1910 caucus. In June it was re-emphasized in Ontario where Whitney and his lieutenants made a point of being at Borden's side during a brief tour of the province. And in August E. C. Tanner and J. J. Ritchie, leading spokesmen for the Nova Scotia Conservatives, accompanied Borden on an excursion through his home province. But the provincial leaders could not help Borden solve his most challenging problem. He alone had to find a way to accommodate the differences between his colleagues on naval policy. As long as he advocated an emergency contribution Borden's French-speaking followers would support him on other issues but go their own way on the primary public question of the day. "The convictions we hold upon the naval question differ so greatly from those of our fellow members on our side of the House that . . . I think it is perhaps better for each to follow our own course," Monk had written in January.[1] In May, *L'Evenement*, the only French-language Conservative organ in Quebec, demanded the formation of a new party headed by Monk, Bourassa, and Lavergne.[2] By the summer Monk and his followers were sharing platforms with Bourassa and his friends, all of them denouncing both the Naval Service Act and Borden's policy. At St. Eustache, in July, Monk and Bourassa damned both policies and seemed to suggest that Canadian naval policy should be tied to a Canadian voice in Imperial foreign policy.[3] In September, after he attended a meeting addressed by Monk at Montmagny, William Price told the Ottawa *Citizen* that the "Nationalists or Independents could carry fully one-half of the ridings in Quebec against the Laurier Government".[4]

Quebec sentiment on the naval issue had been tested just before the parliamentary session opened in November, 1910. Sir Wilfrid had appointed Louis Lavergne to the Senate and opened his constituency, Drummond–Arthabaska, to a by-election. The Conservatives stayed out of the contest. After all, the seat had once been Laurier's, it embraced his hometown, and had been solidly Liberal since 1887. Lavergne assured the Prime Minister that the party candidate, J. E. Perrault, would be returned easily. But neither party reckoned with the strength that the other candidate, Arthur Gilbert, a nominal Liberal opposed to the government's naval policy, would draw from the Nationalist crusade. Monk, Bourassa, Armand Lavergne, provincial MLA's J. M. Tellier and E. L. Patenaude, Albert Sévigny, Conservative MP's Nantel and Blondin, and a host of others supported Gilbert and even took the Nationalist message to Montreal. There, on October 20, Bourassa charged that the establishment of a Canadian navy would inevitably lead to conscription. And there, ten days later, Laurier himself replied with a vigorous defence of his policy and an absolute denial of conscription. Sir Wilfrid observed that the once-proud Conservative party in Quebec had betrayed its tolerant past and become the refuge of "The Pharisees of Canadian Catholicism, those who set themselves up with ostentation as the defenders of religion, which no one attacks; those who handle the holy water sprinkler like a club, those who have arrogated to themselves the monopoly on orthodoxy". These men, Laurier added, had attracted younger Liberals like Bourassa and Lavergne, men who "having nothing Liberal in their nature, have found, after several efforts at groping in the dark, their true home in the waters of the Castors".[5]

Belatedly, some English-speaking Tories jumped into the unexpectedly bitter contest. In response to a questionnaire by the Montreal *Herald*, Foster and Sam Barker advised Conservatives to vote against Perrault. "Hon. Bob" Rogers wired from Winnipeg that "every Conservative and loyal Canadian ... should recognize that his first duty to his country is to vote against the Laurier Administration". Other Conservatives were plainly less anxious to get involved. McBride told the voters to follow "the advice of our leader at Ottawa". Borden found that piece of Pacific political sagacity of little comfort. Clearly, he could support neither Perrault nor Gilbert, the apparent protégé of Bourassa and Monk. When asked for an opinion, Borden said that he had just returned

from a Virginia holiday and was not aware of the issues in the
by-election. He lamely advised the electors to "vote according to
the dictates of their own consciences".[6]

To everyone's surprise, the Nationalist candidate won the
election by two hundred votes. As late as polling day Bourassa
had expected defeat. He prepared an editorial for publication in
his paper, *Le Devoir*, next day, explaining Perrault's victory as
the result of Liberal party corruption. It was one piece he was
delighted not to print. For Laurier and his party Gilbert's victory
was a severe blow. And the Conservatives found the result
scarcely more comforting. William Price reported that for the
time being the French-Canadian MP's would not attend the party
caucus. "Our presence," Monk had told Price, "could only em-
barrass our friends with whom I desire to remain on the same
old friendly terms."[7]

"The same old friendly terms," of course, meant no meeting of
minds on the naval issue. The government was delighted and
most of the Opposition appalled when Monk moved his own
amendment to the Speech from the Throne. He regretted the lack
of consultation of "the people on its naval policy and on the
general question of the contribution of Canada to Imperial
armaments".[8] Borden, who had already spoken, was forced to
rise again and offer a sub-amendment. It was a desperate attempt
to cover up the split in his ranks, to try once again to bridge the
gap between Monk's followers and his own. He made two important concessions to Monk. First, he said, if he were in power
and if an emergency contribution was necessary (and he thought
it would be), "I would appeal to parliament for immediate and
effective aid, and if parliament did not give immediate and
effective aid I would appeal from parliament to the people of this
country". This was as close as Borden could come to Monk's
demand for consultation of the people on an emergency contribution. Second, with apparent reference to Bourassa's demand
that naval policy be tied to a voice in Imperial foreign policy,
Borden said that Canadians should not agree to "contributing to
the defence of the empire" while they had "no voice whatever in
the councils of the empire touching the issues of peace or war
throughout the empire". His sub-amendment regretted the lack
of consultation of "the people on the naval policy of Canada",
without making any distinction between emergency and permanent policy.[9] Naturally, both amendments were defeated. The in-

teresting point of the votes was that sixty-seven Conservatives supported Monk's amendment.[10]

Some of the English-Canadian Tories were furious at Monk's display of independence during the Throne Speech debate. Monk's amendment had highlighted the division in the party on naval policy. A. E. Kemp sent Borden a series of letters warning of the dangers of further association with the Quebec Nationalists and Herbert Ames reported that the Montreal *Star* was threatening not to support the party in the next election unless Borden broke all ties with Monk and Bourassa. But Borden refused to break openly with the French Canadians. Despite their differences on naval policy, Monk and his colleagues were still Conservatives, still allies. Once the Throne Speech debate was over the naval issue would recede from public notice as the parliamentarians prepared for their Christmas holiday. Borden looked forward to the opportunity to spend a few relaxing days with Laura and to plan his strategy for the remainder of the session.

He knew there would be much work to do in the next few months. Laurier's government was expected to present a full legislative program to Parliament, including a Bill to aid the construction of Mackenzie and Mann's Canadian Northern Railway in Ontario. And following the decennial census there would be a redistribution of House of Commons representation. The most crucial matter would be the results of negotiations with the United States on Canadian-American trade that had begun in November. Despite the protective tariff barrier each nation mounted against the other's goods, the United States was Canada's most important trading partner. Any significant reduction in the tariff of either country could have a profound effect on the Canadian economy. Moreover, ever since the introduction of Macdonald's National Policy tariff Canadian-American trade relations had become a highly emotional political issue. For most Conservatives the tariff had become a symbol of Canada's separate nationhood on the North American continent, the first line of defence against annexation by the United States. Any significant reduction in the Canadian tariff on American imports would be interpreted by the Conservatives as a threat to the Canadian identity, as the introduction of the thin edge of the wedge of continentalism.

A number of factors had led to the current trade talks. In one sense they were the capstone to a series of Canadian-American agreements which had finally settled disputes reaching well back into the nineteenth century and which had established agencies, like the International Joint Commission, to resolve twentieth-century cross-border problems. In the parlance of the day, a trade agreement would be the culmination of "cleaning the slate" with the United States. Then, too, the effect of the 1907 Fielding tariff and the 1909 Payne-Aldrich tariff in the United States had been to force the Americans either to apply discriminatory duties on Canadian imports or to seek a reciprocity agreement with Canada. Both Democrats and insurgent Republicans in President Taft's own party, supported by a number of commercial interests dominated by importers of Canadian pulp and paper products, had urged Taft to choose negotiation rather than retaliation. It was a unique experience for Canadians; not they, but the Americans, had initiated the trade negotiations.

Laurier's government was especially receptive to the American initiative because agrarian discontent with established national economic policy had grown steadily since 1900. By 1910 the western wheat farmers were organized into powerful protest groups, the United Farmers of Alberta and the Grain Growers' Associations of Saskatchewan and Manitoba. They had made common cause with Ontario agriculturalists in the Canadian Council of Agriculture. During Sir Wilfrid's western tour in the summer of 1910, the Prime Minister had been besieged with demands to right the farmers' grievances and tariff relief had topped the agriculturalists' list. Then, just before the Christmas holiday, eight hundred farmers from the west and Ontario, with a few scattered delegates from the Maritimes and Quebec, had descended upon Ottawa to present their demands and petitions to the government. It was an impressive display of strength and its political significance was obvious to both parties.

The farmers presented a long list of essential reforms. They wanted government-owned and -operated terminal elevators, government-owned and -operated facilities for the chilled meat industry, government construction, ownership and operation, through an independent commission, of the Hudson's Bay Railway, amendments to the Railway Act and the Bank Act, legislation to facilitate the incorporation of co-operative societies, an increase in the British preference, and, of course, reciprocity with the United States. Sir Wilfrid's response was decidedly cool.

"Government ownership is not altogether in my line," he told the farmers.[11] In fact, Laurier thought most of the demands were politically impossible. He told an Ontario Liberal that "the requests of our farming friends are too radical to stand the test of discussion and have no chance of being adopted in the east".[12]

But there was one point, the point most discussed at the mid-December confrontation between the farmers and the government, where diplomatic and political advantage neatly converged: reciprocity. Free trade, freer trade, or some other formula for surmounting the North American tariff barrier, had always been a part of Liberal lexicon, even if it had had more rhetorical than practical support during the party's decade and a half occupancy of the government benches. To satisfy both President Taft and Canadian farmers with one stroke of the diplomatic pen would be sheer political genius. Borden's party would be crushed again; it might even collapse completely under the weight of its own dissension. And the Liberals could go on, well—perhaps forever! When Fielding and William Paterson, the Minister of Customs, went to Washington early in January 1911, to resume negotiations with the United States, they had just such visions in their minds.

They were back in two weeks, looking obviously pleased with themselves. An American negotiator had let it be known on January 18 that there was an agreement "satisfactory to both countries". But the government kept its counsel for days amidst increasing mystery and anticipation in Ottawa. Then, on the 26th, the Finance Minister revealed his secret to a hushed, expectant House of Commons. That there was an agreement came as no surprise. That it would be effected not by treaty, but by concurrent legislation did. More astonishing was the scope of the concord. Fielding droned on through the dreary language of his resolutions, as if he would never stop. There was going to be free trade in natural products, a huge list from "poultry, dead or alive" through "asbestos not further manufactured than ground" to "fish-oil, whale-oil, seal-oil and fish of all kinds". There would be identical lower duties on another long list of processed and manufactured products including food stuffs, farm implements, and motor vehicles. And there was still more. The United States would grant special customs rates on a select list of Canadian goods including aluminum and iron ore and Canada would give lowered rates to a similar list of American exports. At last Fielding was done. Throughout, the House had been silent, clearly stunned by the magnitude, some Conservatives thought the enormity, of it all. He resumed his chair beside Laurier and, as the Montreal *Herald* reported, "the Liberals cheered and cheered again".[13]

Across the aisle, Borden had listened to Fielding with growing concern. He had not expected anything like this. After all, a temporary reciprocity agreement the preceding year, made to avoid the necessity of applying discriminatory duties to Canadian imports by the United States, had been limited to a few token items like photographs and prunes. He anticipated the new arrangement would go further, but not much. But as he listened, as the items on the free list and the reduced duty schedule accumulated, as the economic benefits to Canadian farmers, miners, lumbermen, fishermen, and consumers and even some manufacturers grew and grew, one after another of his arguments vanished. When he rose to reply he was deliberately brief. Like everyone else, he expressed his amazement at the scope of the agreement. He, for one, did not like it. Its implementation by concurrent legislation made it inherently indefinite and hence disruptive to business and trade regularity. Moreover, the trade agreement was unnecessary; domestic political pressures upon President Taft were so strong that the Americans would soon have to make the same concessions to Canada, whether or not Canada gave up anything in return. His party's policy was for "reciprocity within the British Empire", for fiscal freedom, for freedom from "all entangling treaties or alliances or understandings".[14] And that was all.

This was not a moment for commitment. Rather it was a time to gather his forces, to assess the impact of Fielding's shattering blow upon them. At a hastily called caucus the following morning he found his troops in despair. "There was the deepest dejection in our party, and many of our members were confident that the Government's proposals would appeal to the country and give it another term of office."[15]

The despair so evident in the caucus was not echoed in other Conservative circles. There was neither doubt nor dejection in Winnipeg. The day before Fielding's dramatic announcement Borden had asked Robert Rogers to send him his immediate reaction to the news. "Hon. Bob" knew an election issue when he saw one. "A severe blow has been struck at our Canadian National development," he wired on the morning Borden's caucus met in gloomy conclave. Reciprocity sacrificed the Imperial preference, impaired Canadian commercial independence; it was a "departure from Imperialism to continentalism".[16] In short, Laurier had issued a call to battle. Premier Whitney's message was similar. He had long thought that the Liberal governments in both Ottawa and London were opposed "to what I call sane Imperialism". Reciprocity was the final proof of the Laurier government's anti-imperialist, indeed, anti-nationalist attitude. Whitney believed Fielding was the worst of the lot, he "has never been loyal to Confederation", his vision limited to "the desirability of getting a hake of fish and a bag of potatoes into the Boston market on the most favourable terms".[17] Whitney's advice was indirect, but clear enough. The Conservatives should rally round the flag.

Borden was still hesitant. He agreed that reciprocity would "destroy the whole meaning of Confederation" but, at least in the short run, its economic benefits would go to a "considerable portion of the community".[18] Many of his men were going to be hard-pressed to oppose it. He thought they "should be at liberty to attack strongly in committee, letting the Government take responsibility in the end for the proposals".[19] He was not going to compromise further his party's unity by insisting on a common front until he had firmer evidence of reaction against reciprocity from the country.

Very soon there were signs that that might be the case. Some of his colleagues returned from the weekend in their constituencies with renewed heart. And Kemp reported from Toronto that "the best thinking people in the community—Bankers, and nearly everyone whom I have consulted who are in business in a large way, look at the question from the broad standpoint of our national existence. . . . Some of the strongest Liberals in this City would be willing to take almost any legitimate steps if they could prevent this Treaty [*sic*] coming into force."[20]

A line of attack was gradually emerging. The agreement itself would be challenged, but the full assault would be on its inner meaning, its apparent threat to nationhood and the imperial connection. The appeal would be to loyalty, to patriotism, and to support from an indignant business community. The first theme was clear in the resumed Parliamentary debate on February 9. All that was most meaningful to Canadians, all that the Fathers of Confederation had fought to establish, was threatened by this agreement, Borden told the House of Commons.[21] "We faced geography and distance and fought them to a standstill," Foster added a few days later. "The plains were shod with steel, the mountains tamed and tunnelled, our national arteries were filled with the rich blood of commerce, our industries grew, our workmen multiplied, our villages became towns and our towns became cities, with astonishing rapidity."[22] Was all this to be thrown away for a mess of Yankee pottage? The second theme was more delicate, more private. Courting the businessmen had to be done through discreet channels. Confident that Whitney would pass the message on, Borden told the Ontario Premier that "if the business interests of the country believe that this crisis can be met by a few casual meetings and an occasional vigorous protest, they are living in a fool's paradise. We have got to fight and fight hard."[23]

Laurier's support in the business community quickly disintegrated. One highlight of the revolt of the entrepreneurs was the publication of an anti-reciprocity manifesto by eighteen Toronto businessmen and financiers on February 20.[24] Another was the anti-reciprocity speeches of Liberal businessmen Clifford Sifton, William German, and Lloyd Harris in the House of Commons. Sifton set the tone for the campaign of the interests on the 28th. Their appeal would not be based on the presumed threat to their profits. Rather it was the anti-national and anti-imperial stance of the Laurier government which offended their sensibilities. Reciprocity was a blow to Canada, the Naval Act a threat to the Imperial connection. "Up to this present time we have been somewhat of a nuisance to the Empire," Sifton said,

> but now we come to a point where we may be of use to the Empire, when we can send men and ships if necessary, to her aid, then when we can be of some use to the Empire that gave us our liberty and our traditions of citizenship—at the first beckoning hand from Washington we turn to listen; the first time anyone beckons we turn from the path that leads to the centre of the Empire and take the path that leads to Washington. So far as I am concerned, I say, "Not for me".[25]

The next day Sifton, Lloyd Harris, Toronto lawyer Zebulon Lash, who headed the newly formed Canadian National League to propagandize against reciprocity, and Willison were in Borden's office. Harris, whose business interests included Massey-

Harris, Stelco, and a long list of other manufacturing, insurance, and financial concerns, had contacted Borden sometime before this and found the Conservative leader "afraid of the division in his own following, and disinclined to fight".[26] Harris had gone away to rally the "recalcitrant Liberals". Now he was back with the others, ready, as Willison politely put it in his notes of the meeting, "to arrange a basis of co-operation with Mr. Borden".

In return for the support they could command, the visitors asked Borden to agree to a number of conditions if he came to power. Proper representation should be given to Quebec and the Catholic Church, but Borden "should not be subservient to Roman Catholic influences in public policy or in the administration of patronage". Borden should resist American "encroachments" and "blandishments", conduct a "staunchly and definitely Canadian" fiscal policy and preserve the Imperial connection. Borden should consult Willison, Lash, and Sir Edmund Walker about his Cabinet in which "the views of those Liberals who may unite with Conservatives against the policy of Reciprocity" should be represented. The outside service should be brought under the Civil Service Commission, a Tariff Commission should be appointed, and the Department of Trade and Commerce reorganized under "a strong Minister without undue regard to party considerations". Finally, Borden should place in his Cabinet "a number of men of outstanding national reputation and influence in order to give confidence to the progressive elements of the country and strength and stability to the Government".[27]

Borden had no difficulty in concurring with these points. He himself had advocated identical positions on fiscal policy, the civil service, and a tariff commission many times. He had no sympathy with subservience to any religious interest, Catholic or Protestant, and that, too, was a matter of record. And what of the other matters, the really important aspects of the political deal? Did his agreement to consult two Liberals (Willison was a Conservative) about his Cabinet constitute an insidious alliance? Would his agreement to include "men of outstanding national reputation" from "outside Parliament" in his cabinet be part of a corrupt bargain? No. The rebelling Liberals had every right to expect to be consulted in return for their support. And Borden would have been incredibly inept, incredibly naive about the strength of his backbenchers, if he did not consider appointing outsiders of national influence to his Cabinet. He was neither. To the conditions, then, he pledged "to use every possible endeavour to give them effect". He even went further; he would step down if another leader would be more effective.[28] But Sifton, who spoke for the visitors, would have none of it.[29]

There was just one more matter to tidy up to seal the Conservative party's alliance with the business community. Kemp wrote in early March expressing concern over talk among Conservatives about "increasing the British Preference". The businessmen wanted no more of Borden's "reciprocity within the Empire" than they did of Laurier's reciprocity with the United States. "There can be no good reason advanced for such action," Kemp warned. "Such a movement would have a further unsettled effect upon business." Borden replied immediately: "I do not think you will hear anything of that kind."[30]

The Leader of the Opposition announced his policy to the House of Commons on March 8. "Take the Census, give the West its increased representation, then submit this question to the people of Canada and let them decide." By then Roblin and McBride had carried anti-reciprocity resolutions in their legislatures. And soon nearly every provincial Assembly was debating reciprocity. Expectedly, Whitney got a 74 to 17 vote against the agreement in mid-March and Hazen brought up the rear of the Conservative provincial parade in early April. The Liberals got pro-reciprocity resolutions through the Nova Scotia, Prince Edward Island, and Saskatchewan houses.[31] In Saskatchewan the vote was unanimous, much to Borden's embarrassment and anger. Haultain made a vigorous speech in favour of reciprocity, breaking a promise he had given to Rogers the preceding day to "make his [anti-reciprocity] resolution as strong as possible".[32]

Reciprocity became the dominate subject of debate in the House of Commons. The parties pledged to fight out Fielding's resolutions to the bitter end. The members divided their time between bi-partisan condemnation of annexationist utterances by American statesmen in the concurrent debate in Congress and partisan shafts of fiery rhetoric at their opponents across the aisle. Borden threatened to hold up supply. Laurier countered by proposing to cancel his trip to the Coronation and Imperial Conference. Finally the Grits accepted a two-month adjournment for Sir Wilfrid to go to London and the Tories allowed a supply vote to pass covering the government's expenses until September. Buoyed up by what he considered a tactical victory, Borden decided to take his message to the enemy's country. He would use the adjournment for a tour of the prairie provinces.

Borden left Ottawa on June 16 with Perley, Bergeron, Broder, and Middlebro. Crothers and Ontario MPP Hugh Clark would join them at Sudbury; Roche, W. D. Staples, and the eager MP from Portage, Arthur Meighen, in Winnipeg.[33] Sir Thomas Shaughnessy had agreed to provide "free special service to the same amount of mileage Sir Wilfrid had [last year]" on the Canadian Pacific and in Winnipeg Rogers had arranged that a fleet of luxurious Canadian Northern lounge, sleeping, and dining cars would be added to the train.[34] As the train wound around the sharp curves of the Superior shore Borden recast again and again the paragraphs of his message to the west.

At Winnipeg Rogers and Roblin pulled out all the stops for their leader's reception. There were four bands, 186 automobiles, brilliant illuminations, and an "enormous" crowd for the welcoming procession.[35] Borden, Perley, Bergeron, and Crothers stayed at Roger's "most beautiful" home, Incherra, where the Manitoba Minister of Public Works arranged a huge reception for the leader. And Rogers was in the Chair at the Walker Theatre when Borden rose to give his first speech on the 19th.

It was one of the best of his career. He faced a skeptical audience, little impressed by the showmanship of the Manitoba Tory machine, doubtful that Borden had anything to match Laurier's reciprocity agreement. Laurier had offered them a Yankee bargain. Borden would not do that. He would give them "state control and operation" of terminal elevators, "aid and encouragement by the State" of the chilled meat industry, a government-constructed and -owned Hudson's Bay Railway operated by an independent commission, a permanent Tariff Commission, provincial control of public lands and natural resources in the prairie provinces, and the long desired extension of Manitoba's boundaries. In effect, Laurier had responded to the farmers' demands of last December with reciprocity alone. He would give them more; all they asked, except reciprocity and an increased British preference. There were many reasons why Borden could not give them reciprocity. But in the end they all boiled down to this: "it will lead to Commercial Union and Commercial Union will inevitably end in political absorption."[36]

Over and over again Borden repeated his pledges, in major speeches in large cities and in small towns, in crisp sentences at innumerable five-minute whistle stops. Over and over again, like Laurier a year before, he was met by stern delegations of farmers, their passionate petitions fired by the righteousness of their cause. Borden listened patiently to the interminable rhetorical denunciations of greedy-handed manufacturers and rapacious eastern interests. Only once did he reply sharply. At Macleod he told the Grain Growers that their address was couched "in a lecturing tone which might have been omitted".[37] But he never wavered in his answer. The farmers had their convictions about reciprocity; he had his, and he would no more budge than they. "If you had 60 per cent of the votes of Canada in your right hand and offered to make me Prime Minister to-morrow I would not support it."[38] Unlike Laurier, he did not think their other demands were "too radical"; they would have his support. But not reciprocity.

The seemingly endless processions, banquets, petitions, and speeches were part of every tour. But this journey was somehow different. Borden had always dreaded these affairs. But this time he was truly enjoying himself. He responded to the crowds with a sense of confidence and enthusiasm that his colleagues had seldom seen before. His letters to Laura were spirited, optimistic; there was scarcely a hint of the self-pity which was so characteristic of his correspondence when they were separated. Certainly the splendid facilities Rogers had provided helped. On the train he did not isolate himself in the seclusion of his room. The travelling Tories relaxed in the lounge car. There was plenty of talk, good men's talk, a hilarious, slightly-off-colour story from Bergeron or Broder, a not-quite-believable tale by Perley about his fishing prowess or the one that got away from Borden at Echo Beach. When they got round to politics, the leader's confidence was infectious. As the train turned back toward the east at the end of June, the "boys" were convinced they had a winning issue, perhaps even in the west. The farmer leaders were "in league with" and "possibly" in the pay of Laurier's government, but all the Tories were impressed by the honesty and sincerity of the ordinary farmers. When they got back to Ottawa they were determined to force an election.[39]

The session reconvened on July 18 for ten more days of recrimination and partisan posturing. On the 24th Sir Wilfrid announced that "it was Reciprocity or nothing at this Session". Suddenly, on Saturday, the 29th, the eleventh Parliament was dissolved. "This is going to be a good hard fight," Borden hurriedly wrote to Whitney. "I feel even more convinced than ever that it involves the British connection and the future destiny of this country. I do hope you will make this fight your own in Ontario."[40]

The prospect of power brought the Parliamentary party together. Both the English and French-speaking Conservatives eagerly joined the fight against Laurier's trade agreement. But even the chance to end a decade and a half of Grit rule was not enough to dispel all the factional feuds among the MP's. Some of Borden's strongest defenders at the show-down caucus in April 1910, the old party regulars, had been deeply offended by his reorganization of the Parliamentary party in November. The veterans felt that they had been cast aside, as indeed they had, that Borden had given the key positions in the Parliamentary party structure to younger men who were admittedly close to the leader but who were bumbling amateurs at the game of politics. Sam Hughes gave a typically colourful account of the sentiments of the old hands. Borden is "a most lovely fellow; very capable, but not a very good judge of men or tactics; and is gentle hearted as a girl," he wrote. Perley's appointment as Chief Whip and Ames as organizer had been "galling" to men like "Doc" Reid, Billy Northrup, and William Price—himself a junior MP but very close to the regulars and a key figure in the organization of the Quebec district. That powerful trio "have more brains and organizational power in five minutes, than such fellows would have in a lifetime," Hughes said. Perley, Ames, and Crothers were "d—— noodles". Nor was that all. J. S. Carstairs, Borden's appointee as Ontario organizer, was a "featherheaded fellow"; Hughes would not let him set foot in his riding.[41]

Hughes would complain—he usually did about one thing or another—but he had one virtue some of the regulars did not; he was totally committed in his loyalty to Borden. The others brooded, bided their time, anticipating another maladroit move by the leader. They did not have long to wait. Word of the March 1 meeting with Sifton, Harris, Lash, and Willison soon leaked out and they were furious. A deal with any Grits was bad enough but—God forbid!—Borden had combined forces with the most hated of all the enemy, Clifford Sifton. "Many of the Conservatives are frantic at the prospect of their funds being managed by Sifton & not by themselves," C. F. Hamilton reported.[42]

Incredibly, just at the moment when the party had its first real chance to gain power, the malcontents again challenged Borden's leadership. They denounced his agreement with the Liberals. At a stormy caucus they forecast the destruction of the party. Borden, as in 1910, again appeared to offer the leadership to McBride. McBride, probably by a pre-arrangement with Borden, again refused.[43] Borden also arranged for Crothers to meet Whitney in Toronto, apparently with a request from the insurgents that the Ontario Premier assume the leadership, or at least enter the federal party. Whitney was not in the least interested. After all, he told Borden, as far as the leadership question was concerned, "I am one at least of those who are responsible for your remaining at your post".[44]

Borden again threatened to resign, letting his intentions be known to "two or three intimate friends", probably Perley and Ames. Perley quickly rallied the troops. A round-robin begging the leader to stay at his post was presented to Borden on March 28. Sixty-five members signed the petition, including most of the old time Tories, despite their worries over the deal with Sifton. Twenty did not. Of them, Borden later wrote that Sam Barker, Andrew Broder, George Gordon, and Arthur Meighen were unquestionably loyal but out of town. The hard core of dissent was again made up of the French Canadians, Blondin, Rodolph Forget, Girard, Lortie, Monk, and Nantel. Their English-speaking allies were led by Reid, Northrup, and Price. Again they were beaten back, intimidated by the display of loyalty to the leader in the round-robin. "Price and Reid are very frightened," wrote Hamilton. "Price was declaring 'Whatever fault there is it is all mine!' "[45]

The reciprocity issue was the opportunity for the Conservative provincial premiers to redouble their efforts on Borden's behalf. Neither Whitney nor McBride nor Roblin, all of whom had been asked at one time or another during the early months of 1911, were willing to join him in Ottawa. But within their own domains all three, and even Hazen in his peculiarly lethargic way, used their enormous political resources to support him. For all of them reciprocity was but the latest manifestation of a greater malady, Laurierism and the growing power of the central government. Each had provincial interests to defend and enhance. None had found Laurier co-operative. McBride had been campaigning against Laurier's government for "better terms" for years. Similarly, Roblin demanded an extension of Manitoba's boundaries and Whitney wanted to implement new federal-provincial cost-sharing programs with Ottawa. Borden's strong advocacy of provincial rights throughout his years as Opposition leader held out the promise of a new deal in federal-provincial relations, a better deal for the Conservative provincial premiers. Moreover, each of the Tory premiers was a stout defender of what Whitney called "sane imperialism". On that score Laurier was unquestionably weak. His "tin pot" navy was an insult to their concept of a proper imperial relationship and they would have rejoiced had he been turned out on the issue. Reciprocity gave them the occasion to marshall their forces against Laurier that the navy question had not afforded.

The dissolution of Parliament at the end of July was a formality. In fact, the Conservatives' election machinery was well oiled and ready to go long before the dissolution. As one New Brunswick MP put it, "I came away from Ottawa on the adjournment . . . with the feeling that the election would be won or lost during the vacation".[46] While Borden was touring the west, his followers were hard at work on electoral organization.

The most reluctant support came from Hazen's government in New Brunswick. Hazen was the last of the Tory premiers to put an anti-reciprocity vote through his legislature. Later, during the election campaign, he found it convenient to stay out of the fight until the last moment when he put in a token appearance with Borden. His "Provincial Organization Committee" decided in May to give its blessing to, but remain "entirely independent" from federal election organizational work.[47] Borden tried to inject some power into the New Brunswick campaign by persuading Sir Max Aitken to run in Northumberland. Sir Max refused, but did contribute handsomely to the campaign with $10,000 for Northumberland and another $16,000 for use elsewhere.[48]*

The reason for Hazen's reticence was quite simple and a good

*"I think I am the most traduced person to the square mile in all Canada," Aitken told Hazen. "Living in Montreal, with interests in Ontario, a power plant in Calgary, another in Vancouver, born in New Brunswick, and having resided in Nova Scotia, I was deluged with demands."

illustration of the workings of Maritime politics. Hazen was not going to bet his own prestige and the power of his provincial organization on a losing horse. Only when he was convinced that he had a sure winner would he back Borden. Even then he demanded his pound of flesh, exacting a promise from Borden of a railway subsidy for his St. John Valley line.[49] The MP for York, O. S. Crocket, was quite frank about the whole matter. "It is very difficult here to get even party men active until they see an election actually in sight," he wrote in June, "and it is simply out of the question to get any enthusiasm unless some prospect of victory throughout the country is visible."[50] In the end William Price, who was also busily engaged with organization in Quebec, assisted Crocket with the organization of the party in New Brunswick.[51]

In British Columbia, McBride's response was very different. "Our organization . . . is still in excellent shape," the British Columbia Premier assured Borden in June, "and I am satisfied that when the call comes it will be very well answered."[52] To ensure that nothing was left to chance, McBride's men got up an elaborate handbook for the faithful "to implement the Party's return to power, [and] to provide a permanent opportunity for the electorate to participate in its Country's Government".[53] When the election came on "the people's Dick" himself carried the Tory banner back and forth across the province from remote lumber camps to Vancouver's crowded city wards.

Similarly, the whole weight of the Roblin government in Manitoba was thrown into the fight. As soon as he returned from the Coronation, Roblin went on the stump. For him it was a very personal fight, a fight not only for a concept of empire in which he deeply believed, but also for a proper settlement of Manitoba's boundary dispute with Ontario and Ottawa. "Every vote polled for a Laurier candidate is a vote polled to shackle Manitoba," he declared in late August.[54] He had already agreed to let the genius of his party organization, Robert Rogers, apply his full talents to the federal campaign. In February Rogers had been in Montreal lining up Sir Hugh Graham's support.[55] He was back again in March and in April Borden informed him that Price "is very desirous of getting in touch with you without delay".[56] In Manitoba itself Rogers signed up the civil service manpower of the government for the duration.

Whitney, too, gave all that was in his power. Despite the

formalities of separate federal and provincial organizations in Ontario, in the constituencies, where it counted, the party worked as one. J. D. "Doc" Reid was given responsibility for twenty some ridings in eastern Ontario and had them well in hand before dissolution.[57] A. E. Kemp, whose pocketbook had kept the Ontario organization alive since 1908, headed the Ontario campaign until ill health forced him to step down just before dissolution. Then Frank Cochrane, Whitney's Minister of Lands and Forests and a man whose appreciation of the subtleties of political arrangements was as keen as Roger's, took over.[58]

Whitney and Borden kept a sharp eye on the work of their lieutenants. There was a brief disagreement in mid-April when Whitney discovered that J. S. Carstairs, Borden's appointee as secretary-organizer of the federal organization, had been lining up his backbenchers to run as federal candidates. "During the past year I have spoken to him several times on the subject objecting strongly to his tampering with these men without first consulting me on the subject," Whitney wrote. Borden quickly instructed Carstairs and other organizers that they must approach MPP's who were potential candidates through Whitney. He did tell the Premier, however, that there were several ridings which could be carried by a number of men for the provincial house but which only the strongest man in the riding, who might be the MPP, could carry federally. "I have always understood that in such case you were perfectly willing that such an arrangement might be made as to the candidature that the riding could be carried for the party in both cases."[59] The misunderstanding quickly passed and the federal and provincial Tories in Ontario settled down to the business of dishing the Grits. Borden, much to Whitney's delight, arranged a tour at which the Premier would be the star attraction—"there should be no other speaker except perhaps the Provincial Member and the Conservative candidate".[60] And Cochrane urged Borden to try to get Adam Beck to take a personal hand in the defeat of Mackenzie King in Waterloo North.[61]

In the remaining English-speaking provinces Conservative prospects varied. There Laurier had sympathetic provincial government machines. But by August Blount, who was looking after Maritime political affairs for Borden, thought the outlook in Atlantic Canada was "very good".[62] No one held out much hope for success in Saskatchewan and Alberta. In the former province, as the editor of the *Canadian Annual Review* observed, "the Conservative struggle . . . was not an organized effort". Haultain's pro-reciprocity speech had dashed Tory spirits and his later recantation, his appearance on the platform with Borden at Regina, and his speeches against reciprocity in August were to no avail. In Alberta Charlie Magrath in Medicine Hat and W. A. Griesbach in Edmonton put up strong fights, but the main party effort was to elect R. B. Bennett in Calgary.[63]

In Quebec the provincial organizers were profoundly discouraged. "The one black spot is the position in this blessed Province. Monk has again put us into a most horrible mess," wrote William Price.

> He has made a definite alliance with Bourassa and the Nationalists, and this new combination is calling itself an Independent Conservative Party, under the leadership of Monk. They will not be able to obtain much funds for organization, but they will, at any rate, take several seats from the Liberals.
>
> I was up in Montreal on Tuesday last and Judge Doherty and I tried to arrive at an understanding with Monk and he is to let us know today or tomorrow what can be done, but personally I feel sure that nothing will come of it. At any rate if we are lucky we should return about ten English Conservatives this time which, with Forget, and possibly one or two other French Conservatives that we can rely on to stand solidly, may be sufficient to pull through.[64]

That was the situation in a nutshell. The English-speaking Conservatives and a few French Canadians with traditional sympathies fought one campaign. Monk and Bourassa fought another. Both groups desperately wanted to defeat Laurier in his home province. Beyond that, they had little in common. Borden stayed out of the province, neither blessing nor condemning either group publicly.*

The alliance had been long in the making. It was firmly rooted in the opposition of Monk and Bourassa to Liberal party power in Ottawa and Quebec City. It was nourished by their common opposition to the naval policies of both Laurier and Borden. Both men shared an alienation from power and influence in regular

---

*Significantly, there is no mention of the Monk–Bourassa alliance in his discussion of the election of 1911 in Borden's *Memoirs*.

party affairs. Despite Monk's opposition to reciprocity, he had not been reconciled to his party. "Je sens ma solitude de plus en plus," he told Bourassa in February. And he thoroughly disapproved of the deal with Sifton. "Il se passe ici des manigances que je ne comprends pas parfaitment," he reported, "mais que ne me disent rien de bon." It was just Borden up to his old tricks again, a repeat of the Tarte and Blair affairs.[65]

The extent of Conservative support for the Monk–Bourassa alliance is not clear and may never be known. In so far as it would take votes and seats away from Laurier it was certainly welcomed by the party hierarchy. The alliance did not receive official endorsement by the party. Bourassa later claimed that it did receive financial support from Sir Hugh Graham.[66] Charles Murphy, Secretary of State in the Laurier Government, reported that Bourassa "had a long conversation with Borden" on May 18 and charged that Bourassa was going to use an increase in the capital stock of his publishing company, approved by the Laurier government, against the Grits. "My information," Murphy told Laurier, "is that the additional $200,000 of stock will be largely subscribed for by our opponents, who have taken this means of assisting the most active agency against us in Quebec."[67]

Borden indeed may have seen Bourassa on May 18 and have given his private blessing to the alliance with Monk. That Borden had welcomed and encouraged support from Bourassa in the past is beyond doubt. He and Bourassa were equally convinced— though not for entirely the same reasons—that Laurier had to go. And Borden could have thought that the link with Bourassa through Monk would be just as rewarding a marriage of convenience as his agreement with Sifton. He probably recognized that the alliance could spell trouble if he came to power. But that was in the future. The immediate objective was to get Laurier out of office. For that purpose Bourassa could be a most potent ally.

If Bourassa was an ally not entirely to be trusted, the manufacturers were like wayward sons returned. They had been encouraged to affluence by the party and its National Policy. In the lean years of opposition they had wandered to sup in the tents of the Liberals. Now their ever easy equation of self-interest with national interest drove them back home. They received a cordial welcome and they responded with a determination to put their patrons back in power.

The most interesting manifestation of business support came

from the "non-partisan" Canadian Manufacturers' Association. In March the CMA's Tariff Committee, chaired by T. A. Russell, established a Tariff Educational Fund. Members of the Association were asked to subscribe annual pledges for three years to the fund whose treasurer was the Assistant Secretary of the CMA, H. D. Scully. The money was to be "used in conducting a non-partisan tariff educational campaign among all classes of Canadian citizens" and articles were to be prepared with a special emphasis upon the benefits of protection to Canadian farmers.[68] In April the Fund committee, during a meeting in Montreal, took the name of the Canadian Home Market Association. Its executive committee was chaired by Russell and the other members were G. E. Drummond, A. E. Kemp, W. K. George, R. Hobson, Paul Galibert, and J. H. Sherrard. Norman Lambert, a staff writer with the *Globe* who was already preparing anti-reciprocity articles for the committee, was named secretary.[69]

The manufacturers contributed handsomely to the "educational fund". In mid-May the annual subscriptions were listed as $23,500. By the end of the month the fund had grown to $28,000 and only seven of the firms contacted had refused to contribute. In August the secretary reported that $15,000 had been received from the CMA itself, that $40,000 had been pledged on an annual basis, that only one-third of the members had yet been canvassed and that by January the CHMA could expect an annual contribution of $100,000.[70]

The articles prepared for the Canadian Home Market Association ranged from "The Barley Question" and "Farmer Jones and his City Partners" to "The Repatriation of French Canadians". They were distributed through the Canadian National League, the vigorous propaganda organization headed by Zebulon Lash, and by use of various corporate and political mailing lists.* Abbreviated versions of papers, edited by Lambert and Professor Stephen Leacock of McGill, were given to printing companies which then supplied "ready press service" or "boiler plate" distribution to literally hundreds of country weeklies. Contracts were made with the British Colonial Press Agency for 140 country weeklies, with Toronto Type Foundry for 239 western country

*The T. Eaton Company refused to give its mailing list to the CHMA. Apparently one list was acquired from Massey-Harris and Kemp arranged access to voting lists from the Conservative party.

papers, with Publishers Press Ltd. for Maritime and Quebec (French) weeklies, and with Wilson Publishing Company for 200 Ontario papers. In addition, the CHMA gave large financial support to a number of popular journals including *Bullman's Magazine*, whose name was changed to *Western Canadian Country Life*, *The Dominion*, *Canadian Century*, and *Country Life in Canada*. By late August the CHMA had distributed nearly nine and one-half million copies of its material and was sending out twenty thousand items a day.[71]

Every effort was made to keep the work of the CHMA out of the public's eye. Initially, Kemp was so secretive about his involvement with the organization that he wrote darkly to Borden of "another organization . . . the details of which I cannot go into with you".[72] But in July he privately arranged a meeting between Scully and Borden, explaining that the members of the CHMA were "largely liberals" and that Scully might be able to assist in raising campaign funds.[73] Complaints within the CHMA about issuing material anonymously led to a decision to publish its pamphlets under the name of the Canadian National League. By July the CHMA made a pretence of a separate existence. It had its own office and letterhead, the latter with Scully simply listed as secretary. The Executive Committee was constantly worried that its activities would be "traced back to the CMA" and agreed "the details of the operations of the committee . . . did not concern the public and they should be withheld".[74]

The subterranean work of the Canadian Home Market Association complemented the open co-operation between anti-reciprocity businessmen and the Conservative party. Most striking was the support the party received from prominent Liberal businessmen. Borden encouraged them all, but Whitney advised him to pay particular attention to one man. He was W. T. White, the prominent young Toronto financier, generally regarded as an up-and-coming figure in Canadian business, a man without strong attachments to either party but a signer of the Toronto Eighteen's manifesto. All that was needed was a word from Borden and "he will be ready to take the stump. If so, he will be a very valuable assistant indeed—perhaps the best in the ranks of our Grit friends," Whitney wrote.[75] Within days White had been contacted and had joined the team. The organizational effort had been completed and the battle begun.

The election of 1911 was a classic political confrontation. The Liberals saw it as a contest between Borden and the business interests and Laurier and the people and they did their best to exploit the "unholy alliance" between Borden and Bourassa. A Bengough cartoon in the Toronto *Globe* on September 18 pictured Bourassa entertaining two attractive misses, Tory Party and Nationalist Party. His feet were firmly planted on the Union Jack, his coat was decorated with fleur-de-lis, and he manipulated a tiny wooden puppet—Borden—with a string labelled "anti-British". Laurier himself bemoaned his fate as the master of political accommodation: "In Quebec I am branded as a Jingo and in Ontario as a separatist. In Quebec I am attacked as an Imperialist and in Ontario as an anti-Imperialist. I am neither. I am a Canadian."[76] Quebec Nationalists had a different perception of the issues in the election. They distrusted the imperialist designs of both parties. But more important, they waged a bitterly personal campaign against Sir Wilfrid Laurier, against the corruption of his government, against what they believed to be his vacillation in the protection of the values and rights of French Canada.[77] On August 2 Bourassa demanded the election of "men of honour and men of their word" to "settle the vital problems of the nation, which are Canadian autonomy, the preservation of national unity and the rights of minorities".[78] Finally, the Conservatives quickly identified the election as a struggle between those who would preserve nation and Empire and those who would not. "We are face to face with the fight of 1891 but under circumstances of greater difficulty," Borden wrote.[79] As he put it in his final campaign speech, the issue was quite simple: "We must decide whether the spirit of Canadianism or of Continentalism shall prevail on the northern half of this continent."[80] There was a bit of truth, and an abundance of rhetorical hyperbole, in each of these impressions.

Laurier had the advantage of being in office. As in all his previous electoral battles with Borden, he had the weight of power and patronage on his side. He could expect substantial assistance from five well-established provincial Liberal governments including that of his home province. In Quebec, Bourassa, with Conservative backing, might be a serious threat, but not enough to undermine Laurier's mastery of Quebec federal politics. And Laurier did have a very popular campaign issue. Reciprocity might have been a time-worn solution to the ever-changing problem of trade relations with the United States, but

the very intensity of the anti-reciprocity campaign by the Conservatives and the businessmen demonstrated its appeal as a
vote-catcher for the Liberals. Last, but far from the least of the
Prime Minister's advantages, was his very great personal prestige.
Sir Wilfrid was the architect of twentieth-century Canada. He
still seemed the very personification of a prosperous and confident nation.

But beneath the surface of the Liberal party was a creaking
worn out party machine. In the Maritimes the deft hands of
Fielding and Sir Frederick Borden had kept the party in good
repair. The west, however, was no longer the exclusive preserve
of the Grits; Roblin and McBride had seen to that. And in Ontario,
so often the key province in federal elections, the party was
deeply divided. Sir Allen Aylesworth, old, tired, and painfully
aware of his weakness, was but a token leader. In 1910 Newton
Rowell, the provincial party leader, had warned the Prime
Minister that the situation was desperate, that Liberals would
not follow Aylesworth's hesitant, ineffective lead.[81] And it was in
Ontario that a firm hand was most imperative. In Ontario
reciprocity posed the gravest threat to established interests.
Neither its truck garden farmers nor its fruit-growers liked the
trade agreement. If the Conservatives would be believed, its
growing industrialized towns and cities were in peril. There too,
the full weight of the manufacturers' propaganda campaign was
impressed on the voters. And behind the scenes the truly great
political strategists of the era, Sifton and Silent Frank Cochrane,
with an occasional helping hand from "Hon. Bob", quietly went
about their business.

The party leaders played out their accustomed, ritualized roles.
Neither Borden nor Laurier went to the west, the seedbed of the
demand for reciprocity that now sent them from city to town to
farmyard to speak with ever-more raspy voices of the virtues of
their program and party. The Governor General reported that
both parties were confident of victory; the Liberals expecting a
majority of twenty and "Conservative wire pullers" predicting a
gain of thirty to thirty-five seats.[82] Borden wrote enthusiastically
about the great crowds and warm welcomes which greeted him
in Ontario.[83] He had issued his platform on August 14. Included
were the promises he had made to western farmers in June. He
added pledges of assistance to provincial governments for agricultural education, subsidies for public highways, extension of
rural mail delivery, and civil service reform. He ended with a

vague reference to a policy in foreign relations which "will find its highest ideal in the autonomous development of Canada as a nation within the British Empire". Significantly, there was no mention of naval policy.[84]

Two days later, in London, he took up that contentious subject. Talk of an emergency contribution was carefully put in the past tense now: "We believed that the Empire was confronted by a grave emergency and we urged immediate and effective aid." Any permanent naval policy developed by his government would be "submitted to the people for their approval". On August 23, W. T. White, R. S. Gourlay, and W. K. George shared the platform with him at Massey Hall. Borden had warm words for the Grit businessmen. "They are entitled to just recognition as men who have stood shoulder to shoulder with us in this fight to prevent a national disaster." In Montreal, a week later, Doherty, Bergeron, Marechal, G. F. Johnston, and Charles Cahan were with him. Monk and Bourassa were conspicuous by their absence. Borden then made a quick two-day dash through the eastern townships into the Maritimes, giving Quebec pointedly less attention than he had on any previous tour since he had become party leader. Hazen was briefly at his side in Prince Edward Island and Sir Charles Hibbert Tupper joined him for a great meeting in Halifax on September 12. By the 19th the tour was over.[85] On the 21st the people cast their ballots for "Canadianism" or "continentalism".

The jubilation in Halifax party headquarters that night was unbounded. The parties had split Nova Scotia and the Island, each winning nine and two seats respectively. In New Brunswick the Tories won five and Grits eight—all in all a very respectable showing of sixteen Conservatives from the Maritimes. From Quebec came even better news, an increase from eleven to twenty-seven seats. It was true that many of the Quebec seats had been won by Monk and Bourassa rather than by Borden, but that problem could be dealt with in due time. Late in the evening an astonished Borden learned that Whitney, Kemp, White, Sifton, and Cochrane had done their work with unprecedented thoroughness. No less than seventy-three of eighty-six Ontario constituencies had returned Conservative majorities. Later still the leader was informed that Roblin and McBride had also fulfilled their promises. All seven B.C. seats went Conservative as did eight of Manitoba's ten. One additional member each from Alberta, Saskatchewan, and the Yukon gave Borden a margin of 134 Conservatives to 87 Liberals. Seven of Laurier's Ministers had been defeated including Fielding and Sir Frederick Borden in Nova Scotia and William Paterson, George Graham, and Mackenzie King in Ontario. The key to the victory was the campaign of the politicians and the businessmen in Ontario. Their work resulted in an amazing 56.2 per cent of the popular vote going to Borden's party. In Quebec the party's percentage of the popular vote rose from 40.8 in 1908 to 48.1 in 1911 and in British Columbia from 46.8 per cent to 58.8 per cent. Across the nation the Conservatives had earned a majority of the popular vote for the first time since 1891. It was very much like Macdonald's last great victory. But in Halifax that night there was no time for reflection amidst the handshakes, the cheers, the shouts of joy, the tumult of victory.

Ten and a half years before, Robert Borden had assumed the leadership of the Liberal-Conservatives of Canada. At the time they had been a weak, disheartened and confused band of men with little common purpose. Borden had suffered many defeats and countless humiliations during his decade as leader of the Opposition. Slowly he had established his leadership of the party, only to see it challenged just months before his moment of triumph. Twice he had been beaten in general elections by Laurier. But in the process he had matured as a politician. After 1905, when he gave up his law practice, he had devoted all his time, his energy, his patience, to building a strong party, effective in Parliament and commanding broad support across the country. He had won the confidence of the powerful Conservative provincial premiers and gone some way towards giving the federal party an effective organizational foundation.

Throughout the years his most persistent problem had been holding the total loyalty of his colleagues from Quebec. He had not succeeded, but neither had he driven them from the fold. Many of his English-Canadian followers had repeatedly urged him to have done with Monk and the other French-Canadian MP's. A complete break with Monk would have been neater and much less taxing on Borden's limited reserve of tact than a continued effort at an uneasy compromise between the demands of his French- and English-Canadian followers. But Borden had chosen a more constructive course. On certain questions, like the naval issue, he and Monk had finally agreed to disagree, and to publicly acknowledge their differences, without destroying the Conservative party. The result was the informal "unholy alliance" with Monk and Bourassa in the 1911 election. The alliance more than doubled his Quebec representation in the House of Commons.

Men as different as the calculating Liberal businessman-politician, Lloyd Harris, and the temperamental professional parliamentarian, Sam Hughes, interpreted Robert Borden's deliberate caution as evidence of weakness and indecision. But Borden's caution and persistence had kept him in the party leadership and was the key to the elaborate coalition of parliamentarians, provincial politicians, Quebec Nationalists and former Liberals he constructed and led to victory in 1911. His victory was evidence of the skill he had acquired as a political strategist and a vindication of his style of political leadership.

Even more skill, more persistence, would soon be demanded of him. He would have a dual accountability to his party and to his country. Shortly he would be called upon to form a government, to develop and implement policies and programs that would effect the lives of all Canadians. It was an awesome, almost frightening responsibility.

The day after the election Borden rose early and took the train to Grand Pré. A few hours later he stepped onto the station platform where his father had spent so many hours gaily trading tales with all who would listen. His beloved mother, now in her eighty-sixth year, met him at the station. Together they rode up the hill to his boyhood home. For a day or so he rested between visits from a stream of neighbours who came to pay their respects to the boy from the Valley who had become the nation's leader. His sister Julia was quite taken with the importance of the occasion and Rob had to remind her that just because he would be Canada's First Minister gave her no right to put on airs with the neighbours. The Bordens were still a humble farm family upon whom pretence sat uneasily. Still, there was no hiding of his mother's quiet pride. Eunice Borden had given her first born son a sense of ambition, a yearning for accomplishment in the world of men and affairs. He had succeeded beyond her fondest expectations. She hoped he could stay at home longer, to tell her more about the trials and rewards of a life she hardly comprehended. But he could not. Borden was needed in Ottawa.

CHAPTER TEN

KEEPING PROMISES

Borden's train arrived in Ottawa at noon on Sunday, September 24. He immediately went to Glensmere where, while Laura shielded him from well-wishers and colleagues, he thumbed through piles of congratulatory telegrams Blount had brought from the office. At tea they speculated on the changes high public office would bring in their life-style. Since their move to Ottawa Laura had taken an increasingly active role in the life of the nation's capital. In 1910 she had become President of the Ladies' Golf Club and she was Regent of the local chapter of the Daughters of the Empire, a Councillor of the Victorian Order of Nurses, and a Vice-President of the National Council of Women of Canada. As the wife of the Prime Minister designate, she expected even greater public demands upon her time. Robert anticipated, regretfully, that he would have fewer opportunities to slip away to the rustic fishing camp at Echo Beach for a few days of fly-fishing with his friend Perley. And they knew that they would be called upon to do much more entertaining both at home and at the Rideau Club or their golf club, the Royal Ottawa. Neither one relished the prospect of giving up more of their privacy, but it could not be avoided.

That was apparent the next morning when reporters began to gather at the gate at the end of the curved drive leading into Glensmere. For the next two weeks they would keep a constant vigil, noting the names of the important personages Borden summoned to his house for advice on appointments to his government. On Monday Borden kept pretty much to himself, thinking through the promises he had made to his supporters and the pledges he had made in his platform. Hundreds of hungry Conservatives had arrived in Ottawa seeking the luscious fruits of office and place. Many, indeed most, whose sudden loyalty and ardour for the Conservative cause was coincident with victory, could be safely ignored. But the men who had played a major part in fashioning his electoral triumph and his loyal colleagues in the caucus over so many years could not. Even their expectations could not all be met; some would not get the posts they wanted in the Cabinet, the demands for new legislative programs of others would have to be weighed in the delicate balance of political possibility and national responsibility.

On Tuesday the local faithful arranged a noisy joyful reception for their leader. A triumphal procession through the downtown streets was headed by Borden's carriage, pulled by an even hundred broad-shouldered Tories. With him rode the two local Members of Parliament, Doctor John L. Chabot, a prominent Ottawa surgeon, and Alfred E. Fripp, a popular lawyer who had resigned his seat in the Provincial Assembly and carried the federal riding with Chabot. But pride of place was reserved for George Perley, the only other MP in Borden's carriage. It was another sign of the close friendship of the two men, of Borden's trust in Perley's judgment and political ability. Borden enjoyed the celebration, the cheers that filled the air when he waved to the crowds lining the streets. It was the last care-free moment he would have for a long time.

He was already under pressure from the Governor General to move quickly in the selection of his Cabinet. Lord Grey was retiring and his successor, the Duke of Connaught, the uncle of King George V, was about to embark for Canada. Grey wanted to effect the transfer of power before Connaught's arrival.[1] Borden did his best to accommodate Grey's plans, but he could not be rushed. He moved deliberately, calling for those whose advice he needed and desired. One who was not summoned was George Foster who fumed at his absence from the inner circle. His exclusion, he thought, was a sure sign of Borden's indecisiveness. "B. doesn't know his mind from day to day," Foster wrote on Friday evening.[2]

What infuriated Foster was that so many others were being summoned to Wurtemburg Street. Whitney was the first with Monk quickly following.[3] By Saturday, September 30, Clifford Sifton had made a number of calls and was on his way to Toronto to consult Walker, Lash, and Willison. He carried with him a nearly complete list of proposed Cabinet appointments.[4] Willison was called to Ottawa on the following Tuesday.[5] By then many others had made their appearance or arranged to do so. "Hon. Bob" Rogers, Premier Hazen, E. B. Osler, Casgrain, Forget, and Armand Lavergne all offered advice. Henri Bourassa, despite his later claim to have "left for the country . . . to be disinfected", was in Ottawa over the weekend conferring with Monk.[6]

Borden's choices reflected the forces behind his electoral victory. First consideration was given to the provincial premiers, each of whom had a claim to a Cabinet seat if he wished it. Only Hazen accepted. As Minister of Marine, Fisheries and Naval Service, he and Borden represented the Maritime provinces.[7] Whitney, who was rumoured to have been offered the Justice portfolio,[8] preferred the security of provincial premiership to the vagaries of federal politics as did Roblin and McBride. Each named a willing and able surrogate to represent his interests in Ottawa.

Frank Cochrane, the Ontario Minister of Lands, Forests and Mines, had taken over the Ontario organization from Kemp and engineered the stunning sweep of the province in the election. He was a close confidant of the Premier and henceforth would be regarded—at least by Whitney—as "Whitney's man" in Ottawa.[9] "Silent Frank" was dramatically fetched by canoe from a holiday in Algonquin Park and rushed to Ottawa to accept the Ministry of Railways and Canals. That appointment was a disappointment to Roblin's designated spokesman, Robert Rogers. He very much wanted the patronage-rich Railways portfolio but had to accept a traditional western post, Minister of Interior. There was some compensation for the energetic Winnipegger, however. Interior was not quite as prestigious as Railways, but the Department was extremely complex and offered ample opportunity for the enthusiastic distribution of largesse.[10] Rogers' appointment was very controversial. Sir William Van Horne had told Borden that "Hon. Bob" was "well, decidedly not the man for a place in a Cabinet such as yours" and the ever pious Joseph Flavelle thought him "a politically immoral man".[11] Rogers' appointment would not bolster Borden's image as a champion of clean government. On the other hand, Rogers had the confidence of French-speaking Catholics in both Manitoba and Quebec and the support of influential party figures like William Price, John Willison, and Clifford Sifton. As Price so delicately put it, Rogers and Cochrane were "men who can do things". The other surrogate was quite different. Though no novice in the game of politics, Martin Burrell, McBride's man, was better known as an experienced agriculturalist, something of a scholar and writer, a charming and literate conversationalist. Borden first met him in 1902 and was immediately taken by his charm and intelligence. He had long been a link between McBride and Borden. Though seldom noticed by the public, he would be an effective and innovative Minister of Agriculture.

Sifton's trip to Toronto fulfilled Borden's pre-election commitment to consult with Walker, Lash, and Willison about Cabinet appointments. They would be interested in all the names on the list in Sifton's pocket. But Walker, the president of the Canadian Bank of Commerce, and Lash, a partner in the distinguished law firm of Blake, Lash, Anglin, and Cassels and chief counsel for the Bank of Commerce, the Canadian Bankers' Association and the Canadian Northern Railway, were especially interested in the Ministry of Finance. Borden and Sifton had already agreed that William Thomas White was the man for the job. While Sifton was in Toronto, Whitney, who had been instrumental in bringing White into the anti-reciprocity campaign, wrote to tell Borden that "if he should decline—it would be bad. I feel that he is the keystone of the arch."[12] Sifton reported back to Borden on Tuesday, October 3, that the others agreed. White was immediately summoned to the capital.

The young financier (he was 46) was a man of considerable talent. An honours graduate in classics at Toronto, he had gone on to be a scholarship winner and gold medallist at Osgoode Hall. He had tried his hand at poetry and published some undistinguished verse. Instead of practising law, after brief careers at the *Telegram* and in the city's Assessment Department, White had joined the National Trust Company. He had recently been promoted to the vice-presidency of that company and was recognized as one of the leading young men in the Canadian financial community. White had had no political experience but Borden persuaded him to enter the Cabinet as Minister of Finance and the two men very quickly established an easy rapport of trust and confidence.

Naturally enough, the most unhappy man in Ottawa was George Foster. The thought that White had the post he cherished was almost too much for the gallant old campaigner to bear. Foster was not surprised by White's appointment. In fact, as early as Tuesday the 26th, the day of Borden's grand procession through Ottawa, he had been told by George Taylor that Borden did not intend to include him in the Cabinet. Instead, Foster was offered the Chairmanship of the proposed Tariff Commission at a very handsome salary of $10,000 a year. Foster refused and immediately began a campaign for a place at the Council table. His political cronies from both New Brunswick and Toronto were quickly organized. As W. K. McNaught, prominent Conservative Toronto businessman, put it, "you should at once get all of your friends of the 'Old Guard' to put in a good word *for you at once*".[13] Support also came from W. F. Cockshutt of Brantford, another of the "Old Guard", and from E. S. Clouston, General Manager and first Vice-President of the Bank of Montreal. Clouston had "never been consulted about it" and was doubly worried. He wanted Foster in Finance because, with the revision of the Bank Act pending, "I do not want a Minister who has to learn his business". Even more important, the appointment of White threatened the very close traditional relationship between Ottawa and the Bank of Montreal and its allied interests in Canada's largest city.[14]

Foster's campaign illustrated the "wire-pulling" he daily condemned in his dairy, and it did force Borden to reconsider. But Finance was out of the question. Borden needed a man of impeccable credentials for the Finance portfolio and Foster had never recovered from the Foresters' Affair. Indeed, in 1908, in an attempt to clear his name, Foster sued the *Globe* and its editor, Rev. J. A. Macdonald, for libel for a series of articles written during the election campaign against Foster. The suit finally came to trial in 1910 and Foster lost.[15] It was a further blow to his public reputation.

Still, Foster had sufficient power in the party to force his entry into the Cabinet. On Thursday the 28th, Rogers told him that he would have "a portfolio but not F.M.". Late Saturday evening, Borden offered to appoint him Secretary of State. Foster again refused, waited for his campaign to develop, and privately condemned his leader: "More people—more wire pulling. . . . B. seems helpless on the surf." Finally, on Thursday, October 5, the "Chief" summoned him again. "Offered Trade and Commerce. Ask why F.M. not given. Ans. reasons of high politics. My capabilities, honesty & service fully recognized." He accepted and went away to reflect sourly on the fate he shared with Sir Richard

Cartwright. In 1896 Cartwright also thought he deserved Finance. Both ended up in Trade and Commerce.[16]

Another member of the "Old Guard" was Borden's nominee as Minister of Militia and Defence, the redoubtable member for Victoria–Haliburton, Colonel Sam Hughes. Hughes was an extraordinary character with a well established reputation as a controversial figure in federal politics. A year older than Borden, he had attended the University of Toronto and taught English and history in the public schools. Between 1885 and 1897 he was the editor and proprietor of the Lindsay *Warder*. A vociferous proponent of the strenuous life, Hughes had achieved some prominence as an amateur athlete. He had risen to high rank in both the Orange Order and Masonry. And since his youth his first love had been the military life. Hughes served in the South African War, was chairman of the board of visitors of the Royal Military College, President of the Dominion Rifle Association, and a self-proclaimed expert on any and all military matters. His second love was politics. After an initial defeat in the 1891 general election, Hughes won a by-election in Victoria in 1892 and had represented the constituency ever since. He was an able and knowledgeable politician who skillfully used his political position to enhance his status in the voluntary militia and his military rank to buttress his political reputation.

He was outspoken, aggressive, and vain. Not for Hughes the agonizing game of waiting to be called that Foster played. As soon as he knew that the Conservatives had won the election he put his claims before Borden. It was a classic Hughes letter that deserves full reproduction.

> This morning I was 'phoned from Toronto by one of the most prominent gentlemen there, to inform me that steps were being taken to prejudice me with you by raising the cry that I am not looked upon kindly by a certain ecclesiastical organization.
>
> I do not know what such could have to do with the matter. Everyone has ever had fair play from me; and so long as others do not kick at the appointment of those of that creed they should be quite content.
>
> The movement, I am informed, is boomed not by those of that faith; but by Protestants who would eliminate me from the Government.

It is needless to review here my principles—or my services to the party. For some years a few so-called Tories have made it uncomfortable for me over the Ross Rifle; but when you consider the great success attending that rifle, and the fact that Britain is today perfecting a new rifle, and that the vital principles of the Ross as perfected by my committee are [its] essentials, you will realize the futility of the attack. The aim then was, as I can prove, to "kill Sam Hughes politically" and advance another to be minister under the to be new Tory leader, when you would be driven to retire. Well, neither before their attacks on the Ross Rifle, nor when they twice tried to get rid of our Leader, did I *flinch*—you found me true as steel.

In your coming Cabinet operations difficulties may from time to time arise. It strikes me that it might be that again, my tact, firmness and judgement might come in to help matters along.

My military record is open—and will bear comparison with any. Sir Fred. [Borden] himself has always done me the credit of saying that the vast majority of the democratic and effective changes are due to my suggestions.

It is every honest man's desire to be recognized. Has or has not my line for years been vindicated in this fight? Had our Western men begun a year or two years ago, every Province would have given us a majority. But anon things will come better out there.

I'll explain personally the work in Ontario.

In my walks through life easy management of men has ever been one of my chief characteristics—and I get the name of bringing success and good luck to a cause.

Hoping you will pardon this.[17]

This was so typical of Sam. His boastfulness and hyperbole were at once infuriating and comical, and the root cause of his past, present, and future problems in the party. Moderation was not in his catalogue of manly qualities. His attacks on French Canada and Catholicism knew no more bounds than his defence of the Ross Rifle or his advocacy of imperial centralization. There was nothing to suggest that the power and responsibility of office would temper his perspective of public affairs. Yet Hughes was also a powerful and able man and his letter touched another point that meant much to Borden. Sam was the first colleague to offer to give up his seat for Borden in the humiliating days after his defeat in Halifax in 1904. His loyalty to his leader had been unquestionable. Throughout the disappointing decade of Opposition, Sam had indeed been "true as steel".

Sam's abrasive personality won him the friendship of few but the respect, sometimes grudging, of many in both parties. Sifton agreed that he should have a seat in the Cabinet. Hughes' accomplishments in the militia and his party loyalty made him the obvious choice for the post. Over the objections of the Governor General, Borden offered Colonel Sam the job, coupled with a stern warning. He clearly thought he could control his erratic Minister-to-be. "I sent for Colonel Hughes," Borden later recalled, "and discussed with him his past vagaries, his lack of tact and his foolish actions and words on many occasions. He frankly admitted his faults and told me that he realized his impulsiveness but that he would be more discreet in the future."[18] It was a promise Hughes could not keep.

The third representative of the "Old Guard" in the Cabinet was John D. Reid, physician, businessman and, since 1891, party politician. He had not had a distinguished career in the House but has exhibited considerable flair as a politician's politician. Like Rogers and Cochrane, he was a skilled practitioner of organization and fund raising and had the support of the "practical" men in the party. Borden reluctantly included Reid in his cabinet. The good Doctor, after all, had conspired against Borden's leadership in both 1910 and 1911. On the other hand, once the latter revolt was quashed, Reid, under the supervision of Borden and Cochrane, had been given charge of twenty-four eastern Ontario seats in the election and had demonstrated his worth to the party. Twenty of the twenty-four seats had returned Conservative members. And now Cochrane made a strong case for Reid instead of Andrew Broder, the friend of Whitney and Borden, as the eastern Ontario representative. Borden relented, much to Whitney's dismay, and offered Reid the Customs portfolio. Like Hughes, Reid received a stern lecture from his leader before he was given his reward. "He promised," Borden wrote, "to observe certain rules of conduct which I enjoined and to be loyal at all times in the future."[19] Unlike Hughes, Reid was as good as his word.

Another Ontario member of the Cabinet was Thomas W. Crothers, a former teacher and lawyer from St. Thomas. Crothers was probably a party to the 1910 revolt but had soon made his peace with Borden. He was a relative newcomer to federal politics, being elected for the first time in 1908. In the fall of 1910 Borden made him chairman of the caucus, thus identifying him with that group in the party, led by Perley and Ames, which was closest to Borden. He had played an important organizational role in southwestern Ontario in the campaign and he had the support of Whitney and Sifton. Borden made him Minister of Labour.

Borden may have considered Arthur Meighen as a second Manitoba representative in the Cabinet. He certainly thought the young MP from Portage La Prairie was one of the most brilliant and effective parliamentarians in his caucus. Meighen was loyal and hard working and obviously of Cabinet calibre. In 1913 he would be appointed Solicitor-General, but for the moment he had to be passed over in favour of Doctor William James Roche, a more senior Manitoba member. The first medical doctor to graduate from the University of Western Ontario, Roche began to practice his profession in Minnedosa in 1883. He was first elected to Parliament for Marquette in 1896 and since then had earned a reputation as a reliable if not distinguished member. Borden chose him as Secretary of State and, by virtue of that office, he was also Secretary of State for External Affairs until 1912 when the Prime Minister took over the latter portfolio. The final western representative was James A. Lougheed, a well-known Calgary lawyer who had given long service to the party. He had been appointed to the Senate by the Macdonald government in 1889. In 1906 Lougheed succeeded Sir Mackenzie Bowell as Conservative leader in the Senate. Borden named him government leader in the Senate and Minister without Portfolio.

Two other Ministers without Portfolio were very much Borden's personal choices. A. E. Kemp, the Toronto industrialist, had done more than any other man to keep a semblance of vitality in the Ontario organization through the lean years of Opposition. Sifton was strongly opposed to Kemp, but Kemp deserved and got a place at the Council table. So too did George Perley. The Member for Argenteuil could conveniently serve as the Quebec Protestant representative in the Cabinet, but, as one of the few party men who had the complete confidence of Borden, he would have been there in any case. Quite deliberately, Perley was not given a portfolio, though he was to have "first claim" upon one when opportunity arose.[20] For the time being Borden had a more important task for Perley. He was to be the Prime Minister's right-hand man, generally charged with supervising the overhaul of the administration of government business.

The other English-speaking Quebec member of the Cabinet was equally a personal choice. Charles Joseph Doherty had left a distinguished career at the Bar and on the Bench to enter politics. First elected to Parliament for Ste-Anne in 1908, he quickly earned Borden's favour. He had strong connections with the Montreal business community and was an able spokesman for Irish-Catholic interests in Parliament. Before he finished his first parliamentary term Doherty had replaced Foster as Borden's deskmate. The "Judge" was named Minister of Justice.

Borden had considerable latitude in the selection of the English-speaking Quebec ministers because, as Charles Cahan observed, the appointments did "not effect ninety percent of the Quebec electorate". For the very same reason, Borden's choice of French-speaking ministers was more circumscribed. This was the one subject upon which nearly everyone wanted to offer advice. Only Sifton and Willison had little to say. Sifton's slate of Quebec ministerial prospects was almost contemptuously cryptic: "Quebec—Doherty Perley 2 French".[21] Willison conceded that Quebec should be dealt with "generously", but expected little from Quebec and was prepared to write the province off and concentrate attention elsewhere. "Surely," he wrote, "it is in the West that the Conservative party must chiefly build for the future."[22]

The cause of concern was, of course, the Monk–Bourassa alliance. All sorts of people, from the Governor General to the editors and proprietors of the Toronto *Globe*, were worried about the effect of Nationalist representation in the Cabinet upon naval policy. Lord Grey was characteristically meddlesome. On the 29th he fretted over rumours that Borden was going to submit his naval policy to a plebiscite. "I should expect you to give me an opportunity of explaining to you my opinion on the matter, before you committed yourself," he wrote. Three days later a brief talk with Borden left him "a little uneasy and apprehensive . . . that the presence of Mr. Monk as one of your colleagues on the Treasury Bench does not mean a weak or retrogressive Naval Policy".[23] The *Globe*, hardly a champion of Borden's political welfare, let it be known through a friendly Tory reporter that the paper "would give Mr. Borden no trouble on the naval question unless he backs up on it".[24] The doubts and fears about Monk ignored a fundamental political fact. Monk was, after all, the acknowledged leader of the Quebec Conservatives. Whatever his views on naval policy were, Monk had to be in the Cabinet. That point was not debatable. He was given the Public Works portfolio, an apparently strange choice for a man of Monk's sensitive conscience. But Monk's scrupulous honesty suggested that the Department might be run with less concern for patronage than at any time since Confederation.

If Monk's place in the Cabinet was a foregone conclusion, the selection of the other French Canadians was not. Both the Nationalists and the Old Bleus fought for place and power. There was some support for Bourassa. Van Horne thought that Bourassa as a Minister would be "a power for good instead of evil in Quebec" and Monk pressed Bourassa to join him at the Council table.[25] William Price urged that Bourassa's lieutenant, Armand Lavergne, be appointed as Minister for the Quebec district and Lavergne later claimed that he was offered a portfolio. Van Horne and Price reasoned that the Nationalist leaders could be controlled in the Cabinet. As Price said of Lavergne, he "would be tied to us & would be a future asset".[26] But neither Bourassa nor Lavergne agreed to come in. Instead they placed their support behind less notable and controversial Conservative-Nationalists, L. P. Pelletier from Quebec and W. B. Nantel from the Montreal district. Pelletier was a lawyer of some local standing who had had a moderately successful political career. In earlier days he had supported Mercier's nationalism. In 1908 he failed to win a seat in either the provincial legislature or the House of Commons, but he had been elected for Quebec County in 1911. He was the President of the Quebec Railway, Light, Heat & Power Company. He had the qualified support of Price who reported that he was "able, an excellent debater & of good executive ability" but "not trusted" and "generally unpopular". Charles Cahan, who had close contacts with Bourassa, was more blunt about Pelletier: he "is alleged to have been a grafter, and is now without political influence even in his own constituency". Nantel, also a lawyer, was a Conservative backbencher who had represented Terrebonne since 1908. He too had Price's support as "a straight level headed man of good ability but lacking in experience in the larger sense".[27]

The Cabinet candidates of the "orthodox" Conservatives were more prominent men. L. T. Marechal, a well-known Montreal lawyer, and J. M. Tellier, the provincial Conservative leader, were given some consideration. But the chief contenders were Casgrain and Rodolphe Forget. Casgrain's reputation was impeccable but it was generally agreed that in the climate of 1911 it would be impossible to elect him in the province. His association with the "wrong" side in the prosecutions of both Riel and Mercier, as Cahan put it, "have caused him to be execrated to this day throughout Quebec". Forget, the leading French-Canadian financier in the province, had been elected in two constituencies. But he, too, had political liabilities. Forget was supported by Sir Hugh Graham but nearly every other correspondent warned Borden not to put a "stock broker" in the Cabinet. George Drummond wrote that Forget was "a speculator, first, last and always". Price said he would be a "good man" "were it not for his large business interests" and Cahan observed that "the gambling game engrosses Forget soul and spirit".[28]

Making a choice of his Quebec colleagues was the most difficult problem Borden had in selecting his Cabinet. The Prime Minister clearly had the final word, but he was not going to appoint anyone Monk opposed. For two weeks they weighed the alternatives and by Friday, October 6, they had agreed upon Pelletier and Nantel. But that same evening Forget departed from Ottawa to Montreal "in great anger", and organized a campaign to force his way into the Cabinet. This roused another protest from his opponents.[29] On Saturday Borden was deluged by telegrams and telephone calls from Montreal. He stood by his decision; Pelletier would be Postmaster-General and Nantel, Minister of Inland Revenue.[30]

By Monday evening, October 9, the last details had been tidied up and the Ministers-designate assembled in the capital. The Governor General returned from the opera to receive a call from Borden who reported that his cabinet was complete. After midnight the crowd of reporters at the gate were called into the Prime Minister's house and given the news. Then, at noon on Tuesday, seven cabs, with Borden and Perley leading the procession, made their way to Rideau Hall. The swearing-in ceremony was soon over and every one rushed away to pack his bags. His Majesty's new Canadian Government was on its way to Quebec to take leave of Lord Grey and to welcome the new Governor General, Prince Arthur, the Duke of Connaught and Strathearn. Two weeks later, October 27, the Ministers, who had to resign their seats when they accepted Cabinet appointments, were re-elected in their constituencies without opposition.

The selection of his Cabinet colleagues did not complete the difficult task of finding suitable rewards for the party faithful. Places were found for Casgrain, Charles Magrath, who had lost his seat in Medicine Hat, and Henry Powell, a Saint John lawyer and long-time friend of Borden, on the recently established International Joint Commission with the United States.[31] And despite his repeated advocacy of Senate reform, Borden found the Upper House just as convenient a last refuge for deserving party troopers as every other Prime Minister before or since. Three of the MP's who gave up their seats to Cabinet nominees, J. W. Daniel in Saint John, George Taylor in Leeds, and George Gordon in Nipissing, were rewarded with comfortable sinecures in the Senate. The fourth, Alexander Haggart, who surrendered his Winnipeg seat to Robert Rogers, was appointed to the Manitoba Court of Appeals in 1912.[32]

The impending change of government caused a ripple of fear among the senior civil servants that their jobs were in danger. Joseph Pope, the Under-Secretary of State for External Affairs, was so worried that he urged Lord Grey to give Laurier "plenty of time to close up matters and to fill all vacancies". But, as Perley assured him, his anxiety was groundless.[33] Borden neither desired nor could he afford to strip the civil service of its established and experienced senior members. At the junior levels the inside service, under the supervision of the Civil Service Commission, was relatively secure. The outside service, the customs officers and thousands of other federal employees outside Ottawa, was not, and the potential for a plentiful patronage harvest was great. Borden adopted exactly the same policy Laurier had in 1896. A civil servant could be dismissed for active political partisanship. The question of guilt was established by the personal assurance of a member of Parliament or a defeated candidate, or, failing either of these, by an appointed commission of inquiry.[34] It was a crude system at best—Borden later referred to it as an "expedient"[35]—which was open to partisan and personal abuse. And doubtless it was so abused by both parties in turn. But it did serve to prevent wholesale dismissal of Dominion civil servants. In 1911 some 150 employees were dismissed by Monk, two-thirds of them temporary appointments not subject to protection of the Civil Service Act. And about fifty correspondents of the *Labour Gazette* were let go by Crothers.[36]

The pressure to do more was intense. "Le patronage . . . absorbent le 9/10ième de mon temps depuis que je suis entré en fonctions," Monk told Bourassa. "Rien de plus penible et de plus attristant que cette phase de mes devoirs."[37] Next to Monk, probably most pressure was put upon Frank Cochrane. On the Intercolonial Railway, Monk told Bourassa, "il a abolé les passes et les faveurs, il a abandonné les améliorations utiles non pas strictement essentielles, il a découragé la réintégration des employés congédiés sans raisons en 1896, et, avec cette reforme justifable mais brutalement brusque, nous avons causé un vil mécontentement."[38]

Finally, Borden and his colleagues tried to find men of acknowledged technical competence to head some of the more important of the Government's regulatory bodies. Their first success was the appointment of R. W. Leonard as Chairman of the National Transcontinental Railway Commission. Leonard was a trained civil engineer with wide experience in both hydro-electric and railway construction. Then, in July of 1912, White reported that "after a hard week's work I landed [H. L.] Drayton". Drayton was a lawyer who had served as solicitor for the city of Toronto and on the Toronto Hydro-Electric Commission. His appointment as Chairman of the Board of Railway Commissioners brought a "chorus of approval from all the press of both stripes".[39]

The most important of Borden's appointments, of course, were his choices of Cabinet colleagues. These were the men who would establish the character and shape the policies of his administration. They were an incongruous lot! Imperialists like Hughes and Foster seemed to have little in common with Monk, Pelletier, and Nantel, or the politically inexperienced Liberal businessman, White, with the Tory party managers, Rogers, Reid, and Cochrane. They were short on administrative experience. Only Foster had ever headed a federal government department and the men with backgrounds in provincial administration, Cochrane, Hazen, and Rogers, were soon overwhelmed by the magnitude of their responsibilities in Ottawa. Regionally, Ontario had the strongest representation in the Cabinet with seven members, a clear reflection of the influence that province and its Premier would have on the new government. The weakest delegation was from French Canada. Only Monk had sufficient stature to command attention either at the Council table or among his people. Patient, deliberate negotiation had brought them all together under Borden's leadership. And patient, deliberate consultation would be necessary to keep them together when they turned their attention to the policies that would fulfil his election promises.

It was Henri Bourassa who made the one point upon which they all agreed. "The downfall of the Laurier Government had become a necessity," he wrote just after the election.[40] Each of the groups which supported Borden had particular grievances against the Laurier government, but they all wanted a change from what the editor of *Le Devoir* called "the Laurier system". The administration of the public's affairs had not been a very prominent issue in the 1911 campaign. But two of Borden's eleven electoral pledges indicated the concern. He promised "a thorough reorganization of the method by which public expenditure is supervised" and "the extension of civil service reform".

The pledges revealed a deep-rooted suspicion among Borden's followers that the corruption in the Laurier government was the symptom of a more serious disease. There would always be dishonest men in and out of the public service, men who would put party or personal interest above the welfare of the state. But corruption was nourished by inefficiency, by inadequate controls over the actions of public servants and by the incompetence of senior public officials. This was a common assumption; one shared by businessmen who criticized the government for its lack of business methods, by self-styled reformers, many of them in the public service, who demanded civil service reform, and by politicians who had first-hand knowledge of the state of Canada's public service. It followed that efficiency and honesty went hand in hand, that "organization", the use of modern bureaucratic techniques, was the key to clean government. The bland, unemotional words of Borden's electoral pledges conveyed the message that "extravagance" could be curbed simply by "a thorough reorganization of the method" of supervising public expenditure and that a "reformed" civil service would be both honest and efficient. These pledges were freighted with a host of assumptions about public morality and a rather naive faith in the efficacy of business-like administration.

So too was one of the earliest acts of the Borden government, the appointment of the Public Service Commission. In December 1911 the Prime Minister appointed A. B. Morine, a Conservative lawyer and politician who had had a colourful and stormy career in Newfoundland politics, R. S. Lake, who had lost his Saskatchewan seat in the election, and G. N. Ducharme, a Montreal banker, to investigate the state of the federal public service. The object was to "obtain such information as will enable any existing defects or abuses to be remedied, secure the adoption of more efficient methods, remedy any existing abuses and more thoroughly safe-guard the public interest".[41] At the same time A. E. Kemp was asked to head a Cabinet committee inquiring into the purchasing practices of the government departments.[42] Yet another Commission was appointed to investigate the administration and expenditure of the National Transcontinental Railway.

Each investigation was in part politically motivated. Its main purpose was to discover how well, or how badly, the machinery of government worked. But if it unearthed evidence of corruption in the previous administration, so much the better. This was particularly true of the National Transcontinental Railway investigation. When the Commissioners, F. P. Gutelius, a CPR man who became General Manager of the Intercolonial, and G. Lynch-Staunton, a Hamilton lawyer, reported their findings in 1914, the document struck a partisan note. No evidence was presented, but a number of charges of maladministration were made against the NTR under Laurier's government.[43]

Kemp's committee quickly discovered that purchasing practices varied widely from department to department as did the amount of supervision of departmental purchasing systems. Kemp advised Borden that he would await the report of Morine's Public Service Commission before making any recommendations.[44] A preliminary report of the Morine Commission in March, 1912, briefly described the heart of the problem. "Since Confederation," the Commissioners observed,

> the administrative machinery of the Dominion as a whole has never been reported on or reorganized; nor have the various parts been considered in relation to the whole. Owing

to the great development of the country exigencies have arisen from time to time, and services have been created to meet these exigencies, but no organized effort has been made to coordinate these services with the various Departments of the Public Service as a whole, and assign to each its proper status and duties in the general machinery of the administration.

"It is not necessary to assume that corruption or the inefficiency of individuals has been the cause of this improper administration," the Commissioners concluded. "It may be that the fault arises entirely from the neglect of proper methods."[45]

The Morine Commission was soon confronted with unanticipated and embarrassing problems. The first was that neither Borden nor the Commissioners realized the extent of their assignment. The Commission became bogged down in a number of complex specific inquiries and it warned Borden that "the magnitude of the task becomes more than ever apparent as the inquiry proceeds". Then, at the end of March, it was revealed that Morine, at an earlier stage in his political career, had been involved in a serious conflict of interest. For a time he had been both Minister of Finance in the Newfoundland government and, as Morine put it, "general legal Advisor" to R. G. Reid, a railway contractor doing extensive business with that government. Morine explained that his dual role was a well-known public fact and, indeed, a customary practice in Newfoundland. That was small comfort to Borden. Whatever the practices of Newfoundland political life, Morine's Public Service Commission had been charged to uncover and eliminate just such peculiarly flagrant abuses of the public trust. The revelation, said Borden, was of an "exceedingly grave character". He asked for and received Morine's resignation.[46] But the damage had been done. The credibility of the Public Service Commission had been destroyed. Though Lake and Ducharme continued their work, Borden soon concluded that "the present commission is useless and . . . it should be dissolved".[47]

Long before the Public Service Commission embarrassment came to light, Adam Shortt, a former Queen's professor and one of the members of the Civil Service Commission, had convinced Borden that "piecemeal" investigations of government administration and the public service would not do. What was needed was an "impartial" examination of "the whole question" and Shortt recommended that an official of the British Treasury be hired to do the work. In February 1912, Perley reported that Sir George Murray, former permanent Secretary of the Treasury, had agreed to make the investigation.[48] Murray arrived in Ottawa late in September. Borden saw almost nothing of him until he presented his report on November 30. The Prime Minister was preoccupied with the preparation of his naval aid bill and apparently left Murray in White's charge.[49]

Murray's report was a sweeping indictment of the Canadian public service from top to bottom. Murray made the same basic criticism as the Public Service Commission: Canada was a modern industrial state being administered with machinery adopted by and appropriate to its government at the time of Confederation. The "only means" of controlling growth and the development of a complex economy and society, he observed, was by "division of labour and devolution of power". Neither had happened. The result, he warned, was that "the machinery of government must gradually become less efficient and must ultimately break down under the stress imposed upon it". Public services were duplicated in a number of Departments, were assigned to inappropriate Departments, were financed under varying accounting procedures.

The requirements for entrance into the inside (Ottawa) Civil Service were generally satisfactory, but the outside service, by far the largest portion of the Civil Service, remained an open field for patronage. Even in the inside service, public servants found little incentive for hard productive work. Job classification was haphazard, with many highly paid senior civil servants performing tasks appropriate for departmental clerks. "Such a system is fatal to an efficient service in two ways," said Murray: "the higher positions are filled, not by experts, but by amateurs; and the best type of official is not attracted into the service because he recognizes that its prizes are not within his reach." The absence of a pension system also damaged the public service. "Men whose services might well be dispensed with are retained after their powers have begun to fail; and men whom the State would be glad to retain are allowed to be tempted out of the service at a time when their value is highest." In short, the government could not attract the best talent into the public

service, and the best it could attract was soon lost to more
promising careers in private enterprise.

Even more important, in Murray's mind, was the problem at
the top. There, Borden's Cabinet was being run with Macdonald's
machinery. The Ministers, said Murray, "have too much to do
and do too much". It was there that the absence of division of
labour and devolution of power was most apparent and most
serious. Cabinet business ranged "from questions of the highest
importance . . . down to the acceptance of a tender for the
erection of a pump."[50] Murray recommended that many powers
vested in the Governor in Council (Cabinet) should be delegated
to individual departments. The Treasury Board, a committee of
Council which, unlike its contemporary British or modern Canadian counterparts, dealt almost solely with personnel affairs in
the Civil Service and minor patronage,[51] should be abolished and
its business assumed by the departments or an Appointments
and Promotion Board. Most important, a clear distinction should
be drawn between the work of Ministers and their subordinates.
"The business of a Minister is not to administer, but to direct
policy," Murray observed. "The carrying out of this policy . . .
should be left to his subordinates."[52]

Borden did not record his immediate reaction to the Murray
Report. But it is certain that he got more than he bargained for
and Sir George Murray's recommendations were not implemented. Many years later Borden observed that the report "was
very elaborate and far reaching" and, rather unfairly, he alleged
that Murray "went somewhat beyond the scope of the proposed
inquiry".[53] More to the point, most of Murray's report was so
general in its indictment, so devoid of specific evidence of inefficient or incompetent conduct in the public service, that it was
not a good base for detailed reforms. In addition, some of
Murray's remedies were better suited to a mature civil service
than they were to the fledgling bureaucracy in Ottawa. And a
complete reorganization of the Canadian civil service could only
be effected immediately at the expense of a serious disruption of
government services. Equally important, as Borden carefully put
it,there was "strong opposition in various quarters" to a number
of Murray's proposals.

That was the core of the matter. The Civil Service Commissioners objected to having promotions taken out of their control.

A pension system for civil servants, particularly a non-contributory pension system, was very controversial. Stricter classification of jobs within Departments and adherence to appointments and promotion within that classification lessened the ability of Ministers to bestow favours upon their subordinates. And the backbenchers and party managers undoubtedly pointed out that the reform of the outside service would strip the party of its organizational base. Provision was made for the appointment of a third Civil Service Commissioner and some attention was paid to improving the efficiency of the work of the Cabinet over the next few years. But a sweeping reform of the administration of the government's business had to wait for more propitious times.

The results of Borden's first effort at administrative reform were disappointing, but not surprising. First, all the evidence suggested that the more suspicious activities of Laurier's government were less due to willful and rampant corruption than to an outmoded and inefficient system of conducting public business by well-meaning and honest but sometimes incompetent men. Second, the machinery of government had been carefully examined for the first time since Confederation. Many of its creaking, worn, and overloaded parts, particularly the Cabinet, had been identified. Both discoveries were important. And they pointed to a third. Borden and his government had been taught a valuable lesson about the problems of power. They discovered that it was much easier to criticize than to conduct the country's business.

"The development of industry and commerce, the marked progress and advancement in every field of national activity, the marvellous increase in wealth and the inequality of [its] distribution are attended with problems" that test the capacity of "self-government", Borden observed in 1913. "All men are not born equal in their capacity and energy," he noted on another occasion, "and in an individualistic world there can be no expectation of equality of results." Nevertheless, Borden believed that it was the task of "modern democracy" in the industrial era to ensure "to each individual that there shall be accorded, so far as may be humanly possible, equality of opportunity in the national life".[54]

"Equality of opportunity" became the goal of the "progressive and vigorous policy" of his government.[55] He used the phrase repeatedly in defence of his pre-war legislative program. But Borden acknowledged that equality of opportunity for Canadians would not be achieved quickly. Nor could it be imposed by government legislation upon a people either unready or unwilling to accept it. Repeating one of his firmest convictions, he told the American Society of International Law in April, 1912, "that you could teach the people no worse lesson than the enactment of a law so far in advance of public opinion that they felt themselves more or less at liberty to disregard it".[56]

Another important question remained unanswered. Who would determine when the public desired policies to enhance the equality of opportunity in society? The answer, in Borden's mind, varied from situation to situation. In some cases he would act, as had Laurier before him, in response to evident public pressure for new legislation. On other occasions he would sound out policy proposals with trusted advisers in and out of Parliament, just as he had throughout the Opposition years. And on some issues he would act as the sole judge, consulting with at most one or two trusted colleagues. One of these was the tariff. Potentially, it was among the most powerful instruments of government policy to achieve his goal. It was also one of the most contentious politically. In 1913 Borden decided that tariff policy would be decided by White and himself: "told [White] that he and I would settle tariff matters and avoid protracted discussion in Council".[57]

Clearly then, equality of opportunity was not going to be forced by the enactment of a radical legislative program by Borden's government. To do so would have challenged the basic assumptions of the "individualistic world" in which Borden lived. Instead, his government would proceed slowly, cautiously, in step with accepted public attitudes and public opinion. Borden and his colleagues would try to correct the worst abuses of modern Canada's industrial society; they were not about to overturn it.

The election of 1911 suggested that, of all the groups in Canadian society, the farmers seemed to have the most grievances and the most political power to demand that they be corrected. Borden still would not concede their basic demand, reciprocity. In 1912 and 1913 he agreed to reduce the duties on cement and upon some industrial goods and machinery not manufactured in Canada. In 1913, under a new trade agreement with the West Indies, sugar from the islands entered at a reduced tariff rate. And in 1914, with the government contemplating an election, the tariff on agricultural implements was cut. But he and White were basically satisfied with the existing tariff. "Our tariff, like all other tariffs, presents many anomalies," White admitted in 1913:

> but has for over 30 years been based upon the two-fold principle of providing by indirect taxation for our revenue requirements and, by affording a reasonable degree of protection to such production as is properly native to the Dominion, of developing our resources, promoting the establishment of diversified national industries, building upon great commercial centres, creating our home markets for the agricultural producers and generally promoting the welfare of the entire community.[58]

The farmers believed that reciprocity was the first and most important step towards equality of opportunity. But Borden and White argued that a "reasonable degree of protection" promoted "the welfare of the entire comunity" and that reciprocity threatened the economic system which made the gradual achievement of equality of opportunity possible.

Their intransigence on the tariff was in marked contrast to the government's response to other agrarian demands. Almost too quickly it reviewed the pre-election contracts of the Laurier government for the Hudson's Bay Railway, that other panacea for western farmers, and promised completion of a line to Port Nelson by 1914.[59]* And two provisions in the decennial revision of the Bank Act in 1913 were also designed to assist the farmers. One extended the supplemental note issue privileges of the banks from September through February to cover the financing of the grain trade. The other enabled banks to make loans to farmers on the security of their crops and to ranchers on the security of their cattle.

Still more important was the passage of the Canada Grain Act of 1912. Originally introduced by the Laurier government in 1911, it established a Board of Grain Commissioners to supervise grain inspection and regulate the grain trade. The Act also provided for the building or acquisition of terminal elevators by the federal government. The Conservatives' attitude towards the Grain Act differed from the Liberals' in one important respect. Laurier's government had included the clause on government

---

*In 1917, because of the war, construction was halted on the still incomplete line.

elevators in response to a long-standing farmers' demand. But, said their spokesman in the Senate, "it will not be resorted to if we can help it".[60] Borden was not ready to nationalize all terminal elevators (though his electoral platform had suggested that he would). But he was prepared to construct and operate government elevators at strategic locations in competition with the private operators. By 1915 the government had terminal elevators in operation at Port Arthur, Moose Jaw, Calgary, and Saskatoon, and a transfer elevator in Vancouver.

All these measures and some others were designed to give material assistance to farmers to overcome their most persistent marketing problems. But the intent of the Borden government's agricultural program went beyond agricultural marketing or the fulfillment of specific election pledges. Indeed, its purpose was to cure the disease of isolation and alienation that so deeply infected the agricultural community. No one doubted that the problem was serious, that the industrialization of Canada had impaired the farmers' chance for "equality of opportunity" in modern Canadian society, or that the alienation of rural Canada was fraught with peril for the whole country. "Agriculture is not only an occupation which some individuals follow for profit," Dr. James W. Robertson told the Commission of Conservation in 1912; "it is a great national interest, determining in a dominant way the fortunes of this nation and the opportunities and the character of the population."[61] "If conditions are such as to cause the withdrawal of the best blood from the rural districts, or such as to favour the deterioration of rural life, the social and national disaster is imminent," said W. C. Good, Master of the Dominion Grange.[62] Martin Burrell, the Minister of Agriculture, was still more blunt: "Cut away men from the fields and the fruits of the earth and in six months there will be silence in the streets."[63]

One significant step towards ending the isolation of rural Canada was the extension of rural free delivery services by the Post Office Department, a policy Borden had advocated since the introduction of his Halifax Platform. Another was to provide funds to assist the provinces with highway construction. In 1912 and 1913 the government brought in bills to provide conditional grants to the provinces for that purpose. But the keystone of the government's agricultural program was its Agricultural Aid Bill of 1913. "Following the best methods of the most progressive countries," Burrell said, the federal government would provide funds for ten years to assist the provinces in their programs of agricultural education. Here was the crux of "equality of opportunity" for Canada's agrarians. The educated, competent farmer would be a contented and competitive farmer. Even more, a nation of technically skilled farmers would be the base for, as Burrell put it, "the creation of a rural civilization which will at once ensure a fuller and happier life to those in its midst, and prove a source and fount of strength to the State itself".[64]

The government's plans for continued national development complemented its agricultural policies. The opening up of new areas for resource exploitation, the extension of the national network of transport facilities, and huge improvement schemes for designated national harbours all meant more jobs and better jobs for a growing population. Both the Hudson's Bay Railway and the highways bill were parts of the grand scheme. So too were bills providing assistance to the Ontario government's Temiskaming and Northern Ontario Railway and enabling the federal government to acquire branch lines in the Maritime provinces for the Intercolonial Railway. And the final settlement of the long-disputed Ontario-Manitoba boundary question in 1912 was accompanied by the surrender of the enormous territory in the federal districts of Keewatin and Ungava to the provinces of Manitoba, Ontario, and Quebec.

Borden could count upon his comfortable majority in the House of Commons to support his progressive legislative program. What he did not anticipate was that the Senate, dominated by the Liberals, would systematically attempt to block government legislation.* The Senate's obstruction of the government's bills, as its rejection of the highways bill illustrated, was dictated by both principle and partisanship. Many of the Grit Senators thought the principle of conditional grants written into the highways bill was unconstitutional. But others saw the highways bill primary as a pay-off to friendly Tory provincial governments who, they assumed, would get the lion's share of the grants from Ottawa. Knowing that Whitney's government would especially welcome the legislation, Sir Richard Cartwright, the Liberal leader in the upper chamber, made the battle against the highways bill one of the last partisan fights of his long political career. "It is bad in principle, worse in detail, and the motive, I believe,

---

*At the opening of the 1911–12 session there were 62 Liberals and 19 Conservatives in the Senate.

to provide a huge fund for corruption, is worst of all," he said. "Were I to suggest a short title for the Bill, I would recommend the following—that this should be declared a Bill to make the British North America Act so much waste paper, and to provide a permanent corruption fund for the use of the Government of the day."[65]

Obstruction in the Senate came quickly. In the first parliamentary session the Senators turned back Borden's tariff commission bill and added unacceptable amendments to the highways bill and to a bill granting aid to the Ontario government railway. The latter was passed in 1913, but the highways bill was amended a second time and the Intercolonial Branch lines legislation was rejected. In 1914 the chamber of sober second thought amended legislation increasing the representation in the Senate for the western provinces and giving aid to depositors who had suffered in the failure of the Farmer's Bank of Canada.[66] Borden later admitted that the Senate was justified in rejecting the Farmer's Bank legislation.[67] But its amendment to the representation bill was just too much to bear. Borden believed that the motivation was purely political. "The Grit Senators, doubtless in collusion with their friends in the Commons, deliberately violated the agreement to pass the resolutions for increase in Senate representation," he wrote. "Laurier looking uneasy and ashamed but our men believe that he permitted it and connived at it."[68]

The obstruction of the Senate did not destroy the pre-war legislative program of the Borden government. Much of it did become law and part of a modest record of reform. The Prime Minister was especially disturbed, however, by the rejection of the tariff commission and highways bills. He regarded both as reform measures of major importance. The establishment of a tariff commission, he reasoned, would be a first step towards removing the tariff from political influence and aligning it more closely to the economic needs of the country. The highways bill was even more important because it would initiate the principle of conditional grants in Dominion-Provincial relations. Borden argued that conditional grants would not impair provincial autonomy but would introduce a long overdue measure of federal responsibility in Dominion-Provincial fiscal relations. Of course, the traditional federal grants would remain and could be used for any purpose the provincial government thought appropriate.

But new grants from the federal government, administered by the provinces, should be for specific purposes. "It is not only the right but it is also the absolute duty of the government of Canada," he said, "to provide that the money shall be applied to that particular purpose and no other, and that it shall be expended in such a way as to result in permanent benefit and advantage."[69] He did not agree with the Liberal Senators who claimed conditional grants were unconstitutional. They were at once constitutional and a major part of his promise to reorganize the "method" of supervision of federal government expenditure.

Borden's legislative program presumed continued growth in the Canadian economy to finance large expenditures on railways, harbour facilities, grain elevators, and highways. None of this posed any problem in prosperous times. "The phenomenal development and progress of the country," he wrote in 1912, "seems likely to continue in even greater measure for many years to come."[70] At the conclusion of the 1912–13 session the Ministers fanned out across the country with their pockets full of announcements of new public projects. At Halifax on June 14, 15,000 people heard Borden and Cochrane declare that projected harbour improvements would give the city terminal facilities "second to none on the continent of America".[71] A month later Bob Rogers, who had taken over the Public Works portfolio when Monk resigned, reminded Vancouverites that they were soon to have two new postal sub-stations, a new drill hall, a new immigration hall, and expanded port facilities including a large floating dry-dock.[72] These were promises of prosperity, promises based upon a healthy public treasury.

White's pre-war budgets were optimistic, crowded with facts and figures detailing higher revenues than expenditures and consequent reduction in the national debt. But as his colleagues were spread across the country announcing new projects, the Minister of Finance began to worry. His representatives in trading centres throughout Canada were beginning to forecast gloomy business prospects. Their quarterly reports, for so many years filled with descriptions of the "bright outlook" and "the general advances", now contained analyses of "a terrible falling off" in business activity and "the present financial stringency".[73] In October 1913, White warned Borden of a probable decline in government revenue and recommended that tenders for public works be delayed for a year. A month later he thought that "the worst is over and that we may look for better markets within the next few months".[74]

White was wrong. The business downturn in 1913 was not a short temporary interruption in the wave of prosperity; it was the first stage of a serious depression. The London money market was even more reluctant to handle Canadian securities in 1914 than it had been in 1913. In Canada industrial production fell just as dramatically as the rate of unemployment climbed. By mid-1914 the President of Canadian Car and Foundry reported that his work force of 7,500 men in 1913 had been reduced to 2,500 men. "We certainly want every bit of work that we can possibly get hold of," wrote the General Manager of STELCO. "Manufacturing conditions both here and in the United States are in a most depressed condition," he added, "probably worse than they have ever been in my recollection."[75]

Of all the business enterprises in Canada, the most vulnerable were the two new transcontinental railways. Neither was finished and until they were the chances that either would be able to pay its fixed charges were minimal. Moreover, their construction and equipment costs were steadily rising in advance of revenues from completed sections of their lines. Both railways relied upon the London market for financing to finish construction of their lines. But the market was flooded with Canadian securities, and railway issues at four or four and one-half per cent could not compete with Canadian municipal bonds offering five or six per cent.[76] The railways turned to their ultimate benefactor, the Government of Canada. Both the Canadian Northern and the Grand Trunk Pacific brought elaborate schemes for aid from the public purse to Borden's door.

Neither caller was welcome. They were, said George Foster, products of the "foolish and criminal railway blundering" of the Laurier government.[77] Railway politics always seemed to bring out the basest political motivations in both parties and the Conservatives were sorely tempted to let the railways stew in their own juices. But the government could not do that. If either railway went into receivership, it would have a disastrous effect upon Canadian credit in London. In addition, if the Canadian Northern went under, it might take its bank, the Canadian Bank of Commerce, with it. More important still, every province except New Brunswick and Prince Edward Island, through provincial guarantees of various bond issues, was directly tied to the financial health of the railways.[78] Some provinces were so deeply committed that their guarantees on railway bonds exceeded their own annual revenues. However Borden's government looked at the problem, one basic fact was clear: it would have to bail the railways out.

Railway policy was developed by a small group of Cabinet members headed by the Prime Minister. White was always present and Cochrane was usually included until Bright's disease disabled him and "Doc" Reid stepped in as Acting Minister of Railways. And Rogers sometimes attended the frequent informal conferences on railway policy. In addition, Borden sought advice on specific points from prominent outsiders like Sifton, Joseph Flavelle, the president of National Trust Company, Shaughnessy of the Canadian Pacific, and Frederick Williams-Taylor of the Bank of Montreal. Only after policy had been determined did Borden take his plans to Cabinet and caucus. As with the tariff, "protracted discussion" of railway policy in either forum was not encouraged.

The Grand Trunk Pacific's problems with the Borden government preceded the 1913 financial crisis. The railway's notorious support of the Grits in the past coloured the government's attitude in acrimonious negotiations beginning in 1912. At issue was the assumption of the lease of the National Transcontinental by the Grand Trunk Pacific. The Conservatives wanted to hand over the completed sections of the National Transcontinental to the Grand Trunk Pacific under the leasing arrangement in the 1904 contract. The railway refused, saying the terms of the contract specified that a completed line be leased to them. The line was incomplete and the railway suggested that the government continue to operate the National Transcontinental indefinitely. The whole matter was complicated and contentious but, rightly or wrongly, Borden's colleagues came away from the meetings convinced that the Grand Trunk Pacific had evaded its contractual obligations.

Borden had some sympathy for the railway's position. He knew that the reluctance of the Grand Trunk Pacific to lease the National Transcontinental was based on more than incomplete sections between Winnipeg and Moncton. In the contract, after a grace period of seven years, the railway had agreed to pay three per cent per annum of the construction cost of the line for its lease. In 1904 that had been a reasonable deal for the Grand Trunk Pacific; estimates of the cost of construction ranged from sixty-two to sixty-eight million dollars. But by September 1911, the government's chief engineer estimated that the Winnipeg–Quebec City section alone would cost more than one hundred and sixty million dollars to complete.[79] Most of the line ran through non-revenue producing territory. The fixed charges for the lease were going to be enormous, the revenue from the line minimal. Borden thought "the burden would be too great for the Company to bear".[80] Rather than wait for the inevitable collapse of the scheme, in September 1912, Borden suggested that the government take over the whole GTP–NTR system. The government would pay the Grand Trunk Pacific the cost of the lines it had constructed, would assume the company's outstanding liabilities, would relieve the Grand Trunk from any obligation it had incurred, and would finish the line from Moncton to Prince Rupert. A month later Borden's proposal was refused by the Grand Trunk Board of Directors in London.[81]

At the beginning of the financial crisis in the spring of 1913 the GTP asked that a loan of fifteen million dollars, which the government had refused during the argument over the NTR lease, be reconsidered. The railway claimed that assistance was "absolutely necessary" because "securities cannot be floated at any decent price and prospects are not bright".[82] Borden was not prepared to see the system collapse or remain unfinished. By the end of May the details of the loan were worked out and White had gotten assurances from Laurier that the Liberals would support it.[83] A year later the GTP was back for more money. On this occasion, again with Laurier's support,[84] the government guaranteed the principal and interest on sixteen million dollars of Grand Trunk Pacific four per cent bonds. In return for the guarantee, it took a first mortgage on the railway.

Borden knew that Laurier would not give the same magnanimous support to aid for the Canadian Northern. True, Mackenzie and Mann's railway had been generously supported by the Liberals. In fact, just before the election of 1911 the government had guaranteed thirty-five million dollars of bonds for the Canadian Northern Ontario railway from Port Arthur to Montreal. And Mackenzie and Mann had become Sir William and Sir Donald on Laurier's recomendation. But Sir Wilfrid never trusted these brash upstart Canadian entrepreneurs. In gratitude for his favours they, or at least their associates, had turned against him in 1911.

What Borden did not expect was the magnitude of Mackenzie and Mann's demands and the opposition in his own party to the Canadian Northern. He discovered that the railway, contrary to popular speculation, was in very serious trouble, living from hand to mouth, and entirely dependent upon government assistance. He also learned that Mackenzie and Mann had scarcely more friends in his own party than among the Liberals. A subsidy of about five million dollars was arranged without much difficulty in 1912. But when Mackenzie came back again for more in 1913 it was quite a different story.

On January 17 Mackenzie asked for a loan of thirty million and additional subsidies on 2,200 miles of railway. Mackenzie argued that compared to the federal assistance to both the CPR in the past and to the GTP–NTR line, his request was trifling. Borden thought there was considerable merit in the Canadian Northern case but others were not so sure. Both E. B. Osler, a director of the Canadian Pacific, and Shaughnessy regarded Mackenzie and Mann as untrustworthy schemers who ought to be forced to put their own presumably enormous wealth into their line rather than get public aid.[85] White also opposed Mackenzie's plan. Even a scaled down request for twenty-two million in subsidies and no loan was, Borden told Mackenzie, "too large an order".[86] At the end of May the government did decide to grant the Canadian Northern subsidies in excess of fifteen million. The decision caused a "great disturbance" in caucus and an angry western Conservative complained bitterly to White after the subsidy bill passed. "Are we so bound up with the corporations that we neglect and overlook the producers of the country, the very men and women who make it possible for the corporations to exist?" he asked. He and his colleagues had left the caucus "with very little explanation", believing that "the half had not been told" about why the subsidies were being given to these very rich men.[87]

In 1914 the Canadian Northern returned for more aid. Because of the opposition to the railway within his party and the depressed financial conditions, Borden could "hold out no hope" to Mackenzie and Mann.[88] But now the prospect that the railway would crash was very real indeed. If that happened, the provinces, already strapped for funds, would have to pick up the interest payments on their guaranteed bonds. They could not afford to do so. Neither could the federal government allow any government guaranteed securities to default. One way or another, Ottawa was going to have to pay.

White appeared to favour letting the railway go into receivership but Sifton and Williams-Taylor, among others, were horrified by that prospect.[89] In March the government came up with a plan. Arthur Meighen, who had recently been appointed Solicitor-General, and three government officials were sent to Toronto to make a thorough examination of the railway's affairs. When they returned the railway was forced to consolidate its many lines into one company, the Canadian Northern Railway, which would be declared for "the general advantage of Canada". It would be eligible for further assistance but would also be subject to rate regulation by the Board of Railway Commissioners. A debt of more than twenty million dollars owed the Mackenzie and Mann construction company by the railway would be cancelled. The common stock of the company would be reduced to one hundred million dollars and the Government of Canada would take thirty-three million of it. Together with the seven million of stock demanded for assistance in 1913, the government would have a forty per cent interest in the Canadian Northern Railway. In return Borden and his colleagues would give no subsidies nor any cash payment to the railway. Instead, they guaranteed forty-five million dollars of Canadian Northern bonds.

The surprisingly tough terms "greatly pleased" the Cabinet,[90] but not all members of the party. R. B. Bennett and W. F. Nickle broke party ranks when the Canadian Northern bill was presented to the House of Commons. And Bennett got into an unseemly squabble with Meighen, "the gramophone of Mackenzie and Mann", who had charge of the bill in the House.[91] The Liberals put up some opposition to the government plan, but they were no more disposed to see Mackenzie and Mann default than the Conservatives. They used the occasion to taunt Borden and his colleagues for their collusion with the unscrupulous promoters. It was a sham fight and Borden had little patience with it. Out of power the Grits were "ready to spring upon any corporation, take it by the throat, shake it, make it yield up its stock, destroy it, if necessary; have no mercy upon it. But, when they come into power we find them closeted with corporations, linked up with them in every possible way, and treating them as gently as it would be possible to treat their dearest friends." So it was with Mackenzie and Mann. In power, their railway was worthy of every aid; the owners "enterprising, patriotic, pure-minded Canadians". How different, he noted, the vision from the Speaker's other hand. Now Laurier's knights of the realm were "buccaneers"![92]

Pirates or business statesmen, Mackenzie and Mann had their aid. So too did the sober and respectable managers of the Grand Trunk Pacific. Neither railway had gotten what it wanted or all it wanted from Borden's government. What Borden and his colleagues gave, they gave reluctantly and, especially in the case of the Canadian Northern, with conditions that would have been unthinkable a few years before. There were two consequences of Borden's railway policy. He had committed his government to the completion and the successful operation of both of the new transcontinental lines. Getting the railways going was not too difficult a problem. The Grand Trunk Pacific mainline was opened for traffic late in 1914. In 1915 both the Grand Trunk Pacific's eastern counterpart, the National Transcontinental, and the Canadian Northern were in operation. But keeping the railways going was quite another matter.

Borden's government began its work with the optimism characteristic of a party that had just won a stunning electoral victory. Unaccustomed to the reality and complexity of exercising power, it hoped to fulfil its election promises, root out corruption and inefficiency in the federal government, and implement a program of legislative reform that would augment "equality of opportunity" for all Canadians. Neither the Prime Minister nor his Cabinet colleagues expected that the Liberals would use their power in the Senate so consistently or so effectively to obstruct government policy. None of them anticipated that a depression would threaten the growing surpluses that had been the central feature of federal budgets for more than a decade, or that the new transcontinental railways, on the edge of financial collapse, would have to be rescued by the federal government. Even so, the Borden government established a respectable record of legislative accomplishments, especially in agricultural policy, and made a

28. The Tories on tour, 1911. Borden is sitting behind the driver of the lead car.

29. (Left) Planning the sweep of Ontario in the 1911 election: Robert Borden, Edmund Bristol, Hon. Frank Cochrane, Hon. J. O. Réaume, and Sir James Whitney.

30. Borden's first cabinet: (left to right) Hughes, Rogers, Reid, Doherty, Roche, Foster, Hazen, Borden, Pelletier, Crothers, Kemp, Perley, Lougheed, Cochrane, Nantel, Monk, and White

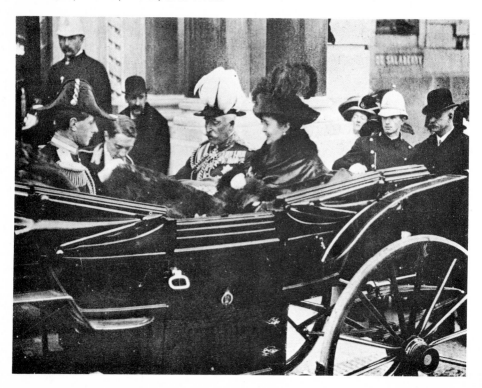

31, 32 & 33. (far left) The Duke and Duchess of Connaught leaving the Parliament Buildings, Quebec City, October 13, 1911. (Below) Robert and Laura aboard the S.S. *Royal George*, summer, 1912

34. The Bordens being greeted at Paddington Station, July 4, 1912

35 & 36. (Left) With Winston Churchill, First Lord of the Admiralty, July 1912.
(Right) The Prime Minister in his Windsor uniform

37 & 38. (Above) Thomas White, Robert Borden, and Sir Wilfrid Laurier at Lansdowne Park, Ottawa, probably 1913. (Right) A practice swing on the lawn at Glensmere, photographed by Laura Borden in 1913

halting start at administrative reform during its first three years in office.

By the summer of 1914 the government had fulfilled most of the pledges it had made in the 1911 campaign. There was one great issue, however, upon which Borden had made no promises. He had purposely avoided any public commitments on naval policy. But that issue, and Canada's relations with the United States, had been at the heart of the 1911 campaign. The bitterness of the anti-reciprocity campaign had strained Canada's relations with its neighbour; the lack of commitment in naval policy had left the Imperial question confused and ambiguous. Both problems demanded the immediate attention of the Prime Minister.

CHAPTER ELEVEN

THE GREAT DEBATE

Five days after the election of 1911 the United States Consul General in Ottawa, John G. Foster, predicted that Robert Borden would "be anxious to counteract [the anti-Americanism] in his own party".[1] Foster was in a good position to know Borden's attitude toward the United States. He and Borden had been friends for many years, going back to the days when they were both in Halifax. And his prediction was correct. A few weeks later he observed that "Mr. Borden, Mr. White and other members of the Cabinet are taking considerable pains to express friendliness to the United States".[2]

Borden had already given one reassuring public statement on Canadian-American relations in New York and in December he would give another. In mid-November, speaking for the government, George Foster told the New York Canadian Society that "we did not reject Reciprocity because we did not want to trade with you".[3] Indeed, Borden's government was determined that the rejection of reciprocity should not undermine the good relations with the United States that had been established in the last few years. He had acted quickly to fill the Canadian positions on the International Joint Commission so that it might begin its work. He recognized that Canada's ever growing trade with the United States was both desirable and necessary to Canadian prosperity. So too was continuing encouragement by his government of American investment in Canadian industrial development. In December 1913, White assured a New York gathering of American life insurance company executives that Canada was "a fine field for the investment of their surplus funds".[4]

Borden, however, thought there was an even greater purpose to be served by a healthy relationship with the United States.

230

Based upon the premise, as White put it, that "no two people understand each other better than the Americans and Canadians",[5] and upon the assumption that Canadians understood their mother country better than the Americans did, the Prime Minister believed that Canada had a unique role to play in North Atlantic diplomacy. "Canada's voice and influence should always be for harmony and not for discord between our Empire and the great Republic," he told a Halifax audience in November 1911.[6] A month later the New York Canadian Society heard him proclaim that it was "the duty of Canada to become more and more of a bond of goodwill and friendship between this Great Republic and our Empire".[7]

The idea that Canada should serve as the interpreter and mediator of the Anglo-American relationship was not new. But Borden was the first Canadian Prime Minister to give it forceful and frequently repeated sanction as a Canadian "duty". That emphasis hinted at his desire to play a much more prominent role in external relations than his predecessor. In April 1912, the office of Secretary of State for External Affairs was transferred from the Secretary of State to the Prime Minister. The following year Borden hired Loring C. Christie, a young Nova Scotian who had had a brilliant career in law at Harvard and was a senior official in the United States Department of Justice. Much of the routine work in external relations could be left in the hands of the capable experienced Undersecretary of State for External Affairs, Joseph Pope. But Christie, as "Legal Adviser" to the Department of External Affairs, and as the personal adviser to Borden on external relations, quickly exerted his influence on external policy. He shared Borden's vision. Canada, he wrote, "is destined to be in some sense the mediator between the two great branches of the English-speaking world. . . . Between us we can command the future peace and good order of the world."[8]

Being a partner, even a junior partner, in the command of "the future peace and good order of the world" was a rather tall order for Canada. The nation had scarcely made its presence known in the international arena. Neither of the senior partners in the North Atlantic triangle would readily assent to the proposition that the Canadians understood either of them better than they understood each other. More likely, both London and Washington would regard Canadian attempts at "mediation" in the broad spectrum of Anglo-American relations as both ludicrous and presumptuous. In the past Canada's role in Anglo-American diplomacy had been to be informed and to advise the mother country on the protection of its own interests. Neither the British Foreign Secretary nor the United States Secretary of State would readily think of calling upon Borden and Christie to resolve their differences. Serving as the linchpin in Anglo-American affairs was an ideal to be aimed at, not a role to be assumed immediately by Canada.

In practical terms, Canada's external relations were limited to the protection of perceived Canadian interests. To cite one example, in 1913 both the British and Japanese governments waited patiently for months for Ottawa to adhere to a renewed Anglo-Japanese trade agreement. Borden's government was not opposed to the treaty; indeed, Canadian trade with Japan was not the question at issue. Rather, protracted negotiations were carried on with the Japanese Consul-General in Ottawa in an effort to impose further restrictions upon Japanese immigration. Borden did not believe the Lemieux agreement of 1907 sufficiently protected Canadian interests and he was under constant pressure from McBride to exclude all Japanese immigrants. "We are determined at all hazard to permit of no further encroachment by Japanese on these shores," the British Columbia Premier wrote.[9] In April a bill was presented to the House of Commons to renew the trade agreement with Japan. For three long days the House debated whether adherence to the treaty would impair Canada's power to restrict Japanese immigration. Only after assurance from the government that Canada retained full control of its immigration policy did the bill pass.[10] The question, Borden said as the debate concluded, "is not, at the bottom, one of race or of discrimination against a nationality, but the question is one of economic concern. Therefore, it would be perfectly possible, whether this treaty did come into force or not, for the Government of Canada to pass regulations under the Immigration Act which would prevent the immigration of persons of a certain occupation whose competition would not be fair to the labouring men of Canada."[11]

In December 1913, with the concern growing daily over the rapid rise of unemployment, Borden's government passed an Order-in-Council forbidding "artisans" and "labourers, skilled or unskilled" from landing at any port in British Columbia. Taken together with existing immigration regulations requiring Asian immigrants to have two hundred dollars in their possession and to proceed to Canada only by "continuous voyage" from their country of origin, the Order-in-Council virtually closed the country to Asian immigration. The Order-in-Council was used in July 1914, as the legal justification for the denial of entry of more than three hundred East Indians who had come to Canada on a chartered Japanese vessel, the *Komagata Maru*. The intending immigrants had been holed up on the ship in Vancouver harbour since May 23 while British Columbians demanded their exclusion and the India Office asked that they be admitted. On July 17 Borden told Perley, who was serving as Acting High Commissioner in London, that the Indian Government must "realize fully that public opinion in this country will not tolerate immigration in any considerable numbers from Asiatic countries and that even more drastic measures and regulations will if necessary be provided in order to prevent an influx of Hindus".[12] Six days later the *Komagata Maru* and its passengers sailed out of Canadian waters escorted by the *Rainbow*, one of the two British warships Laurier had acquired for the Canadian Naval Service.[13] British Columbians enthusiastically supported both the passage of the Order-in-Council and the exclusion of the East Indians aboard the *Komagata Maru*. But both the Anglo-Japanese Treaty debate and the *Komagata Maru* incident, under the pretext of protecting Canadian workmen from unfair competition for employment, embarrassed the British government and illustrated the limits of Canadian co-operation in imperial relations.

The same limits were apparent in the consideration of an expansion of the imperial preference by the Borden government. In the United Kingdom the Opposition Unionists interpreted Borden's election victory as evidence of support of their policy of mutual imperial preference agreements.[14] When they learned that Borden was going to visit the mother country in 1912, they spared no effort to see that the colonial was given the proper perspective on the preference issue. There were, however, two difficulties. First, Borden's own commitment to the preference ideal was, at best, shallow; during the election campaign he had assured Canadian manufacturers that he would not support any adjustment of the Canadian preferential tariff which would impair their interests. Equally important was the awkward fact that Borden had to deal with the Liberal government, not the Unionist Opposition. He did tell the Unionist leader, fellow-Canadian Bonar Law, that if the British imposed customs duties which would give a preference to Canadian goods, he would consider some method of increasing the Canadian preference upon British imports. Law anxiously inquired in October 1912, if Borden was going to make such an announcement soon. More than a month later Borden replied that no suitable occasion had arisen but that it might come up at the time of the next budget. In late December 1912, the Unionists party nearly split apart on the question of advocating preferential duties on foodstuffs. Borden seized the occasion to tell L. S. Amery that "since the question of food taxes has become a question of such fierce controversy in the United Kingdom I have endeavoured to abstain from any action which might be regarded as undesirable or obtrusive interference".[15] The 1913 budget contained no announcement concerning the imperial preference. In subsequent months George Foster tried to use his appointment as the Canadian representative on the Dominions Royal Commission on Natural Resources, Trade and Legislation to round up support for mutual imperial preferences.[16] He was not encouraged by Borden.

A broader scheme of mutual preferential tariffs would have been welcomed by some Canadians. Canadian farmers wanted British preferential duties on their food exports. Some advocates of imperial centralization thought an elaborate plan of imperial preferences was the surest way to their ultimate goal. Others, however, including both the British and Canadian members of the Round Table movement, an organization established in 1909 to study imperial problems and promote imperial unity, knew that the preference was so divisive politically in both Britain and in Canada that its promotion could hinder imperial centralization.[17] In Canada, the manufacturers were adamantly opposed to any expansion of the preference on British imports and Borden's studied inactivity reflected the lack of any pressing domestic concern on the preference issue.

By contrast, the revival of the naval debate aroused the deepest political passions. When Borden presented his naval legislation to the House of Commons in December 1912, it touched off one of the longest and bitterest debates in the history of the Canadian Parliament. As in 1909 and 1910, the argument went to the very core of the imperial relationship and aroused the deepest emotions of both proponents and opponents of imperial unity. As in 1909 and 1910, the different perceptions of a proper imperial relationship held by French and English Canadians were put in sharp relief. Both Borden and Laurier strove to deal with the naval issue on the high plane of statesmanship. Both failed. Before the debate was over it became a fierce partisan struggle that did credit to neither party leader.

Borden had carefully evaded the navy issue during the 1911 election. During the Throne Speech debate at the opening of the first session of the twelfth Parliament he was equally non-committal. "It is infinitely better to be right than to be in a hurry," he said. "Permanent cooperation" should be debated at length and any plan should be submitted to the people. He had no immediate recommendations. He simply proposed to discover "what are the conditions that confront the Empire".[18]

Four months later, on March 18, 1912, Borden made a tactical error. He told the House that when his permanent policy was formulated it would be submitted to the people. He added that any Canadian role in imperial naval defence would have to be matched by "a greater voice in the councils of the Empire than [we] have had in past years". That was all very well. But his most important point was the announcement that his government would not continue the naval program passed by the Laurier government in 1910.[19] This was an obvious concession to the Nationalist members from Quebec who had demanded repeal of the Naval Service Act. Borden presented no alternative plan, nor any hint that there would be one in the near future. Consequently, the announcement smacked of partisan politics and antagonized the Liberal opposition. It set the stage for the vigorous party obstruction by the Liberals when Borden did bring a naval program before the House of Commons.

His intention was to develop a different permanent policy for naval defence, a policy which he hoped would have the support of both the Nationalists and the Imperialists in his party. But suddenly there was an abrupt change of plan. Within a week of Borden's suspension of the Naval Service Act, the First Lord of the Admiralty, Winston Churchill, announced a stepped-up Dreadnought building program in response to new German naval construction. A permanent Canadian naval policy was temporarily put aside. The thorny question of an emergency contribution again came to the fore because Churchill's March 18 speech

clearly invited Dominion contributions to the British Dreadnought program.[20]

Borden did not doubt the seriousness of the situation for a
moment. Arrangements were quickly made for a trip to England.
On June 1 he sought advice on naval policy from a number of his
supporters. Borden's letter made it clear that he was already
convinced an emergency situation did exist. He asked Whitney,
among others, to comment upon "the necessity or expediency of
an effective contribution for the temporary purpose of meeting
conditions which undoubtedly confront the Mother Country at
the present time". Whitney quickly replied that an emergency
contribution was both "necessary" and "expedient" to maintain
"our self-respect as a nation".[21]

Borden's conviction that the emergency situation warranted
a Canadian contribution was not shared by his French Canadian
colleagues. He believed they would eventually support him if a
strong case for a contribution could be made. From the very
beginning he and they had agreed, as Burrell had put it in 1910,
"on the desirability of giving a contribution in case of emergency". They differed only on the "fact of emergency". And Borden
was even more insistent than they that a Canadian contribution
to naval defence had to be matched by a Canadian voice in
imperial foreign policy. Neither point could be settled in Ottawa.
Only the Admiralty could establish the fact of emergency beyond
doubt; only the British government could grant a Canadian
presence in the councils of peace and war. On June 26 Borden,
Hazen, Doherty, and Pelletier—Monk was invited and refused to
go—sailed from Montreal on the *Royal George*. Once past Quebec,
Borden and his shipmates settled into a daily round of conferences preparatory to their meetings with members of the British
government. To buttress his arguments, the Prime Minister carefully read through A. B. Keith's recently published *Responsible
Government in the Dominions*.[22]

A large crowd greeted Robert and Laura and the other Canadians when the ship docked at Bristol just before noon on July 4.
After receiving an address of welcome from the mayor, the party
took the train to London. In mid-afternoon Lord Strathcona, the
Canadian High Commissioner in London, and Casgrain and the
Mayor of Ottawa headed the crowd that greeted them on the
platform at Paddington Station. After countless rounds of cheers
Strathcona took them to their hotel where they found a huge pile
of invitations awaiting them.[23]

The visit gave Borden an opportunity to discuss a whole list of questions with the British government. Next to the navy problem the most important was British reaction to proposed amendments of the British North America Act to provide for the appointment of more Senators. For almost two months there was an endless round of conferences, dinners, and weekends with leaders of the Asquith government, prominent Unionists, and some British members of the Round Table movement. Late in July Borden spent four days in Paris. In August he toured British shipyards and discussed with their owners plans for building ships in Canada. And there was an on-going series of ceremonial occasions of which the highlight was his investiture into the Imperial Privy Council on July 19.

But the naval question dominated Borden's thoughts and activity. On his first day in London, Churchill told him the naval situation was "very serious". Ten days later another interview with the First Lord was "quite satisfactory. He is quite willing to play the game. Will give assurance in writing as to necessity [of an emergency contribution]."[24] That seemed to meet the first requirement for French-Canadian support.

The question of a Canadian voice in imperial foreign policy was more difficult to resolve. Numerous discussions were held with Prime Minister Asquith, Colonial Secretary Harcourt, Churchill, and others. Borden defended his demand publicly in a series of speeches and in private in two meetings of the Committee of Imperial Defence. He knew that Asquith had rejected the idea of Dominion participation in the formulation of foreign policy when the question was discussed at the Imperial Conference of 1911. But Asquith now informed him that the Conference had recommended Dominion representation at meetings of the Committee of Imperial Defence when their problems were being discussed. He offered this to Borden who accepted it as a "temporary measure".[25] It was not all Borden wanted. Dominion representatives would only be invited to meetings of the Committee of Imperial Defence when their affairs were being considered. Moreover, though Borden may not have thoroughly understood its role, the CID was a purely advisory committee which did not formulate imperial foreign policy. Still, it was a step forward that he could present to his French-Canadian colleagues.

Just as he was preparing to return home, Borden received a confidential memorandum on the naval emergency from Churchill.

It was not satisfactory. Borden needed two documents, a public statement and a confidential memorandum for his Cabinet. He sat up most of the night of August 26–27 revising the confidential draft and making suggestions for a public paper.[26] He sailed for home on the 29th. A month later Churchill's revised documents reached Ottawa.

Borden found the secret memorandum "very impressive" and immediately read both papers to his Cabinet. Monk's response annoyed him. He now demanded a plebiscite on an emergency contribution. "Long discussion as to consultation of the people. Monk very strong as to this. Nantel merely his echo. It would probably be fatal to us in the English Provinces."[27] The Cabinet debated the emergency contribution for weeks. Monk remained adamant on the necessity of a plebiscite, the English Canadians equally adamant as to its impropriety. On October 11 Monk told Borden he would "retire unless we consult people" and a week later he left the Cabinet.[28] Borden had expected Monk would retire for some time and had already begun considering a replacement for him. He was more concerned whether he could hold the support of the other Nationalists. He already knew that Nantel would stay in the Cabinet, and he still wanted his party to "go united before Parliament".[29] If Monk's resignation was the price to be paid for the apparent unity of his party on the naval question, he was ready to pay it.

On November 27 the Prime Minister called his French-Canadian members together. He offered a number of inducements for their support of an emergency contribution. He proposed to repeal the Naval Service Act. He emphasized the importance of Canadian representation on the CID. And he gave them a preliminary sketch of his plans for a permanent naval policy, including a substantial ship-building industry in Quebec.

> Boulay, Barette [Barrette], Bellemare, Achim and Gailbault [Guilbault] said they agreed the proposals are wise but they are bound by promises. Lavallee and Gauthier said notwithstanding promises they would vote for us. Also Paquet, Rainville, Blondin and Sevigny.[30]

Some of the French Canadians were won over and, along with Pelletier and Nantel, would support Borden's naval policy. But others would not, and he could not go to the House with a united party behind him.

On December 5, 1912, the Prime Minister introduced his naval aid bill. It was an uncomplicated measure with five brief clauses; following White's advice, there was no elaborate preamble justifying the principles behind the emergency contribution, and it did not repeal the Naval Service Act.[31] The bill called for a grant of $35 million to be used for the "construction and equipment of battleships or armoured cruisers of the most modern and powerful type". When built, the ships would be placed "at the disposal of His Majesty for the common defence of the Empire".[32] Negotiations with the British Government on the question of returning the ships "to [the] Canadian government whenever Canada is prepared to maintain them" were still pending when the naval aid bill was introduced.[33]

Borden's speech emphasized the emergency nature of the contribution. The Prime Minister looked to the not too distant day when a huge shipbuilding industry in Canada would supply smaller vessels for the Royal Navy and construct the ships of a Canadian force. And he made much of the demand for a Canadian voice in imperial foreign policy. "When Great Britain no longer assumes sole responsibility for defence upon the high seas, she can no longer undertake to assume sole responsibility for and sole control of foreign policy which is closely, vitally associated in that defence in which the Dominions participate."[34] The British government, he said, "would welcome the presence in London of a Canadian minister during the whole or a portion of the year."

> Such a minister would be regularly summoned to *all* meetings of the Committee of Imperial Defence and would be regarded as one of its permanent members. No important step in foreign policy would be undertaken without consultation with such a representative of Canada.[35]

This extraordinary statement was not an accurate account of his agreement with Asquith. It greatly exaggerated the role any Canadian representative in London might be expected to play in the formation of imperial foreign policy. Five days later a despatch from the Colonial Secretary pointedly reminded Borden that a Canadian minister "would at all times have free and full access to the Prime Minister, Secretary of State for Foreign Affairs and Secretary of State for the Colonies for information on all questions of Imperial policy". But "full and free access" to "information" was not the same thing as "consultation". Moreover, the Canadian minister would not be "regularly summoned to all meetings of the Committee of Imperial Defence". Rather, he would attend "when questions of naval and military defence affecting the Overseas Dominions are under consideration". Finally, Harcourt noted that during their discussions with Borden he and Asquith had "pointed out to him that the Committee of Imperial Defence is a purely advisory body and is not and cannot under any circumstances become a body deciding on policy".[36] It is not clear whether Borden fully understood the subtle but very important differences between his and Harcourt's versions of the agreement reached in London during the summer. At any rate, Borden did not modify his account of the role the proposed resident Canadian minister in London would play in the formation of foreign policy during the naval debate.

A week later Sir Wilfrid presented the policy of the Opposition. Laurier said Borden's emergency contribution was "not an adequate or satisfactory expression of the aspirations of the Canadian people in regard to Naval defence", demanded "speedy" reinstatement of the Naval Service Act, and asked for the construction of two fleet units which would be stationed on the Atlantic and Pacific coasts of Canada.[37]

Borden's resolution and Laurier's amendment initiated the most acrimonious debate the House of Commons had ever witnessed. The Conservatives held the floor and marshalled every possible argument for a contribution in the first few days of debate in January 1913. Then the Liberals mounted a parade of speakers between January 31 and February 13 to denounce Borden's policy. "We are asked to give an amount of money which is not needed," claimed L. J. Gauthier, in return for having "an adviser when an adviser is not requested".[38] "Canada is to embark on the whirlpool of European politics," warned H. S. Beland.[39] On the 13th, Laurier's amendment was defeated, 122 to 75 and, later in the day, Borden's resolution carried, 115 to 83. After two more weeks of debate the naval aid bill passed second reading. As they had on the 13th, seven Conservative Nationalists voted with the Liberals.*

On Monday, March 3, the naval aid bill went into committee stage. From then until Saturday, the 15th, except for Sundays,

---

*The seven were H. Achim, J.-A. Barrette, A. Bellemare, H. Boulay, E. Guilbault, P.-E. Lamarche, and A.-A. Mondou. Monk, who was ill, was not present for any of the recorded votes on the naval aid bill.

the House sat in continuous session. The Liberals openly admitted their purpose was obstruction. "We are going to sit until Christmas time, if necessary," J. P. Molloy threatened, "to prevent the passage of this Bill".[40] Borden quickly became impatient with colleagues and Opposition members alike. When one of his backbenchers forced him to return to the Commons chamber to straighten out a procedural point, Borden scathingly denounced the poor man for his error. Later, regretting his flare of temper, he "wrote Currie consoling letter. He wept. Geo. Lafontaine also wept today when I spoke kindly to him."[41] Laurier was equally restive. Donald Mann, who was acting as an intermediary between the party leaders, reported on Saturday, March 8, that Sir Wilfrid was "very angry and will fight to the end. Laurier says I practically agreed not to sit beyond midnight. This is of course not true."[42] Over the night of March 14–15 the business of the House dissolved into a chaotic scene. Borden recorded the events in his diary:

> I went to the office early [Friday] morning and remained in House until 8 Saturday morning. Ruled Laurier's amendments out of order. Points of order all night and appeals therefrom. Objected that Deputy Speaker absent and Chairman not qualified. I made short speech in French. Quebec members congratulated me. Returned to House this afternoon after two hours sleep. Very warm and even bitter feeling between the two parties. As midnight approached Speaker twice had to take the chair amid scenes of great disorder. The whole opposition on their feet gesticulating and bellowing. Dr. Clarke was named by Speaker who showed great decision and firmness. I prepared resolution suspending Clarke but first asked him to apologize which he did. Our men angry at end and both sides wanted a physical conflict. Primeval passions.[43]

Borden warned the Governor General that he was considering introducing closure. "The present position of the House is painful to its credit and incompatible with the performance of its inherent functions. When obstruction reaches the point of destroying Parliamentary Government it must be arrested, condemned and banished," he argued. "Liberty of speech ought to be preserved: but, as Mr. Gladstone said, it must be prevented from descending into frivolity and license."[44] For some time his caucus had been urging him to restrict the ability of the Opposition to obstruct the naval aid bill. In mid-February he appointed a small committee of private members to consider amendments of the rules of the House. Led by Arthur Meighen, the committee devised additions to House Rule 17 which defined the circumstances requiring closure and the procedure for applying it. Meighen also suggested a clever device which would deny Laurier the opportunity to make amendments when Borden introduced the rule changes. On April 7 Laurier told Borden that the Liberals "would make no arrangement" to bring the naval debate to an end.

Two days later, after the Conservative caucus was instructed "not to raise points of order and not to interrupt", Borden introduced the rules to apply closure. Laurier was denied the customary right of reply to the Prime Minister when the Speaker recognized Hazen who moved the previous question. William Northrup then moved that Hazen be heard. "Laurier and Grits very angry and demonstrative," Borden dryly wrote in his diary.[45] When Laurier finally got a chance to speak later in the day, he was bitter. "The poison he offers us to-day will come to his own lips at some future day; we are in the minority; we can be gagged; we can be prevented from expressing our opinions; they can trample upon our rights. But, Sir, the day of reckoning will come and it comes as soon as we have a dissolution of the present Parliament."[46]

For another two weeks the short-tempered MP's debated the closure motion. The original question at issue, whether an emergency contribution should be made to the imperilled Royal Navy, had almost vanished from the scene. Instead, members' attention was firmly focused on partisan bickering and wrangling. The cry of "gagging" was used by both sides. "If there has been gagging," Borden said on April 22, "it has been the gagging of the majority of this House who have been prevented by Hon. gentlemen on the other side, with taunts and insinuations, from recording their votes on measures which have been presented to this Parliament."[47] The next day the closure rules were adopted, 108 to 73. And finally, on May 15, the naval aid bill passed third reading. "Laurier and Guilbault contended for the honour of moving six months hoist," Borden sourly noted, "and Laurier won by a neck or rather by a mouth. Five Nationalists (Achim, Barrette, Bellemare, Boulay and Guilbault) against us and we had a majority of 33."[48]

There was little sense of jubilation in the government camp—only exhaustion, a collection of tainted recollections of five months of partisan insults, and a very real fear that Laurier's promised "day of reckoning" might come long before dissolution. Borden had known for some time that there would be trouble in the Senate. He asked James Lougheed, the government leader, to negotiate a compromise with Sir George Ross, the Liberal leader in the upper chamber. Ross, an ardent Imperialist, was as anxious as anyone to make a contribution to the Royal Navy. But to sweeten the proposal in the Senate, he suggested that some small appropriation for a permanent policy be added to Borden's bill. Borden wanted to keep a clear distinction between emergency and permanent policy, but he probably was willing to accept such an amendment from the upper house. However, neither Ross nor Borden fully appreciated the anger of the Liberals in the Commons. Borden had inflicted the greatest possible insult on their policy; he had virtually declared the Naval Service Act of 1910 a dead letter. More important, he had gagged their leader, the most eloquent and respected parliamentarian of the day. The talks with Ross collapsed. At the end of May, the Senate returned the naval aid bill to the House of Commons with a short, cutting message: "This House is not justified in giving its assent to the Bill until it is submitted to the judgement of the country."

The great naval debate was over. The Senate amendment killed the naval aid bill and challenged the Borden government to take its naval policy to the people. At various times between June 1913 and the beginning of the Great War, Borden threatened to push forward with one form or another of his emergency contribution policy. As early as June 6 he told the House of Commons that before the additional ships laid down by the British were completed he would "introduce a bill to pay for them and take them over".[49] He had already assured Churchill and Colonial Secretary Harcourt that "Canada will ultimately defray the cost". But the British government was not impressed. "The Cabinet were unanimous that this suggestion could not be entertained," Prime Minister Asquith reported to the King. "It would be in the nature of a gambling transaction, and would be construed in Canada as a direct intervention by the Imperial Government in her party controversies." Churchill produced an alternative plan for naval construction that took no account of a Canadian contribution. In February 1914, Asquith again reported on Borden's "continued default" and his "admitted inability to make any progress with the Canadian contribution this year".[50] Canada would enter the war with neither the naval force Laurier had planned nor the Canadian Dreadnoughts Borden had proposed.

Another victim of the naval debate of 1913 was Borden's own plan for a permanent naval policy. During March 1913, he had given an outline of his plan to the Duke of Connaught. It differed from Laurier's naval service in three respects. First, Borden proposed a much broader development of Canadian maritime services, including the building of commercial vessels. Second, as Hazen had hinted in 1912, the Borden government rejected the concept of separate navies in wartime. The "defence of the Empire upon the high seas cannot be successfully accomplished by a series of scattered navies." But there could be Imperial fleet units, contributed by and recallable to the Dominions. The three Dreadnoughts of the naval aid bill, Borden suggested, might form the nucleus of a Canadian "unit or units of the Imperial Navy". And finally, Borden again tied the navy and imperial foreign policy together.

> It has been said in Great Britain that any such proposal would abnegate the control by the people through their representatives of foreign policy relations. This argument seems to proceed upon the assumption that the people who can properly be entrusted with such control reside wholly within the United Kingdom. The people are undoubtedly entitled to control foreign policy but there are at least fifteen millions of them outside the United Kingdom.

"Cooperation" in naval defence was, in short, inseparable from "responsibility and voice in foreign policy".[51] Borden's ambitious plan was never put in legislative form. Given the mood of the Senate and the Opposition, there would have been no point to the effort.

The inconclusive naval debate left unresolved the fundamental question implicit in the naval issue over the last four years. In mid-December 1913, Loring Christie prepared a memorandum for his chief on Canada's role in external relations. His reflections were pessimistic. "The Canadian people must sooner or later assume a control over foreign policy (i.e., over the issues of peace and war) no less than that now exercised by the people of Britain or by the U.S.A." Christie saw only two routes to the goal. Canadians could separate "their own foreign policy from that of the Empire" and control "it through their own Dominion Government", or they could insist "that the foreign policy of the Empire be separated from the domestic affairs of Britain and entrusted to a government responsible no less to Canadian than to British voters". Canadians, Christie concluded, "do not grasp the reality of these two alternatives, neither of which is palatable, nor do they understand that it is impossible to evade one or the other."[52] Borden agreed that neither alternative was palatable. One was tantamount to a declaration of independence from the Empire, the other implied far more centralization of imperial foreign policy than he could accept. He thought Christie's conclusions were too rigid, that autonomy and responsibility in external policy could be achieved by more gradual steps which would eventually give Canada "control" over her own foreign relations and a voice in imperial foreign policy. His naval policy had been an attempt to achieve that goal in external affairs. But it had been blocked by the Senate.

Finally, the great naval debate was the major test of Borden's support in French Canada. The first public sign of a break in French-Canadian support was Monk's resignation in October 1912. No one doubted the sincerity of Monk's conviction on the naval issue. He did not believe in an emergency contribution and, in fact, he never had. But it was also true that Monk was looking for an appropriate occasion to resign. He did not like his position as Minister of Public Works; the demands of the job overwhelmed him and the patronage aspects of the work discouraged him. More important, he was not well[53] and after his resignation from the Cabinet he was seldom seen in the House of Commons again. And during his tenure of office he was under constant pressure from his friend Bourassa to oppose Borden's policies on both the navy question and on a renewal of the age-long dispute over separate schools in Canada.

The Borden government's first association with the separate schools issue occurred in the spring of 1912 when it fulfilled an election promise by extending the Manitoba boundary to annex the District of Keewatin. Bourassa and Lavergne and Paul Emile Lamarche, one of Borden's backbenchers, insisted that the government provide constitutional guarantees for Keewatin's Catholic schools in the Act transferring the territory. Monk, to Bourassa's dismay, defended the government's refusal to write constitutional safeguards into the legislation by arguing that Ottawa could not force Manitoba to provide guarantees for separate schools which, in fact, did not exist at the time of the transfer. Robert Rogers persuaded his friends in Winnipeg and among the French-Canadian Conservatives to accept a compromise, whereby the Roblin govenment would promise to deal justly and tolerantly with Manitoba Catholics on the schools issue. "Hon. Bob" arranged a banquet in Winnipeg in April to seal the bargain publicly. Armand Lavergne and Lamarche, Eugene Paquet, J. H. Rainville, and Louis Coderre from Borden's party were all present to congratulate Premier Roblin on the expansion of his province.[54]

Just two days after the Winnipeg banquet the Whitney government announced new regulations for bilingual schools in Ontario which insisted that instruction in English begin as soon as a child entered any Ontario school, either public or separate, and that instruction in French not be allowed after the first two years of schooling. The new rules, soon known simply as "Regulation 17", caused an immediate protest in French Canada. By the fall of 1912, when Borden was trying to convince his French-Canadian colleagues to accept his emergency naval aid policy, the pressure from Quebec for Ottawa to intervene was so intense that Borden and Pelletier wrote to Whitney expressing their concern.[55] Whitney was not about to make any deals with his federal colleagues in a matter within his jurisdiction. On October 17 he gave Borden a vigorous defence of his policy, in effect telling the Prime Minister that "Regulation 17" was none of his business.[56] Monk knew that Borden could not afford to do anything more which might provoke a quarrel with Whitney and he knew that Borden was determined to have his naval aid bill. He gave his resignation to Borden the next evening.

Borden had mixed feelings about Monk's departure. On the one hand he seemed relieved to see his troublesome colleague go. Just after Monk's resignation, Borden called some reporters from Tory papers to his office. The pressmen found the Prime Minister "in an extraordinary good humour, far removed from his customary formality". But he cautioned them to be "very tender in [their] treatment of Mr. Monk". "Monk has been handled delicately," Borden told them, "has needed such handling, & if the process is kept up may take up an advantageous attitude."[57] Over the next several months Borden offered his former lieutenant a number of positions. All were refused. Monk was too tired, too sick, and too full of politics. He died on May 15, 1914.

Of the remaining nineteen French-Canadian members from Quebec, seven consistently voted against Borden's naval policy and twelve, including Pelletier and Nantel, supported it with equal regularity. But, like Monk, the other seven members, Achim, Barrette, Bellemare, Boulay, Guilbault, Lamarche, and Mondou, did not leave the party. Indeed, on nearly every other issue brought to a vote in the House of Commons before the war, they supported the government.[58]

For four years, in opposition and in power, the naval issue had confounded Borden's efforts to keep his party united on policy questions. He had tried to find a policy all could support. He was prepared to submit his permanent policy to the people. He thought that he could convince all of his French-Canadian members of the "fact of emergency" that would justify his naval aid bill. And, in response to a demand from them, he had suspended the implementation of the Naval Service Act of 1910. But that concession set the stage for the bitter prolonged debate in the House of Commons and led directly to the Senate amendment challenging him to take his emergency policy to the people. The Conservative majority in the House and the Liberal majority in the Senate were in deadlock. Only the electorate could break it.

CHAPTER TWELVE

THE LAST DAYS OF PEACE

Since the election of 1911 Robert Borden had focussed his attention on the drafting and implementation of government policy. He was attracted to this kind of work and found the business of governing the country rewarding. He spent days drafting, redrafting, and redrafting again the major speeches he was going to make in the House of Commons. He prided himself upon his "business-like" presentation of major policy statements and carefully noted the responses they received in his diary. By contrast, the Prime Minister found the continuing responsibilities of party leadership more irritating than ever before. Especially irksome were the endless complaints about the distribution of patronage. Every region, every interest, every religious group demanded its fair share and each differed as to what the others' fair share was. Every position awarded made one friend and many enemies; every project begun in one region slighted another. Wherever Borden went he was badgered by seekers of offices and contracts. During one trip to Halifax they were "as thick as autumn leaves in Vallombrosa" and he suffered through a "meeting of County Executive and Ward Chairmen and listened to more than two hours [of] complaints as to distribution of patronage".[1]

When he could safely do so, he delegated the resolution of the party's quarrels and disputes to a few of his colleagues. Most often the assignments were given to J. D. Reid and Robert Rogers, men who were respected in party circles for their "practical" approach to politics. Rogers was very effective at patching up differences. He was always going somewhere, carefully and smoothly explaining why projects were delayed or contracts not let and testing the local political winds before a scheduled by-election.

But many problems could not be delegated. Major appointments, for example, went right to the heart of party life and were the object of fierce competition. Only the Prime Minister could make the choices. Near the top of the list were Senate appointments and in the spring of 1913 there was a nasty quarrel in the Cabinet over a proposal to appoint four new Senators from Ontario. At a regular Saturday mid-day Cabinet meeting on May 24 there was a "fierce controversy between Pelletier and Doherty; also between Crothers and Cochrane. Very unpleasant. After Council had conference with Doherty and Pelletier but made no progress. Pelletier came in afternoon in a condition bordering on delirium." Sunday was worse. "A terrible day with Pelletier and Crothers about Senate appointments. Pelletier to see me from 12 to 1. In afternoon Crothers from 5 to 6 almost crying." And Monday was no better.

> Very tiring and worrying day, especially as to Senate appointments. Doherty has to some extent become sane on the subject, but the Frenchmen, especially Pelletier, are absolutely delirious and wild. Innumerable conferences with them until 1:30 a.m. Pelletier says he must resign unless a Frenchman appointed. I gave best of reasons why it cannot be done now but said it would be done on next occasion.[2]

Monk's resignation raised an even more contentious problem, finding another Quebec representative to sit in the Cabinet. Casgrain was approached and again refused. Marechal, whose name had also been put forward in 1911, considered, hesitated, and then declined, causing Borden to reflect that it was "very difficult to make progress as Frenchmen are so variable and unstable".[3] George Drummond urged that Herbert Ames be appointed to give English-Protestant Quebeckers representation and claimed that Ames had the support of the French-Canadian Conservatives.[4] But that would not do. Borden needed a French-Canadian replacement who would support his naval policy. In the end, Louis Coderre, a Montreal lawyer who had first been elected to Parliament in 1911, accepted the Secretary of State portfolio. Pelletier desperately wanted to switch from the Post Office to Public Works but Borden refused. Rogers, who had done so much to maintain party harmony, was given Monk's old position and Doctor Roche moved from Secretary of State to Interior. And Coderre left Ottawa to seek re-election in Hochelaga.

For a time Borden planned to join his campaign. But with the naval issue still to be resolved, with French-Canadian support wavering, Borden's presence in Hochelaga became, as he put it, "not only unnecessary but undesirable".[5] Pelletier, White, Doherty, Crothers, Nantel, Rainville, Ames, and Marechal all campaigned for the new Minister.[6] Coderre won easily, increasing his majority by nearly a thousand votes. The Prime Minister, unwanted, stayed in Ottawa.

It was very suggestive of Borden's relationship with his French-Canadian ministers. Only Monk had a significant following in Quebec, and he alone was really respected by Borden. He tolerated the others, Pelletier and Nantel, and then Coderre, consulting them only when necessary. Pelletier was the most bothersome. He seemed to have a penchant for resigning and offered his resignation to Borden in both 1913 and 1914. On the later occasion Borden dismissed the threat with the comment, "annual resignation received from Pelletier".[7]

Pelletier was forever getting into trouble. At the beginning of 1914, without consulting the Cabinet, the Postmaster General authorized the distribution of bilingual postcards, which had always been used in Quebec, throughout the country. There was an immediate outcry in English Canada. "My people are kicking," warned J. H. Burnham, the Tory member for Peterborough West. Burnham and correspondents from numerous Orange Lodges across the country contended that the use of bilingual postcards contravened the British North America Act. Kemp, who was himself a prominent Orangeman, told Borden that he "regards situation as very serious".[8] Pelletier and his Deputy Minister argued just as forcefully that issuing the cards was well within the bounds of the BNA Act.[9]

It was the political ramifications of Pelletier's administrative blunder, not the constitutional case, which upset Borden. "Whether the course which you took was or was not constitutionally justifiable, it had never before been adopted in the half century of Confederation," he told Pelletier in early February. "For this reason and because it involved not only a question of administration but a question of policy in a very delicate and difficult matter, you should have consulted Council and especially myself, before taking such a course."[10] Two weeks later the

Prime Minister "spoke strongly to Pelletier about detriment to the party which his stupidity and vanity have occasioned".[11] It took more than a year to resolve the problem by distributing bilingual postcards only in Quebec and the portion of eastern Ontario where the population was predominantly French-speaking.[12] But Borden's brusque dressing-down of Pelletier and his apparent dismissal of the constitutional case for bilingual postcards offended his French-Canadian colleagues.

Monk's departure and Borden's treatment of Pelletier, Nantel, and Corderre did not help the party in Quebec. Quebec Tories found themselves with no effective spokesman in Ottawa. The party leader could keep neither the ministers nor the party members from quarreling. In the Quebec district a patronage dispute between Pelletier's men and the followers of Sir Rodolphe Forget was so intense that William Price threatened to withdraw his support for the party.[13] In 1913 Borden turned to an old friend, Sir Charles Fitzpatrick, former Liberal Cabinet minister for the Quebec district and now Chief Justice of the Supreme Court of Canada, to settle the problem. At first sight it was an extraordinary choice. But "Fitz", despite his position, was still very much involved in Quebec politics, had close connections with Quebec City businessmen like the influential contractor, M. P. Davis, and was willing to lend a hand.

Fitzpatrick quickly reported that the chief problem in Quebec City was the delay in building the National Transcontinental terminals. R. W. Leonard, the NTR Commissioner, was arguing with both the Minister of Railways, Cochrane, and the contractor, Davis, about the terminals and related matters. "Davis is incensed beyond expression and an explosion may come at any time," Fitzpatrick warned. Moreover, the failure to complete the terminals could result in the Grand Trunk Pacific diverting all its grain shipments into the lake ports or the United States, depriving Quebec City of its promise to be a major grain export centre. The whole business community was "grumbling".[14] Rogers was sent to Quebec City to "cooperate" with Fitzpatrick in patching up the political rifts and getting construction underway. By the fall of 1913 "Hon. Bob" and the Chief Justice had arranged for Borden to lay the cornerstone for the new National Transcontinental shops and to be the guest of honour at a "nonpartisan" banquet in Quebec City.[15]

At the last moment Pelletier had been brought into the discussions and, Fitz reported, had "really done good work". But it had been Rogers and Fitzpatrick who had solved the troubles in Quebec City and the impression left upon the city's businessmen was not entirely favourable. As they saw it, the Borden government had been responsible for the long delay in construction of the terminals. The government had not acted until party powers like Price threatened trouble. And then the chief government emissaries were a Manitoba minister and the former Liberal minister for the district. Their own representative in the Cabinet had played a secondary role. None of this augered well for Conservative fortunes in Quebec.

A year later, though the terminals were being constructed, the central problem of patronage remained unresolved. French-speaking Conservatives complained that they were cut out of the disposal of party favours. The president of the Conservative Association of the Quebec District told Borden that "nous nous sommes plusieurs fois plaints, que la direction des affaires fédérales, au point de vue du patronage, était faite de manière à annuler complètement notre travail, et même, avait pour résultant trop fréquent de favoriser nos adversaires".[16] Similarly, in the Eastern Townships, Senator Rufus Pope and the regional organizer were being accused of systematically ignoring the French-speaking party members on questions of both policy and patronage.[17] In Montreal it was much the same story. The business community worried over the dominant influence of Ontario, and especially Toronto interests, in the Cabinet and gave only grudging support to Borden's government. The refusal to take Ames into the Cabinet left them, they believed, without a spokesman for their interests. With Monk gone, the French-speaking Conservatives had lost any influence in Ottawa. Both groups complained to Borden that there was no effective organization in the city.[18] "There is nothing doing here," Casgrain wrote, "no organization, no stirring up of the masses; no educational campaign; no telling our people what we have done, what we intend doing; nothing to inspire the young men with confidence in the future of the Conservative Party!"[19]

The party in Quebec suffered from weakness and from negligence. By 1914 few of Borden's French-speaking MP's gave more than token lip-service to the Nationalist principles and rhetoric which had been so important in 1910 and 1911. But none of them had been included in the inner circle Borden consulted on government and party policy. The truth was that they neither had the confidence of the party leader nor did they have sufficient influence in Quebec to force their views upon him. In consequence, as the years passed, the estrangement between Borden and his French-Canadian colleagues deepened and the Conservative party in Quebec grew ever weaker. It was a dangerous situation for a party planning an election.

By the spring of 1914 there was abundant evidence that Borden and his colleagues were doing just that. The preceding summer the Ministers had set out East and West to promote the government and to bestow favours from Halifax to Vancouver. In September 1913, the Prime Minister had gone to Halifax to defend his "progressive and vigorous policy" in a fighting partisan speech. Anyone who observed the announcements of government programs in the spring of 1914 would not have guessed the country was in the midst of a depression. White told the House of Commons that the duty on agricultural implements would be reduced and that the government had finished the preceding fiscal year with a surplus of $24 million. The Militia Council reported that fifty-one drill halls had been or were being completed in 1913–14 and Hughes announced the expenditure of another two and one-half million on drill halls and armouries for 1914–15. Pelletier reported that 940 new routes had been established in the rural free delivery system in 1913–14. Rogers appointed a royal commission to study the feasibility of constructing the Georgian Bay Canal and his Department had spent more than $27 million in public works during the year, an increase of more than 50 per cent over the previous year's expenditure.[20] The intended message was clear enough. Sound businesslike government could result in fiscal surpluses and continued development, even in bad times.

The Conservative's political prospects appeared equally rosy. Since the 1911 election there had been provincial contests in Ontario, Prince Edward Island, British Columbia, Quebec, New Brunswick, Saskatchewan, and Alberta. Whitney, McBride, and J. K. Flemming, Hazen's successor in New Brunswick, as well as Premier J. A. Mathieson of Prince Edward Island, had all been returned to power with huge Conservative majorities. Expectedly, the Liberals had taken one-sided victories in Quebec,

Saskatchewan, and Alberta. The Conservatives, then, had gained one more provincial government and Whitney and Roblin were expected to easily win again in provincial elections announced for June and July. The results of Dominion by-elections were even more encouraging. The Tories had won five of seven contests in 1912 and six of seven (two by acclamation) in 1913. In short, the party might be even weaker in Quebec than it had been in 1911 but the dominion and provincial electoral results suggested that the voters were not ready to bring Sir Wilfrid Laurier back to power.

The party's organization in Ontario, which had been allowed to slip after the 1911 election, had been revitalized by another infusion of funds from Kemp.[21] Perley, Rogers, and Reid had been delegated to set up a "Federal Press Bureau" to disseminate propaganda favourable to the governing party.[22] Rogers made preliminary arrangements for a September 1914, tour of the west by the Prime Minister.[23] And while the electoral machinery was being warmed up, Borden worried about the political effect of accepting a knighthood. He had been offered the honour once before in December 1912, and had declined it. On the evening of June 17, 1914, a messenger came to his house with a letter from the Governor General saying that the King would be "very disappointed" if Borden did not accept his nomination as Knight Grand Cross of the Order of St. Michael and St. George. Borden quickly decided to accept the knighthood. Then he had second thoughts and took the matter to Cabinet next day where Doherty agreed "that it is rather a detriment from the purely political point of view". However, after some discussion "all thought I should accept" and the public announcement was made on the 22nd.[24]

The Conservative's election platform was ready-made. A vigorous defence of the "equality of opportunity" program would be coupled with an attack on Liberal obstructionism and a demand for major reform of the Senate. The experience of his administration had transformed Borden's ideas on Senate reform from academic musings into a question of very practical politics. The Senate's rejection of his naval aid bill had provoked howls of protest and demands for change in Conservative circles. The Montreal *Star* called the Senate "a band of licensed wreckers", the Halifax *Herald* condemned "the deliberate, disloyal attitude of the Liberal majority in the Senate", and the Winnipeg *Tele-*

gram complained that "the people do not rule when it is left in the power of the Leader in that irresponsible Chamber to dictate and insult the responsible Chamber. That is not democracy; it is oligarchy." McBride and Roblin demanded the Senate be made responsive to the people's will and Premier Mathieson pithily proclaimed that "the Senate must speedily be ended or mended".[25]

In July 1913, Borden had asked Christie to prepare an "abstract of the provisions relating to the elections or appointment of the Senate or upper house" in a long list of countries in the Empire and in the United States, France, Germany, Switzerland, and Italy.[26] At the time he was not sure just how far he wanted to go with Senate reform. But another calculated rebuff from the upper chamber in the 1914 session fixed his determination on fundamental reform. During the session he and Laurier had agreed to redistribute the seats in the House of Commons before the next election on the basis of a report from a bi-partisan committee of MP's. As a corollary to the agreement, Laurier had promised to support Borden's proposal to increase the number of Senators from seventy-two to ninety-six. The redistribution bill and the bill to increase the size of the Senate both received unanimous approval in the House of Commons. But the Senate amended the latter, adding a provision that it would not take effect until after the next election.

Borden was furious. He was absolutely convinced that Sir Wilfrid had broken his promise. On June 9, when Borden asked about Senate reaction to the bill increasing Senate representation, Laurier had told him "there would be no difficulty there so far as he knew". Three days later "*the Grit Senators, doubtless in collusion with their friends in the Commons*, deliberately violated the *agreement* to pass the *resolution for increase in senate representation*."[27] It was the last straw, the final humiliation from Laurier's partisan partners in the chamber of sober second thought.

A resolution was drafted calling for a plebiscite on Senate reform "as soon as possible after the conclusion of the present session". "Since 1867," it declared, "the evolution and development of Federal systems both within the British Empire and in foreign countries has strongly tended in the direction of election of members of the Upper House instead of appointment thereto by the Executive." The people would be asked: "Are you in favour of abolishing the Senate of Canada as at present constituted and of substituting therefor a Senate elected by the people?"[28] In the last days of the 1914 session the resolution was not presented to the House of Commons. Instead, Borden decided to appeal to the people for an elected Senate.

"Everything is happening in a way that makes it wise for you to go to the country in accordance with the several talks we have had on the subject," Perley wrote from London where he was serving as Acting High Commissioner. By early July Whitney's government had scored another overwhelming victory in Ontario and Perley assumed Roblin would do the same in Manitoba. Both railways had been given aid and would "continue their large employment of labor". The financial situation was not good, but there was no expectation that it would be any better in 1915. "The general opinion," Perley concluded, "is that you could win the elections this year."[29] The same advice came from Hector McInnes in Halifax and from correspondents in Saskatchewan and British Columbia.[30]

And then, suddenly, between Thursday, July 9 and the following Wednesday, Borden changed his mind. A combination of circumstances caused Borden to draw back. The critical factor was the Manitoba election, where a revitalized Liberal party led by T. C. Norris threatened to defeat Roblin's government which was plagued with charges of corruption. Rogers, Roche, and Meighen, who were on the spot, reported that "victory is assured" but Borden was "apprehensive".[31] On the 10th he discussed the forthcoming federal election with Sir William Mackenzie. The same day Manitoba electors gave Roblin the barest of majorities; one Minister had been defeated, another won by four votes, others had very small majorities, and the Liberals took four of the six Winnipeg seats. That night, with the voting trend running strongly against the Conservatives, the press reported "that Roblin Gov't. had been defeated".

Manitoba was no longer safe. A decisive victory by Roblin would have assured Borden of substantial support from Winnipeg in the federal campaign. But now Roblin would have to fight to save his own skin and would have little time for federal politics. What made that so serious was that Borden could not count on Whitney either. The Ontario Tories had won another impressive victory in June, but their leader was ill. He had nearly died in January and, though he had recovered enough to take a small part in the election, his health was very precarious. Borden had little confidence in Whitney's colleagues. "Outside of Whitney there seems to be no very outstanding figure in the Ontario Gov't." he had observed at the end of June.[32]

In effect, Borden had lost the effective support of his two strongest allies, Whitney and Roblin. When he turned to his own colleagues the prospects were not very promising. In Manitoba, Rogers, Roche, and Meighen had been supremely confident and had been proven wrong. In Ontario, Reid was in trouble with the local party chiefs because of his proclivity for making appointments without consulting them. Hughes was totally erratic and unreliable. White, whatever his virtues, was scarcely the person to run an election. The job was too big for Crothers, and Kemp, Borden remembered, had had to withdraw from the active work of organization early in the 1911 election. His replacement, Cochrane, now had chronic Bright's disease.

At this point the Quebec situation assumed fundamental importance. Borden, clearly, had been prepared to let Quebec go, much as he had in 1908. He had hoped that Whitney's recovery would be quicker and more substantial than it proved to be, and that Roblin again would win decisively in Manitoba. Neither had happened and the weakness of the party in Quebec could no longer be ignored. Monk was dead, Bourassa was gone, and Pelletier, Nantel, and Coderre could not deliver the votes of French Canadians. Doherty might rally the Irish, but with Perley in London and Ames not in the Cabinet, the English Protestants had no voice. Beyond that, throughout the province organization was in a shambles.

During that decisive week in July Borden considered the sudden turn of events. If he called an election he could expect reduced support in Manitoba and Ontario and a decisive rejection of the Conservative government in Quebec. McBride, Flemming, and Mathieson could still be counted on, but their forces were not enough. The "equal opportunity" platform was a mixed bag of some policies implemented, others rejected by the Senate. Senate reform was a perpetual topic of debate among politicians, a perpetual bore to the electorate. There would be no election. And Borden decided to put off a decision on his proposed western tour until after he had returned from a long awaited vacation in Muskoka.[33]

Late Wednesday evening, July 22, Robert and Laura boarded the sleeper for the overnight trip to Toronto. At noon next day they were on their way to Muskoka. Slowly the Grand Trunk train climbed the grade that separated the Lake Ontario and Georgian Bay watersheds. From the parlour-car window they watched the landscape change from the rich black soil of the Holland Marsh to the harsh splendour of the shield which stretched in a great long arc from Labrador to Manitoba. It was very different from the shore at St. Andrews or Atlantic City's beaches or the rolling hills, red soil, and tall southern pines of the Carolinas and Virginia where they had often vacationed before. It was a land lumbered over and slow to recover from the devastation of the woodsmen's axe, a land of stunted cedars, small oaks, maples, poplars and, in vivid contrast, clumps of glistening white birch, a land more rock than soil, of shallow bogs, and cold clear lakes.

Major H. C. Maclean, a founder of the Maclean Publishing Company, had met the Bordens on the train and took them from Gravenhurst to Port Carling in his launch. The Mayor and councilmen, having been told that Sir Robert and Lady Borden were going to stay at the hotel, met them at the dock. Nervously, His Worship read a formal address of welcome. Then Maclean took them away again for tea at his cottage with Mrs. Timothy Eaton, "a very bright, happy and shrewd old body".[34] Later Robert and Laura returned to the hotel for a light supper and restful evening.

They would always remember this last pre-war vacation. The business of state and party had followed them on most of their previous flights from Ottawa. Just a year before, at St. Andrews, there had been correspondence from Churchill to answer and a day of conferences with Reid about the Quebec terminals. "Telegrams and correspondence continue to pour in about various political matters," Borden had complained. "Many persons apparently consider that my attempt at a holiday gives me ample opportunity to attend to their personal applications or grievances."[35] But this summer Blount was under strict instructions to leave his master in peace. They could be alone or with new found friends, as they chose, when they chose. They played golf on a course which was "quite crude but good enough for exercise". Borden swam at least once each day. And on Friday Mrs. Harriet Sanford, the widow of the late Senator W. E. Sanford of Hamilton, took them on a cruise through Lakes Rosseau and Joseph.

The peace and freedom of Muskoka was a refreshing change from the routine of an Ottawa day. In the capital there was always too much work to do, there were always too many people to see. Borden rose early, around six, and had a light breakfast of fruit, toast, or muffins, perhaps a bit of bacon, and coffee. After an hour or so of work Laura would see him to the door around nine and, if Parliament was sitting, he would invariably tell her, "well, Old Girl, I'm on the way up to face the wild beasts of Ephesus".[36] Robert never owned a car and never learned to drive. He thought an electric brougham given to Laura by the ladies of the Conservative party in 1913 too unreliable after its battery gave out several times some distance from home. He usually walked the mile and a half to his office, though he occasionally rode on the streetcar to Parliament Hill.[37]

The Cabinet met almost daily, Monday through Saturday. Before it, without fail, there was an important person, a delegation, an unhappy colleague to see. If there was time Borden went home for a light lunch and a short walk in the park across Wurtemburg Street from Glensmere. In the afternoon Borden would be at his desk in the House of Commons, answering questions, keeping his followers in line. When the House was not sitting Blount always managed to have more callers for Borden to see, more meetings for him to attend. Between six and seven, he would go home. Miss Lowe, the housekeeper, had a simple, carefully prepared meal waiting. But the work of the day was not over. Borden either returned to the House or repaired to his library where a mass of papers and documents awaited him. Towards midnight he would dutifully record a dozen or so cryptic lines in his pocket diary. Only then would he go to his room, thumb through the pile of daily papers that had been left by his bed and perhaps read a speech by Demosthenes or Cicero in the orignial Greek or Latin from the volume that was always present on his bedside table.[38]

If the routine was broken, it was seldom for relaxation from the cares and responsibilities of office. The Prime Minister was expected to greet and entertain the long line of distinguished visitors who passed through Ottawa, to attend banquets and make solemn speeches to half-caring audiences. During the session the Members of Parliament had to be entertained, forty at a time gracing his table. After the service at All Saints Anglican Church on Laurier Avenue, Sunday was another working day.

Every Sunday afternoon the Bordens had an open house. Ottawa's finest ladies came to take tea and pay their respects; Borden's colleagues came to talk politics. And every Sunday evening the faithful Blount appeared with the routine correspondence of the week under his arm for Borden to answer.

Day after day, week after week it went on like that with no respite. There might be an infrequent game of golf with Laura, or Perley, or White on Saturday afternoon, or an occasional chat for an hour with Campbell Laidlaw, Borden's doctor and close friend, about some medical topic which Borden found fascinating. But it was never enough to break the tedium and the pressure of the work. After months of effort Borden would suddenly be played out. His diary entries would then emphasize his exhaustion, his irritability, his impatience with his work and his colleagues, and a rather exaggerated concern for his health. Often he had some minor ailment, "myalgia of muscle of neck" in June 1913, and a very painful carbuncle and slightly enlarged liver, the latter a periodic recurrence of the nervous dyspepsia he had always lived with, some months later.[39] None of these was serious. His friend Laidlaw later recalled that he was "very rugged".[40] But Borden would become preoccupied with his ailments and worry about them unduly.

His work would be hastily finished and a vacation arranged. If he was left alone, both his health and his attitude soon improved. The local baths would be taken regularly. The local doctors would be consulted and, after a week or so, assure him that his "liver has become normal". They would "[give] me good advice as to conduct of life &c.", as often as not an admonishment to change his work habits, to find more time for relaxation and recreation.[41] After three or four weeks Borden would return to Ottawa and plunge right back into the same dreary exhausting routine.

What happened was that Borden, because of his work habits, suffered minor but regular bouts of hypochondria. The experience, and the behaviour which led to it, was probably not uncommon in the lives of public men who were forced to work intensively, without interruption, for months at a time. There are numerous hints in Borden's diary that some of his colleagues followed much the same work patterns and suffered much the same consequences.[42] The episodes of hypochondria were short-lived and did not seriously affect the conduct of the government.

But when they occurred Borden's tolerance for the foibles of his colleagues, never great, disappeared completely and minor policy decisions were temporarily shelved.

Borden's concern for his own health was, perhaps, intensified by his anxiety about his youngest brothers, Hal, and his mother. Hal, who was carrying on a modest law practice in Halifax and looking after Robert's investments, had never really recovered from the tragic death of his wife in 1905. For a time Robert thought a change of scene might help and considered bringing Hal into his office as a private secretary. In June 1913, Hector McInnes was prepared to offer Hal a partnership in his Halifax law firm and in January 1914, Borden and Doherty discussed an appointment for Hal in the Justice Department.[43] But nothing came of any of these plans. More worrisome was his mother's health. In the winter of 1912–13, when she was eighty-eight, Borden brought her and Julia to Ottawa. He was shocked to find her "much changed" when she arrived in early November. Her condition varied from week to week as Rob made his regular Sunday visits to her apartment at the Roxborough. By April, a month before she and Julia went back to Grand Pré, she was "very much weaker. She has been unable to walk for a week." She had not improved when Borden visited the homestead in the fall of 1913. And just before he went to Muskoka, Borden made another short trip to Grand Pré. "Found mother better than last autumn but entirely an invalid. Very difficult to understand her."[44]

The problems of government and party, the routine of Ottawa life, and the cares of family had all been put aside for the Muskoka vacation. Golf, swiming, evening bridge, and quiet parties with old and new friends filled the days for Robert and Laura at Port Carling. Late Monday afternoon, July 27, Borden read in the papers which had just been delivered at the hotel that "war declared by Austria against Serbia and stock markets in panic".[45] He noted the next day that it would be "almost impossible for us to keep out" of a general European war, but he was not especially concerned. He played golf in the morning with Laura on Tuesday and Wednesday and Thursday, and they visited the falls at Bala with Mrs. Sanford on Wednesday afternoon. Thursday morning when he came off the golf course he found a telegram telling him that the ministers in Ottawa thought he should be prepared "to leave on short notice". That evening he received a more ominous letter from Blount who had been surveying the cables from London. He immediately wired Blount to summon all the Cabinet members to Ottawa and to recall the Governor General from his western tour. He asked that his private railway car be sent to Toronto to meet him next day. Laura was going to stay in Muskoka "for a few days in case I am able to return".[46]

Friday morning Borden took the boat to the Lake Joseph station to meet the Canadian Northern train to Toronto. During the trip south he was impressed by the opulence of the parlour- and dining-cars on Mackenzie's railway. In Toronto he was met by Billy Northrup and C. H. Ritchie, a distinguished Toronto lawyer, and taken to the Albany Club. That evening he attended a small dinner party at the Yacht club. When he finally got to the station the reporters, inevitably, hovered about, insistent to have a statement. "Everyone anticipates war," he observed. "Told reporters merely that situation so serious as to demand my immediate return."[47]

After breakfast in his car, Borden took a cab through the almost empty streets of an early Saturday morning in Ottawa to his office. Blount was waiting for him, ready to summarize the growing pile of cables on his desk. Before the first Cabinet meeting of the day Borden drafted a message for the Colonial Secretary. "If unhappily war should ensue," he wrote, "the Canadian people will be united in a common resolve to put forth every effort and to make every sacrifice necessary to ensure the integrity and maintain the honour of our Empire."[48] Then began an almost continuous round of Cabinet meetings that lasted until Parliament opened on the 18th. At 8:55 on Tuesday evening, August 4, a cable from the Colonial Secretary arrived reporting that the last desperate efforts for peace had failed. The Empire was at war. In the hectic days that followed and amidst rumours that the Austrians were attacking Glace Bay and that German cruisers in the Pacific had sunk the *Rainbow*, the government passed dozens of Orders-in-Council required for the defence of Canada and discussed drafts of the war legislation Borden would present to Parliament. Monday evening, August 17, Borden gave Laurier copies of the Throne Speech and the bills he had prepared. The next night he worked until 1 o'clock on his speech. It would be long and detailed, as most of his speeches were. As he sketched out the last paragraphs, the concluding phrases easily fell into place. He could not foretell how or when this war would end, or what its cost in blood and treasure would be. But of this Borden was sure: the cause was just and Canada's duty was clear.

> Not for love of battle, not for lust of conquest, not for greed of possessions, but for the cause of honour, to maintain solemn pledges, to uphold principles of liberty, to withstand forces that would convert the world into an armed camp; yea, in the very name of the peace that we sought at any cost save that of dishonour, we have entered into this war.[49]

A NOTE ON SOURCES

The principal source for the study of Sir Robert Borden's life is the large collection of Borden Papers at the Public Archives of Canada. This collection was organized after Sir Robert's retirement from public life by W. F. O'Connor to aid Sir Robert in the preparation of his *Memoirs*. Mr. O'Connor divided the main body of the papers dealing with Sir Robert's public career into three series, O.C., O.C.A., and R.L.B., in a manner which apparently made sense to himself and Sir Robert but which has confused researchers ever since the Borden Papers were opened to the public in 1952. A fourth series, the Post-1921 Series, includes Sir Robert's correspondence after his retirement from public life. Fortunately for the student of Borden's life, the Public Archives of Canada has numbered the papers in these four series consecutively and in my footnotes I have referred only to the present volume number and page numbers of the documents. Finally, W. F. O'Connor prepared an extensive body of notes for Sir Robert, and these, together with three volumes of correspondence from 1900 to 1911 and some other material, make up a separately numbered series of twenty volumes called the Memoir Notes Series. When citing from this series, I have included the designation "Memoir Notes" in my footnotes. I have listed all the public Borden Papers as "Borden Papers".

Another set of papers, which includes several hundred pages of family correspondence and Sir Robert's diaries, is housed at the Public Archives of Canada. This collection also merits a few words of explanation. The correspondence, which is presently closed to the public, contains a valuable exchange of letters between Robert and Laura Borden. There are no letters from Laura to Robert Borden after 1905, when the Bordens moved from Halifax to Ottawa, and there are only a few letters from Robert to Laura Borden after that year. In short, almost no correspondence relating to Borden's private life exists after 1905. Sir Robert made frequent entries in a little diary during the year 1873–74 when he was teaching school in Matawan, New Jersey. On June 25, 1912, the day he left Ottawa for England to discuss his naval policy with the British Government, Sir Robert began making daily entries in a small pocket diary, a practice he continued until his death. There are two sets of diaries in the private Borden Papers; the originals, which are written in French for a number of years beginning in 1918, and a typed (and translated) transcript for the years 1912 to 1921 which has often been referred to as the "Extended Diaries". In a few places the typed transcript differs from the original diaries. Where this occurs, I have cited the original diary entry. For many years the diaries have been open to scholars with the permission of Henry Borden. The material in this set of papers is referred to in my footnotes as "Borden Papers Private".

Even in this substantial collection of more than four hundred volumes of public papers and the private papers there are some serious gaps. This is particularly true for the portion of Sir Robert's life covered in this volume. I have not, for example, been able to locate any papers relating to Sir Robert's law firm. Consequently, I have had to rely upon *The Canadian Law Times*, the *Dominion Law Reports*, and Great Britain, *Law Reports*, *Appeal Cases*, for an assessment of his legal career. Nor are there any papers in Borden's pre-1911 correspondence for the year 1908. And the three slim volumes of correspondence before October 1911 are in striking disproportion to the more than three hundred volumes of correspondence covering the years after Sir Robert became Prime Minister. Additional information on Borden's life may be found in *Robert Laird Borden: His Memoirs*, 2 volumes, Toronto, 1938 and in *Letters to Limbo*, Toronto, 1971, both edited by Henry Borden.

The papers of many of the public men associated with Borden and the records of the Parliament of Canada, the Canadian Government, and the British Government contain a wealth of material on Sir Robert's public career. A list of the collections I have used in the preparation of this book and of some of the unpublished theses by other scholars who have written on subjects related to Borden's career follows.

MANUSCRIPTS
Public Archives of Canada
Ballantyne, Charles Colquhoun
Bennett, Rt. Hon. Richard Bedford
Blount, Austin Ernest
Bourassa, Henri
Cahan, Charles H.
Christie, Loring C.
Foster, Sir George Eulas
Fitzpatrick, Sir Charles
Grey of Howick, fourth Earl
Kemp, Sir Albert Edward
Landry, A.-C.-P.-R.
Laidlaw, Dr. Campbell (taped interview)
Laurier, Sir Wilfrid
Law, Andrew Bonar
Magrath, Charles A.
Meighen, Arthur
Minto, fourth Earl
Monk, Frederick Debartzch
O'Connor, W. F.
Perley, Sir George Halsey
Pope, Sir Joseph
Sifton, Sir Clifford
Thompson, Sir John S. D.
Tupper, Sir Charles
White, Sir William Thomas
Willison, Sir John S.
The Canadian Pacific Railway Papers, Series 1, President's
    Papers (Shaughnessy)

Public Archives of Nova Scotia
Borden, Sir Frederick W.

University of New Brunswick
Crocket, O. S.
Hazen, Sir John Douglas

McGill University
Ames, Sir Herbert Brown

Queen's University
Flavelle, Sir Joseph W.

Foster, John G.
Lambert, Norman

Archives Deschâtelets, Ottawa
Belcourt, Napoleon-Antoine

Public Archives of Ontario
Whitney, Sir James P.

University of British Columbia
Tupper, Sir Charles Hibbert

Public Archives of British Columbia
McBride, Sir Richard

GOVERNMENT RECORDS
Public Archives of Canada
Record Group 2, The Privy Council
Record Group 7, The Governor General
Record Group 9, The Department of Militia and Defence
Record Group 19, The Department of Finance
Record Group 25, The Department of External Affairs
C.O. 42, The Colonial Office
Great Britain, Cabinet Papers (Microfilm)

PUBLISHED RECORDS
Canada, Parliament, *Sessional Papers*
Canada, House of Commons, *Debates*
Canada, House of Commons, *Journals*
Canada, Senate, *Debates*
Canada, Department of External Affairs, *Documents on Canadian External Relations, I, 1909–1918*, Ottawa, 1967

INTERVIEWS
Barnstead, Arthur
Borden, Henry
Tupper, Reginald Hibbert

THESES
Acheson, T. W., "The Social Origins of Canadian Industrialism: A Study in the Structure of Entrepreneurship," Ph.D., Toronto, 1971.
Barber, Marilyn J., "The Ontario Bilingual Schools Issue, 1910–1916," M.A., Queen's, 1964.

Bothwell, Robert, "Loring Christie: The Failure of Bureaucratic Imperialism," Ph.D., Harvard, 1972.

Clippingdale, Richard T., "J. S. Willison, Political Journalist: From Liberalism to Independence," Ph.D., Toronto, 1970.

Copp, John Terry, "The Canadian General Election of 1908," M.A., McGill, 1962.

Crunican, Rev. Paul E., "The Manitoba School Question and Canadian Federal Politics, 1890–1896: A Study in Church-State Relations," Ph.D., Toronto, 1968.

Eagle, John Andrew, "Sir Robert Borden and the Railway Problem in Canadian Politics, 1911–1920," Ph.D., Toronto, 1972.

English, John Richard, "Sir Robert Borden, The Conservative Party and Political Change, 1901–1920," Ph.D., Harvard, 1973.

Hall, David John, "The Political Career of Clifford Sifton, 1896–1905," Ph.D., Toronto, 1973.

Humphries, Charles W., "The Political Career of Sir James P. Whitney," Ph.D., Toronto, 1966.

LaPierre, Laurier J. L., "Politics, Race and Religion in French Canada; Joseph Israel Tarte," Ph.D., Toronto, 1962.

Levitt, Joseph, "The Social Problem of the Nationalists of Quebec, 1900–1914," Ph.D., Toronto, 1967.

Lupal, M., "Relations in Education Between the State and the Roman Catholic Church in the Canadian North-West with Special Reference to the Provisional District of Alberta from 1880 to 1905," Ph.D., Harvard, 1963.

MacIntosh, Alan W., "The Career of Sir Charles Tupper in Canada, 1864–1900," Ph.D., Toronto, 1959.

McLaughlin, K. M., "Race, Religion and Politics: The Election of 1896 in Canada," Ph.D., Toronto, 1974.

Muise, D. A., "Elections and Constituencies: Federal Politics in Nova Scotia, 1867–78," Ph.D., Western, 1971.

Regehr, T. D., "The Canadian Northern Railway, Agent of National Growth, 1896–1911," Ph.D., Alberta, 1967.

Smith, Brian, "Sir Richard McBride," M.A., Queen's, 1959.

Stevens, Paul Douglas, "Laurier and the Liberal Party in Ontario, 1887–1911," Ph.D., Toronto, 1966.

Stewart, Kenneth Fenwick, "R. B. Bennett as M.P., 1910–1917," M.A., Queen's, 1971.

Warner, Catherine P., "Sir James P. Whitney and Sir Robert L. Borden: Relations between a Conservative Provincial Premier and his Federal Party Leader, 1905–1914," M.Phil., Toronto, 1967.

NOTES

CHAPTER ONE

1. An 1864 map of King's County lists thirty-one householders in the "Grand Pré Business Directory" and has a separate listing for Lower Horton, the distinction being between the residents living on the hill (Grand Pré) and those living on the lowland adjacent to the meadow (Lower Horton). John Lovell's *Directory* for 1871 lists one hundred thirty-one households under the inclusive title, Grand Pré. I have used Lovell's designation here and assumed that, taking account for moderate growth, there were about one hundred households in Grand Pré in the 1850s. Public Archives of Canada, Map Division, "King's County Map, 1864" (hereafter cited as PAC); *Lovell's Canadian Dominion Directory for 1871* (Montreal: John Lovell, 1871), pp. 1596–97; Henry Borden, ed., *Robert Laird Borden: His Memoirs*, I (Toronto: Macmillan, 1938), ch. 1 (hereafter cited as *Memoirs*).
2. J. S. Martell, "Intercolonial Communications, 1840–1867" in G. A. Rawlyk, ed., *Historical Essays on the Atlantic Provinces*, Carleton Library, no. 35 (Toronto: McClelland and Stewart, 1967), pp. 177–206.
3. I am indebted to my friend and colleague, Professor Charles W. Humphries of the University of British Columbia, for bringing this information on the Windsor and Annapolis Railway to my attention. There is a colourful description of the opening of the railway at Grand Pré in Marguerite Woodworth, *History of The Dominion Atlantic Railway* (Kentville, 1936), ch. v.
4. Archibald MacMechan, *Red Snow on Grand Pré*, Toronto, 1931.
5. C. Bruce Ferguson, "The Expulsion of the Acadians," *Dalhousie Review*, 1955, 127–35.
6. J. B. Brebner, *The Neutral Yankees of Nova Scotia*, Carleton Library, no. 45 (Toronto: McClelland and Stewart, 1969), p. 47.
7. *Lovell's Canadian Dominion Directory for 1871*, pp. 1596–97.
8. Duncan Campbell, *Nova Scotia, in its Historical, Mercantile, and Industrial Relations* (Montreal, 1873), pp. 482–83.
9. A. W. H. Eaton, *The History of King's County, Heart of Acadian Land* (Salem, 1910), pp. 458–60.
10. *Ibid.*, pp. 338, 343–44.
11. *Ibid.*, p. 579.
12. Borden Papers Private, II, Eunice Laird Borden to Robert, 4 and 10 June, 1887. I have used this designation for a collection of private family papers owned by Mr. Henry Borden which is housed at the Public Archives of Canada and is not, at present, open to public examination. (Hereafter referred to as BPP.) Other information in this and the preceding and following paragraphs is gathered from genealogical records of the family which are owned by Mr. Borden and currently in the possession of the author.

13. BPP, Diary, October 4, 1873.
14. *Memoirs*, I: 5.
15. BPP, Robert to Eunice Laird Borden, December 31, 1876.
16. *Ibid.*, William P. Laird to J. W. Borden, August 21, 1900; *Memoirs*, I: 4.
17. *Memoirs*, I: 7–9.
18. Eaton, *The History of King's County*, p. 345. See also M. V. Marshall, *A Short History of Acacia Villa School*, privately published, 1963.
19. PAC, Borden Papers, 300. Address to the Graduating Class at Acadia University, May 25, 1932, no. 175282. (Hereafter referred to as BP.)
20. *Ibid.*, no. 175233–34.
21. BPP, Diary, October 2, 1873.
22. *Ibid.*, September 19, 1873.
23. Borden systematically recorded the order, genus, species, common name, and location of fifty-three plants in the back of his diary. BPP, Diary, 1873–74.
24. BPP, Diary, September 30 and October 24, 1873.
25. *Ibid.*, March 31, 1874.
26. *Ibid.*, April 25, 1874.
27. *Ibid.*, March 8, 1874.
28. BPP, William P. Laird to Robert Borden, November 13, 1873.
29. Eaton, *The History of King's County*, p. 158.
30. BPP, Diary, September 19, 1874.

CHAPTER TWO

1. David Erskine, "The Atlantic Region" in John Warkentin, ed., *Canada. A Geographical Interpretation* (Toronto: Methuen, 1968), pp. 231 ff.; J. M. S. Careless, "Aspects of Metropolitanism in Atlantic Canada" in Mason Wade, ed., *Regionalism in the Canadian Community, 1867–1967* (Toronto: University of Toronto Press, 1969), pp. 117–29; Thomas H. Raddall, *Halifax Warden of the North* (Toronto: McClelland and Stewart, 1948), pp. 224–52.
2. Phyllis R. Blakeley, *Glimpses of Halifax, 1867–1900* (Halifax: Public Archives of Nova Scotia, 1949), pp. 99–100.
3. Raddall, *Halifax*, p. 101.
4. Cited in George Rawlyk, "The Maritimes in the Canadian Community" in Wade, *Regionalism in the Canadian Community*, p. 101.
5. A detailed sketch of Halifax business life can be found in Miss Blakeley's *Glimpses of Halifax*, especially in Chapter III. Her evidence, though not her interpretation of it, appears to support my contention that Halifax experienced steady growth in the 1870s, 80s, and 90s. I am indebted to Dr. D. A. Muise for statistical evidence, some of it alluded to above, of the growth of Halifax. See especially Appendices I–VIII of his "Elections and Constituencies: Federal Politics in Nova Scotia, 1867–78," Ph.D. Thesis, University of Western Ontario, 1971, pp. 395–412. See also T. W. Acheson, "The Social Origins of Canadian Industrialism: A Study in the Structure of Entrepreneurship," Ph.D. Thesis, University of Toronto, 1971, Chapter II and the same author's valuable essay, "The National Policy and the Industrialization of the Maritimes, 1880–1910," *Acadiensis*, I, 2 Spring, 1972, 3–28.
6. Muise, "Elections and Constituencies," Appendix IV.
7. *McAlpine's Halifax City Directory, 1875–76*, p. 90; *Memoirs*, I: 14.
8. "Address by Hon. A. G. Archibald" in *The Inaugural Addresses, etc., Delivered At the Opening of the Law School in Connection With Dal-*

housie University, Halifax, Nova Scotia. At the Beginning of the First Term in 1883 (Halifax, 1884), p. 37.

9. BPP, II: 6, Graham to Borden, November 13, 1887. The "exception," doubtless, was his former partner, Weatherbe.
10. *Ibid.*, Daybook, October 14 and 28, 1874.
11. *Ibid.*, November 4, 1874.
12. *Ibid., passim: McAlpine's Halifax City Directory, 1875–76*, pp. 90, 427.
13. *Ibid., Memoirs*, I: 15; PAC, R. G. 9 (Militia Records), II F6, vol. 144 and II J5, vol. 25; Henry James Morgan, ed., *The Canadian Men and Women of the Time* (Toronto, 1898), pp. 1026–27 (biography of Sir Charles Hibbert Tupper).
14. *Ibid.*, Daybook, November 16, 1874.
15. *Ibid.*, VI, Borden to Mother, September 23, 1877, November 16, 1877 and n.d. (between November 16 and Christmas, 1877).
16. *Ibid.*, Borden to Mother, n.d.
17. *Memoirs*, I: 18; *McAlpine's Halifax City Directory, 1883–84*, "List of Barristers and Attornies of the Supreme Court of Nova Scotia," pp. 493–98. Chipman was made a Q.C. (Canada) in 1884 and appointed County Court Judge in 1890. Morgan, *Canadian Men and Women, 1898*, pp. 184–85.
18. *Memoirs*, I: 19.
19. BPP, II: 1, Borden to Laura Bond, May 21, 1886; II: 2, Laura Bond to Borden, September 21, 1886; II: 5, Borden to Sir John Thompson, June 11, 1887 and Thompson to Borden, June 25, 1887. See also Robert Craig Brown, *Canada's National Policy, 1883–1900* (Princeton, 1964), pp. 29–33 for a description of the "David J. Adams" and "Doughty" cases.
20. PAC, Sir John S. D. Thompson Papers, 60, Wallace Graham to Thompson, September 30, 1887. Professor Peter Waite, who is currently preparing a biography of Thompson, kindly brought this letter to my attention.
21. Graham's point here was that Borden would surrender his "professional" independence as a lawyer by accepting Thompson's offer.
22. BPP, II: 6, Graham to Borden, November 13, 1887. In 1890 the Deputy Minister of Justice received a salary of $4,000 per annum. I think it reasonable to assume that Borden was offered approximately the same amount in 1887. *Canadian Almanac, 1890*, p. 47.
23. PAC, *Thompson Papers*, 65, Borden to Thompson, February 6, 1888.
24. *Memoirs*, I: 21.
25. BPP, II: 5, C. H. Tupper to Borden, May 14, 1888.
26. *Ibid.*, Borden was named a Q.C. (Canada) in 1890 and a K.C. (Ontario) in 1908.
27. PAC, R.G. 9, II F6, vol. 144 and II B4, vol. 4.
28. Interview with Mr. Arthur Barnstead, June 1965.
29. Borden was a vestryman at St. Paul's from 1891 to 1904. Reginald V. Harris, *The Church of Saint Paul in Halifax, Nova Scotia, 1749–1949* (Toronto: Ryerson, 1949), p. 265.
30. See Canada, *Supreme Court Reports*, 16–26, 1887–1896.
31. BPP, II: 1, Robert to Laura Borden, November 21, 1893.
32. *Ibid.*, Robert to Laura Borden, November 27, 1893 and December 1, 3, 5, 6, 9, and 11, 1894; *Memoirs*, I: 39–40.
33. *Geldert* v. *The Municipality of Pictou* (1891), 23 NSR 483; *Great Britain, Law Reports, Appeal Cases* (1893), p. 524. Borden's other case before the JCPC was *Reynolds* v. *Attorney General for Nova Scotia* (1896), p. 240, where the position he took for the Province of Nova Scotia in a matter concerning a mining licence was upheld.
34. *Memoirs*, I: 30.

35. *McAlpine's City Directory of Halifax, 1895–96*, pp. 623-24. Borden became a Director of the Bank of Nova Scotia in 1900. At the beginning of the year he owned ninety-five shares of Bank of Nova Scotia stock. He purchased an additional seventy-five shares during the year. The value of the shares varied from a high of $229 to a low of $220 during 1900. J. S. Burchell, Secretary, The Bank of Nova Scotia, to the author, September 26, 1967.

36. See *Preliminary Conference and First Meeting of the Canadian Bar Association, Montreal, 1896* (Toronto, 1896), pp. 1–15.

CHAPTER THREE

1. BPP, II: 5, Sir Charles Hibbert Tupper to Borden, January 27 and February 3, 1896; *McAlpine's Halifax Directory, 1896*, p. 227.

2. *Ibid.*, II: 1, Borden to Laura, April 27, 1896.

3. *Memoirs*, I: 42.

4. PAC, C. H. Cahan Papers, Cahan to Grattan O'Leary, November 25, 1930. Cahan ran in Shelburne and Queen's in 1896 and was defeated.

5. Canada, *House of Commons Debates*, September 23, 1903, p. 12192 (hereinafter referred to as HCD); University of British Columbia Library, Sir Charles Hibbert Tupper Papers, C. H. Tupper to Borden, May 23, 1917. Tupper's letter, written in grief over the death of his son in the war and in resentment of Borden's failure to secure a commission for his son before his death, began: "I cannot refrain from letting you know how keenly I feel and resent your official attitude towards me since your term of office began, since on reflection it snaps the personal regard I have hitherto retained and struggled to retain for you."

6. *Ibid.*

7. *Memoirs*, I: 42.

8. Cited, P. B. Waite, *Canada, 1874–1896: Arduous Destiny* (Toronto: McClelland and Stewart, 1971), p. 186. Professor Waite ably discusses the "Repeal" election in Chapter 10. See also the detailed account in Bruce Ferguson, *Hon. W. S. Fielding, Vol. 1, The Mantle of Howe* (Windsor, N.S., 1970), Chapter 4.

9. BPP, II: 5, F. W. Borden to Borden, June 15, 1887, February 2, 1888, and April 11, 1888.

10. *Memoirs*, I: 42.

11. BPP, II: 5, Thompson to Borden, February 7, 1892. A running account of the legal manoeuvres Borden employed may be found in PAC, Thompson Papers, vols. 127, 128, 132, 133, 141, 142, 144 and 145, *passim*. Borden also acted on Cahan's behalf and put up $2,000 in Cahan's cases. Cahan appears not to have repaid Borden. See Thompson Papers, 130, J. A. Chisholm to Thompson, June 5, 1891.

12. *Ibid.*, II: 5, A. E. Calkin to Borden, January 17, 1894, and Borden to Calkin, January 23, 1894; Halifax *Herald*, February 23, 1894.

13. *The Morning Chronicle*, May 4, 1896.

14. BPP, II: 2, Laura to Robert, May 4, 1896.

15. *Morning Chronicle* and the *Herald*, May 1, 1896.

16. BPP, II: 1, Robert to Laura, May 4, 1896 (2 letters).

17. Halifax *Herald*, May 12–23, 1896, *passim*.

18. See K. M. McLaughlin, "The Canadian General Election of 1896 in Nova Scotia," M.A. Thesis, Dalhousie, 1967, which discusses this point in great detail. On the Manitoba School Question see Waite, *Arduous Destiny*, Chs. 11–13 and Robert Craig Brown and Ramsay Cook, *Canada,*

1896–1921, A Nation Transformed (Toronto: McClelland & Stewart, 1974), Ch. 2.

19. Cited, K. M. McLaughlin, "Race, Religion and Politics: The Election of 1896 in Canada," Ph.D. Thesis, Toronto, 1974, p. 288.
20. *Halifax Herald*, May 15, 1896.
21. *Ibid.*
22. BPP, II: 1, Robert to Laura, August 18, 1896.
23. In 1899, returning to Ottawa from Halifax, his Pullman was not connected to the Ottawa train at Montreal and he had to complete his journey by coach. "Herewith," he wrote Laura, "I send my Pullman check on which I am entitled to a refund of 50 cents as the Pullman did not come further than Montreal. Please ask Hal to attend to it." *Ibid.*, Robert to Laura, July 2, 1899.
24. *Ibid.*, Robert to Laura, July 25, 1899.
25. BPP, II: 5, Sir Charles Hibbert Tupper to Borden, June 27, July 7 and 9, 1896; Borden to Tupper, July 2, 1896; *McAlpine's Halifax Directory, 1897*, p. 615.
26. *Ibid.*, II: 1, Robert to Laura, August 22, 29, and 30 and September 9, 1896.
27. *Ibid.*, II: 2, Laura to Robert, June 15, 16 and 21, 1897.
28. *Ibid.*, II: 1, Robert to Laura, August 21, 1896.
29. *Ibid.*, Robert to Laura, September 4, 1896.
30. BP, 261, Bourassa to Borden, October 18, 1935, no. 146826.
31. *Memoirs*, I: 47.
32. *Ibid.*, Robert to Laura, July 7, 1899.
33. HCD, August 28, 1896, pp. 387–91.
34. BPP, II: 1, Robert to Laura, August 27 and 28, 1896.
35. HCD, May 13 to June 23, 1897, *passim.*
36. *Ibid.*, May 18, 1899, pp. 3425–40; May 25, 1899, pp. 3560–77. See also June 13, 1899, pp. 4951–61 for his speech on Third Reading of the Bill and G. R. Stevens, *Canadian National Railways*, vol. 2 (Toronto, 1962), pp. 273–74 and 354.
37. BPP, II: 1, Robert to Laura, July 6 and 7, 1899; *Memoirs*, I: 56–59; Canada, House of Commons, *Journals*, XXXIV, 1899, Appendix 2.
38. *Ibid.*, Robert to Laura, July 4 and 11, 1899.
39. *Memoirs*, I: 58–59; HCD, March–June, 1900, *passim.*
40. BPP, II: 1, Robert to Laura, July 16, 1899.
41. BP, 328, "memorandum", no date [1900], no. 193503-05; letter from Miss Alice Lowe, Sir Robert and Lady Borden's housekeeper, to the author, March 25, 1966.
42. BPP, II: 1, Robert to Laura, July 8 and 24, 1899.
43. *Ibid.*, Robert to Laura, July 24, 1899.
44. *Memoirs*, I: 68.
45. *Morning Chronicle*, October 13, 1900.
46. Cited, J. M. Beck, *Pendulum of Power: Canada's Federal Election* (Toronto, 1968), p. 88.
47. *Morning Chronicle*, November 9, 1900.
48. BP, 350, Memoir Notes, Borden to Sir C. H. Tupper, November 8, 1900, no. 5616.
49. PAC, Sir Charles Tupper Papers, Journal, November 7, 1900.
50. *Memoirs*, I: 48.
51. *Halifax Herald*, October 20, 1900.
52. U.B.C., Sir Charles Hibbert Tupper Papers, Borden to Tupper, December 5, 1900.
53. *Memoirs*, I: 73.

CHAPTER FOUR

1. BP, 362, Speech at Massey Hall, May 27, 1901.
2. *Ibid.*, Speech at Halifax Banquet, July 1, 1901.
3. BPP, II: 1, Borden to Laura, November 6, 7, and 9, 1901.
4. BP, 362, Speech at Winnipeg, October 13, 1902, *Memoirs*, I: 87–92.
5. U.B.C., Sir Charles Hibbert Tupper Papers, A. C. Galt to Tupper, September 10, 1902.
6. BP, 350, Memoir Notes, Borden to R. B. Bennett, March 19, 1903, no. 5675-77.
7. *Ibid.*, Borden to Chairman, Moose Jaw Convention, March 17, 1903, no. 5671-74. See also Borden to F. W. Haultain, April 6, 1903, no. 5678-79.
8. *Memoirs*, II: 401.
9. BPP, 350, Memoir Notes, Thomas Chase Casgrain to George Taylor, March 7, 1904, no. 5832-37.
10. BPP, II: 1, Borden to Laura, July 9, 18, and 24, 1903.
11. BP, 350, Memoir Notes, Monk to Borden, November 18, 1903, no. 5782-84.
12. Laurier J. L. LaPierre, "Politics, Race and Religion in French Canada: Joseph Israel Tarte," Ph.D., University of Toronto, 1962, Ch. VII. For Borden's views see HCD, March 10, 1902, pp. 954–56.
13. Cited, *ibid.*, p. 464.
14. *Memoirs*, I: 94–96.
15. BP, 350, Memoir Notes, Hugh Graham to Borden, October 25, 1902, no. 5655.
16. *Ibid.*, Tarte to Borden, June 6, 18, and 19, 1903, nos. 5696-97, 5699, 5700.
17. *Ibid.*, Macnab to Borden, "Friday" and "Monday", [August] 1903, nos. 5737 and 5739.
18. BP, 334, Memoir Notes, nos. 27 and 42.
19. *Ibid.*, no. 44.
20. BP, 350, Memoir Notes, Borden to George Taylor, February 13, 1901, no. 5620.
21. BP, 306, Borden to Mr. Wright and Mr. Leavitt, May 17, 1901, no. 179191.
22. HCD, April 26, 1901, p. 3902.
23. See, for example, his speech on the revision of the Coronation Oath, HCD, March 1, 1901 and *Memoirs*, I: 77–79.
24. HCD, April 15, 1902, p. 2747.
25. *Ibid.*, March 14, 1904, p. 66.
26. Cited, *Memoirs*, I: 83.
27. HCD, March 18, 1902, p. 1339.
28. BP, 350, Memoir Notes, Borden to Stairs, March 24, 1902, no. 5643-44.
29. *Ibid.*, Borden to Stairs, April 17, 1903, no. 5681-83.
30. BP, 324, Amherst Speech, January 14, 1903.
31. HCD, April 17, 1903, pp. 1494–95.
32. *Canadian Annual Review* (1902): 222–24.
33. T. D. Regehr, "The Canadian Northern Railway, Agent of National Growth, 1896–1911," Ph.D., University of Alberta, 1967, and *Canadian Annual Review* (1902): 224-26.
34. BP, 350, Memoir Notes, Borden to Sandford Evans, December 16, 1902, no. 5664-67.
35. Brown and Cook, *Canada, 1896–1921*, pp. 148–53.
36. HCD, August 18, 1903, pp. 8994–9006.
37. BP, 350, Memoir Notes, Flavelle to Borden, August 16, 19, and 24, 1903, nos. 5748-59, 5760-61, and 5762-64.
38. *Ibid.*, Flavelle to Borden, August 19, 1903, no. 5748–49.
39. *Ibid.*, Stairs to Borden, August 6, 1903, no. 5716-18.

40. *Memoirs*, I: 117.
41. HCD, April 5, 1904, pp. 725–88.
42. *Ibid.*, May 26, 1904, p. 3572.
43. *Canadian Annual Review* (1904): 82–84.
44. BP, 350, Memoir Notes, Macnab to Borden, July 7, 1904, no. 5895-96.
45. *Ibid.*, Watson Griffin to George Taylor, June 2, 1904, no. 5878-82.
46. *Ibid.*, Borden to Sandford Evans, May 30, 1904, no. 5869-70.

CHAPTER FIVE

1. BP, 327, Thomas Tweed to Hugh Graham, May 18, 1904, in Graham to Borden, May 26, 1904, no. 192936-40.
2. *Ibid.*, 350, Memoir Notes, Borden to Stairs, April 7, 1904, no. 5846-47; 327, Borden to W. H. Thorne, August 29, 1904, no. 192946.
3. *Canadian Annual Review* (1903): 99; (1904): 166.
4. BPP, II: 1, Borden to Laura, July 13, 1904.
5. BP, 350, Memoir Notes, Borden to Stairs, April 7, 1904, no. 5846-47.
6. BPP, II: 1, Borden to Laura, July 29, 1904.
7. *Mail and Empire* and *The News*, September 21, 1904.
8. *The News*, October 5, 1904.
9. *The Globe, Mail and Empire*, and *The News*, September 22, 1904.
10. BPP, II: 1, Borden to Laura, October 18, 1904.
11. BP, 350, Memoir Notes, Borden to Barker, October 18, 1904.
12. *Ibid.*, Borden to Barker, October 27, 1904.
13. J. M. Beck, *Pendulum of Power: Canada's Federal Elections* (Scarborough, 1968), pp. 96, 106.
14. BP, 350, Memoir Notes, Borden to McMaster [*sic*], November 5, 1904, no. 5937.
15. *Canadian Annual Review* (1904): 221–24.
16. *Ibid.*, 226.
17. *Ibid.*, 258.
18. Most of this correspondence is in volume 327 of the Borden Papers. Some additional letters may be found in volume 350. Graham, who delighted in vaguely conspiratorial dealings, seldom wrote to Borden *en clair* in those years. He used the Conservative party's "Z" code, a copy of which is in the finding aid to the Borden Papers, and an "A" code which is not available. In the following citations Borden is "Ameer" and Graham is "Baker" or "Arpents".
19. BP, 327, "Arpents" to Borden, May 13, 1903, no. 192886-87, "Baker" to Borden, June 30, 1903.
20. Regehr, "The Canadian Northern Railway", pp. 130–31.
21. BP, 327, B. A. Macnab to Borden, September 17 and 24, 1903, nos. 192920-22 and 192923. Stress mine.
22. BP, 350, Memoir Notes, Borden to Russell, September 29, 1904, no. 5933; *Canadian Annual Review* (1904): 221–22.
23. Regehr, "The Canadian Northern Railway", pp. 135–36.
24. BP, 327, A. E. Blount to Borden, December 27, 1904, no. 192958-61.
25. Regehr, "The Canadian Northern Railway", pp. 136–42. BP, 327, D. Waters to Manager, Montreal, November 16, 1904, no. 193091; W. P. Hunt to General Manager, Toronto, November 18, 1904, no. 193090; H. C. McLeod to Manager, Montreal, January 9, 1905, no. 193088 and January 19, 1905, no. 193085; W. P. Hunt to General Manager, Toronto, January 17 and 18, 1905, no. 193086-87. Hunt was the Montreal Manager for the Bank

of Nova Scotia and McLeod was the bank's General Manager in Toronto.

26. BP, 327, Hunt to General Manager, October 17, 1904, no. 193097-98; McLeod to Manager, October 18, 1904, no. 193096; Hunt to General Manager, October 18, 1904, no. 193094-95; unsigned memo "Montreal" [October 18, 1904?], no. 193093; Hunt to General Manager, October 19, 1904, no. 193092.

27. *Ibid.*, Borden to Graham, October 19, 1904, no. 192948-49.

28. *Ibid.*, McLeod to Borden, December 10, 1907, no. 193084.

29. *Ibid.*, [Graham] to "Arthur" [Monk], May 26, 1903, no. 192891.

30. *Ibid.*, Graham to Borden, July 18, 1903, no. 192902.

31. *Ibid.*, Graham to Borden, July 15, 1904, no. 192942-44.

32. *Ibid.*, Graham to Borden, August 19, 1904, no. 192880-81.

33. *Ibid.*, Sir C. H. Tupper to Graham, December 10, 1904, no. 192955; Graham to Borden, October 31, 1917, no. 193284-85.

34. BP, 350, Memoir Notes, Borden to Barker, November 8, 1904, no. 5940-41.

35. *Ibid.*, Borden to Taylor, November 8, 1904, no. 5942.

36. PAC, Willison Papers, 36, C. F. Hamilton to Willison, November 7, 1905.

37. BPP, II: 1, Borden to Laura, July 5, 1904.

38. BP, 350, Memoir Notes, Borden to Hughes, December 9, 1904, no. 5951; BPP, II: 8, Borden to [Joseph Chamberlain], December 17, 1904.

39. BP, 334, Memoir Notes, no. 58.

40. BP, 350, Memoir Notes, Borden to McBride, December 15, 1904, no. 5952-53.

41. The resignation was dated January 7, 1905. See BP, 14, no. 3401-04.

42. BP, 327, Blount to Borden, December 27, 1904, no. 192958-61.

43. PAC, Willison Papers, 7, Borden to Willison, August 5, 1905.

44. *Ibid.*, Borden to Willison, February 11, 1905.

CHAPTER SIX

1. BPP, II, 3, Julia Borden and Eunice Borden to Robert, June 22, 1905; interview with Mr. Henry Borden, October 23, 1973.

2. *Memoirs*, I: 144-45.

3. BPP, II: 1, Borden to Laura, June 15, 1905.

4. *Ibid.*, Laura to Borden, June 14 and July 1, 1905; Borden to Laura, June 25, 1905.

5. M. C. Urquhart and K. A. Buckley, eds., *Historical Statistics of Canada* (Toronto: Macmillan, 1965), pp. 14, 351, 352, 362 and 371.

6. *Canadian Annual Review* (1905): 22.

7. *Historical Statistics*, p. 23.

8. Both quotations are cited in Brown and Cook, *Canada, 1896–1921*, pp. 72–73.

9. *Canada, 1896–1921*, p. 74.

10. BP, 334, Memoir Notes, 62-65; *Memoirs*, I: 142.

11. Cited, *Canada, 1896–1921*, p. 75.

12. HCD, February 21, 1905, p. 14621

13. *Ibid.*, March 22, 1905, p. 2929.

14. *Ibid.*, February 21, 1905, p. 1463.

15. See M. Lupal, "Relations in Education Between the State and the Roman Catholic Church in the Canadian North-West with Special Reference to the Provisional District of Alberta from 1880 to 1905," Ph.D., Harvard, 1963.

16. *Canada, 1896–1921*, pp. 77–78; O. D. Skelton, *Life and Letters of Sir*

Wilfrid Laurier, II (New York, 1922), 226–41; David John Hall, "The Political Career of Clifford Sifton, 1896–1905", Ph.D., Toronto, 1973.
17. PAC, Willison Papers, 36, C. F. Hamilton to Willison, March 5, 9, 20, and 24, 1905.
18. HCD, March 31, 1905, pp. 3528–29.
19. HCD, March 22, 1905, pp. 2932–33.
20. *Ibid.*, pp. 2944–45.
21. BP, 350, Memoir Notes, Borden to Flavelle, March 24, 1905, nos. 6014-5 and 6016-19.
22. *Ibid.*, Casgrain to Borden, 24 March, 1905, no. 6024.
23. *Ibid.*, Prieur to Borden, March 27, 1905, nos. 6035-38.
24. BP, 302, Speech at Quebec City, August 29, 1907, no. 176902.
25. BP, 350, Borden to Joseph Flavelle, April 8, 1905, no. 6056-58.
26. See above.
27. BPP, II: 1, Borden to Laura, June 14, 1905.
28. BP, 350, Memoir Notes, Flavelle to Borden, April 1, 1905, no. 6052-55.
29. BPP, II: 1, Borden to Laura, June 28, 1905; *Memoirs*, I: 148, note 8.
30. *Ibid.*, Borden to Laura, July 8, 1905.
31. *Memoirs*, I: 152, note 12.
32. PAC, Willison Papers, 37, C. F. Hamilton to Willison, October 30, 1908.
33. BP, 350, Memoir Notes, Notes enclosed in Borden to Dr. Thompson, November 10, 1905, no. 6116-19.
34. *Ibid.*, Borden to C. A. Pentland, July 10, 1905, no. 6093-94.
35. *Ibid.*, H. A. Powell to Borden, November 24, 1905, no. 6130-31; *Canadian Annual Review* (1905): 124.
36. *Canadian Annual Review* (1905): 127–30.
37. BPP, II: 1, Borden to Laura, July 20, 1905.
38. *Canadian Annual Review* (1905): 127.
39. Queen's University, Flavelle Papers, "Copy" in Borden to Flavelle, February 24, 1906.
40. BP, 350, Memoir Notes, Whitney to Borden, February 6, 1906, no. 6153-54; 351, Roblin to Borden, February 9, 1906, no. 6188-90 and Tupper to Borden, February 12, 1906, no. 6217-22.
41. Queen's University, Flavelle Papers, Borden to Flavelle, February 24, 1906.
42. BP, 350, Memoir Notes, Borden to Blount, January 23, 1905, no. 5974-76.
43. PAC, Willison Papers, 36, C. F. Hamilton to Willison, April 4, 1905.
44. BP, 306, "Report of Committee to Consider Convention", no. 179203-04; Borden to Foster, April 12, 1905, no. 179200. Borden's nominees were: New Brunswick: J. W. Daniel, G. W. Fowler, and G. W. Ganong; Prince Edward Island: A. A. Lefurgy and A. Martin; Quebec: H. B. Ames, J.-G.-H. Bergeron, J.-E.-E. Léonard, F. D. Monk, E. Paquet, G. H. Perley, and R. N. Walsh; Ontario: S. Barker, W. H. Bennett, R. Blain, A. Broder, G. A. Clare, A. Ingram, and A. E. Kemp; Manitoba: W. J. Roche and Wm. Staples; Saskatchewan: R. S. Lake; Alberta: J. Herron and M. S. McCarthy.
45. *Ibid.*, Undated memorandum, "Organization of the Dominion Liberal–Conservative Association for the Province of Ontario," no. 179220-3.
46. PAC, Willison Papers, 36, C. F. Hamilton to Willison, October 5, 1905; October 27, 1905; December 18, 1905; and March 7, 1906.
47. *Ibid.*, C. F. Hamilton to Willison, November 7–8, 1905.
48. BP, 350, Memoir Notes, J. A. Macdonell to Borden, November 23, 1905.
49. *Ibid.*, 327, Graham to Borden, October 15, 1905, no. 192963-68.
50. PAC, Willison Papers, 36, C. F. Hamilton to Willison, November 23, 1905.
51. *Canadian Annual Review* (1905): 37.

52. BPP, II: 1, Borden to Laura, July 16 and 20, 1905.
53. *Canadian Annual Review* (1906): 576–77.

CHAPTER SEVEN

1. *Canadian Annual Review* (1906): 560; HCD, June 20, 1906, p. 5634.
2. BP, 351, Memoir Notes, Borden to L. T. Marechal, June 29, 1906, no. 6278.
3. HCD, June 29, 1906, pp. 6593–6600.
4. *Ibid.*, July 6, 1906, pp. 7353–57.
5. *Canadian Annual Review* (1907): 449.
6. *Ibid.*
7. BP, 351, Memoir Notes, Borden to Sir C. H. Tupper, December 4, 1906, no. 6327-29.
8. See Stuart Marshall Jamieson, *Times of Trouble: Labour Unrest and Industrial Conflict in Canada, 1900–66* (Ottawa, 1968), ch. 2, for a discussion of the strike.
9. On this subject see Desmond Morton, "Aid to the Civil Power: The Canadian Militia in Support of Social Order, 1867–1914," *Canadian Historical Review*, LI, no. 4, December, 1970, 407-25.
10. HCD, January 9, 1907, pp. 1150–52.
11. *Ibid.*, p. 1165.
12. *Ibid.*, p. 1155.
13. *Ibid.*, December 17, 1906, pp. 1042–43. See also Brown and Cook, *Canada, 1896–1921*, pp. 121–22.
14. *Ibid.*, February 14, 1907, pp. 3032–45.
15. *Memoirs*, I: 181.
16. BP, 350, Memoir Notes, Borden to "Dear Mr. [Conservative members of the House of Commons]," January 26, 1906, no. 6142-43.
17. *Canadian Annual Review* (1908): 28.
18. *Canadian Annual Review* (1906): 572–76; (1907): 469–72; (1908): 42–44 and 56–77; HCD, pp. 1906, 1906–07, 1907–08, *passim*.
19. See J. E. Hodgetts, *et al, The Biography of an Institution: The Civil Service Commission of Canada, 1908–1967* (Montreal, 1972), pp. 19–28.
20. PAC, Willison Papers, 36, C. F. Hamilton to Willison, March 24, 1906.
21. *Canadian Annual Review* (1906): 574–75.
22. PAC, Willison Papers, 36, C. F. Hamilton to Willison, April 4, 1906.
23. *Ibid.*, C. F. Hamilton to Willison, May 20, 1906.
24. BP, 351, Memoir Notes, E. A. Hardy to Borden, March 30, 1907, no. 6385.
25. *Ibid.*, Barker to Borden, February 11, 1906, no. 6215-16.
26. *Memoirs*, I: 170; Foster charged that the member of the Government was A. B. Aylesworth, the Minister of Justice. Aylesworth denied it. *Canadian Annual Review* (1907): 442–43.
27. *Memoirs*, I: 169–70; *Canadian Annual Review* (1906): 580.
28. BP, 351, Memoir Notes, E. W. Thompson to Senator Kirchoffer (1906?), no. 6280-82. Foster's former colleague and sometime rival, Sir Charles Tupper, was unconvinced by Foster's defence. He wrote that Foster "has made fatal blunder that will destroy his usefulness as a public man". *Ibid.*, Tupper to Borden, December 17, 1906, no. 6333-34.
29. Cited, *Memoirs*, I: 177. See also Henry Borden, ed., *Letters to Limbo* (Toronto: University of Toronto Press, 1971), pp. 66–77, on this point and for Robert Borden's extended equivocal assessment of Foster's actions.
30. The scandal campaign is discussed in more detail in my essay, "The Politics of Billingsgate" in C. Berger and Ramsay Cook, eds., *The West*

and the Nation (Toronto: McClelland and Stewart, 1976).
31. BP, 351, Memoir Notes, Borden to McBride, January 22, 1907, no. 6343-44.
32. *Ibid.*, C. A. Pariseault to Borden, January 24, 1907, no. 6347-48; Louis Coderre, Secretary, Executive Committee of the Conservative Party of the Province of Quebec, to Borden, January 28, 1907, no. 6349.
33. *Ibid.*, Whitney to Borden, January 24, 1907, no. 6350-51.
34. *Ibid.*, Ross to Borden, February 7, 1907, no. 6357; Tanner to Borden, February 23, 1907, no. 6363-65; Walsh to Borden, February 13, 1907, no. 6361-62; McBride to Borden, March 5, 1907, no. 6366; Roblin to Borden, March 29, 1907, no. 6378-80.
35. *Memoirs*, I: 197.
36. PAC, Willison Papers, 37, C. F. Hamilton to Willison, October 15, 1909.
37. *Ibid.*, 36, C. F. Hamilton to Willison, June 11, 1907.
38. BP, 351, Memoir Notes, Tupper to Borden, December 10 and 15, 1906 and January 3, 1907, nos. 6330, 6324, and 6331-32.
39. *Ibid.*, A. L. Davidson, December 12, 1907, no. 6469-70.
40. PAO, Sir J. P. Whitney Papers, Borden to Whitney, January 23, April 19 and July 11, 1906. For a detailed examination of Borden's negotiations with Whitney see Catherine P. Warner, "Sir James P. Whitney and Sir Robert L. Borden: Relations between a Conservative Provincial Premier and His Federal Party Leader, 1905–1914," M.Phil., Toronto, 1967, Ch. III. See also Charles W. Humphries, "The Political Career of Sir James P. Whitney," Ph.D., Toronto, 1966, p. 444.
41. PAO, Whitney Papers, Borden to Whitney, January 11 and May 4, 1907.
42. *Ibid.*, Whitney to Borden, December 31, 1906; Whitney to W. F. Nickle, August 4, 1908.
43. *Ibid.*, Whitney to Pope, June 17, 1907. Stress original.
44. BP, 351, Memoir Notes, Pariseault to Borden, January 24, 1907, nos. 6347-48; 327, Borden to ———, May 15, 1907, no. 192987.
45. BP, 327, Macnab to Graham, July 9, 1907, no. 192998-193004.
46. *Ibid.*, Macnab to Borden, July 18, 1907, no. 193006-07.
47. PAC, Willison Papers, 37, C. F. Hamilton to Willison, May 19 and July 3, 1908.
48. BP, 351, Memoir Notes, Borden to Roblin, August 2, 1907, no. 6412-13.
49. BP, 350, Memoir Notes, Roblin to Borden, January 31, 1906, no. 6147-50.
50. BP, 351, Memoir Notes, Borden to Ferguson, March 23, 1906, no. 6248.
51. *Ibid.*, Ames to Borden, February 7, 1906, no. 6172-75; Kemp to Borden, February 7, 1906, no. 6177-78; Broder to Borden, February 7, 1906, no. 6179-82; Bell to Borden, February 10, 1906, no. 6194-95; Monk to Borden, February 10, 1906, no. 6203-04; Ferguson to Borden, February 10, 1906, no. 6205-08; Ingram to Borden, February 12, 1906, no. 6223-26; Foster to Borden, February 18, 1906, no. 6229-30.
52. BP, 79, "Extracts from Speeches of R. L. Borden, K.C., M.P.", Sydney Mines, N.S., September 3, 1906, and Truro, N.S., September 8, 1906, no. 41044.
53. *Memoirs*, I: 171.
54. BP, 351, Memoir Notes, Borden to Sir Charles Hibbert Tupper, December 4, 1906, no. 6327-29.
55. *Ibid.*, Roblin to Borden, March 29, 1907, no. 6378-80.
56. "The Liberal-Conservative Platform As Laid Down by R. L. Borden, M.P., Opposition Leader, at Halifax, August 20, 1907," *passim.*
57. *Canadian Annual Review* (1907): 459–68.
58. BP, 351, Memoir Notes, Shaughnessy to Kemp, September 11, 1907, no. 6436-37.
59. *Ibid.*, Ames to Borden, August 28, 1907, no. 6430-35.

60. PAC, Willison Papers, 36, Hamilton to Willison, September 20, 1907.
61. *Memoirs*, I: 201.
62. BP, 294, Borden to Macnab, October 14, 1907, no. 172512-15.
63. BP, 327, "List of those invited . . .", no. 192986; draft, Borden to ———, May 17, 1907, no. 192995; Borden to Graham, June 3, 1907, no. 192997.
64. BP, 351, Memoir Notes, Whitney to Borden, September 11, 1907, no. 6440-41, 6443.
65. HCD, May 12, 1908, p. 8297.
66. *Canadian Annual Review* (1908): 48–56.
67. *Ibid.*, 161, 171.
68. *Ibid.*, 170.
69. *Memoirs*, I: 222.
70. *Canadian Annual Review* (1908): 223.
71. Norman Ward, ed., *A Party Politician: The Memoirs of Chubby Powers* (Toronto: Macmillan, 1966), pp. 9–10.
72. Borden later claimed, unconvincingly, that it cost him a majority, *Memoirs*, I: 227–29.
73. *Canadian Annual Review* (1908): 198. Two accounts of the 1908 election agree with this general point. See the brief description in J. M. Beck, *Pendulum of Power, Canada's Federal Elections* (Scarborough: 1968), pp. 107–19, and the much more detailed analysis in John Terry Copp, "The Canadian General Election of 1908," M.A., McGill, 1962. On the Conservative side all accounts, including the present one, suffer from the absence of any correspondence in Borden's papers for the year 1908.
74. PAC, Willison Papers, 7, Borden to Willison, September 12, 1908.
75. *Ibid.*, 37, C. F. Hamilton to Willison, November 1, 1908 and Willison to Hamilton, November 4, 1908.
76. *Ibid.*, 36, C. F. Hamilton to Willison, July 29, 1907.
77. *Canadian Annual Review* (1908): 228.
78. PAC, Willison Papers, C. F. Hamilton to Willison, November 3, 1908.
79. PAO, Whitney Papers, Whitney to H. A. Gwynne, December 2, 1908.
80. Henry Borden, ed., *Letters to Limbo*, pp. 28–31.
81. *Memoirs*, I: 229.

CHAPTER EIGHT

1. PAC, Willison Papers, 37, C. F. Hamilton to Willison, January 26, 1909.
2. BP, 351, Memoir Notes, Willison to Borden, January 11, 1909, no. 6482-83.
3. *Ibid.*, Borden to Willison, January 23, 1909, no. 6502-03.
4. *Ibid.*, Borden to Willison, February 13, 1909, no. 6484-85.
5. *Ibid.*, "Memorandum" in Borden to Willison, January 13, 1909, no. 6488-89.
6. *Canadian Annual Review* (1909): 208; *Memoirs*, I: 232.
7. BP, 351, Memoir Notes, Borden to Willison, March 20, 1909, no. 6542-43.
8. HCD, March 30, 1909, p. 3597.
9. *Ibid.*, February 1, 1909, pp. 355–71.
10. *Canadian Annual Review* (1909): 189–91 and 217. On the Commission of Conservation see F. J. Thorpe, "Historical Perspective on the 'Resources for Tomorrow' Conference," *Resources for Tomorrow* (Ottawa, 1961), I: 1–13; C. Ray Smith and David R. Witty, "Conservation, Resources and Environment: An Exposition and Critical Evaluation of the Commission of Conservation, Canada," *PLAN*, XI, 1, 1970, 55–70, and XI, 3, 1972, 199–216; Robert Craig Brown, "The Doctrine of Usefulness: Natural Resources and National Parks Policy in Canada, 1887–1914" in

J. G. Nelson, ed., *Canadian Parks in Perspective* (Montreal, 1970), pp. 46–62; and Brown and Cook, *Canada, 1896–1921*, pp. 96–98.

11. HCD, January 18, 1910, pp. 2058–59.
12. R. MacGregor Dawson, *William Lyon Mackenzie King, A Political Biography, 1874–1923* (Toronto: 1958), pp. 204–06; Lloyd G. Reynolds, *The Control of Competition in Canada* (Cambridge: Cambridge University Press, 1940), pp. 132–39.
13. BP, 352, Memoir Notes, Flavelle to Borden, February 21, 1910, no. 6797-6812.
14. HCD, April 26, 1910, pp. 7995–96.
15. Cited, Brown and Cook, *Canada, 1896–1921*, p. 164.
16. *Ibid.*, p. 163.
17. BP, 300, "The Influence of Canada upon Imperial Policy," March 14, 1902, Lindsay Collegiate Institute, no. 174809-10.
18. BP, 352, Memoir Notes, Borden to L. S. Amery, April 23, 1909, no. 6574-77.
19. *Memoirs*, I: 219-21.
20. The Foster resolution did not, as Professor Preston puts it, call "for immediate financial support for the Royal Navy". R. A. Preston, *Canada and "Imperial Defense"* (Toronto, 1967), pp. 389.
21. J. C. Hopkins in *Canadian Annual Review* (1909): 49.
22. *Canadian Annual Review* (1909): 49–61. The best study of the 1909 naval scare is in Arthur J. Marder, *From the Dreadnought to Scapa Flow, I, The Road to War, 1904–1914* (London, 1961), chs. VI–VII. On the strategic and diplomatic aspects of the crisis see also Samuel R. Williamson, Jr., *The Politics of Grand Strategy, Britain and France Prepare for War, 1904–1914* (Cambridge, Mass., 1969), chs. 2–4.
23. BP, 352, Memoir Notes, Casgrain to Borden, March 25, 1909, no. 6560-62.
24. *Ibid.*, Borden to Casgrain, March 26, 1909, no. 6563-64.
25. *Ibid.*, Casgrain to Borden, March 27, 1909, no. 6565.
26. PAC, Willison Papers, 37, C. F. Hamilton to Willison, March 23 and 25, 1909.
27. Summaries of the debate may be found in *Canadian Annual Review* (1909): 56–61 and in Gilbert Norman Tucker, *The Naval Service of Canada*, I (Ottawa, 1952), 122–28. For the debate see HCD, March 29, 1909, pp. 3483–3564.
28. *Canadian Annual Review* (1909): 60.
29. Borden had first suggested "immediate" but compromised with Laurier on the word "speedy". BP, 352, Memoir Notes, Borden to J. L. Maxse, May 20, 1909, no. 6614-16.
30. *Ibid.*, Laurier to Borden, March 29, 1909, no. 6568.
31. *Canadian Annual Review* (1909): 91–93. The Governor General, Lord Grey, though hardly a champion of the Tories, shared the view of the provincial Conservative leaders. He told the Colonial Secretary that Laurier's speech in the debate and his resolution were "Flap Doddle and nothing more". PAC, Grey of Howich Papers, 15, Grey to Crewe, March 30, 1909. Hereafter cited as Grey Papers.
32. BP, 352, Memoir Notes, Borden to Amery, April 23, 1909, no. 6574-77; Borden to J. L. Maxse, May 10, 1909, no. 6614-16.
33. *Ibid.*
34. *Canadian Annual Review* (1909): 96.
35. *Ibid.*
36. Marder, *From the Dreadnought to Scapa Flow*, I: 159–77.
37. *Ibid.*, chs. V and VIII; *Canadian Annual Review* (1909): 112–16.
38. Marder, *From the Dreadnought to Scapa Flow*, I: 180.

39. PAC, Grey Papers, 15, Grey to Crewe, May 12, 1909.
40. BP, 352, Memoir Notes, Grey to Borden, June 5, 1909, no. 6623-36 and Grey to Monk, May 20, 1909, no. 6637-40.
41. *Canadian Annual Review* (1909): 92–93.
42. BPP, VI, misc., daybook page, June 17, 1909. Borden noted a "satisfactory interview with Monk on previous day".
43. BP, 352, Memoir Notes, Monk to Borden, October 29, 1909, no. 6686-87.
44. *Canadian Annual Review* (1909): 98.
45. BP, 352, Memoir Notes, Monk to Borden, November 2, 1909, no. 6690-91.
46. Canada, Department of External Affairs, *Documents on Canadian External Relations, I, 1909–1918* (Ottawa, 1967), p. 234.
47. PABC, Sir Richard McBride Papers, Martin Burrell to McBride, November 15 and 28, 1909.
48. Queen's University, Flavelle Papers, Borden to Flavelle, November 19, 1909. PAC, Willison Papers, 7, Borden to Willison, November 19, 1909.
49. BP, 352. Memoir Notes, White to Borden, November 22, 1909, no. 6697, and Wallis to Borden, November 22, 1909, no. 6698-99.
50. *Ibid.*, Willison to Borden, November 22, 1909, no. 6700-03; Flavelle to Borden, November 23, 1909, no. 6704-09; Whitney to Borden, November 24, 1909, no. 6713-15; Roblin to Borden, November 23, 1909, no. 6710-11; Sir C. H. Tupper to Borden, November 25, 1909, no. 6719-20; Kemp to Borden, November 29, 1909, no. 6725-28; Bennett to Borden, December 7, 1909, no. 6761-66; Casgrain to Borden, December 4, 7, and 9, 1909, nos. 6754-56, 6767-69, and 6770-71.
51. HCD, January 12, 1910, p. 1735.
52. *Ibid.*, p. 1761.
53. PABC, McBride Papers, Burrell to McBride, January 23, 1910.
54. BP, 352, Memoir Notes, Monk to Borden, January 28, 1910, no. 6787-88.
55. PABC, McBride Papers, Burrell to McBride, February 6, 1910.
56. *Ibid.*
57. *Canadian Annual Review* (1910): 166.
58. BP, 134, Hughes to Borden, March 23, 1910, no. 70813.
59. *Ibid.*, Hughes to William MacArthur, March 23, 1911, no. 70829-35; PAC, Willison Papers, 37, C. F. Hamilton to Willison, March 8, and April 5, 1910.
60. BP, 351, Memoir Notes, Casgrain to Borden, January 29, 1909, no. 6508-13.
61. *Canadian Annual Review* (1909): 232.
62. BP, 352, Memoir Notes, Borden to W. B. Ross, October 22, 1909, no. 6688-89.
63. PABC, McBride Papers, Burrell to McBride, March 10, 1910.
64. *Ibid.*
65. *Canadian Annual Review* (1910): 288.
66. PABC, McBride Papers, Burrell to McBride, March 10, 20, and 24, 1910.
67. *Ibid.*, Burrell to McBride, March 24, 1910.
68. BP, 15, W. B. Northrup to "Dear Sir", October 18, 1909, no. 3532.
69. Borden tactfully did not name the three in his *Memoirs*, I: 288. But A. E. Blount identified them in the margin of his copy. PAC, A. E. Blount Papers, 2, copy, *Memoirs*.
70. BP, 134, Hughes to Borden, November 24, 1910, no. 70823-27; Toronto *Star*, April 7, 1910.
71. PABC, McBride Papers, Burrell to McBride, March 10, 1910.
72. Burrell's correspondence implies that McBride was not at all interested in moving to Ottawa. Mr. Brian Smith suggests the same in his "Sir Richard McBride," M.A. Thesis, Queen's, 1959.

73. John Richard English, "Sir Robert Borden, The Conservative Party and Political Change, 1901–1920", Ph.D. Thesis, Harvard, 1973, 105, n.87.
74. BP, 352, Memoir Notes, Borden to Hugh Clark, April 6, 1910, no. 6818-19. Roblin to Borden, April 6, 1910, no. 6824-27.
75. *Ibid.*, Hugh Clark to Borden, April 4, 1910, no. 6816-17.
76. *Ibid.*, Roblin to Borden, April 6, 1910, no. 6824-27.
77. BP, 294, Burrell to Borden, October 17, 1932, no. 172623-27.
78. PABC, McBride Papers, A. E. Blount to J. T. Robinson, April 13, 1910.
79. *Canadian Annual Review* (1910): 293.

CHAPTER NINE

1. BP, 352, Memoir Notes, Monk to Borden, January 28, 1910, no. 6787.
2. *Canadian Annual Review* (1910): 290.
3. Robert Rumilly, *Histoire de la province de Quebec, XV*, Montreal, 1945, 70–74; H. Blair Neatby, *Laurier and a Liberal Quebec: A Study in Political Management* (Toronto, 1973), pp. 192–93; *Canadian Annual Review* (1910): 188.
4. *Canadian Annual Review* (1910): 190.
5. Cited, Neatby, *Laurier*, p. 194.
6. *Canadian Annual Review* (1910): 198.
7. BP, 352, Memoir Notes, Price to Perley, November 7, 1910, no. 6877-79.
8. HCD, November 22, 1910, p. 133.
9. *Ibid.*, November 24, 1910, pp. 218–27.
10. *Canadian Annual Review* (1910): 211.
11. *Canadian Annual Review* (1911): 335.
12. Cited, Brown and Cook, *Canada, 1896–1921*, p. 161.
13. *Canadian Annual Review* (1911): 31.
14. HCD, January 26, 1911, p. 2501.
15. *Memoirs*, I: 303.
16. BP, 133, Telegram, Borden to Rogers, January 25, 1911, no. 70347; Telegram, Rogers to Borden, January 27, 1911, no. 70349.
17. BP, 5, Whitney to Borden, January 27, 1911, no. 532.
18. BP, 16, Borden to A. E. Kemp, January 30, 1911, no. 3640.
19. BP, 133, Borden to Rogers, January 30, 1911, no. 70351.
20. BP, 16, A. E. Kemp to Borden, February 1, 1911, no. 3643-44.
21. HCD, February 9, 1911, pp. 3294–3316.
22. *Ibid.*, February 14, 1911, p. 3562.
23. PAO, Whitney Papers, Borden to Whitney, February 14, 1911.
24. See *Canadian Annual Review* (1911): 47–49.
25. HCD, February 28, 1911.
26. Queen's University, Norman Lambert Papers, Diary, February 9, 1919. An account of a conversation between Harris and Lambert on the date indicated.
27. PAC, Willison Papers, 105, Memorandum, no. 38488-92.
28. *Ibid.*
29. BP, 268, Borden to J. W. Dafoe, December 17, 1931, no. 150602.
30. BP, 16, A. E. Kemp to Borden, March 6, 1911, no. 3652; Borden to Kemp, March 7, 1911, no. 3653.
31. *Canadian Annual Review* (1911): 96–110.
32. BP, 133, Rogers to Borden, March 8, 1911, no. 70359.
33. BPP, II: 1, Borden to Laura, June 16, 1911.
34. PAC, Canadian Pacific Railway Papers, Series 1, President's Papers,

Shaughnessy Letterbooks, 99, Shaughnessy to Ames, May 18, 1911; *Memoirs*, I: 315.

35. BPP, II: 1, Borden to Laura, June 30, 1911.
36. *Canadian Annual Review* (1911): 90–92.
37. *Ibid.*, 94.
38. *Ibid.*, 95.
39. BP, 16, Borden to Kemp, July 10, 1911, no. 3732; 131, Perley [?] to T. B. Cole, June 23, 1911, no. 69481.
40. BP, 16, Borden to Whitney, July 31, 1911, no. 3749.
41. BP, 134, Hughes to Wm. McArthur, March 23, 1911, no. 7829-35.
42. PAC, Willison Papers, 37, C. F. Hamilton to Willison, March 31, 1911, no. 14234-38. Borden's secretary and political manager, A. E. Blount, Hamilton added, "remarked that it would be a fine thing to let the other fellows carry the onus of the campaign fund".
43. Professor John English convincingly argues that McBride's rejection of the leadership was pre-arranged in his "Sir Robert Borden, the Conservative Party and Political Change, 1901–1920", Ph.D., Harvard, 1973, pp. 112–13. Borden's telegram offering the leadership, on March 25, is cited in *Memoirs*, I: 309. See also PABC, McBride Papers, Telegram, Toronto *Star* to McBride, March 28, 1911 and Telegram, McBride to Toronto *Star*, March 31, 1911. There is some evidence that McBride had the support of Hugh Graham, "all the leaders in Quebec", and Donald Mann of the Canadian Northern. See C. H. Mackintosh to McBride, March 27, 1911; Telegram, Mann to McBride, April 1, 1911.
44. BP, 16, Borden to Whitney, March 30, 1911, no. 3660; 5, Whitney to Borden, April 7, 1911, no. 561.
45. PAC, Willison Papers, 37, C. F. Hamilton to Willison, March 31, 1911. Borden's account of the incident is in *Memoirs*, I: 309–11. It includes a full list of those who did and did not sign the round-robin. The original round-robin list is in BP, 14, no. 3414-5. See also BP, 268, Borden to J. W. Dafoe, December 17, 1931, no. 150602-06.
46. U.N.B., O. S. Crocket Papers, Crocket to Borden, May 27, 1911.
47. *Ibid.*, A. R. Slipp to Crocket, May 11, 1911.
48. U.N.B., Sir Douglas Hazen Papers, Aitken to Hazen, October 22 and 28, 1911.
49. U.N.B., Crocket Papers, Crocket to Borden, June 10 and 12, 1911.
50. *Ibid.*, Crocket to William Price, June 12, 1911.
51. *Ibid.*, Crocket to William Price, May 10 and June 12 and 28, 1911; Crocket to Borden, May 27 and 30 and June 10 and 12, 1911.
52. PABC, McBride Papers, McBride to Borden, June 7, 1911.
53. *Ibid.*, "British Columbia Conservation Association, 1911, Information concerning Registration of Voters, Naturalization, Courts of Revision, Suggestions in Organization Work with suggested Constitutions for Central and Local Associations".
54. *Canadian Annual Review* (1911): 240–41.
55. BP, 327, Graham to Borden, February 18, 1911, no. 193107-10.
56. BP, 133, Borden to Rogers, April 8, 1911, no. 70363.
57. *Ibid.*, Reid to Borden, April 15 and 19 and June 27, 1911, no. 70406-07, 70408-10, and 70433-36.
58. BP, 16, A. E. Kemp to Borden, July 27 and 28, 1911, no. 3748 and 3754. See also Scott Young and Astrid Young, *Silent Frank Cochrane* (Toronto, 1973), p. 116. Mr. and Mrs. Young incorrectly assume that "Silent Frank" was in charge of the Ontario campaign from the beginning.

59. BP, 16, Whitney to Borden, April 12, 1911, no. 3665; Borden to Whitney, April 13, 1911, no. 3666-67.
60. *Ibid.*, Borden to Whitney, July 31, 1911, no. 3749; Whitney to Borden, August 1, 1911, no. 3755.
61. BP, 133, Reid to Borden, August 3, 1911, no. 70445.
62. BP, 16, Blount to Kemp, August 21, 1911, no. 3775-76.
63. *Canadian Annual Review* (1911): 243–47. On Bennett see also Kenneth Fenwick Stewart, "R. B. Bennett as M.P., 1910–1917", M.A., Queen's, 1971, ch. IV.
64. U.N.B., Crocket Papers, Price to Crocket, June 23, 1911.
65. PAC, Bourassa Papers, Monk to Bourassa, February 22 and March 7, 1911.
66. See "Nationalism and the parties", a series of fourteen articles by Henri Bourassa, *Le Devoir*, 14th of May to 6th of June, 1913, Translation, in BP, 4, no. 204. This remarkable series of articles remains the fullest account of the origins and development of the alliance.
67. PAC, Laurier Papers, Murphy to Laurier, May 20, 1911, no. 186373-75.
68. Minute Books of the Canadian Home Market Association, meeting of March 21, 1911 of the Tariff Committee of the CMA. The minute books, currently in the possession of the author, were presented to Mr. Henry Borden by Mr. Hugh D. Scully in November, 1964. The CHMA continued its work after the election and eventually became the Canadian Reconstruction Association.
69. Minutes, April 22, 1911. Scully replaced Lambert as secretary when Lambert was sent to the west on CHMA business. Lambert apparently retained his connection with the CHMA through 1912. See Queen's Library, Lambert Papers, Diaries, April and November, 1912.
70. Minutes, May 12 and 29 and August 24, 1911.
71. Minutes, April 22, May 12 and 29, July 3, and August 24, 1911.
72. BP, 16, Kemp to Borden, June 6, 1911, no. 3714-15.
73. *Ibid.*, Kemp to Borden, July 16, 1911, no. 3735-36.
74. Minutes, May 12 and July 3, 1911.
75. BP, 16, Whitney to Borden, August 1, 1911, no. 3755-58.
76. *Canadian Annual Review* (1911): 165.
77. PAC, Bourassa Papers, Bourassa to W. D. Gregory, September 26, 1911.
78. *Canadian Annual Review* (1911): 185–86.
79. BP, 16, Borden to Kemp, January 30, 1911, no. 3640.
80. Cited, *Memoirs*, I: 328.
81. P. D. Stevens, "Laurier, Aylesworth and The Decline of the Liberal Party in Ontario," CHA, *Historical Papers* (1968): 101.
82. PAC, Grey Papers, Grey to "London", September 14, 1911.
83. BPP, II: 1, Borden to Laura, September 2 and 7, 1911.
84. *Memoirs*, I: 324–25; *Canadian Annual Review* (1911): 171.
85. *Canadian Annual Review* (1911): 169–79.

CHAPTER TEN

1. BP, Grey to Borden, September 25 and 26, 1911, nos. 592-94, 643 and 596.
2. PAC, Foster Papers, Diary, September 29, 1911.
3. PAO, Whitney Papers, Borden to Whitney, September 25, 1911; PAC, Monk Papers, Borden to Monk, September 27, 1911.
4. BP, 16, Sifton to Borden, September 30, 1911, no. 4197-4197A.
5. PAC, Willison Papers, Borden to Willison, October 3, 1911.

6. Henri Bourassa, "Nationalism and the parties", no. 12; Heath N. Macquarrie, "The Formation of Borden's First Cabinet," *C.J.E.P.S.*, XXIII, no. 1, February, 1957, 98. See also Roger Graham, "The Cabinet of 1911" in Frederick Gibson, ed., *Cabinet Formation and Bicultural Relations*, Studies of the Royal Commission on Bilingualism and Bicultural Relations, no. 6, Ottawa, 1970, pp. 47–62.
7. BP, 6, Hazen to Borden, October 5, 1911 (two telegrams), nos. 649 and 650, and October 7, 1911, no. 653.
8. *Canadian Annual Review* (1911): 288.
9. Catherine L. Warner, "Sir James P. Whitney," 103. See also Scott Young and Astrid Young, *Silent Frank Cochrane*, pp. 125–31.
10. See David John Hall, "Sifton", *passim*, for many illustrations of the sources of patronage in the Interior Department.
11. BP, 6, Van Horne to Borden, September 24, 1911, no. 630-37; Queen's University, Flavelle Papers, Flavelle to W. M. Grigg, October 31, 1912.
12. BP, 16, Whitney to Borden, Sunday P.M. [October 1] 1911, no. 4198-4201.
13. McNaught to Foster, September 30, 1911, cited, Wallace, *The Memoirs of the Rt. Hon. Sir George Foster*, pp. 158–59.
14. PAC, Foster Papers, 12, Cockshutt to Foster, October 4, 1911 and Clouston to Foster, October 3, 1911.
15. *Canadian Annual Review* (1910): 294–95.
16. PAC, Foster Papers, Diary, September 28–October 5, 1911.
17. BP, 118, Hughes to Borden, September 25, 1911, no. 65082.
18. *Memoirs*, I: 33.
19. *Ibid.*, 331.
20. BP, 118, Perley to Borden, February 24, 1911, no. 65049-50.
21. BP, 16, Sifton to Borden, September 30, 1911, no. 4197A.
22. BP, 132, Willison to Borden, October 5, 1911, no. 69918-20.
23. BP, 6, Grey to Borden, September 29 and October 2, 1911, nos. 597-99 and 601-2.
24. BP, 132, F. W. L. Smith to Fred [Hamilton], October 2, 1911, no. 69917.
25. BP, 6, Van Horne to Borden, September 24, 1911, no. 630-37; Bourassa, "Nationalism and the parties", no. 12.
26. BP, 6, Price to Borden, October 2, 1911, no. 640-42.
27. *Ibid.*; BP, 152, Cahan to Borden, October 1, 1911, no. 81819-21.
28. BP, 252, Drummond to Borden, September 29, 1911, no. 142221; BP, 6, Price to Borden, October 2, 1911, no. 640-42; BP, 152, Cahan to Borden, October 1, 1911, no. 81819-21.
29. BP, 6, Monk to Borden, "Saturday 1 P.M." [October 7, 1911], no. 663; PAC, Monk Papers, Lavergne to Borden, October 8, 1911.
30. A more detailed account of the complex negotiations over the Quebec representation in the Cabinet may be found in Roger Graham's excellent essay, "The Cabinet of 1911", *op. cit.*
31. William R. Willoughby, "The Appointment and Removal of Members of the International Joint Commission", *Canadian Public Administration*, 12, 1969; 411-26.
32. See *Canadian Annual Review* (1911): 302 and (1912): 198 and 672; J. K. Johnson, *The Canadian Directory of Parliament, 1867–1967*, Ottawa, 1968, *passim*.
33. PAC, Sir Joseph Pope Papers, Diary, September 23 and 27 and October 7, 1911.
34. BP, 24, "Memorandum as to Dismissals for Offensive Partisanship" [1913], no. 8473-74.
35. Sir Robert Borden, "The Problem of an Efficient Civil Service", *Canadian Historical Association Annual Report, 1931*, 8.

36. *Canadian Annual Review* (1911): 299.
37. PAC, Bourassa Papers, Monk to Bourassa, November 10, 1911.
38. *Ibid.*, Monk to Bourassa, Fevrier 11, 1912.
39. BP, 23, White to Borden, July 1, 1912, no. 7697-7700.
40. PAC, Bourassa Papers, Bourassa to W. D. Gregory, September 26, 1911.
41. BP, 24, P.C. 2928, December 21, 1911, no. 8385.
42. BP, 22, Kemp to Borden, January 11, 1912, no. 7313.
43. Stevens, *Canadian National Railways*, pp. 2, 459; *Canadian Annual Review* (1912): 179; (1914): 734-35.
44. BP, 22, Kemp to Borden, January 11, 1912, no. 7313-18.
45. BP, 24, A. B. Morine to Borden, March 15, 1912, no. 8370-83.
46. *Canadian Annual Review* (1912): 204-05.
47. BPP, Diary, September 19, 1912. Lake and Ducharme resigned in November, 1912. Their final report was presented to Parliament in December. It is summarized in *Canadian Annual Review* (1912): 205.
48. PAC, Grey Papers, Shortt to Grey, January 22, 1912; BP, 22, Perley to Borden, February 5, 1912, no. 7324-26.
49. BPP, Diary, September 14, October 24 and November 7 and 30, 1912.
50. Canada, Parliament, *Sessional Papers*, 1913, no. 57a, "Report on the Public Service of Canada by Sir George Murray".
51. See BP, 23, White to Borden, May 11, 1912, no. 7687-90.
52. For a detailed discussion of the Murray Report see J. E. Hodgetts, *et al*, *The Biography of an Institution. The Civil Service Commission of Canada, 1908-1967* (Montreal, 1972), Ch. 2. See also Dawson, *The Civil Service of Canada*, pp. 83-85, and Borden, "The Problem of an Efficient Civil Service", pp. 14-15.
53. Borden, "The Problem of an Efficient Civil Service," pp. 14-15.
54. BP, 371, Speech to American Bar Association, September 1, 1913; *Memoirs*, I: 344, Speech to Canadian Society in New York, December 8, 1911.
55. *Ibid.*, Halifax Speech, September 16, 1913.
56. BP, 300, Speech, April 24, 1912.
57. BPP, Diary, January 3, 1913.
58. HCD, May 12, 1913, p. 9640.
59. *Canadian Annual Review* (1912): 179-81; Stevens, *Canadian National Railways*, 2: 439-40; Zaslow, *The Opening of the Canadian North, 1870-1914*, pp. 219-22.
60. Canada, *Senate Debates*, 1911, p. 306.
61. Canada, Commission of Conservation, *Report of the Third Annual Meeting* (Ottawa, 1912), p. 89.
62. W. C. Good, *Farmer Citizen: My Fifty Years in the Canadian Farmers' Movement* (Toronto, 1958), p. 94.
63. HCD, January 24, 1913, p. 2149.
64. *Ibid.*, pp. 2149-50.
65. Cited, *Canadian Annual Review* (1912): 233.
66. *Ibid.*, 228-35; (1913): 256-59; (1914): 752-53.
67. *Memoirs*, I: 444.
68. BPP, Diary, June 12, 1914.
69. BP, 334, Memoir Notes, 334.
70. BP, 153, Borden to G. E. Drummond, June 24, 1912, no. 82043.
71. *Canadian Annual Review* (1913): 200.
72. *Ibid.*, 212-13.
73. PAC, Department of Finance, Deputy Minister's Correspondence, 281, 298. (Reports from Deputy Receiver General in Victoria and Winnipeg).

74. BP, 10, White to Borden, October 11 and November 18, 1913, no. 2424 and 2439-40.
75. PAC, Sir W. T. White Papers, N. Curry to George Foster, n.d. [June, 1914]; R. S. Hobson to White, June 24, 1914.
76. For a detailed analysis of the problem as it affected the Canadian Northern, see ch. XIII of T. D. Regehr, *Of Dreams and Schemes* (Macmillan, 1976).
77. PAC, Foster Papers, Diary, March 18, 1914.
78. Queen's University, Flavelle Papers, Joseph Flavelle to William Flavelle, May 2, 1911.
79. Stevens, Canadian National Railways, 2: 214, 219.
80. BP, 25, A. W. Smithers to Borden, October 18, 1912, no. 8683-88.
81. BP, 17, handwritten "Outline of Proposed Agreement", n.d., no. 4745-46; BPP, Diary, September 12, 14, 15 and 25, 1912; BP, 25, A. W. Smithers to Borden, October 18, 1912, no. 8683-88.
82. PAC, White Papers, Wm. Wainwright to Borden, May 7, 1913.
83. BPP, Diary, May 30, 1913.
84. *Ibid.*, April 29, 1914.
85. BPP, Diary, January 7 and February 21, 1913; BP, 27, E. B. Osler to Borden, March 2, 1913, no. 10494-5, Shaughnessy to Borden, March 5, 1913, no. 10496-500.
86. BPP, Diary, May 1 and 16, 1913.
87. *Ibid.*, June 2, 1913; PAC, White Papers, F. L. Schaffner to White, September 4, 1913.
88. BPP, Diary, January 22, 1914.
89. *Ibid.*, February 19 and March 2, 1914; Regehr, Ch. XIV.
90. *Ibid.*, April 28, 1914.
91. See Roger Graham, *Arthur Meighen, I, The Door of Opportunity*, (Toronto, 1960), pp. 77–82.
92. HCD, May 28, 1914, p. 4552.

CHAPTER ELEVEN

1. Queen's University, J. G. Foster Papers, Foster to C. M. Pepper, September 26, 1911.
2. *Ibid.*, Foster to R. M. Patchin, November 6, 1911.
3. *Canadian Annual Review* (1911): 296.
4. *Canadian Annual Review* (1913): 247.
5. *Ibid.*
6. *Canadian Annual Review* (1911): 295.
7. BP, 141, Speech to the New York Canadian Society, December 8, 1911, no. 74859. Many years later Borden observed that "Sometimes, with that self-conceit which is so characteristic of Canadians, we have thought that possibly we might be a helpful medium of interpretation between the great republic and the mother country beyond the ocean." Address to the British Commonwealth Relations Conference, September 13, 1933 in Henry Borden, ed., *Letters to Limbo*, p. 48.
8. Cited, Robert Bothwell, "Loring Christie: The Failure of Bureaucratic Imperialism", Ph.D., Harvard, 1972, p. 59.
9. BP, 22, McBride to Borden, July 12, 1913, no. 7491-96.
10. HCD, April 2–4, 1913, *passim*.
11. Cited, *Memoirs*, I: 397–98.
12. *Documents on Canadian External Relations*, I: 649.
13. BPP, Diary, July 23, 1914. On the *Komagata Maru* affair see Eric W.

Morse, "Some Aspect of the *Komagata Maru* Affair, 1914", *C.H.A.A.R.*, 1936 and *Documents on Canadian External Relations*, I: 643–55.
14. See, for example, BP, 131, Milner to Borden, June 16, 1912, no. 69402.
15. BP, 5, Bonar Law to Borden, October 26, 1912, no. 488-90; Borden to Bonar Law, December 3, 1912, no. 491; Amery to Borden, January 6, 1913, no. 492-96; Borden to Amery, January 20, 1913, no. 497-98.
16. Suzann C. Buckley, "Sir George Foster's 'Imperial Junket': The Failure to Promote Imperial Economic Organization, 1912–1917," *The American Review of Canadian Studies*, III, 2, Autumn, 1973, 14–29 and "Attempts at Imperial Economic Cooperation, 1912–1918; Sir Robert Borden's Role", *Canadian Historical Review*, LV, 3, September, 1974, 292–306.
17. John Kendle, *The Round Table Movement and Imperial Union* (Toronto, 1975), p. 166.
18. HCD, November 20, 1911, pp. 59–60.
19. *Ibid.*, March 18, 1912, pp. 5356–57.
20. Marder, *From the Dreadnought to Scapa Flow*, I, ch. XI.
21. BP, 125, Borden to Whitney, June 1, 1912, no. 67279; Whitney to Borden, June 4, 1912, 67149-54.
22. BPP, Diary, June 26 to July 4, 1912.
23. *Ibid.*, July 4, 1912.
24. *Ibid.*, July 5, and 16, 1912.
25. *Documents on Canadian External Relations*, I: 268.
26. BPP, Diary, August 26–27, 1912. Churchill's first draft was also opposed by the Sea Lords at the Admiralty. See Randolph S. Churchill, *Winston Churchill*, II (London, 1967), pp. 629–30.
27. BPP, Diary, September 30, 1912.
28. *Ibid.*, October 11 and 18, 1912.
29. *Ibid.*, October 2, and 15, 1912.
30. *Ibid.*, November 27, 1912.
31. BP, 23, White to Borden, no date, no. 7720.
32. BP, 6, "The House of Commons of Canada (1912–13), Bill 21," no. 730A.
33. BP, 23, Governor General to Colonial Secretary, draft, December 11, 1912, no. 8110.
34. HCD, December 5, 1912.
35. *Ibid.*, 692.
36. *Documents on Canadian External Relations*, I: 276–77.
37. Cited, *Canadian Annual Review* (1913): 140.
38. HCD, January 17, 1913, p. 1721.
39. *Ibid.*, January 31, 1913, p. 2562.
40. *Ibid.*, March 14, 1913, p. 5719.
41. BPP, Diary, March 6, 1913.
42. *Ibid.*, March 8, 1913.
43. *Ibid.*, March 14–15, 1913.
44. BP, 10, Borden to Connaught, March 8, 1913, no. 2292-2300.
45. BPP, Diary, April 7 and 9, 1912. See also Graham, *Meighen*, I: 70–72.
46. HCD, April 9, 1913, p. 7441.
47. *Ibid.*, April 22, 1913, p. 8251.
48. BPP, Diary, May 15, 1913.
49. *Ibid.*, June 6, 1913.
50. PAC, Reel A903, British Cabinet Papers, C.A.B. 41, Vol. 34, No. 18, Asquith to the King, June 5, 1913; Vol. 35, No. 3, Asquith to the King, February 11, 1914.
51. BP, 125, "Confidential Memorandum to Governor-General, March 24, 1913". An incomplete version of this document is printed in *Documents on Canadian External Relations*, I: 279–81.

52. BP, 126, "Memo from L.C.", December 10, 1913, no. 67875.
53. BP, 5, Monk to Borden, November 18, 1912, no. 512 and F. A. Finley, M.D., to Monk, November 18, 1912, no. 513.
54. See Ramsay Cook, "Church, Schools and Politics in Manitoba, 1903–1912", *Canadian Historical Review*, XXXIX, 1, March, 1958, 1–23.
55. PAO, Whitney Papers, Borden to Whitney, October 16, 1912 and Pelletier to Whitney, October 21, 1912.
56. *Ibid.*, Whitney to Borden, October 17, 1912.
57. PAC, Willison Papers, Hamilton to Willison, October 16 and 18, 1912.
58. This conclusion is based on a survey of forty-four divisions in the House between November 1911 and June 1914. Barrette, Bellemare, Guilbault, Lamarche, and Mondou did vote against the government on the Manitoba Boundary legislation in 1912.

CHAPTER TWELVE

1. BPP, Diary, September 16–17, 1913.
2. *Ibid.*, May 24–26, 1913.
3. *Ibid.*, October 25, 1912.
4. BP, 153, Drummond to Borden, October 18, 1912, no. 82048.
5. BP, 5, Borden to Bonar Law, December 3, 1912, no. 491.
6. *Canadian Annual Review* (1912): 252–54.
7. BPP, Diary, May 29, 1914.
8. BP, 110, Burnham to Borden, n.d., no. 59923; Resolutions from Wingham Loyal Orange Lodge, King Edward Loyal Orange Lodge (Vancouver), Lord Salisbury Loyal Orange Lodge (Regina), nos. 59899a, 59901, 59901a; BPP, Diary, February 19, 1914.
9. *Ibid.*, Pelletier to Borden, January 19 and February 12, 1914, nos. 59899, 59912; Memorandum by E. J. Lemaire, February 10, 1914, no. 59912-14.
10. *Ibid.*, Borden to Pelletier, February 6, 1914, no. 59903c.
11. BPP, Diary, February 21, 1914.
12. BP, 110, Casgrain to Borden, April 29, 1915, no. 59927a-b.
13. BP, 28, Casgrain to Borden, April 14 and 24, 1913, nos. 11056-57A, 11059-60.
14. BP, 25, Fitzpatrick to Borden, July 14, 1913, no. 8576-80. *See also* Fitzpatrick to Borden, July 24, 1913, no. 8589; Fitzpatrick to Cochrane, August 15, 1913, no. 8604-06; Fitzpatrick to Borden, August 27 and September 5, 1913, nos. 8608 and 8612-13.
15. BPP, Diary, October 22–24, 1914.
16. BP, 28, Dr. N. A. Dussault to Borden, August 21, 1914, no. 11115-6.
17. *Ibid.*, Dorais Panneton to Pelletier, December 3, 1913, no. 11089-92.
18. *Ibid.*, Casgrain to Borden, September 17, 1913 and May 18, 1914, nos. 11083-85 and 11099; G. F. Johnston to Borden, December 31, 1913, no. 11096.
19. *Ibid.*, Casgrain to Borden, September 17, 1913, no. 11083-85.
20. *Canadian Annual Review* (1914): 744–49.
21. PAC, Kemp Papers, 3, Carstairs to Borden, May 23, 1912.
22. BPP, Diary, October 17, 1913.
23. PAC, Willison Papers, Arthur Ford to Willison, July 24, 1914.
24. BP, 336, Memoir Notes, no. 807-09; BPP, Diary, December 10, 1912 and June 17, 18 and 22, 1914.
25. *Canadian Annual Review* (1913): 170–71.
26. PAC, Christie Papers, Borden to Christie, July 7, 1913.
27. BPP, Diary, June 9 and 12, 1914. Stress original.
28. BP, 33, undated resolution on Senate reform [1914], no. 13883.

29. *Ibid.*, Perley to Borden, July 6, 1914, no. 13423-24.
30. *Ibid.*, McInnes to Blount, July 20, 1914, no. 13427; Willoughby to Borden, July 20, 1914, no. 13426; Matson to Borden, July 31, 1914, no. 13429.
31. BPP, Diary, July 9, 1914.
32. *Ibid.*, June 28, 1914.
33. *Ibid.*, July 22, 1914.
34. *Ibid.*, July 23 and 26, 1914.
35. *Ibid.*, July 26, 1913.
36. PAC, Sound Archives, Tape 285. A CBC interview with Dr. Campbell Laidlaw, Borden's doctor, July 28, 1971. Hereafter "Laidlaw interview".
37. Letter from Miss Alice Lowe, the Borden's housekeeper, to the author, March 25, 1966.
38. Laidlaw interview.
39. BPP, Diary, June 15 and 16, October 21–26 and November 11, 1913.
40. Laidlaw interview.
41. BPP, Diary, November 11 and 25, 1913.
42. See, for example, the references to White in his diary, 1912–14.
43. BPP, Diary, November 9, 1912; June 21 and 23, 1913; and January 13 and 16, 1914.
44. *Ibid.*, November 8, 1912; April 13, 1913; July 4, 1914.
45. *Ibid.*, July 27, 1914.
46. *Ibid.*, July 28–30, 1914.
47. *Ibid.*, July 31, 1914.
48. *Documents on Canadian External Relations*, I: 37.
49. Cited, *Memoirs*, I: 461.

INDEX

Abbott, Sir John, 31
Acacia Villa Seminary, 7
Acadians, 2
Achim, Honoré, 238, 240, 242, 247
Agricultural Aid Act (1913), 219–20
Aitken, Sir William Maxwell, 185
Alaska Boundary Award, 62–3
Alberta: provincial status (1905), 92–102
American Federation of Labor, 93
Amery, Leopold Stennett, 150, 155, 156, 234
Ames, Sir Herbert Brown, 76, 100, 122, 128, 134, 169, 173, 184, 249, 257
Anglo-Japanese trade treaty (1913), 232–33
Annapolis Valley, 1
Asian immigration, 232–33
Asquith, Herbert Henry, 156; and Borden, 237, 239; on Borden's naval policy (1913–14), 243–44
Australia, 152
Autonomy Bills of 1905, 90–102
Aylesworth, Sir Allen Bristol, 123, 193

Bank Act (1913), 218

Bank of Nova Scotia: Borden becomes director of, 26; and *La Presse* Affair, 82
Barker, Samuel, 61, 86, 102, 123, 171, 184; and *La Presse* Affair, 82
Barnstead, Arthur, 42
Barnstead, Ethel, 91, 112
Barnstead, Mabel, 42, 90
Barrette, Joseph-Arthur, 238, 240, 242, 247
Bay of Fundy, 1
Beck, Sir Adam, 187
Beland, Henri Sévérin, 240
Bellemare, Adélard, 238, 240, 242, 247
Bennett, Richard Bedford, 54, 155; Alberta party leader, 109; on Canadian Northern Railway, 227; election of 1911, 188; on naval policy, 160
Bennett, W. H., 69
Bergeron, J. G. H., 46, 100, 112, 128, 139, 181, 194
Beresford, Lord Charles, 157
Blair, Andrew George, 46; and *La Presse* Affair, 78–82; resigns from Cabinet, 67
Blondin, Pierre-Édouard, 162, 171, 184, 238
Blount, Austin Ernest, 88, 88–89, 107, 109, 111, 258, 259, 260,

262; on election of 1908, 138; election of 1911, 187; on party convention, 127, 169

Board of Grain Commissioners, 218

Booth, J. R., 68

Borden, Andrew: death of, 42; marriage to Catherine Fuller, 5; marriage to Eunice Jane Laird, 5; Robert's opinion of, 6

Borden, Eunice (daughter of Henry Clifford), 90–91

Borden, Eunice Jane (*née* Laird), 42, 196; health (1912–14), 261; influence on Robert, 5; marriage to Andrew Borden, 5

Borden, Sir Frederick William, 36, 159; defeated in 1911, 195; Hughes on (1911), 203; supported by Robert (1882), 30–31

Borden Government: agricultural legislation (1912–14), 217–20; Anglo-Japanese trade treaty (1913), 232–33; Keewatin Schools, 245–46; Ontario Schools Question, 246; preferential tariffs, 233–34; preparation for war, 262; railway policy (1912–14), 224–28

Borden, Henry (son of Henry Clifford), 90–91

Borden, Henry Clifford (Hal), 5, 112, 261; attends Dalhousie Law School, 25; death of his wife, 90–92; in Robert's firm, 42; marries Mabel Barnstead, 42

Borden, John William, 5, 91; in Department of Militia and Defence, 36, 42

Borden, Julia, 5, 196

Borden, Laura (*née* Bond), 32, 86; accompanies Robert on Ontario tour (1904), 74; accompanies Robert on western tour (1902), 52; accompanies Robert to England (1912), 236; and "Glensmere", 140; and Robert, 36, 37, 43, 112; as public figure, 74, 197; marries Robert (1889), 24; Muskoka vacation (1914), 258–62; prepares "Pinehurst" for sale, 89

Borden, Mabel (*née* Barnstead), 42, 90

Borden, Mabel (daughter of Henry Clifford), 90–91

Borden, Sir Robert Laird: ancestors, 4; birth, 4; childhood, 6; education, 7; teaching career, 7–11; health, 10, 21, 25, 43, 260–61; legal training, 11–12, 17–19; Fisheries Commission of 1877, 18–19; in militia, 19–20; admitted to the Bar (1878), 20; partnerships with Ross and Chipman, 20–21; with Graham and Tupper, 21; invited to be Deputy Minister of Justice (1888), 22; establishes his own firm (1889), 23; marries Laura Bond (1889), 24; purchases "Pinehurst" (1894), 25; Supreme Court Cases, 25; friendship with Charles Hibbert Tupper,

25–26; business interests, 26, 86; *Municipality of Pictou* v. *Geldert* (1893), 26; president of Nova Scotia Barristers' Society, 26, 28; runs for Parliament, 28, 33–36; daily routine in Ottawa, 36–38, 259–60; connections with Conservative Party, 29–32; represents Halifax interests, 40; election of 1900, 44–46; becomes party leader (1901), 47–49; western tour of 1902, 52–55; maritime tour of 1903, 55; and Monk, 55–59; and Tarte, 57–59; and caucus, 60–61; railway policy (1902–04), 65–71; election of 1904, 72–89; Ontario tour of 1904, 73–76; defeated in Halifax, 77; *La Presse* Affair, 78–85; elected in Carleton (1905), 89; gives up legal practice, 89; death of Mabel Borden, 90–92; and party convention, 107–11, 126–27; and Jacques Cartier Club, 109–10; scandal campaign, 120–25; Foresters' Affair, 123–25; cooperation with Bourassa (1907–08), 129; Halifax Platform, 129–35; tour of 1907, 133–35; election of 1908, 135–39; purchases "Glensmere", 140; naval question (1909–10), 151–64, 172–73; challenge to his leadership (1910), 165–69; reciprocity (1911), 176–83; western tour of 1911, 181–82; election of 1911, 183–96; challenge to his leader-

ship (1911), 184; naval question (1911), 194; selects his Cabinet, 197–208; and civil service reform, 211–16; and Grand Trunk Pacific Railway (1912–14), 224–25; and Canadian Northern Railway (1912–14), 225–28; becomes Secretary of State for External Affairs, 231; employs Christie, 231; permanent naval policy (1912–14), 235, 238, 243–44; Naval Aid Bill of 1913, 236–43; trip to United Kingdom, 1912, 236; and Churchill, 237–38, 243; and Committee of Imperial Defence, 237, 239–40; support in French Canada (1912–14), 245–47, 249–53, 257; as party leader (1912–14), 248–57; Senate appointments (1913), 249; and Pelletier, 250–52; election plans (1914), 253–57; accepts knighthood (1914), 254; Manitoba election of 1914, 256; vacation (1914), 258–62; preparations for war, 261–63

Views on:
Asian immigration, 53, 232; Autonomy Bills (1905), 96–101; Canada in World War I, 263; Canadian-American relations, 230–32; Canadian Pacific Railway, 53; Civil Service, 39; closure (1913), 241–42; Combines Investigation Act, 146–47; conditional grants, 221–22; conservation, 144–45; Conservative caucus,

87; Drummond–Arthabaska,
171–72; education, 8;
English-French relations,
61–2, 116; his father, 6;
Foster (Sir George), 136;
French Canadians, 73, 101,
143, 249; government owner-
ship, 69–70, 131–34; Grand
Trunk Railway, 143–44;
Haultain (F.W.G.), 54–55;
Hughes, (Sir Samuel), 204;
Imperial relations, 62–4,
149–51, 244–45; indemnity
legislation, 102–03; Industrial Disputes Investigation
Act, 118–20; industrial
economy, 52, 216; Laurier
(Sir Wilfrid), 136, 241, 242,
255; the law, 27, 217; Lord's
Day Observance Act, 116–17;
Maclean (W. F.), 104;
Manitoba Schools Question,
34–35; Monk (F. D.), 238,
246–47; his mother, 5, 261;
National Policy, 34; Parliament, 39, 61, 103–04; party
convention, 164–65; party
organization, 55, 111; patronage, 248, 258; preferential
tariff, 40, 63–4, 180, 234;
prohibition, 75; provincial
rights, 99–101; railway
policy, 131–32; the Senate,
130, 221, 255–56; the tariff,
52–53, 65, 117–18, 217; Tariff
Commission Bill, 221;
Tupper, (Sir Charles), 39
Borden, Ritchie, Parker and
Chisholm, 26; agency work
for Department of Justice, 24
Borden, Sara, 10

Borden, Sophie, 5
Borden, Thomas, 5, 10
Boulay, Herménegilde, 238, 242,
247
Bourassa, Henri, 138, 199, 257;
and Autonomy Bills of 1905,
97; and Borden's Cabinet,
207; and Conservative Party
(1907–08), 128–29; and
Conservative Party (1909),
164; and Foresters' Affair,
125; and South African War,
44; boards with Borden, 38;
election of 1911, 188–89, 192,
194–96; Keewatin Schools,
245; on immigration policy,
95–96; on Laurier Govern-
ment, 211; on Lord's Day
Observance Act, 116; on
naval question, 170–72
Bowell, Sir Mackenzie, 28
British Government:
and Borden's visit (1912),
237–38;
and naval question (1909–
10), 152, 156
British North America Act, 150;
and Autonomy Bills of 1905,
97, 99–100; Borden seeks
amendment of (1912), 237
Broder, Andrew, 130, 181, 184,
204
Brodeur, Louis-Philippe, 159
Bruchési, Archbishop: sup-
ports Lord's Day Observance
Act, 115
Bulyea, G. H. V., 97
Burnham, John Hampden, 250
Burrell, Martin, 139, 162, 163,
165, 167; Minister of Agriculture, 199–200; on Agricul-

tural Aid Act (1913), 219–20; on Borden's leadership (1910), 166; on Monk (1910), 165; on rural life, 219

Cahan, Charles H., 194, 206; on Borden, 29–30; on Rodolphe Forget, 208; on Pelletier, 207
Canada–Atlantic Railway, 68, 92
Canada Grain Act (1912), 218–19
Canadian-American relations. *See* Borden, Sir Robert Laird; Election of 1911; Foster, John G.; Laurier, Sir Wilfrid; Reciprocity (1911); United States
Canadian Bank of Commerce, 66, 223
Canadian Bar Association: founded (1896), 27, 28
Canadian Home Market Association, 190–91
Canadian Manufacturers' Association, 70, 93, 115; election of 1911, 189–91; on tariff of 1907, 117
Canadian National League, 178
Canadian Northern Railway, 66, 68, 173; and *La Presse* Affair, 80–82; seeks government aid (1912–14), 223–28
Canadian Pacific Railway, 53, 66, 68, 70; and *La Presse* Affair, 81
Carstairs, J. S., 127, 187
Cartwright, Sir Richard: Borden on, 39; on highways bill of 1912; 220–21
Casgrain, Thomas Chase, 47, 76,

164, 199, 236; considered for Borden's Cabinet, 208, 249; I.J.C. appointment, 209; on Monk, 56; on naval question, 152–53, 160; on organization in Montreal (1913), 252
Chabot, Doctor John L., 198
Chamberlain, Joseph, 63
Chapais, Sir Thomas, 110
Chipman, John P., 20
Chisholm, Joseph Andrew, 31; joins Borden's firm, 23
Christie, Loring C., 255; on external policy, 231, 244–45; legal adviser in External Affairs, 231
Churchill, Winston Spencer, 258; and Borden, 237–38, 243; and naval crisis of 1912, 235
Civil Service Amendment Act (1908), 122
Civil Service Commission, 122, 209, 213, 215–16
Clancy, James, 36
Clark, Hugh, 181
Clark, Michael, 241
Clark, Sir William Mortimer, 164
Clarke, Edward F., 47, 61, 69, 74
Clouston, Sir Edward Seaborne, 201
Cochrane, Francis, 128, 193, 204, 224, 249, 251, 257; election of 1911, 187; Minister of Railways and Canals, 199
Cockshutt, William Foster, 201
Coderre, Louis, 246, 257; appointed Secretary of State (1912), 249
Combines Investigation Act, 144, 145–47

Commission of Conservation, 144–45

Committee of Imperial Defence: Canadian representation on, 237, 239–40

Connaught and Strathearn, Duke of, 198, 241, 244; becomes Governor General, 209; recalled from western tour, 262

Conservative caucus: Autonomy Bills of 1905, 98–102; Borden's relationship to, 60–61; his resignation (1904), 88; his leadership (1910), 167–69; his leadership (1911), 184; Canadian Northern Railway, 226–27; closure (1913), 242; National Policy, 64; party convention, 126, 169; party organization, 59–61; preferential tariff, 63–64; railway policy (1904), 71; reciprocity (1911), 176

Conservative Party, 41, 50–51; Borden's view of, 32; by-election results (1912–13), 254; convention plans, 107–11, 126, 164–69; election of 1896, 35–36; election of 1900, 45; election of 1904, 73–78; election of 1908, 135–39; election of 1911, 183–96; Halifax Platform, 133–34; indemnity legislation, 104; leadership candidates (1900), 46–47; Naval Aid Bill of 1913, 236–45; naval question (1909–10), 152–65; organization, 108, 127, 254; party contributions (1904), 79; in

Quebec, 55–59, 110, 128–29, 250–53; railway policy (1904), 70

Corby, Henry, 60

Craigie, Henry, 36

Crocket, Oswald Smith, 165, 167; election of 1911, 186

Crosby, Adam B., 138

Crothers, Thomas Wilson, 139, 165, 167, 181, 249, 257; appointed Minister of Labour, 205

Crown Life Insurance Company: Borden and Tupper as founders of, 26

Currie, John Allister, 241

Dalhousie Law School: founded (1883), 18

Daniel, J. W., 209

Davin, Nicholas Flood, 46

Davis, Michael Patrick, 251

Doherty, Charles Joseph, 139, 194, 249, 257; accompanies Borden to England (1912), 236; Minister of Justice, 206

Dominion-Provincial relations: Borden argues for conditional grants, 221–22

Dominions Royal Commission on Natural Resources, Trade and Legislation, 234

Drayton, Henry Lumley, 210

Drummond–Arthabaska by-election, 171–72

Drummond County Railway, 40

Drummond, George Edward, 190, 249; on Rodolphe Forget, 208

Ducharme, Guillaume Narcisse, 212–13

Dundonald, Earl of, 149

Eaton, Mrs. Timothy, 258
Election of 1896, 32–36
Election of 1900, 44–46
Election of 1904, 72–89
Election of 1908, 135–39
Election of 1911, 183–96
Emmerson, Henry Robert: and
  La Presse Affair, 78
English-French relations:
  and naval question (1909–
  10), 147–49; and School
  Question of 1905, 95–102;
  Borden on (1906), 116;
  Keewatin Schools, 245–46

Farmers' Bank of Canada, 221
Fielding, William Stevens,
  election of 1900, 45; election
  of 1904, 77; election of 1911,
  195; on tariff of 1907, 117;
  Premier of Nova Scotia, 30;
  reciprocity (1911), 175–76
Fisher, Lord John, 157
Fisher, Sydney, 145
Fitzpatrick, Sir Charles, 81, 140;
  and Autonomy Bills of 1905,
  97; helps Borden with
  patronage, 251–52
Flavelle, Sir Joseph Wesley,
  89*n*, 105, 128, 160, 224; on
  Autonomy Bills of 1905, 102;
  on railway policy (1903), 68
Flemming, J. K., 253, 257
Fripp, Alfred E., 198
Foresters' Affair, 123–25, 201
Forget, Sir Joseph David
  Rodolphe, 128, 184, 199, 251;
  considered for Borden's
  Cabinet, 208

Forget, Louis-Joseph, 134
Foster, Sir George Eulas, 41, 46,
  50, 53, 64, 74, 88, 102, 129, 130,
  137, 142, 171, 178; and
  Foresters' Affair, 123–25, 201;
  appointed to Dominions
  Royal Commission, 234; elec-
  tion of 1908, 136; Minister of
  Trade and Commerce, 200–
  02; naval resolution of 1909,
  151–55; on Borden (1911),
  198, 201; on Canadian–
  American relations, 230; on
  Laurier's railway policy, 223;
  on tariff of 1907, 117
Foster, John G.: on Borden's
  attitude towards U.S., 230
Fowler, George: and Foresters'
  Affair, 123–24
Fuller, Catherine, 5

Galibert, Paul, 190
Ganong, Gilbert, 60
Gauthier, Louis-Joseph, 240
Gauthier, Louis-Philippe, 238
George, William Kerr, 164, 190,
  194
Georgian Bay Canal, 253
German, William Manly, 178
Gilbert, Arthur, 171–72
Girard, Joseph, 184
"Glensmere", 140
Glenwood Institute, 9
Good, William C.: on rural life,
  219
Gordon, George, 209
Gourlay, Robert S., 194
Graham, George Perry, 195
Graham, Sir Hugh, 59, 137, 186,
  189; and Jacques Cartier
  Club, 110; and *La Presse*

Affair, 78–85; contributions to Conservative Party, 83–84

Graham, Wallace, 19; appointed to the Bench, 23; invites Borden to be partner, 21

Grand Pré, 1, 196, 261; Covenanters' Church, 2; educational facilities in 1860s, 3; "massacre", 2; occupations (1871), 2; settlement of, 2

Grand Trunk Railway, 66, 67, 92

Grand Trunk Pacific Railway, 67, 68, 69, 79, 143–44; seeks government aid (1912–14), 223–25

Grant, Principal George M., 148–49

Greenshields, J. N.: and *La Presse* Affair, 78

Grey, Lord, 198, 209; on Monk and naval question, 206–07; on naval question (1909–10), 157–58

Griesbach, W. A., 188

Griffin, Watson, 70

Guibault, Édouard, 238, 240, 242, 247

Gutelius, Frederick Passmore, 212

Hackett, M. F., 57, 59

Haggart, Alexander, 209

Haggart, John Graham, 61, 65

Halifax, 1; Borden announces public works in (1913), 222; business community, attitudes of, 14–15; description of, 13–17; Imperial ties of, 14; investment capital in, 15–16;

leisure activities, 16–17

Halifax City and County: represented by Borden and Russell (1896–1900), 35; represented by Roche and Carney (1904–08), 77; represented by Borden and Crosby (1908–11), 138

Halifax *Herald*: on Borden (1896), 33; on Senate, 254

Halifax *Morning Chronicle*, 15; on Borden (1896), 32–33

Halifax Platform, 129–35, 137

Hamilton, Charles F., 9, 18, 184; on Conservative Party and Borden's leadership, 122–23; on election of 1908, 137; on Foster (1908), 142

Hamilton, James Henry, 7, 9

Harcourt, Lewis, 237, 243; on Canadian representation on C.I.D., 239–40

Harrington, C. S., 27

Harris, Lloyd, 196; reciprocity (1911), 178–80

Haultain, Frederick W. G., 155; and Autonomy Bills of 1905, 96; election of 1911, 188; leads Provincial Rights Party, 109; meets Borden (1902), 54; on Conservative Party leadership (1905), 107; reciprocity (1911), 180

Hazen, Sir John Douglas, 138, 199, 242, 244; accompanies Borden to England (1912), 236; election of 1911, 184–85, 194; Minister of Marine, Fisheries and Naval Service, 199; on naval question, 155; reciprocity (1911), 180

Highways Bills (1912–13), 219, 221

Hobson, Robert, 190

Hochen, H. C., 137

House of Commons: closure (1913), 241–42; naval debate of 1913, 241–42

Howe, Joseph, 1

Hudson's Bay Railway, 136, 174, 181, 218, 220

Hughes, Sir Samuel, 61, 74, 129, 164, 183, 196, 253, 257; Minister of Militia and Defence, 202–04; offers his seat to Borden (1904), 88

Hunt, W. P., 82–83

Hutton, Colonel Edward, 149

Imperial Defence Conference (1909), 158–59

Imperial relations, 62–64, 148–63, 232–45

Indemnity legislation (1906–07), 102–06

Independent Order of Foresters, 123

Industrial Disputes Investigation Act, 115, 118

Intercolonial Railway, 13, 68, 220, 221

International Joint Commission, 174

Jacques Cartier Club, 109–10

Johnston, George Franklin, 194

Judicial Committee of the Privy Council, 26

Keewatin Schools, 245–46

Keith, A. B., *Responsible Government in the Dominion*: read by Borden, 236

Kemp, Sir Albert Edward, 130, 139, 173, 180, 190, 212, 250, 257; election of 1911, 187; Minister without Portfolio, 205; on naval policy, 160–61; reciprocity (1911), 177

Kenny, Thomas Edward, 29, 32, 34, 45

Kidd, Edward, 88, 103, 142

King, William Lyon Mackenzie, 119, 145–47, 187, 195

King's County, Nova Scotia: religious affiliation of people in, 3

Kingston *Standard*, 152

Komagata Maru Incident, 233

La Presse, 152

La Presse Affair, 78–85

Lafontaine, George, 241

Laidlaw, Doctor Campbell: on Borden's health, 260

Laird, John, 7

Laird, William P., 11

Lake, Sir Richard Stuart, 103, 109, 212–13

Lamarche, Paul-Émile, 240, 245–47

Lambert, Norman Platt, 190

Lash, Zebulon Aiton, 178–80, 190, 198, 200

Laurier, Sir Wilfrid, 50, 96, 180; and closure (1913), 242; and Drummond–Arthabaska, 171–72; and Imperial relations, 62; and *La Presse* Affair, 81; and Tarte, 57; becomes Prime Minister, 35; election of 1904, 73; election of 1908, 135–38; election of 1911, 183–96; naval resolution (1909), 154; Naval Service Act (1910), 161–63; on Borden, 136; on government ownership, 174–75; on Industrial Disputes Investigation Act, 119; on Naval Aid Bill (1913), 240

Laurier Government, 44, 72–73; and Imperial relations, 149; appoints Commission of Conservation, 145; immigration policy of, 93–96; on terminal elevators (1911), 218–19; railway policy of, 67, 92; reciprocity (1911), 174–83; tariff policy of, 92–93

Lavallee, Joseph-Octave, 238

Laverge, Louis, 171

Lavergne, Armand, 128, 138, 148, 171, 199, 245–46

Law, Andrew Bonar, 234

Leacock, Stephen, 190

Le Nationaliste: and *La Presse* Affair, 78–79, 85

Lemieux, Rodolphe, 119

Lennox, Haughton, 69

Leonard, Reuben Wells, 210, 251

L'Evenement, 170

Liberal Party, 77, 192–95; aid to Canadian Northern Railway, 225–28; aid to Grand Trunk Pacific Railway, 225. *See also* Laurier Government; Laurier, Sir Wilfrid

Lord's Day Alliance, 115

Lord's Day Observance Act, 115–17

Lortie, Joseph-Arthur, 162, 184

Lougheed, Sir James Alexander: becomes Government leader in Senate, 205; and Naval Aid Bill (1913), 243

Lowe, Miss Alice, 259

Lynch-Staunton, George, 212

McBride, Sir Richard, 73, 88, 127, 171, 253, 257; and party leadership (1910), 166–67; and party leadership (1911), 184; election of 1911, 184–86; meets Borden (1902), 54; on Asian immigration, 232; on naval question, 155; on party convention, 127; on Senate, 255; reciprocity (1911), 180

Macdonald, Sir Hugh John, 46, 50

McInnes, Hector, 256

MacKeen, David, 36

Mackenzie, Sir William, 66, 67, 226–28

MacLaren, Alexander, 36

Maclean, Major H. C., 258

Maclean, William Findlay, 47, 85, 89, 104, 106, 138, 164, 167

McLeod, H. C., 82–83

MacMaster, Donald, 77

Macnab, Brenton, 59, 80–81, 128

McNaught, William Kirkpatrick, 201

Magrath, Charles, 139, 165, 167, 169, 188; appointed to I.J.C., 209

Manitoba Schools Question, 33–35

Mann, Sir Donald, 66, 67, 241

Marcil, Charles, 142–43

Marechal, Louis Theophile, 116, 128, 194, 208; considered for Cabinet (1912), 249

Mathieson, J. A., 253, 255, 257

Matawan, New Jersey, 9

Meighen, Arthur, 139, 181, 184, 256; aid to Canadian Northern Railway, 227; and closure (1913), 242; appointed Solicitor-General, 205

Middlebro, William Sora, 181

Molloy, John Patrick, 241

Mondou, Albérie-Archie, 240, 247

Monk, Frederick Debartzch, 47, 53, 73, 76, 112, 123, 128, 130, 166, 184, 198, 240, 250, 257; and Borden, 55–59, 100, 195–96; and Tarte, 58–59; election of 1911, 188–89, 194; Minister of Public Works, 206–07; naval question, (1909–10), 157–58, 160, 162, 170–72; on immigration policy, 95; on Keewatin Schools, 245–46; on patronage, 210; Quebec leadership, 56–59, 164; Quebec party convention, 110; resigns from Cabinet, 238, 245–47

Montreal *Herald*, 133, 171, 176

Montreal *Gazette*, 160

Montreal *Star*, 59, 78, 104, 124, 128, 152, 254

Morine, Alfred Bishop, 212–13

Municipality of Pictou v. *Geldert*, 26

Murphy, Charles, 189

Murray, Sir George, 214–15

Nantel, Wilfrid Bruno, 139, 158, 162, 171, 184, 238, 257; Minister of Inland Revenue, 207–08

National Trades and Labour Congress, 93

National Transcontinental Railway, 67, 68, 122; investigation of, 212; Quebec City terminals, 251–52

Naval Aid Bill (1913), 235–43

Naval Service Act (1910), 147–63, 238, 243, 247; suspended by Borden, 235

New Zealand: and naval question (1909), 152

Nickle, W. F.: opposes aid to Canadian Northern Railway, 227

Norris, T. C., 256

North Atlantic Trading Company, 121

Northcliffe, Lord, 157

Northrup, William Barton, 123, 162, 167, 184, 242, 262

Northwest Territories: educational ordinances of 1901, 95, 98; school system of 1875, 95

Nova Scotia, 1; Repeal campaign in, 29–30

Nova Scotia Barristers' Society, 17, 26, 28

Nova Scotia Railway, 1

Oliver, Frank: on immigration policy, 94–95

O'Mullin, J. C., 77

Ontario–Manitoba Boundary, 220

Ontario Schools Question, 246

Orange *Sentinel*, 137, 138

Osler, Sir Edmund Boyd, 199, 226

Ottawa *Citizen*, 152

Ottawa *Free Press*, 152

Paquet, Eugène, 162, 238, 246
Parker, W. F., 22, 23, 28, 31
Paterson, William, 175, 195
Patterson, Arthur McNutt, 7
Patenaude, Esioff-Léon, 171
Pelletier, Louis-Philippe, 57,
    59, 76, 238, 246, 249, 251–53,
    257; accompanies Borden to
    England (1912), 236; and
    Jacques Cartier Club, 110;
    appointed Postmaster-
    General, 207–08; issues
    bilingual postcards (1914),
    250–51
Perley, Sir George Halsey, 181,
    184, 198, 254, 256; Chief
    Whip, 169; Minister without
    Portfolio, 205–06
Perrault, J. E., 171–72
"Pinehurst", 25, 42, 89
Pope, Sir Joseph, 209, 231
Pope, Rufus Henry, 41, 60, 128,
    252; on Borden's leadership
    (1910), 167
Powell, Henry, 36, 46, 209
Preston, W. T. R., 121
Price, William, 136, 139, 158,
    170, 184, 207–08, 251; on
    Armand Lavergne, 207; chal-
    lenges Borden's leadership,
    167; election of 1911, 186
Public Service Commission,
    212–13
Pugsley, William: and
    La Presse Affair, 78

Rainville, Joseph-Hormisdas,
    238, 246
Reaume, Doctor J. O., 110

Reciprocity (1911), 173–83
Reid, Doctor John Dowsley,
    184, 224, 248, 254, 257, 258;
    appointed Minister of
    Customs, 204; challenges
    Borden's leadership, 167;
    election of 1911, 187
Reid, Robert Gillespie, 213
Ritchie, Charles Henry, 262
Ritchie, William Bruce Almon,
    23–24, 31, 91
Robertson, James Wilson: on
    rural life, 219
Roblin, Sir Rodmond, 73, 109,
    127, 246, 256; election of 1911,
    185–86; Manitoba election of
    1914, 256; meets Borden
    (1902), 53; on Borden's
    leadership (1910), 167–68;
    on government ownership,
    132; on indemnity legislation,
    105; on naval question, 155,
    158, 160; on party conven-
    tion, 127; on party platform,
    130; on Senate, 255; reciproc-
    ity (1911), 180
Roche, Doctor William James,
    45, 60, 181, 256; Minister of
    Interior, 250; Secretary of
    State, 205
Rogers, Robert, 109, 127, 181,
    193, 199, 222, 224, 246, 248–
    49, 251, 253, 254, 256; election
    of 1911, 186; Minister of
    Interior, 199; Minister of
    Public Works, 249–50; on
    Drummond–Arthabaska,
    171; reciprocity (1911), 176–
    77
Rosamond, Bennett, 36
Ross, Sir George: and Naval

Aid Bill (1913), 243
Ross, John T., 20, 24
Ross Rifle, 122, 203
Ross, William B., 24, 126
Round Table Movement, 234, 237
Rowell, Newton Wesley, 193
Royal Commission on Life Insurance, 123–25
Rural free delivery, 219
Russell, Benjamin, 35
Russell, David: and *La Presse* Affair, 78–83
Russell, T. A., 190

Saint John, 1
Saint John *Telegram*, 80
Sanford, Mrs. Harriet, 258, 261
Saskatchewan: provincial status (1905), 92–102
Sbaretti, Mgr.: and Autonomy Bills of 1905, 97
Scandal Campaign of 1906–08, 120–25
Scully, H. D., 190
Sedgewick, Robert: Deputy Minister of Justice, 23
Senate: and Conservative election plans (1914), 254–56; Conservative Party and elective Senate, 130; obstructs Borden's legislative program, 220–22, 228; rejects Naval Aid Bill (1913), 243
Sévigny, Albert, 171, 238
Shaughnessy, Sir Thomas, 68, 84, 131, 133, 181, 224, 226
Sherrard, James Henry, 190
Shortt, Adam, 213
Sifton, Sir Clifford, 46, 145, 164, 224, 227; and Autonomy Bills

of 1905; 96–99; and Borden's Cabinet, 198–206; and immigration policy, 93–96; and *La Presse* Affair, 81–82; election of 1911, 193; reciprocity (1911), 178–80
Smith, Goldeven: and South African War, 44
South African War, 44, 62, 70, 148
Sproule, Thomas, 61, 129; on immigration policy, 94
Stairs, John F., 33–34, 64; member for Halifax City and County, 29
Stanfield, John, 138; elected in Colchester (1907), 127
Staples, William, 181
Strathcona and Mount Royal, Lord, 236
Supreme Court of Canada, 25, 36

Taft, President William Howard, 174–76
Tanner, E. C., 77; opposes party convention, 126–27
Tariff of 1907, 115, 117, 174
Tariff Commission Bill, 221
Tarte, Joseph Israel, 83; and Borden, 57–59; on Lord's Day Observance Act, 115–16; on National Policy, 58
Taylor, George, 86, 167, 201, 209; appointed Chief Whip, 60
Tellier, J. M., 128, 158, 171, 208
Temiskaming and Northern Ontario Railway, 220
Thompson, Sir John S. D., 31; appointed to Bench, 21;

invites Borden to be Deputy Minister, 22; Minister of Justice (1885), 22; partner of Graham and Tupper, 21

Tisdale, Colonel David, 61

Toronto *Globe*, 76, 97, 201; on Borden's naval policy (1911), 206–07; election of 1911, 192

Toronto *Mail and Empire*, 76, 128, 138, 160

Toronto *News*, 75, 76, 78, 124, 138; becomes Conservative paper (1908), 128

Toronto *Star*, 78, 133, 166

Toronto *World*, 47, 138; and *La Presse* Affair, 79

Trades and Labour Congress, 93

Trans-Canada Railway, 66

Tupper, Sir Charles, 1, 26, 41, 50, 53; asks Borden to run for Parliament, 28; becomes Prime Minister (1896), 28; defeated in election of 1900, 46; election of 1896, 33, 34; selects Borden as party leader, 47–49

Tupper, Sir Charles Hibbert, 19, 31, 36, 84, 127, 131; considers joining Borden's firm, 28; elected to Parliament (1882), 21; election of 1896, 33; election of 1900, 46; election of 1908, 138; election of 1911, 194; joins Borden's firm, 37; Minister of Marine and Fisheries (1888), 23; on indemnity legislation, 105; on naval policy, 160; partner of Graham and Thompson, 21;

passes Bar examination, 20

Tupper, Reginald Hibbert, 26

Union Trust Company, 123

Unionist Party (United Kingdom), 237; and Borden's victory in 1911, 233

United States: Canada's relations with after 1911, 230–32; reciprocity (1911), 173–83

Vancouver *World*, 138

Van Horne, Sir William: on Bourassa, 207; on Rogers, 199

Victoria *Colonist*, 104

Walker, Sir Byron Edmond, 164, 179, 198, 200

Wallace, Nathaniel Clarke, 47, 61

Wallace, W. B., 45

Wallis, A. F., 160

Weatherbe and Graham, 18; Borden articles at, 12

Weatherbe, R. L., 11–12, 18, 32

West Indies: Canadian trade agreement with (1913), 217

White, Richard, 160

White, Sir William Thomas, 164, 194, 224, 226, 227, 253, 257; budgets of 1912–14, 222; election of 1911, 191; encourages U.S. investment in Canada, 230; Minister of Finance, 200; on depression of 1913–14, 222–23; on tariff policy (1913), 218

Whitney, Sir James Pliny, 127–28, 198, 253, 256; and Jacques Cartier Club, 109–10; election of 1908, 139; election of 1911, 185–87, 191; Halifax Platform, 134–35; illness of, 256–57; on Borden's leadership, 128, 184; on indemnity legislation, 105; on naval question, 155, 160; on party convention, 108, 126; on White, 200; Ontario elections of 1905, 106; Ontario Schools Question, 246; reciprocity (1911), 177, 180

Williams-Taylor, Sir Frederick, 224, 227

Willison, Sir John S., 89, 134, 160, 164, 198, 200; on Foster, 137; reciprocity (1911), 178–80

Windsor and Annapolis Railway, 1, 6

Winnipeg *Telegram*: on Senate, 254–55

Wood, Edward Rogers, 164

World War I: Canadian Government prepares for, 262–63